The Ruin Dwellers

∴

The Ruin Dwellers

∴

PROGRESS AND ITS DISCONTENTS IN THE
WEST GERMAN COUNTERCULTURE

Jake P. Smith

THE UNIVERSITY OF CHICAGO PRESS
CHICAGO AND LONDON

The University of Chicago Press, Chicago 60637
The University of Chicago Press, Ltd., London
© 2025 by The University of Chicago
All rights reserved. No part of this book may be used or reproduced in any manner whatsoever without written permission, except in the case of brief quotations in critical articles and reviews. For more information, contact the University of Chicago Press, 1427 E. 60th St., Chicago, IL 60637.
Published 2025

34 33 32 31 30 29 28 27 26 25   1 2 3 4 5

ISBN-13: 978-0-226-82359-1 (cloth)
ISBN-13: 978-0-226-82361-4 (paper)
ISBN-13: 978-0-226-82360-7 (e-book)
DOI: https://doi.org/10.7208/chicago/9780226823607.001.0001

Library of Congress Cataloging-in-Publication Data

Names: Smith, Jake P., author.
Title: The ruin dwellers : progress and its discontents in the West German counterculture / Jake P. Smith.
Description: Chicago : The University of Chicago Press, 2025. | Includes bibliographical references and index.
Identifiers: LCCN 2024050258 | ISBN 9780226823591 (cloth) | ISBN 9780226823614 (paperback) | ISBN 9780226823607 (ebook)
Subjects: LCSH: Counterculture—Germany (West)—History. | Youth movements—Germany (West)—History. | Germany (West)—Civilization. | Germany (West)—Politics and government—1945–1990.
Classification: LCC HN460.S62 S65 2025 | DDC 306/.1—dc23/eng/20241226
LC record available at https://lccn.loc.gov/2024050258

Contents

INTRODUCTION · 1

CHAPTER ONE
The Allure of Progress in Postwar Germany · 14

CHAPTER TWO
The Countercultural "Off-Modern" · 40

CHAPTER THREE
The Youth Revolts of 1980–81 and the
Radical Potential of the Present · 68

CHAPTER FOUR
Perpetual Motion: Ritualization and Rebirth in the 1980s · 100

CHAPTER FIVE
Insurgent Dwelling and the Cultivation of Place
in Hamburg's Hafenstraße · 129

CHAPTER SIX
Carnival Time and Creative Destruction in the New Berlin · 155

EPILOGUE · 181

Acknowledgments 187
Notes 189
Bibliography 233
Index 255

Introduction

In the October 1981 edition of the prominent leftist journal *Kursbuch*, author and activist Benny Härlin provided readers with an inside account of a peculiar new youth movement that had been gaining momentum in cities like Freiburg and West Berlin since the late 1970s.¹ In his article, Härlin described how he and a group of friends took part in the illegal occupation of an abandoned, turn-of-the-century apartment building in the Schöneberg neighborhood of West Berlin; how they engaged in do-it-yourself repair work and mobilized an eclectic array of artistic techniques to redesign the space; how they came together with like-minded activists in West Berlin's "Squatter's Council," in street protests, and at punk concerts; and how they sought to utilize the unique material attributes of the houses to experiment with new forms of collective living. Although Härlin wrote primarily about his experiences in West Berlin, his description of the movement could have applied equally well to any number of the other squatting and youth cultural milieus that were emerging in cities across West Germany—and to varying extents across Western Europe—in these years.²

In large part, this remarkable consistency across different locales was a result of the widespread circulation of self-produced media, including films, magazines, posters, and music, which described and thus helped to define the movement, often by highlighting the differences between youth protest in the early 1980s and the forms of leftist activism that had prevailed in the 1960s and 1970s. Härlin, in particular, was at pains in his essay to differentiate the new youth movement from earlier iterations of new leftist protest. Many of the practices that he described, however, would likely have seemed quite familiar to *Kursbuch* readers, especially those who had taken part in the waves of protest that ebbed and flowed during West Germany's "Red Decade" (1967–77).³ His description of the West German state as "a machine, an apparatus, a computer" that had infiltrated all areas of postwar life, for example, would certainly have resonated with veterans of earlier movements.⁴ So would his contention that, although the state "has the power," its attempts to exert total control over society had made it "vulnerable" to an array of leftist counterattacks.[5] Like their predecessors in the Red Decade, Härlin and his fellow squatters tended to imagine such acts of militant resistance to state power as more than just mechanisms for defending leftist infrastructure from the forces of order, though this was certainly an important component. These acts were also understood as liberatory, since it was only by overturning dominant forms of state power, many activists believed, that one could begin to clear a path for the emergence of a different world.[6]

Although the political, economic, and military infrastructure of West Germany and its NATO allies served as the most concrete instantiations of "The State," activists of both generations also tended to conceptualize state power as a widespread, insidious network of domination that had suffused the bodies, built environments, and social forms of postwar life. Subverting the power of the state thus required more than militant resistance in the streets; it also necessitated a radical transformation of the everyday.[7] One way activists sought to go about this was by creating "autonomous" enclaves within which they hoped to cultivate lives liberated from power. Communes, living co-ops (*Wohngemeinschaften*), underground clubs, and alternative youth centers were all significant in this regard, but it was the squatted houses—of which there were more than 160 in West Berlin alone in the summer of 1981—that came to play the most important role for many youth activists in the 1980s. As spaces that were by definition illegal, the squatted houses represented ideal locations for cultivating autonomous, antiauthoritarian modes of collective living. Not only were the occupants of the squatted houses subversively experimenting with new aesthetics and new forms of sociability, they were doing so in direct opposition to the established legal codes of the state.

The infrastructure of the movement more broadly also helped to facilitate the development of antiauthoritarian organizational forms. Härlin described meetings of the "Squatters' Council," for example, as chaotic affairs in which there were no leaders, no meeting agenda, and no established principles for making decisions. Instead of taking their cues from the established canon of leftist texts or from a central cadre of leaders, as they imagined the participants in the 1960s student movements to have done, squatters from different occupied houses periodically gathered in venues like the "KuKuCK" (Art and Culture Center of Kreuzberg) to share ideas, debate tactics, and establish new connections. As is true of anarchist movements more broadly, the intention here was to create a movement that emerged from the ground up, rather than from established political programs.[8] This had strategic benefits as it made activists "fast, fantastical, and above all totally unpredictable" (an assessment with which city officials, property owners, and the police came to agree), but it was also more than this.[9] Organizing their everyday lives according to antiauthoritarian principles served both as a strategic tool for combating, and potentially overturning, state power—thus paving the way for the emergence of another world—*and* as a way to "prefigure" this other world. Antiauthoritarianism and radical autonomy, in other words, represented both the goals toward which activists were working and the surest way to reach these goals.

As historian Terence Renaud has argued, such prefigurative practices have long been a hallmark of European new leftist politics. Time and again, Renaud shows, new generations of leftist activists sought to differentiate themselves from more established leftist groups by bringing the means and the ends of revolutionary practice in alignment, often by calling for a more wide-ranging implementation of antiauthoritarian principles.[10] They reasoned that if the postcapitalist future was to be a world without hierarchy, then the means employed to reach that end also needed to be antihierarchical in nature. In a number of respects, the youth activists of the 1980s continued to operate within the established prefigurative traditions of older new lefts. As in earlier leftist movements, participants in the youth movements of the 1980s also sought to differentiate themselves from established leftist parties by centering antiauthoritarian practices and by rejecting the "poetry of the past." At the same time, though, youth activists in these years also radicalized many of these ideas by jettisoning some of the core principles of Marxist theory, which, despite their anarchist inclinations, earlier new lefts had largely retained.

They steadfastly refused, for example, to serve as intellectual guides for the so-called revolutionary masses. Härlin makes this point in no uncertain terms in his essay, declaring matter-of-factly: "We're not engaged in any politics of representation."[11] Throughout the previous decade, much—though, as I argue in the following chapter, certainly not all—of the West German New Left had imagined themselves as a detached vanguard whose primary task was to encourage marginalized populations (whether in the form of the working class, racialized minorities, colonized peoples, or even, in some cases, frustrated teenagers) to recognize and embrace their innate revolutionary potential. The acts of resistance and negation in which these supposedly "prepolitical" revolutionary actors engaged had to be channeled into appropriately "dialectical" logics in order to serve as effective catalysts of revolutionary change. Marginalized groups, in this view, represented systemic contradictions who had the power to overturn capitalist modes of production and domination, but only if they followed the course prescribed by dialectical theory. They were meant to serve as the negative term in the dialectical equation, whose positionality would allow them to counteract dominant forms of power and thus bring society one step closer to its prescribed utopian end.

As is evident in Härlin's essay, participants in the squatting and youth movements largely rejected such dialectical and representational politics, a point which he emphasizes by including a quote from the January 1981 issue of the far-left journal *Radikal* in which the authors claimed that the "68er Grandpas [APO-OPAs] still haven't realized that we're not fighting for the public but for ourselves [. . .] for a self-determined life in all areas."[12] Although street protests were important venues for enacting these ideas of a nonrepresentational revolutionary movement, they were often overshadowed by acts of domestic transgression in which squatters occupied, explored, and repaired empty houses in order to use them as venues for constructing liberated forms of being together. As Härlin and his friends began exploring "their" new house with "candles, water in canteens from the neighbor, sleeping ten to a room in sleeping bags," their main concerns were not with radicalizing the masses in order to spark a revolutionary transformation of society sometime in the future, but with building new autonomous communal forms in the present.[13] They were literally living out the utopian future in the "free spaces" of the squatted houses, underground clubs, and youth centers.

The new youth movement's rejection of traditional leftist politics centering on representation and dialectical activism often took the form of an overt embrace of absurdism. This is clearly evident in much of the language employed by participants in the movement, especially the slogans that were spray-painted on and around the squatted houses. Whereas some of these slogans—"Germany, Germany, it's all over" and "Berlin has to burn so that we can live"—evince activists' belief that a militant overturning of the West German state would allow them to construct fully autonomous lives, others—"nonsense instead of consensus," "no dialogue with anyone," "say no to salad!" and "free time during the end times"—point to their tendency to reject coherent ideological narratives in favor of provocative absurdity and seemingly irrational acts of transgression. Unable to take such discourse on its own terms, many commentators at the time sought to explain the outbreak of youth unrest in the early 1980s by mobilizing well-established social, economic, and psychological theories, arguing, for example, that youth protesters were simply frustrated by the constraints of adolescence.

Dismissing the interpretations of the self-appointed experts who sought to explain the emergence of the new youth movement by employing sociological and economic theories, Härlin defines it affectively as "a state of being, both individual and collective [which] one can feel when things are going down in the streets [. . .] as a trembling of desire and fear in your gut, when the glass shatters from the freeing flight [of a rock], when you're laughing and running." It was a movement that drew strength from perpetual transgression, from "the break with the known, with [their] parents' house, with school, [. . .] with the public consensus, with the always defensive leftist certainties, with the achievable. It's a feeling of breaking through."[14] Earlier generations of postwar leftists had also been drawn to this feeling of breaking through into the new, which they often interpreted as a dialectical means toward a larger revolutionary end, however vaguely defined. In the squatting and youth movements, by contrast, acts of transgressive negation were treated as ends in themselves, breakthroughs shorn of directionality and logic, less prefigurations of the utopian future than endless reconfigurations of an expansive and unpredictable present. Despite the squatting movement seeming to operate within the prefigurative traditions of earlier new lefts, then, something strange was afoot, something that called into question some of the central ideological tenets of the Marxist left, ranging from ideas of representation to conceptions of revolutionary time.[15]

Participants in the youth movements of the 1980s exhibited extremely unorthodox understandings of revolutionary time. Throughout the 1960s and 1970s new leftists in West Germany had largely subscribed to a progressive vision of revolutionary temporality in which the present and the past had to be repeatedly "overcome" in order to clear the way for the promised future. Squatters and their allies, by contrast, tended to reject such teleologically oriented conceptions of progressive time altogether, a tendency they shared with segments of the "alternative milieu" that proliferated in the wake of 1968.[16] However, whereas the alternative milieu often looked for ways to slow time down, squatters and their allies sought to speed it up. Indeed, as Härlin's constant references to novelty, momentum, and breakthroughs suggest, participants in the youth movements of these years tended to conceptualize time in some fundamentally modernist ways. These feelings of breathless anticipation for the new come through clearly in the oft-repeated lyrics from the band Fehlfarben, which implore listeners "not to take a breath" because "history is being made. It's moving ahead."[17] It was essential in this formulation that history be moving ahead. Where exactly it was moving, though, was much less important. The future toward which the new youth movement was so breathlessly striving was not one that included any clearly established teleological end points, whether Marxist, capitalist, or liberal. It was an ecstatic search for constant negation and endless becoming, an anarchist temporal imaginary that paralleled some of the ideas being produced contemporaneously by radical European philosophers like Gilles Deleuze and Félix Guattari.[18]

Beyond rejecting teleological futures, the anarchist temporal practices that were emerging in the new youth movement also diverged from more mainstream iterations of modern progressive time in that they resisted any sort of inclinations toward obfuscating or overcoming the past. In contrast to more orthodox iterations of progressive time in which attaining the future is premised on repeatedly staging the separation of the past from the present, participants in the youth movement relished the constant presence of the unruly past.[19] This was evident in their fashion choices, with Härlin, for example, describing the styles on display at a punk concert as consisting of a disorienting array of clothing made from discarded consumer goods, fashion items from the 1950s, glitter, and mismatched (and often mutually contradictory) political symbols.[20] Far from being seen as a problem, such seemingly illogical mixtures of temporal and political signifiers became one of the hallmarks of the early 1980s youth movement, even the ideology which Härlin described as a collection of "dusty fragments from previous movements."[21] While clothing styles, musical performances, and modes of embodiment were all important tools for experimenting with temporal categories, the asynchronous qualities of the squatted houses—almost all of which were built before WWII—made them the ideal mediums for cultivating these practices of temporal pastiche.

Take, for example, Härlin's reflections on his first few days in the squat, where alongside lines describing his excitement about building a new, autonomous life, he muses about previous residents of the house: "For more than 100 years people had lived [in the house]. They loved, hated, were scared, couldn't stand one another or slept together, were born there and died there. It lived. Yet when we occupied the house, it was dead." Coming into contact with the layered remains of the past that littered the building, ranging from threadbare furniture to a tattered issue of the Nazi-era newspaper the *Völkischer Beobachter*, Härlin and his fellow squatters initially felt as if they were "strangers in a dead land," adventurers tasked with building a new world on top of the ruins of the old.[22] In this sense, they were operating squarely within the destructive temporal logics of progressive modernity in which meaningful being in the world is tethered to acts of temporal differentiation. The modern self, in this formulation, gains value by repeatedly staging its separation from and superiority to the outmoded other. Unlike most iterations of progressive time, however, Härlin and his fellow squatters were not interested in erasing or narratively subsuming these uncanny traces of the German past. Instead, their goal was to dwell among them.

Making sense of this peculiar desire to dwell amid the ruins of the twentieth century is the primary task of this book.

∴

As is clear in Härlin's essay, the squatting and youth movements of the early 1980s diverged from their more Marxist-oriented predecessors in a number of respects, in particular regarding their understandings of and commitment to established conceptions of progressive time. Whereas previous generations of new leftists had largely subscribed to an ideology of temporal progress in which reaching the prescribed future was premised on repeatedly overcoming (or otherwise subsuming) the past, squatters and their allies imagined a world in which the jumbled, overlapping presence of multiple different pasts facilitated what, in an earlier historical moment, the philosopher Walter Benjamin called "a leap into the open air of history."[23] The openness of the future, in other words, depended on the constant presence of the "unmastered past." Dwelling amid the uncanny traces of the past served both as a means for undermining the progressive conceits of modern time (namely, that the past is actually past), and as a fulfillment of its promises of constant becoming. In a sense, these "ruin dwellers" of the early 1980s were attempting to occupy and subversively repurpose the logics of progress. How, though, should we go about making sense of this peculiar, anarchist temporal imaginary? Why did it take root with such intensity in the squatting and youth movements of the early 1980s? How did it relate to the progressive temporalities that had infused the ideologies, the built environments, and even the bodies of postwar Germany? And what effects did it have on urban practices and temporal consciousness in German society more broadly?

One way to begin answering these questions would be to interpret the experimental temporal imaginaries that arose in these years as part and parcel of a broader shift toward "presentism" within late twentieth-century capitalist societies. A number of scholars have drawn attention to the presentist temporal imaginaries which, they claim, have infiltrated almost all dimensions of contemporary life. French historian François Hartog, perhaps the most well known of these critics, has described presentism as "the sense that only the present exists, a present characterized at once by the tyranny of the instant and by the treadmill of an unending now."[24] He goes on to claim that the waning power of progressive futures has led to a concomitant explosion of pasts. The growing popularity of heritage sites, of memory studies, and of history more broadly are, according to this interpretation, all components of a broader "crisis of time" associated with the advent of presentism.[25] Others have tended to agree. The German literary theorist Hans Ulrich Gumbrecht, for example, argues that under contemporary conditions of presentism (which he refers to as the "broad present") "*pasts* flood our present," which "has turned into a dimension of expanding simultaneities."[26] In a somewhat similar vein, Marxist critic Fredric Jameson, whose most influential essay on the subject appeared just as the first wave of the 1980s youth revolts were winding down, has called attention to the emergence and rapid spread of "postmodern" social, cultural, and aesthetic forms, the attributes of which (depthlessness, intensity, spatialization, nostalgia, and collapsing futures) closely resemble those Hartog associates with presentism.[27] Despite their differences, these authors all contend that the rapid transformation of social, cultural, and aesthetic forms, which began in the late twentieth century and continues today, stems from underlying changes in the structuring of time and that this represents a worrisome threat to the progressive values of modernity.

Although useful and perceptive in many respects, these paradigms are inadequate for grasping the experimental practices that emerged in the youth movements of the 1980s. There are a number of reasons for this. First, the idea that presentist social, cultural, and aesthetic forms merely *reflect* underlying structural transformations in the organization of time is difficult to sustain, at least in the case of the experimental countercultures analyzed in this book. Drawing from close readings of activist texts and practices, *The Ruin Dwellers* shows that squatters and their allies in the early 1980s youth movements were active agents in processes of temporal change, that their experiments with aesthetic forms and autonomous living helped to produce some of the social, cultural, and aesthetic phenomena commonly associated with presentism. In making this argument, I emphasize not only the agency of leftist and countercultural actors but also the creative and productive dimensions of their activism. Contrary to the interpretations developed by Hartog and others who see presentism as a dangerous and unwelcome challenge to the modern time regime, I follow a number of recent works in Marxist and queer theory which have called attention both to the ways that the modern time regime functions within a larger economy of power and to the radical possibilities opened up by its collapse.[28] Finally, in contrast to theorists who have posited external causes such as shifts in the mode of production or the emergence of new technologies as the prime initiators of presentism, *The Ruin Dwellers* illuminates how presentist practices emerged, in part at least, from *within* progressive temporal logics as activists experimented with and subversively repurposed the dynamic temporalities of modernity. I thus refer to these practices not as presentist but as postprogressive. Accounting for the emergence, spread, and ramifications of these postprogressive temporalities will be the primary task of this book. It's a narrative that moves from the ascent of capitalist progress in 1950s West Germany, to its fragmentation in the 1970s, and finally to the emergence and codification of new spatiotemporal practices in the 1980s and 1990s.

∵

In many respects, this is a book about the "afterlives of 1968" in West Germany.[29] This is by no means an understudied topic. Indeed, over the past years a number of scholars have made provocative arguments detailing the ways in which radical movements in 1960s and 1970s West Germany galvanized late twentieth-century social, cultural, and political transformations. Some have argued that the student movements and alternative cultures of the long 1960s contributed to the liberalization of West German society.[30] Others have pointed to their significance in the shift toward postmaterialist values, arguing, among other things, that the left-alternative milieu of the long 1960s played an essential role in the transformation of social codes and conceptions of the self.[31] Some historians have also begun to analyze the temporal dimensions of new left politics—calling attention, for example, to the role played by the Nazi past in the West German left, to the ways that shifting ideas about the future catalyzed transformations in leftist imaginaries during the 1960s and 1970s, and, in a few cases, to the peculiar temporal practices of the youth movements of the early 1980s.[32] Building on, and at times challenging, this scholarship, *The Ruin Dwellers* begins by situating the 1960s New Left within a more widespread embrace of progressive temporalities in the postwar period. It then goes on to investigate the manifold ways in which leftist and countercultural experimentation with these temporal forms in the 1960s and 1970s helped spark the development of postprogressive practices in the youth movements of the 1980s. Drawing from recent historical and theoretical scholarship on the temporal dimensions of modernity, *The Ruin Dwellers* shows how participants in the youth movements of the 1980s simultaneously operated within and radically reconfigured the progressive temporalities that had infused the lifeworlds of postwar Germany.[33]

The Ruin Dwellers also engages with recent scholarship on the role of cultural production in leftist milieus to explore the centrality of aesthetic experimentation for the early 1980s youth movements.[34] Here, I analyze not only the incredible array of artistic expression that emerged in the context of the youth movement (including films, music, fashion, poetry, and sculpture) but also some of the philosophical texts produced in these years.

I treat these philosophical texts in much the same way as I treat other types of cultural and aesthetic expression: namely, as forms of media that both reflected upon and helped to produce the embodied innovations of their historical moment.[35] Whether it was an artistic installation consisting of discarded cars and washing machines outside of a squatted house, an experimental music performance where everyday objects from different historical eras were transformed into instruments that conjured the past, or a philosophical tract reflecting on the subversive qualities of temporally layered places, cultural, aesthetic, and philosophical experimentation were essential in forging and codifying postprogressive temporal imaginaries. I should note, at this point, that this investigation into the aesthetic and cultural dimensions of the new youth movements would have been impossible were it not for the extraordinary work of a number of archivists who have collected objects, films, artworks, photographs, and brochures from these years and made them available for researchers like me. The Papiertiger Archiv and the Umbruch Bildarchiv in Berlin, the Social Movement archives in Freiburg and at the Rote Flora in Hamburg, the Medienpädagogik Zentrum in Hamburg, the Swiss Social Archives in Zurich, and the International Institute of Social History in Amsterdam deserve special mention in this regard.

Sculpture, poetry, graffiti, novels, music, films, and theoretical tracts were all significant tools for experimenting with and subversively repurposing the progressive temporalities of modernity, but perhaps the most important medium was the palimpsestic built environment of cities like West Berlin. As had also been the case in the immediate postwar period, squatters and their allies used the historical traces encased within the temporally layered environments of urban spaces as backdrops against which to forge new lives. Yet, unlike their predecessors in the reconstruction years and in the antiauthoritarian movements, the youth cultures of the early 1980s were under no illusions that the past could ever actually be separated from the present. Nor, for that matter, would they have wanted it to be. Given that modernist organizations of time depend on continued contact with the past in order to fuel the drive toward the future, definitively separating the past from the present would have meant the end of temporal dynamism, of the feeling of breaking through into something new. Thus, squatters continually sought out environments in which the past had not been fully erased, haunted spaces where the presence of "the outmoded" facilitated endless leaps into the new.[36] As spaces teeming with traces of the past, the squatted houses became preeminent locales within which to prolong this rush of untethered development. They were spaces where progress—both the liberal variant of progress that suffused the discourses and practices surrounding

West Germany's miraculous postwar rebirth, and the dialectical progress of the left—could be repeatedly staged in ever new configurations. As environments marked by multiple pasts, the squatted houses came to serve as spaces of productive asynchronicity where residents could both critique the violent erasures of the modern time regime and endlessly reproduce the feelings generated by progressive breakthroughs into the new. They were, in other words, preeminent locations for cultivating postprogressive forms of being in time, spaces where one could dwell indefinitely in a state of liminality.

In his 1980 analysis of "the practices of everyday life," the French philosopher Michel de Certeau wrote that "haunted places are the only ones people can live in."[37] This sentiment was clearly visible in the countercultural practices that developed in and around the squatted houses, youth centers, and concert venues of the late 1970s and early 1980s, which posited that it was only by dwelling alongside the ghosts of the past that one could begin to build a meaningful life outside of the restrictive logics of progress—an existence where one could, to quote Christina Sharpe, engage in a "re/seeing, re/inhabiting, and re/imagining [of] the world."[38] The hauntological practices that emerged in these years were thus not only critiques of progressive temporalities; they were also mechanisms by which to reformulate meaningful being in the world.[39] This was by no means, however, a phenomenon that was limited to late twentieth-century countercultural milieus in Europe. Indeed, the practices that arose in the fractured urban spaces of cities like West Berlin bore a striking similarity to social, cultural, and political forms from other times and places.[40] Due to limitations of space and of expertise, I am unable to offer a full comparison of these different movements. Throughout the course of this book, though, I do engage with an array of different theoretical perspectives to explore some of the broader contours of postprogressive thought and practice, as well as the modern time regime from which it emerged. In so doing, I point to what Walter Benjamin called "the chips of Messianic time" that inevitably shadow modern life.[41]

This exploration will include periodic engagement with Marxist-inspired interpretations of shifting temporal regimes. *The Ruin Dwellers* takes seriously the argument that the logic of capitalism, like that of modernity more broadly, is premised on a relentless process of identifying and subsuming nonsynchronous temporal forms, and that the constitutive necessity of this process has resulted in the continued presence of divergent temporal rhythms in the present. The peculiar logics of capitalist modernity, in other words, help to enable subversive milieus such as those studied in this book to imagine and enact alternatives. In making this argument, I look to a diverse group of authors and thinkers who have posited that the ever-increasing disruptions to the flow of dominant temporal logics can spark experiments with new modes of being, moments, to quote the novelist Ben Lerner, when "what normally [feels] like the only possible world [becomes] one among many, its meaning everywhere up for grabs."[42] Svetlana Boym has referred to this marginal mode of being in time, or being in the margins of time, as the "off-modern," which, she claims, "acknowledges the syncope and the off-beat movements of history that were written out from the dominant versions" and which "proceed[s] laterally, not literally, to discover missed opportunities and roads not taken."[43] Various iterations of off-modern imaginaries have allowed people, she continues, "to think beyond the directional arrows of time pointing at the Past or Future and to inhabit multiple temporal regimes of the Present, with their different pace, rhythm, and duration."[44]

Whereas progressive regimes of temporality are premised on attempts to erase, subsume, or otherwise contain the past in the service of creating feelings of forward momentum toward a teleologically constituted version of the future, the postprogressive countercultural milieus analyzed in this book sought to bring the past into the present so as to radically open the future. Instead of viewing the upsurge in nostalgic practices among the left as retrograde attempts to hide from or counteract the collapse of utopian futures, or as unselfconscious enactments of capitalist fragmentation, we might, then, view them as constituting a shift toward postprogressive values in which dwelling with the ruins of futures past served as a means for opening the future's future.

My arguments regarding the late twentieth-century reconfiguration of progressive time emerge over the course of six main chapters and an epilogue. The first chapter, "The Allure of Progress in Postwar Germany," relies primarily on existing historical and theoretical scholarship to trace how progressive temporal logics came to infuse many different areas of life in postwar West Germany. While much of the New Left enthusiastically embraced these visions of progress, the 1960s and 1970s also witnessed the emergence of various "off-modern" experiments in the realms of politics, art, and everyday life. The second chapter, "The Countercultural 'Off-Modern,'" draws from a range of sources to analyze some of these experiments. The following two chapters—chapter 3, "The Youth Revolts of 1980–81 and the Radical Potential of the Present," and chapter 4, "Perpetual Motion: Ritualization and Rebirth in the 1980s"—examine the squatting and youth movements that roiled West German and other Central European cities in the late 1970s and early 1980s, paying particular attention to the development, spread, and transformations of postprogressive social, cultural, and political forms. The final two chapters—chapter 5, "Insurgent Dwelling and the

Cultivation of Place in Hamburg's Hafenstraße," and chapter 6, "Carnival Time and Creative Destruction in the New Berlin"—shift into an exploration of the built environment and its role in the continued development of postprogressive practices in the 1980s. Finally, the epilogue situates these movements within some recent literature on the collapse of the modern time regime.

[CHAPTER ONE]

The Allure of Progress in Postwar Germany

In his 1966 book *Journey through a Haunted Land*, the Israeli journalist Amos Elon offers a particularly damning account of life in 1960s West Germany, writing of a "harmless present camouflag[ing] a noxious past" and comparing West Germany to a "a pretty modern Technicolour photo superimposed on the black-grey shadows of a massacre."[1] Along with a number of like-minded critics, Elon viewed West Germany's attempts to reinvent itself in the wake of Nazism with intense skepticism. Not only did the Federal Republic fail to properly "master" the Nazi past, but in embracing Americanized visions of progress and capitalist abundance, it also threatened to imbricate West Germans in new systems of exploitation and violence.[2] Initially, though, such skeptical outlooks on the value and utility of progress were in the minority. Indeed, in the immediate postwar period, many Germans enthusiastically embraced the progressive temporal imaginaries promoted by the victorious Allied powers, which seemed to offer them the opportunity to start their lives anew.

In the wake of Nazi Germany's defeat, many of those who had supported or even just tacitly accepted the regime found themselves intensely disoriented, trying to make sense of a state of affairs that, according to the temporal imaginaries championed by the Nazi regime, should not have been possible. Having been in existence for only twelve years, the "Thousand Year Reich" had come to an end, leaving in its wake death and destruction on an unfathomable scale. No longer able to temporally orient themselves within the narrative parameters of Nazism, many began looking for alternative frameworks with which to conceptualize and constitute some sense of meaningful being in time.[3] In her diary documenting the collapse of Nazism and the onset of the occupation, the anonymous author of *A Woman in Berlin* gave early voice to this desire, writing, "I feel something nagging at me, boring into me. [...] I need to move, I have to act, start doing something."[4] In both the western and eastern occupation zones, new ideologies and ideas began to fill this void, offering alluring visions of the future with which Germans could begin reorienting themselves in time.

Films from the immediate postwar period are illustrative of this process. Wolfgang Staudte's 1946 film *The Murderers Are among Us*, to take one of the best-known examples, explores themes of guilt and the desire for rebirth amid the ruined landscape of postwar Berlin.[5] The film, one of the first produced in Germany after the war and thus eerily populated by actors who had experienced the Nazi years firsthand, follows the veteran Dr. Hans Mertens (Ernst Wilhelm Borchert) and the concentration camp survivor Susanne Wallner (Hildegard Knef) as they seek to rebuild their lives after the war. Upon her return from a concentration camp (the reason she was there remains unspecified in the film), a very smartly dressed Susanne finds an alcoholic and psychologically distressed Hans squatting in her old apartment. Although they agree to share the space, their outlooks on life and on the possibilities for a better future remain worlds apart. Committed to rebuilding a meaningful life out of the ruins of the past, Susanne cleans the apartment, prepares dinners, paints signs for a campaign to "Save the Children," and looks wistfully into the distance as the camera lingers on her face. Hans, meanwhile, is convinced that the future will be nothing more than a bleak continuation of the traumatic past. He stumbles drunkenly around the ruined city periodically facing the camera to make pronouncements like "Forgotten? I've forgotten nothing." Eventually, Susanne's overwhelming desire to start "living life, at last" wins Hans over, and, against a dramatic backdrop of bombed-out buildings, they join hands, declare their love for one another, and take their first steps into a new future. In this sense, the film served as an early example of the optimistic, progress-oriented language that would come to suffuse West German life during the Economic Miracle of the 1950s, which held that domesticity, heterosexual love, and bourgeois ethics were essential tools for bracketing the pain of yesterday and moving into a brighter tomorrow.[6]

Things become more complicated, however, when Hans discovers that his old captain, Ferdinand Brückner (Arno Paulsen), is not only still alive but thriving in the new order—a turn of events which one might categorize as an early filmic example of what Philipp Felsch and Frank Witzel have described as the unsettlingly noirish character of the Federal Republic.[7] Faced with this unwelcome return of the past, the blissful domestic state Hans had begun to forge with Susanne quickly unravels. Increasingly, he succumbs to traumatic flashbacks of wartime violence, especially the moment when Brückner ordered the murder of more than a hundred civilians during Christmas of 1942. While Hans is tormented by these memories, Brückner

FIGURE 1.1. Still from *The Murderers Are among Us* (1946). Directed by Wolfgang Staudte, photography by Eugen Klagemann. Photo: Eugen Klagemann. Source: DEFA Film Library.

seems entirely unperturbed. Indeed, his success making "saucepans from helmets" and his seemingly idyllic bourgeois family life—in which, for example, he tells his children heroic war stories about his "days in the gray uniform" during dinner—wholly overshadows any sense of guilt concerning his actions during the war. At one point, we even see him happily drinking coffee and eating toast on top of a newspaper with the headline "2 Million People Gassed: Report from Auschwitz." With figures like Brückner not only still walking free but even finding ways to prosper in the new order, the film suggests that something more than romantic love, hard work, and domestic bliss would be necessary for Germans to come to terms with their past. In the final scene, the film thus offers a supplementary mechanism for dealing with the legacies of the war. Upon discovering his plans for vengeance, Susanne seeks to prevent Hans from shooting Brückner, arguing "We cannot pass judgment," to which, lowering his gun, Hans replies, "That's right, Susanne, but we must bring charges and demand atonement on behalf of the millions of innocent victims." As the film fades out to a scene of Brückner behind bars, the audience could take solace in the fact that the truly guilty would face justice for the crimes of the Nazi years, thus leaving everyone else free to reorient themselves toward the horizon of a brighter future.

The two solutions presented by the film—rebuilding a meaningful, future-oriented private life, and punishing those deemed responsible for Nazi crimes—both proved to be essential strategies for recalibrating narratives of temporal progression in the postwar, especially in what would soon become West Germany. Punishing the perpetrators of genocide would, theoretically at least, separate the fascist past from the democratic present and the guilty from the innocent, and thus liberate individuals to pursue personal renewal; while domesticity, democratic politics, and mass consumption offered concrete tools with which West Germans could rebuild meaningful, future-oriented lives after genocide. In other words, both were strategies for reconstituting what Aleida Assmann has termed a "modern regime of time" in the wake of Nazi Germany's spectacular collapse.[8] Drawing from Assmann's analysis, the modern time regime can be understood as a loose organization of temporality consisting of continually accelerating attempts to separate the past from the present (whether by destroying it, historicizing it, adjudicating it, or transforming it into heritage) in pursuit of novelty, rebirth, and interminable development. Whether employed by academics, nationalists, or business leaders, this mode of organizing temporality incessantly conjures images of "the past" in order to immediately overcome them and, in so doing, to perpetually recast the present as the new. Movement toward the future, in other words, requires that the past be ritualistically evoked and disavowed. Thus, despite its claims to the contrary, progress necessitates that the past linger as a present absence. Given the close relationship between the modern regime of time and capitalism, it should come as no surprise that this process closely resembles the dynamics of value creation in modern capitalist societies, which depends on the incessant transformation of "use" into "exchange" value, a process that, paradoxically, produces "unevenness as a condition of its own continuing condition," even as it creates the illusion of unstoppable, unidirectional change.[9]

This is not to say, of course, that all modern time regimes are identical (for example, that of Nazi Germany and that of revolution-era France), or that they represent an internally coherent organization of experience. Nor is it to claim that everyone is subjected to them equally. Indeed, as the authors of a recent volume on the subject have argued, temporalities are multiple, conflicting, and inextricably intertwined with the exercise of power.[10] The temporal practices and ideologies associated with modernity (including historicism, creative destruction, progress, and the like) are neither natural nor total—though they are naturalizing and totalizing and have thus readily been employed as disciplinary mechanisms for gaining, maintaining, and reifying various forms of power. In her work on queer temporalities, Elizabeth Freeman employs the term *chrononormativity* in reference to the disciplinary utility of modernist orientations of time, that is, their ability to bind subjects "into socially meaningful embodiment through temporal regulation."[11] As I argue below, occupation authorities and their successors in power utilized progressive temporal imaginaries to remake postwar Germans, to discipline them into chrononormative modes of being in time in which attaining the democratic and capitalist future was premised on repeatedly invoking and overcoming the past. Like Hans and Susanne marching hand in hand out of the rubble of Berlin and into a new tomorrow, Germany's postwar future would take shape against the ever-present backdrop of its nightmarish past.

In the wake of Nazism's collapse, many Germans—particularly those living in the western zones of occupation—evinced a marked desire to remake themselves within these new iterations of temporal progress. Indeed, François Hartog's assessment that, in the years following the second world war, "the modern regime of historicity [. . .] was even cast as the one and only temporal perspective" holds particularly true for West Germany, where occupation policies coupled with the widespread desire to temporally ground (and thus reconstitute) the self resulted in an explosion of practices and ideas centering on renewal.[12] The proliferation of these progressive practices did not, however, result in the wholesale erasure of the painful past. Given that under modern regimes of temporality, progress is constituted by repeatedly enacting the separation of the past from the present, definitively saying "goodbye to yesterday," to quote Alexander Kluge from his 1966 film *Abschied von Gestern*, would prove impossible. What emerged instead was a series of intertwined practices each concerned with cultivating *feelings* of departure, momentum, and progress. In the following pages, I document some of these practices as they emerged in West Germany during the first decades of the postwar period, focusing in particular on the Economic Miracle and the leftist movements of the long 1960s. The arguments in this chapter come mainly from published secondary sources and are meant to serve as a foundation for the primary-source-based analysis of countercultural experimentation in the 1970s and 1980s that follows. Those familiar with this context might want to skip ahead to chapter 2.

⁂

After briefly considering plans calling for immediate and violent retribution, authorities in the western zones of occupation settled on reeducation, denazification, and public trials as the most effective means for ridding Germany of the legacies of Nazism. Germans were forced to watch films such as *The Death Mills*, to visit exhibits documenting the details of genocide, and in some cases to help exhume hastily buried bodies from mass graves.

These techniques were supplemented by the removal of material traces of the Nazi regime from the built environment, from the media landscape, and from professional life. Authorities renamed streets, removed swastikas from buildings, and terminated committed Nazis from their positions in government, education, and public service. In extreme cases, occupation authorities relied on public trials such as those that took place in Nuremberg in 1945–49, which tried almost two hundred defendants and compiled incontrovertible evidence of Nazi crimes. As temporal strategies, denazification and reeducation played an essential role in separating the past from the present and thus enabling postwar Germany to begin reorienting itself toward the future.[13] They represented the necessary foundation of the "zero hour" myth, which held that West Germany had definitively broken with the legacies of Nazism. Such invocations of a fresh start are commonplace in progressive temporal regimes, where they function to generate momentum by performing a definitive separation of the past from the present.

The revival of German democratic thought from the interwar period coupled with the economic recovery that followed the currency reforms of 1948 resulted in an ever-increasing acceptance of liberal democracy throughout the early 1950s.[14] Increasingly, the "task of democratization for the young West German republic lay with building a strong and stable economy, shoring up the political democracy, and forging close economic and military relations with the Western powers."[15] Founded in the immediate aftermath of the war, the Christian Democratic Union party (CDU), and especially leading figures such as Konrad Adenauer and Ludwig Erhard, came to champion this Western orientation for the Federal Republic. Not only did they express support for further integrating West Germany into Western military alliances like NATO, they also advocated for market economies and, up to a point at least, for consumerism.[16] Cognizant of the distrust many Germans still felt for democratic modernity, CDU leaders sought to balance these policies with a renewed focus on the supposedly untainted traditions of the national past. West Germany could begin reconstituting itself within the normative frameworks of modernity and progress, in which the new constantly surpassed the old even as it rested, reassuringly, on "timeless" national traditions.[17]

Consumer objects play a central role in mediating identity and social interactions in almost all capitalist societies. Given the centrality of capitalism for the reconceptualization of German identity in the early postwar years, such objects played an inordinately large role in West Germany. According to Susan Stewart, material objects such as antiques, collectibles, and souvenirs serve as catalysts for narratives of the self—stories in which the owner of the object situates themselves within and against large-scale social, cultural, and temporal logics.[18] Material objects, she argues, mediate not only our conceptions of ourselves and others but also our relationship to (and being in) time. In West Germany, objects evoking the Nazi past were systematically erased, as, for example, with the hundreds upon hundreds of swastikas that were removed from buildings, medals, books, and other media during the occupation. Or they were hidden away in basements and attics, waiting to be found by the proverbial sons and daughters of the perpetrators. In their place came new consumer objects representing democracy, capitalism, and unfettered individuality, which proliferated in magazines, advertisements, shop windows, and other environments that showcased and stoked desire. Even though such objects were initially almost entirely unattainable for the average consumer, they nonetheless infiltrated the West German imaginary as "anticipatory visions of mass consumption."[19]

Whether circulating as images in magazines or as concrete objects in consumer displays, these objects "served as orchestrated moments of forgetting" and as "powerful symbols of renewal," which both represented and helped to realize the progressive temporalities of the postwar.[20] In his 1976 film *Kings of the Road*, Wim Wenders illustrates how thoroughly these dream images of future happiness had suffused West German imaginaries, as one of the characters, gazing at roadside advertisements and humming along to an American song playing on the radio, suddenly has something of an epiphany, exclaiming: "The Yanks have colonized our subconscious."[21] The objects on display at newly stocked department stores such as the aptly named Department Store of the West in West Berlin, and increasingly in peoples' homes and on their bodies, offered concrete proof that capitalist visions of progress were real and, in theory at least, available for everyone.

Nowhere was this more true than in the imagery and discourses surrounding modernized domestic spaces, which came to serve as some of the primary sites within which postwar Germans could begin recasting themselves as characters in the epic drama of progress.[22] As "romanticized sphere[s] of postwar moral and aesthetic idealism," single-family dwellings in the postwar years largely superseded public arenas as privileged sites for imagining and artfully staging novel configurations of past, present, and future.[23] By combining putatively untainted traditions such as the nuclear family and the gendered mores of bourgeois domesticity with modern technologies and sleek architectural forms, the postwar home came to serve as a highly effective machine for enacting and reifying progress. Modern futures in the form of household gadgetry could be staged against the backdrop of traditional domestic iconography (often personified by the housewife), thus providing the necessary forward momentum of progress while also allaying fears of (Americanized) modernity run amok and effacing the actual past against which these domestic spaces emerged: namely, Nazism and its violent racialization of home. The postwar home was a space of salvation, an almost magical realm in which pasts could be mastered, futures could be embraced, and individuals could be reborn. It's no wonder that Härlin and his fellow squatters found it so fantastical when they occupied it years later.

Domesticity also proved to be a highly useful vehicle for American Cold War propaganda. By supporting exhibits like the 1950 "America at Home" exhibit and the 1952 "We Are Building a Better Life" exhibit (which drew thousands of visitors from the East and West eager to see concrete examples of modern domestic life), the US State Department attempted both to provide Germans with an alternative and ostensibly apolitical vision of the good life, and to discredit the visions of their Communist rivals.[24] According to Greg Castillo, events such as the "Better Life" exhibition clearly illustrated the ways in which the "cultural Cold War forged weapons from modern home furnishings."[25] This sentiment is readily apparent in a 1950 speech given by Raymond Loewy at the Harvard Business School, in which he noted: "The citizens of Lower Slobovia may not give a hoot for freedom of speech but how they fall for a gleaming Frigidaire, a stream-lined bus or a coffee percolator."[26] The Cold War focus on domesticity would continue to intensify throughout the 1950s, culminating in the so-called Kitchen Debate between Nixon and Khrushchev in July 1959.

Democracy, consumption, and domesticity all represented concrete mechanisms for rehabilitating modern, progressive temporalities in the wake of Nazism. However, as a 1956 letter from Siegfried Kracauer to Leo Löwenthal illustrates, they were not always successful. The Germans, Kracauer wrote, "live without form or focus, they lack shape (and are disordered within). Everything is there, but nothing is in its proper place. So, they behave in ways that are insincere and overly artificial, use *stilted language*, and are completely insecure. They are *not so much human beings as raw material for human beings*. In short, I don't trust them."[27] Contemporary historians have also drawn attention to the uncanny undertones of postwar life by investigating "the prevalence of mentalities and psychological conditions in postwar society that were difficult to incorporate into the forward looking, achievement-oriented society of the economic miracle" and arguing that West Germany was plagued by "collective anxieties and ongoing nightmares, [by] rumors, magic, miracles, and wandering ghosts."[28] These unsettling asynchronicities clung even to the most trusted symbols of West Germany's postwar rebirth. The Volkswagen, for example, "in which millions [...] imagined driving *away* from their past," also represented "'debris' from the Nazi empire," whose presence in the burgeoning consumer dreamscapes of the postwar disrupted the illusory momentum of progress.[29] The past kept returning because the progressive temporal regime implemented in the wake of Nazism was built on its spectral presence. It adhered to the objects, bodies, and environments of the postwar because they were the mediums through which it was converted into promising futures. As if in a nightmare, the quicker they ran, the closer it came.

I know of very few texts that better convey this tendency of the nightmarish past to cling to the dreamworlds of progressive time than Rainer Werner Fassbinder's deeply unsettling 1979 film *The Marriage of Maria Braun*, which follows Maria as she seeks to rebuild her life after the war. In many respects, Maria serves as the perfect embodiment of the uplifting, progressive rhetoric of the Economic Miracle. In the aftermath of the war, with her husband missing in the East and presumed dead, with no steady employment, living in a crumbling house with her mother, Maria doesn't give in to despair. Instead, like Susanne in *The Murderers Are among Us*, like the anonymous author of *A Woman in Berlin*, and like the endlessly circulated narratives of the "Rubble Women" who helped rebuild German cities, she gets to work. She sells family heirlooms on the black market in exchange for food, befriends American troops and learns English, and uses her wits to gain power, influence, and even a new home. But throughout her ascent into power, wealth, and security, Maria remains shadowed by the past, embodied by her husband Hermann, who, after returning unexpectedly from the East, is sentenced to jail for the murder of Maria's African American GI boyfriend, Bill. As the film progresses, the contradictions between the consumer future and the Nazi past continue to build, culminating in the final scene where Maria, upon realizing that she had herself been transformed into a commodity, blows up her new house along with herself, her husband, and countless other consumer objects. As this scene unfolds, a voice on the radio proclaims "Goal! Goal! Germany is the World Champion!" referencing West Germany's victory in the 1954 World Cup. The inability of progress, consumerism, and modernity to liberate West Germany from its past, Fassbinder suggests—perhaps thinking of leftist terrorism in the 1970s—could only end with a bang.

∴

Over the course of the 1950s, countless West Germans worked tirelessly to transform their ruined cities and their shattered lives into paragons of democratic modernity. They sought to silence the voices of the past beneath a miraculous cacophony of progress, and, to a certain extent, they succeeded. Indeed, the 1950s and early 1960s, the so-called miracle years, were characterized by an astounding economic recovery, political stabilization, and a rapidly expanding consumer culture. Having abandoned its "special path" in favor of a more acceptable route toward modernity, the newly created Federal Republic of Germany seemed well on its way to becoming a normal, modern European nation. Many still worried, though, that the past had not actually been put to rest, that the nightmares of yesterday had not been overcome so much as forcibly repressed under a thin veneer of capitalist abundance. Some even began to suggest that the utopian visions of the postwar order were not only chimeras of progress unable to truly put the horrors of the past to rest, but nightmares in their own right replete with new forms of violence and injustice.

This was especially true for many of the prominent theorists of the nascent New Left such as Theodor Adorno, Alexander and Margarete Mitscherlich, and Herbert Marcuse, who argued that the consumer dreamworlds of the postwar boom years not only prevented West Germans from adequately coming to terms with the Nazi past but also embroiled them in an equally destructive system of global capitalism and imperialism.[30] In his highly influential 1964 book *One-Dimensional Man*, for example, Marcuse—building on Horkheimer and Adorno's analysis from their 1947 *Dialectic of the Enlightenment*—argued that mass consumption, the "culture industries," and technological rationality had robbed citizens of advanced industrial nations of their humanity and blinded them to the destructive effects of capitalism. Believing themselves to be living a fulfilled life of abundance and infinite progress, they were, in reality, captive to an all-encompassing system of capitalist and imperialist domination. Their freedom was pseudofreedom, their individuality was pseudoindividuality, and the feeling of satisfaction they got when purchasing new cars, furniture, or records was pseudosatisfaction. In embracing capitalist modernity, these critics argued, the Federal Republic had traded one skewed developmental path for another. Far from salvational, for many on the left, the postwar embrace of capitalist progress was at the heart of the problem.

Similarly trenchant critiques of postwar dreamworlds can be found in films from the era. In *Abschied von Gestern*, for example, Alexander Kluge illustrates the proclivity of the past to haunt the everyday spaces of the postwar. The film opens with the phrase "We are separated from yesterday, not by an abyss but by the changed situation" and follows Anita G. as she tries to shed her connections to the past by fully embracing the present and its promises of a better future. In scene after painful scene, however, the viewer witnesses how Anita is unable to accomplish this feat. As a Jewish woman in a society that has attempted to eradicate all traces of Jewishness, a homeless person in a world built around the salvational qualities of modern dwelling, and an East German refugee seeking a new life in the capitalist West, Anita embodies many of the groups on whose exclusion postwar dreamworlds were built. As such, she serves as a persistent reminder of the nightmares that lie beneath the surface of the everyday. The past had not vanished; it was biding its time, waiting to resurface. Anita, like tiny Oskar Matzerath from Günter Grass's 1959 novel *The Tin Drum*, "provokes associations that run counter to established patterns of remembering and forgetting."[31] Ghostlike, these characters carry the memories of the past into the present and threaten to reveal the postwar as a hall of mirrors teetering on the edge of catastrophe.

By the early 1960s, these leftist critiques of postwar dreamworlds began gaining traction among West German youth. Somewhat shocked by the eagerness with which young, left-leaning Germans attended his postwar seminars, Adorno mused that "it was as if the spirits of murdered Jewish intellectuals had taken up residence in the bodies of German students."[32] At the same time, though, European youth were also becoming increasingly enamored with the experimental sounds and styles coming from England and the United States. A young person in Frankfurt in the mid-1960s could attend one of Adorno's lectures on Kant, freedom, or the dialectic in the morning, see the latest American blockbuster at a theater in the afternoon, and dance to the Rolling Stones at a local club in the evening. By the late 1960s, these distinct cultural forms began to converge, thus laying the groundwork for the emergence of the antiauthoritarian movements of the late 1960s. It is to this explosive convergence of pop culture and leftist politics that I now turn.

As the Economic Miracle was transforming the citizens and the built environments of the Federal Republic into paragons of modernity, democracy, and capitalism, West German youth were doing their part by eagerly consuming the products of Western (primarily British and American) mass culture.[33] Gathering in public spaces to mimic the rebellious fashions and mannerisms portrayed in American movies like *The Wild Ones* and *Rebel without a Cause* and to blast the latest rock and beat music from portable radios, youth groups known as the Halbstarke embraced transnational youth culture as a way to differentiate themselves from their parents and to carve out a space of their own in postwar society. These practices only intensified over the course of the early 1960s as rising purchasing power and a globalizing media market allowed European youth unprecedented access to new styles, sounds, and aesthetics.[34] Historian Julia Sneeringer has documented this process as it played out in the St. Pauli neighborhood of Hamburg in the early 1960s, an area well known for music and sex and which served as home to the Beatles in their formative early years. "Celebrating the joys of amplified sound and physical connection in a place where the pleasures

FIGURE 1.2. Rock 'n' roll in the "Bathtub" on Nürnberger Straße in West Berlin (1955). Photo by Liselotte and Armin Orgel-Köhne / bpk Bildagentur.

of the body were the coin of the realm," she argues, youth, and especially young women, "used these spaces to create amongst themselves moments of utopia outside of the era's sexual conservatism and social conformity."[35] Although not quite in the way their parents had envisioned, West German youth were proving to be experts at employing the consumerist logics of renewal and self-creation that the older generation had cultivated in the early miracle years.

Musical performances in particular were essential arenas for enacting pop cultural iterations of progress. Early rock 'n' roll concerts were especially significant in this regard as they enabled young people to collectively experiment with new aesthetics and social forms. Take, for example, the Beatles' 1962 New Year's Eve performance at the Star Club in Hamburg. Recordings of this concert convey an intense atmosphere as the young British musicians played American rock 'n' roll hits for a raucous and appreciative crowd of West German rock fans.[36] As the band played popular hits like "Twist and Shout" in quick succession, the energy of the crowd continued to build, unleashing crescendos of barely contained chaos. The palpable sense of electricity that emerged at this and other concerts in these years stemmed, I would like to suggest, from the collective enactment of progressive breakthroughs into the new. As is true of progressive temporalities more broadly, rock performances such as the Beatles' New Years Eve concert in Hamburg generated feelings of momentum and breakthrough by repeatedly staging the separation of the past from the present and by empowering youth to serve as the agents of this process. Taking their cues, perhaps, from the postwar avant-garde or even from the burgeoning fashion industry, popular youth cultural performances in the 1960s tended to enact this separation of the past from the present by negating the values and the aesthetics of polite, bourgeois society, the values and aesthetics, that is, of their parents' generation. Collectively transgressing established aesthetic, sonic, stylistic, and social mores allowed participants in youth subcultures to recategorize dominant aesthetics as hopelessly passé and thus to feel, momentarily at least, as if they were on the precipice of realizing the new.

The desire to play music, try out new styles, and experiment with nontraditional lifestyles led youth in the 1960s to seek out spaces that were set apart from mainstream society. The early 1960s witnessed the founding of a variety of clubs, for example, where progressively minded young people gathered to listen to music, watch movies, and discuss current events. Although in many respects similar to the youth organizations developed under the aegis of larger political parties such as the Jungsozialisten in der SPD (JUSOS), the youth clubs of the 1960s set themselves apart by rejecting established party politics and by embracing new trends in popular culture. While clubs remained influential throughout this period, many came to eschew what they believed to be the clubs' overly structured qualities and instead occupied public spaces like parks and squares to drink, play music, and socialize. These groups of so-called Gammler were especially prominent in the Munich neighborhood of Schwabing and in the area around the Gedächtniskirche in West Berlin.

Although largely apolitical, the Gammler milieu proved to be formative for many of the activists who later took part in the antiauthoritarian movements of the 1960s and '70s. Dieter Kunzelmann, for example, remembered the Schwabing riots of 1962 as a significant moment in his life, noting: "For the first time, I experienced how hundreds of people felt solidarity with the guitar-playing Gammlers, and that it only took a banal occasion to transform quiet and order into glorious chaos. This experience influenced me so deeply, that in the following years I let no opportunity slip by to recreate the experience in different forms."[37] Similarly, Michael "Bommi" Baumann, who would go on to take part in Kommune I, the street battles of the 1960s, and the militant activism of the early 1970s, considered his time in West Berlin's Gammler milieu to be his first step on the road to becoming a revolutionary.³⁸ These were spaces where young people could collectively experiment with the new cultural forms and oppositional politics of the 1960s—spaces, to quote Detlef Siegfried, where "happiness and the enjoyment of life" could be enacted "in the here and now."³⁹

Over the course of the 1960s, leftist youth in West Germany (and in countries across the world) underwent an intense process of radicalization, due in part to the growing awareness of the atrocities being committed in Vietnam, but also for a number of additional reasons, including Mao Zedong's Cultural Revolution in China, the Civil Rights Movement in the United States, the brutal Soviet crackdown on opposition in places like Prague, the rising tide of anticolonial activism across the Global South, the Grand Coalition between the CDU and the SPD under the leadership of the former Nazi Kurt Georg Kiesinger that governed the Federal Republic from 1966 to 1969, the debate over and eventual passage of the Emergency Laws in West Germany in 1968, and the radical proliferation of experimental countercultural milieus. Galvanized by these events, which they tended to interpret through their readings of theorists like Marcuse and Regis Debray, a new generation of leftists began looking for ways to ignite revolutionary passions in cities like West Berlin.⁴⁰ As in earlier revolutionary moments, they increasingly felt that they could no longer wait for the revolution, that the time for radical action was now.⁴¹ The question was how best to proceed.

Following theorists like Marcuse, many activists in West Germany's burgeoning antiauthoritarian movement believed that the working classes of advanced capitalist societies had been lulled to sleep by the dreamworlds of consumption and liberal democracy and were thus no longer able to serve as the vanguard of a revolutionary movement. Many new leftists thus came to believe that they needed to look elsewhere to find dialectical catalysts for the revolution. On the one hand, this meant colonized populations abroad and those suffering from racist persecution in the metropole, groups that were idealized and often co-opted by West German leftist circles throughout the Red Decade. On the other hand, though, proponents of this theory also began calling attention to the revolutionary potential of countercultural youth who were engaged in small-scale rebellions "against the false fathers, teachers, and heroes," and who had "an all but instinctual solidarity" with the "wretched of the earth."⁴² Increasingly, many new leftists in the late 1960s came to believe that they could harness the explosive energies emerging from places like Schwabing for the purposes of the revolution.⁴³ In an April 1967 strategy paper, Reimut Reiche and Peter Gäng, for example, sought to convince members of the SDS to engage more systematically with youth groups in order to operationalize their "unpolitical protest attitudes."⁴⁴ One of the concrete repercussions of these discussions was the creation of groups like the Action Center for Independent and Socialist Students (AUSS), which combined politics and countercultural aesthetics in the hope of galvanizing youth activism. Similarly, the organizers of the International Essen Song Days of 1968 attempted to infuse new left politics into a festival showcasing the latest trends in popular music as well as the new styles and sociabilities of the counterculture. For many attendees and commentators, the "underground" music, art, and lifestyles on display at the festival represented a concrete negation of mainstream, bourgeois society and, as such, a potential dialectical catalyst for a larger revolutionary movement.[45]

Such attempts to make pop culture function dialectically were certainly at the heart of Kommune I, which became one of the most recognizable symbols of the antiauthoritarian revolt in West Germany. Initially dreamed up by various members of the Provo-inspired political group Subversive Aktion (including Rudi Dutschke, Dieter Kunzelmann, and Bernd Rabehl) during a meeting at Kochel am See in July 1966, Kommune I was conceptualized as a form of provocative theater meant both to scandalize the West German public and to politicize countercultural youth.[46] They sought to accomplish these goals in part by organizing spectacular actions such as the infamous "Pudding Attack" in which the police arrested some of the communards for making bombs to attack US Vice President Hubert Humphrey that turned out, much to the embarrassment of the authorities, to have been made of pudding. Shortly thereafter, they grabbed headlines again by distributing flyers on a department store fire in Brussels—including one with the intentionally provocative title "When Will the Berlin Department Stores Burn?" Here, they mobilized the language of advertising to describe the fire, writing: "Our Belgian friends have finally figured out how to let the people really take part in the fun events [lustigen Treiben] of Vietnam: they set fire to a department store, two hundred saturated citizens ended their exciting lives, and Brussels became Hanoi. [. . .] Brussels has provided us with the only answer [to the events in Vietnam]: burn, warehouse, burn!"[47] Arrested for the stunt, the communards proceeded to make a mockery of the court where, among other actions, they accused the state of various crimes and blew bubbles.[48]

These spectacular actions as well as the communards' highly publicized embrace of countercultural aesthetics and practices (drug consumption, sexual experimentation, and a rejection of bourgeois social norms) combined avant-garde shock tactics with pop cultural negations of polite society in an attempt to politicize countercultural youth, who, many believed, could serve as the new agents of the revolution. These attempts to make popular youth culture function dialectically also resulted in a shift in how many new leftists in the 1960s conceptualized themselves, with some beginning to imagine that *they* could assume the role of the authentic agents of revolutionary change. After all, many of these activists were avid participants in the countercultural forms they had identified as having revolutionary potential. This shift helped to spark an intense radicalization of leftist practice in the 1960s. If the feelings of breaking through into the new that suffused popular youth culture in these years represented the dialectically necessary negations of contemporary society, and if new left activists were themselves enthusiastic participants in this new stream of radical negation, then it stood to reason that they could serve as the agents of a new revolutionary movement, which was on the verge of changing the world. As Detlef Siegfried has argued, the melding of the "the cultural revolutionary and political streams" made it seem as if "the revolution [was] within reach."[49] It produced something like a flow state for the new left, a moment when theory and practice came into alignment making it appear as if the future was being born before their eyes.

Peter Schneider's autobiographical account of these years clearly illustrates the ecstatic feelings that emerged as leftists began imagining that the revolution was taking place in the present and that they were its primary protagonists. "It was," he notes, "a rush [*Rausch*] without drugs, the rush of a 'historically necessary' and 'scientifically grounded' utopia, that took possession of our minds and hearts."[50] Operating in this world-historical key, participants felt as if the past didn't exist, as if "there was only the present and the future."[51] Their actions, it seemed, were constitutive of the revolutionary future, which was unfolding in the present. Collapsing self and world, Schneider and others came to assume that their desires represented the unspoken will of the masses.[52] Acting on their desires was thus not only enjoyable, it was a necessary act of revolutionary negation that would help to usher in utopia, a final and definitive act of breaking through into the new. As the tempo of revolutionary events reached a fevered pitch in 1968, participants could lose themselves in the dialectical rush of the imminent transformation of the world. No longer were they merely seeking to identify and guide the chosen agents of dialectical progress; they had become the theoretical vanguard *and* the authentic agents of revolution all at once. They knew the future even as they were charged with bringing it about. As theory and practice melded together, activists felt as if they were on the verge of the new, as if their actions in the present would determine the future of the world. To quote Susan Buck-Morss writing on an earlier revolutionary moment, it was "when existence was just like the movies, just like the advertising or propaganda image, that one felt truly alive."[53] Although short in duration, these events would have a large impact on subsequent West German new lefts.

In the months following the April 1968 assassination attempt on Rudi Dutschke, the sense of being on the verge of total revolution began to dissipate, yet the antiauthoritarian revolts in West Germany were far from finished. Indeed, throughout the Red Decade, leftist groups across the Federal Republic sought to recreate the rush of these years by developing new techniques for breaking through into the new. Although they imagined it differently, many of the leftist groups in the 1970s remained as, if not more, committed to the logics of progress as their predecessors had been. Drawing from Kristin Ross's interpretation of the legacy of the Paris Commune, the experimental practices of the 1970s can be understood as the "*prolongation*" of the original events of 1968, which were "every bit as vital to the event's logic as in the initial acts of insurrection in the streets."[54] The following section details some of these experiments as they played out in the 1970s. It is not meant as a comprehensive survey of leftist activism in 1970s West Germany, but as a brief analysis of how some new leftists continued to experiment with the logics of progress after 1968.

∴

In a March 1970 speech, Udo Knapp, the provisional head of the rapidly disintegrating SDS, proclaimed that "the exhaustion of the student revolts should not simply be viewed negatively [. . .], but must be considered as a process of self-recognition amongst the actors [. . .] who today as socialist intellectuals are no longer interested in the reconstitution of a student organization along the lines of the SDS, but rather treat the organization question as pertaining to the perspectives of the class battle and the organization of the proletariat."[55] As this speech makes clear, some viewed the end of the SDS as an opportunity to jettison the countercultural proclivities of the antiauthoritarian movement and return to the orthodox dialectical practices of the old left. In this vein, activists associated with the burgeoning Communist groups (the so-called K-Gruppen), as well as many of those operating under the aegis of the Neighborhood Groups, reengaged with Communist theorists from Luxemburg to Lenin and returned to more traditional leftist positions.

This meant, first and foremost, that youth culture could no longer be considered a viable medium for revolutionary change. In an August 1969 article in the radical journal *Agit 883* titled "Getting Stoned and Revolution," for example, Werner Olles argued, perhaps with the Hash Rebels in mind:

"It is clear beyond a doubt that where pot is smoked, where flower power is practiced, that there Marx's Kapital and Guevara's Guerilla—Theory and Method are probably seldom read, and it has likewise been shown that the radicalism of the Hascher [stoners] and the members of hippie-like subcultures never go beyond a noncommittal pacifism containing thoroughly bourgeois elements."[56] Whereas many antiauthoritarian leftists in the 1960s sought to spark dialectical progress by politicizing or in some cases co-opting the negated positionalities of the postwar order (ranging from anticolonial activists to members of the Gammler milieu), activists associated with the K-Gruppen turned to idealized images of the revolutionary proletariat, who they viewed as more appropriate mediums for generating revolutionary change. Participants in these groups cut their hair short, dressed conservatively, and spent their time reading Marxist theory and singing socialist songs rather than doing drugs and listening to Jimi Hendrix. They still sought to spark the revolution by representing what they understood to be the authentic agents of revolutionary negation. They simply no longer believed that the aesthetics and sociabilities of popular youth culture could fill that role.

Whereas the K-Gruppen sought to reanimate the spirit of revolution by returning to original principles, other groups took a more experimental tack.[57] I focus in the following pages on three such groups, some of which were already emerging amid the antiauthoritarian revolts: those who centered the body and subjectivity, those who turned to violence, and finally those who cast a wide net looking for ways to hasten the arrival of the revolutionary future.

The turn to the body and subjectivity was already well underway at the height of the antiauthoritarian movement. Many activists believed that attaining the utopian future required that the agents of revolution had to be cleansed of the persistent presence of the fascist past, which clung to the bodies, the social forms, and the built environments of the postwar. What was needed, in this view, were strategies for exorcising the ghosts of the past in order to facilitate the coming of the future, a leftist rehashing of postwar denazification. The Vienna Actionists serve as an early and particularly extreme example of this process. A loose configuration of radical artists operating in 1960s Vienna, the Actionists designed performances centering phenomena that had been repressed in the postwar period, whether these were memories of the traumatic past or more basic biological processes like sex and death. In one performance, artists slaughtered a pig on stage and rolled in its blood while singing "Silent Night, Holy Night." In another event, a group of Actionists marched in step as if in a military unit, while covering themselves in paint and spitting a bloodlike, gelatinous substance into each other's mouths. In what was perhaps the culminating event of the movement, artists engaged in simultaneous actions in front of an outraged audience at an event organized by the Socialist Austrian Student Union in June of 1968. As Otto Muehl gave a speech denouncing the recently assassinated Robert Kennedy, Günter Brus slashed his chest, urinated in his hand, drank the urine, vomited, and then sang the Austrian national anthem while defecating and masturbating on stage.[58] Such performances were clearly designed to shock audiences into an awareness of the false promises of progress. They also, though, served as a form of "catharsis" in which acting out repressed memories and desires could have "a purifying, even healing, and above all also preventative effect."[59] The Actionists' conjuring of repressed pasts can thus be seen as a part of a broader attempt to overcome them and thus liberate the revolutionary self to pursue a different future.

Another early iteration of this mode of thought is Peter Schneider's plans for an "Exorcist Theater," which was based on the notion that "the Germans needed to run screaming through the streets for at least a week before anything could change."[60] Schneider's unrealized performance called for actors to vent their frustrations against society until they were called to silence by a "German Malcolm X" who would incorporate their voices into a chorus resembling "It's the ballot or the bullet."[61] Here, the goal seems to have been to liberate individuals from the legacies of the past in order to transform them into dialectical agents of the future. Members of the Kinderladen movement also sought to exorcise the stain of the past for the purposes of the revolutionary future, though they attempted to do so using experimental child-rearing practices. Drawing heavily from Wilhelm Reich, they argued that repression, and especially sexual repression, produced fascists. Having been raised by such sexually repressive, closeted fascists, they believed that they themselves were too damaged to serve as agents of the revolutionary future. Their own children, however, still had the chance to become agents of change. Practitioners of this movement created special learning environments in which children would not be disciplined or have their desires thwarted in any way and, as such, would naturally grow into antiauthoritarians capable of realizing the revolutionary future. This was a projected prefiguration of utopian futures by way of generational change.[62]

Not all attempts to jumpstart dialectical progress by exorcising the legacies of the violent past were quite so jarring. In his preface to Deleuze and Guattari's wildly popular *Anti-Oedipus*, for example, Michel Foucault, who closely followed developments in the West German counterculture, asked: "How do we rid our speech and our acts, our hearts, and our pleasures, of fascism? How do we ferret out the fascism that is ingrained in our behavior?"[63] The answers, which he argued were provided by Deleuze and Guattari's book, included: "Free action from all unitary and totalizing paranoia." "Do not think that one has to be sad in order to be militant, even though the thing one is fighting is abominable. It is the connection of desire to reality (and not its retreat into the forms of representation) that possesses revolutionary force." And: "Do not demand of politics that it restore the 'rights' of the individual, as philosophy has defined them. The individual is the product of power. What is needed is to 'de-individualize' by means of multiplication and displacement, diverse combinations."[64] If fascism was a form of disciplinary normalization in which individuals felt compelled to internalize the dictates of power as the precondition for subjectivity, and if these mechanisms were as widespread in the postwar period as they had been during the Nazi years, then the answer was simple: denormalize the self. In radically expanding the field of fascist power, these theories of normalization allowed readers to imagine that their own battles against their parents, their bosses, and their teachers were part of a broader fight against the everyday legacies of fascism.

Foucault's suggestions that individuals could combat fascism by freeing themselves and their surroundings of all traces of power were enthusiastically put into practice by many alternative leftists throughout the 1970s. This is not to say that everyone in the left-alternative milieu read Foucault (though many did), but that philosophical inquiries and activist practices tended to overlap. Hoping to rid themselves of the legacies of the fascist past and the capitalist present, many sought to develop strategies to "'fix' their damaged personalities, to overcome their isolation and to develop personal relations based on tenderness and solidarity."[65] Such practices of "emotionality and bodily sensuality became a mode of self-realization" enabling individuals to forge what they believed to be authentic alternatives to imperialist/fascist/bourgeois values.[66] Whether stemming from fascism or from the "protestant ethics" of capitalism, traces of the violent past held them back from reaching their true revolutionary potential and thus had to be identified and eliminated. Freeing themselves from these stains of the past, however, proved to be exceptionally difficult, partially as a result of their continued reliance on the narrative logics of progress, which bound the present to the past even as it stipulated that it was only by overcoming the past that one could reach the future. Instead of liberated subjectivities, they often ended up with an ever growing list of personal deficiencies.

In a similar fashion, many of the activists who turned to revolutionary violence in the 1970s also attributed the stalled revolution to personal deficiencies stemming from their bourgeois upbringings. Their solution was not to attempt to overcome these deficiencies by embracing authenticity and social warmth, though, but with increasingly radical commitments to violence. From the outset, violence, or at least the possibility of violence, had been a defining feature of the extraparliamentary opposition. Over and above the symbolic violence and art-inspired provocations championed by figures like Kunzelmann, many leftist activists came to see insurrection as a very real possibility, especially in the months following the June 1967 murder of Benno Ohnesorg at the protests against the Shah's visit to West Berlin. Armed with theoretical treatises on the necessity of revolution ranging from Lenin and Mao Zedong to Fanon and Regis Debray, student revolutionaries in Paris, Frankfurt, and West Berlin convinced themselves that they were at the center of a global insurrection that was on the verge of sweeping into power. According to Gerd Koenen, this fascination with theoretical blueprints for revolutionary social transformation "exceeded from the outset all definite interests in concrete relationships, the here and now, and actual politics."[67] The complexities of everyday reality, in other words, were in constant danger of being wholly subsumed into the supposedly higher, transcendental truths of revolutionary abstraction.[68]

In part, this willingness to consider violent insurrection as a viable means of combating the state came from the students' engagement with the theoretical corpus of Marxist and anarchist thought, but it also emerged out of their fascination with anticolonial revolutionary movements across the globe. As Quinn Slobodian has convincingly argued, however, this vision often "effaced the particularity of Third World experience by abstracting it from history, making it modular and repeatable in a Western context."[69] If violent insurrection was deemed necessary according to revolutionary theory, and if the students were themselves part of the revolutionary class destined to overthrow the state, then it made sense for them to engage in acts of violence and to imagine that these acts were equivalent to those being concurrently undertaken by anticolonial fighters in the Global South. As the antiauthoritarian movement gained momentum in the late 1960s, many students evinced an ever greater willingness to engage in acts of violent opposition. The International Vietnam Congress, the Springer Tribunal of February 1968, the Easter 1968 attacks on the Springer publishing building following the attempted assassination of Dutschke, the "Battle at Tegeler Weg," and the expansion of militant groups like the Blues all indicate that a large number of leftist youths were increasingly willing to put their ideas of violent insurrection into practice, to trade their books and guitars for rocks and guns. The revolution was real, they were its protagonists, and they were going to prove it.

Although a number of different militant groups, including the Hash Rebels, the Tupamaros, and the June 2nd Movement, emerged from the antiauthoritarian milieu in West Berlin, they were all united by their commitment to anarchist practices, their rejection of ideological orthodoxy, and their stubborn refusal to jettison countercultural lifestyles.[70] Members of these groups also "understood themselves as the excluded, the marginalized, the criminalized, as those who had been banished to the edge of society."[71] With their black leather jackets, excessive drug consumption, and commitment to radical social transformation, these activists were in many respects the ultimate incarnation of the antiauthoritarian rebel ideal, the sort of people Reiche and Gäng likely had in mind when they called for the SDS to pay more attention to the revolutionary potential of countercultural youth. As someone with connections to a number of militant groups, Bommi Baumann serves as a particularly good example of this form of activism. Reminiscing on the Easter 1968 riots in West Berlin, Baumann clearly identifies the moment he was initiated into the cult of violent resistance: "On the spot, I really got it, this concept of mass struggle-terrorism. [. . .] The determined group is there simultaneously with the masses, supporting them through terror. Standing there in front of the flames, I realized that this is how you can get somewhere. [. . .] The general baiting had created a climate in which little pranks wouldn't work anymore. Not when they're going to liquidate you, regardless of what you do. Before I get transported to Auschwitz again, I'd rather shoot first, that's clear now."[72] As Baumann's statement plainly indicates, some participants in the anarchist movements of the late 1960s and early 1970s felt themselves to be part of an activist vanguard, heroically leading the masses in a revolution against any and all forms of domination.

Baumann's statement is also indicative, however, of the astonishingly narcissistic attitudes that characterized some of the participants in this movement. Leftist radicals in the early 1970s such as Baumann often saw themselves not only as revolutionary vanguards leading the masses into battle but also as victims of state power and, in extreme cases, as victims of fascism, who were forced to fight for their very existence and whose goal was not getting "transported to Auschwitz *again*." Whether they were organizing mass hash-smoking parties in the Tiergarten, robbing banks throughout West Berlin, listening to rock music, traveling to the Middle East to learn guerrilla tactics, engaging in shoot-outs with the police, or kidnapping politicians (as, for example, in the case of the June 2nd Movement's kidnapping of West Berlin mayoral candidate Peter Lorenz in 1975), many members of these groups tended to see themselves as *the* embodiment of revolutionary negation engaged in a seemingly cosmic and never-ending battle with the transhistorical agents of domination.

While the anarchist groups of this period certainly traveled a long way down the path of mythologized insurrection, they were eclipsed by the multiple generations of militants associated with the Red Army Faction.[73] Founded in 1970 by Andreas Baader, Gudrun Ensslin, Horst Mahler, and Ulrike Meinhof, the RAF was responsible for numerous violent attacks throughout the 1970s. Unlike the anarchist groups described above who rarely published any statements justifying their actions, the RAF produced a number of highly theoretical communiqués including "The Concept of the Urban Guerilla" (1971), "Urban Guerillas and Class Struggle" (1972), and "The Actions of the Black September in Munich—On the Strategy of the Anti-imperial Struggle" (1972). For the members of the RAF, militance was much more than mere provocation. It was an attempt to definitively prove to themselves and others that they were the ultimate agents of revolution and, in so doing, to reignite the passions that had burned so intensively in the antiauthoritarian revolts. According to Margit Schiller, taking part in the great battle against the demons of history facilitated "a break with the central norms and values" of bourgeois society, a calling that led her to "depart from [her] previous life" and join something bigger.[74] This was revolution as religious calling.

As Gudrun Ensslin argued when she acerbically accused organizations like the June 2nd Movement of juvenile, hedonistic behavior, noting: "This job that we are doing is serious. It is not allowed to be fun," members of the RAF saw themselves as more committed revolutionaries than the anarchist milieus from which they emerged.[75] They were, however, ultimately motivated by similar concerns. Much like the June 2nd Movement, the RAF engaged in a peculiarly ahistorical battle against the demons of the past. Fashioning themselves as redemptive agents, they sought to use violence to punish West Germany "for the sins of the past and for [. . .] their repetition in the present through such things as police repression and German support for American 'genocide' in Vietnam."[76] They were both the victims of fascism and the agents of vengeance. They were the Red Army who had taken Berlin in 1945, the Royal Air Force that had flattened German cities, and the judges tasked with punishing Nazis after the war. Enamored with the feelings of breaking through into the new associated with being on the edge of a radical transformation of the world, the RAF froze revolutionary dialectics at the imaginary fulcrum point of radical change. The future, in this vision, was always imminent even as their actions remained paramount for its realization.[77]

Let me offer one final example before concluding this brief survey of leftist attempts to resuscitate the feelings of progress in the wake of 1968. Borrowing the slogan "we want everything, and we want it now" from the Italian autonomist groups around Lotta Continua, the Spontis sought to keep the energies of the antiauthoritarian revolt alive by constantly experimenting with new configurations of dialectical progress. They attempted to infiltrate factories like Opel in Rüsselsheim to politicize the workers; they mobilized Marcuse's theories of marginal groups in their work with immigrants, students, runaways, and the homeless; they contributed to the budding ecology movements and the protests against nuclear power; and they helped build and support left-alternative infrastructure like bars, kindergartens, and newspapers.[78] This tendency to embrace any and all possibilities for reviving leftist activism was on full display in what was perhaps their most successful venture, namely the housing struggles (*Häuserkämpfe*) of the early 1970s.

Although they came to be the group most closely identified with this movement in Frankfurt, the Spontis joined the conflict only in its final years. Indeed, by the time the Spontis decided to take part in the movement, West German activists and Citizens' Initiatives had been mobilizing against urban renewal projects and the destruction of traditional neighborhood structures for more than a decade.[79] The construction of modernist housing blocks in the 1960s had generated significant critique best represented in the West German case by Alexander Mitscherlich's 1965 book *The Inhospitality of Our Cities,* however it was the shift toward inner-city revitalization programs in the 1970s that sparked a much more vehement opposition movement consisting of preservationists, leftist Christian groups, Citizens Initiatives like the Aktionsgemeinschaft Westend, "guest workers," and older residents being forced from their homes. Once it became clear that their actions were garnering broad interest from the public, the Spontis took notice and wanted in.[80]

The Spontis were not initially interested in protecting traditional forms of dwelling from the wrecking ball. Instead, they saw in the opposition to urban renewal an opportunity to politicize at-risk urban populations and thus reenergize the march toward revolution. In the 1975 brochure *Häuserkampf-info 1,* for example, the authors authoritatively declared: "With the intensification of the political and economic contradictions of capitalism, the severity of the awaited conflict in the state and the factories will also sharpen. This will cause the further growth of the political consciousness of wide swaths of the population. [. . .] Under these conditions the housing battles in 1974 will become sharper and more than ever before a fighting perspective for the masses."[81] Like other activist groups in the Red Decade, the Spontis were not content with radicalizing and guiding the revolutionary masses; they also believed that they could serve as agents of revolution themselves, a belief that was facilitated by the necessarily embodied act of squatting houses. Describing the experience of leaving jail and finding that the house they had squatted had been torn down, for example, one of the activists remarked: "As we came out of jail, we stood before a mountain of rubble. Full of anger, we discovered what it means to be forcibly displaced, what it means when one's home is taken away."[82] In addition, then, to viewing at-risk populations living in urban areas as potential dialectical catalysts for transforming the world, the Spontis also saw in the occupied houses an opportunity to solidify their own status as authentic agents of revolution. Like the RAF and other militant anarchist groups in the 1970s, the Spontis sought to prove that their fight against the agents of the state was not just theoretical but existential and thus to resuscitate the feeling of being an active participant in the imminent transformation of the world.

∴

In his 2007 autobiographical account of leftist activism in West Germany, Götz Aly wrote that "both, the rulers and the left-radical students, spoke endlessly of the future. The latter 'dreamed' [. . .] of a paradise that went by the name of 'real Utopia' while the former paved over the country and gave off the impression that the freeways [*Autobahnen*], and only they, led directly to eternal happiness."[83] Setting aside his obvious irritation with almost all dimensions of new leftist activism, Aly is on point with his observation that the first two decades after the war in West Germany were marked by a widespread obsession with the future, an almost fetishistic attachment to progressive temporalities that was evident in the embrace of consumption and modernist aesthetics during the Economic Miracle, in the antiauthoritarian left's attempts to make popular culture function dialectically, in the utopian hopes that the Kinderladen activists placed in their children, and even in the RAF's mythologization of revolutionary conflict. Despite their many differences, the manifold groups discussed in this chapter all sought to become active participants in the realization of the new. And yet, because the feeling of moving forward, of breaking through into the new, is premised on repeatedly separating the past from the present, their hopes of achieving a definitive temporal break were consistently dashed.[84] Again and again, the past simply refused to be put to rest.

This was certainly frustrating for many of the participants in these movements, but it was also an essential component in the expansion of the modern time regime, which is fueled by the identification and performative exclusion of the past from the present. As is also true of "use value" for capitalism, the presence of the past is a constitutive necessity for progressive temporal regimes. The inability to separate the past from the present and thus to definitively break through into the truly new, led many leftists to engage in ever more radical attempts to find alternative routes into the future. The temporal dynamics of postwar progress, in other words, were structured in such a way as to intensify, and intensify they did.[85] In autumn 1977, the so-called German Autumn, the search for a miraculous route to the utopian future crescendoed in a frenzy of murder and despair. Following the April 1977 assassination of West Germany's attorney general Siegfried Buback and the July 1977 murder of banker Jürgen Ponto, members of the RAF kidnapped Hans Martin Schleyer on September 5, 1977, and demanded the release of Gudrun Ensslin, Jan-Carl Raspe, and Andreas Baader, who were being held in the high-security Stammheim prison. Fearing that Schleyer would prove an insufficient bargaining chip, a group of Palestinian militants loosely allied with the RAF hijacked Lufthansa Flight 181 on October 13. Subsequent events did not, however, proceed according to plan. After an elite West German counterterrorism unit commenced with "Operation Fire Magic" in which they stormed the plane, killed most of the hijackers, and freed the hostages, Ensslin, Raspe, and Baader were all found dead in their cells in Stammheim, and Schleyer's body was left in the trunk of a car near Mulhouse, France. The government's invocation of "magic fire," it seems, had succeeded.[86] The revolution was over. What would come next, though, was less certain.

[CHAPTER TWO]

The Countercultural "Off-Modern"

By the mid-1970s and especially as RAF violence crescendoed in a wave of murder in 1977, many on the left, including former champions of militance like Joschka Fischer and Rudi Dutschke, began to publicly question the morality and the political efficacy of radical violence. Such sentiments were on full display in the infamous "Buback-Nachruf," in which a certain "Göttinger Mescalero," later identified as Klaus Hülbrock, evinced both a "secret joy" at the RAF's murder of West German Attorney General Siegfried Buback *and* an overwhelming desire for a new path to socialism which "cannot be paved with dead bodies."[1] Others, such as the directors of the film *Deutschland im Herbst*, simply wanted the violence to end, noting: "When one reaches a certain point of barbarity, it no longer matters who started it: it should just stop."[2] As violence gradually lost its luster, many West German leftists began to wonder how they had come to this point and where they could go from here. An activist from Munich clearly described these feelings of disillusionment, noting: "Somewhere between Stammheim and Mogadishu, our dreams dissolved. [. . .] We opened our eyes and realized that the entire direction had been false and that we needed a course corrective."[3]

Numerous scholars have characterized the years following the German Autumn as a period in which the various factions of the West German left turned away from radical violence and toward new modes of revolutionary practice. Whereas for many, this meant transitioning into more mainstream forms of democratic politics, for others it implied experimenting with the logics of progressive time.[4] Some of these more experimental groups began looking to the possibility of constructing alternative social and cultural forms in the present by founding communes, developing new forms of critical media like the *Tageszeitung*, and building left-alternative infrastructure in cities throughout the Federal Republic. Others experimented with music or engaged in illegal occupations in an effort to revive the feelings of breaking through into the new that had fueled prior generations of leftist activists.

Galvanized by the growing concerns over environmental collapse, some even attempted to find ways to stop the flow of time altogether. This chapter focuses on three groups that arose in these years: left-alternative lifestyle reformers, neighborhood activists, and punk and New Wave artists, all of whom sought to reimagine revolutionary temporalities in the wake of the German Autumn. Although not always in ways that their practitioners could have foreseen, these experiments resulted in new, off-modern configurations of time that would come to serve as catalysts for the explosion of postprogressive practices in the early 1980s.

∴

As RAF-style militance was careening toward its bloody conclusion, large segments of the West German left—including many who had previously derided countercultural activities as fundamentally apolitical, if not downright counterrevolutionary—began to look to the autonomous lifeworlds, liberated subjectivities, and social "warmth" pioneered by diverse countercultural and leftist groups in the 1970s for a new way forward. In a 1976 article in the journal *Autonomie*, Meinrad Rohner expressed this desire for alternatives to violence, arguing that: "The revolutionary process consists not only of the ability to destroy capitalist relations in mass but also the ability to lead a new life in the present. The party of destruction is nothing without the party of alternatives."[5] In the wake of the German Autumn a group of disaffected Spontis sought to meet this challenge by organizing the TUNIX festival in West Berlin.[6] One of the major events in the development of left-alternative politics in these years, the January 1978 TUNIX (literally "do nothing") festival in West Berlin emphasized the role of leftist networking, public outreach campaigns, and acts of collective fantasy as more effective means for combating what the conference organizers described as the "bleak asphalt-concrete-deserts of the new construction [*Neubau*] areas," "the violence of the police apparatus," and forms of consumer capitalism that "destroy our dreams with Peter Stuyvesant [cigarettes] and Springer's *Bild* [tabloid newspaper], their unchanging TV shows and their Coca-Cola-Karajan-culture."[7] As this statement indicates, the organizers of TUNIX had by no means abandoned the anticapitalist critiques of the 1960s and 1970s. They still believed that capitalism destroyed lives and prevented people from seeing the real conditions of their existence. Increasingly, though, they sought to combat this state of affairs by living alternatively in the present rather than working to ignite a revolutionary movement that would overcome capitalism in the future.

In many respects, this shift can be attributed to the growing influence of the apocalyptic imaginaries associated with the burgeoning environmental and anti-nuclear movements, which had begun to suffuse leftist thought in the mid-1970s.[8] According to Silke Mende, the activists associated with the nascent Green movement "cultivated a properly apocalyptic feeling, which viewed the present as a prelude to the coming end of the world."[9] The nascent Greens were not, however, alone in this. For a variety of reasons (including the economic crises of the 1970s, the growing fears of environmental catastrophe stemming from incidents like the Three Mile Island accident in 1979, and the failure of leftist movements to implement radical change), apocalypse was in the air. According to Fernando Esposito, in the late 1970s, the "telos of history [. . .] was lost, and for a growing number of contemporaries the future had transformed from an open horizon of possibilities conducive to action into a source of various threats on the horizon."[10]

Imagining the future as catastrophe did not, however, necessarily lead to resignation. For many environmentalists and members of the left-alternative milieu such apocalyptic imaginaries pushed them to focus even more intensively on building alternative worlds in the present. If the present was the prelude to the coming apocalypse, then it was only by radically transforming this present that one could begin to salvage the future. For some this meant "marching through the institutions" and attempting to create structures in the present that would counteract impending catastrophes. For others, including many left-alternative activists in the late 1970s, the apocalyptic visions of the future coupled with growing doubts about the necessity of progress for living a radical life (the idea, that is, that one could trade prefiguration for figuration and thus make new worlds in the present rather than revolutions in the future) led them in a different direction. Whereas earlier generations of new leftists had often sought to utilize negated populations as dialectical tools for hastening the arrival of the promised utopian future, many activists in the late 1970s looked for alternative ways of organizing life in the present in order to prevent the catastrophic future from coming to pass. Alternative leftists in the late 1970s became ever more interested in embracing their true inner selves and living authentically with the natural environment and with others. They lived collectively in shared apartments known as *Wohngemeinschaften* (WGs), joined alternative therapy groups, ate at organic restaurants, and sought to avoid participating in consumer culture, not in order to provoke the masses or to prefigure the future, but to forge an authentic life in the present, a right life in the wrong one. In a sense, the goal here was to cultivate practices meant to slow down the passage of time and, in extreme cases, even to stop it in its tracks so as to avert the coming apocalypse.

In some instances, this shift from prefiguration to figuration brought with it a new wave of cultural appropriation. Indeed, many leftists still imagined that the negated others of capitalist modernity represented an authentic alternative to the alienation of contemporary life. Instead of attempting to radicalize these groups and use them as vehicles for breaking through into the utopian future, though, some left-alternative activists sought to become them. A flyer from TUNIX titled (and presumably produced by) the "Council of Tribes of the Berlin Mescaleros," for example noted: "Many tribes have come together in the land of TUNIX, and we will be as countless as the stars in heaven. You will recognize us by our open, brightly painted, cheerful faces, resolved for any struggle. We will wake your stony gray wigwams to life with our bright colors . . . Our dance and our electric guitars will destroy your ears but give us eternal energy and strength. Jimi Hendricks [sic] comes back from the eternal hunting grounds. We will tear down these gray walls that you name prisons. We will blow the smoke from our pipes to the four winds, so that you will know the cheerfulness of our lives."[11] Large numbers of alternative leftists in the late 1970s evinced a renewed interest in non-Western forms of spirituality, in childhood, and in magic—in short, in anything that was deemed obsolete by modernity, capitalism, rationality, and bourgeois culture. According to Joachim Häberlen, they envisioned "a conflict between the dominating forces of rationality, and everything that remained beyond rationality, such as dreams, desires, or feelings," with the latter seeming to offer authentic alternatives that leftists increasingly sought to make their own.[12] They became "dream dancers," "city Indians," "lost tribes," and "Mescaleros" whose authenticity was assured by their uncompromising, existential opposition to all elements of modern bourgeois life.

Although this shift away from revolutionary futures did not go without critique, by the late 1970s it nonetheless became widespread within much of the left-alternative milieu.[13] Not only did leading figures of the antiauthoritarian revolt like Joschka Fischer and Herbert Röttgen come to accept the viability of this position, but even left-leaning academics like the anthropologist Hans Peter Dürr lent authority to these ideas.[14] According to Dürr, the author of the wildly popular 1978 book *Dreamtime: On the Border between Wilderness and Civilization*, thinking about "hunter-gatherer societies," "shows us where we should stop, if possible get out. [. . .] And therefore, you shouldn't underestimate the roles other lifestyles can play. Every revolt needs its myths."[15] Romanticized alterity became one of the primary foundations on which the postrevolutionary left would seek to construct utopia in the present.

The ideology that began to emerge in the months following the German Autumn was thus built on a contradictory foundation. On the one hand, many postrevolutionary activists continued to operate within the established temporal logics of dialectical progress. Whether by marching through the institutions or attempting to politicize marginalized groups, they still subscribed to a narrative of progressive change in which theoretically informed acts in the present could help spark dialectical movement toward the utopian future. On the other hand, however, many were increasingly convinced that that the future toward which the world was heading was bound to be catastrophic and that the only way to prevent it was to find ways to sidestep, or even step outside of, time and thus perhaps stop progress in its tracks. They believed that one could conjure and live utopia in the present and thus prevent the world from hurtling toward apocalyptic collapse. For all of their critiques of the RAF, such attempts to freeze time and dwell indefinitely in the spaces of authentic negation operated in a strikingly similar mythological vein.

∴

As historian Jennifer Allen has argued in relation to the locally focused activists of the Green Party, artists engaged in "spatial interventionist" projects, and the amateur historians who took part in the history workshops, the temporal practices of West German leftists in the late 1970s and early 1980s were not limited to attempts to implement change through mainstream politics or through appropriative acts of left-alternative romanticism. As Allen has noted, a growing number of left-alternative activists abandoned grand utopian visions and began looking for ways to build "sustainable utopias" in the present, not as a way to stop the flow of time but in order implement change in a more systematic, more sustainable fashion. Instead of a revolutionary event that would totally remake the world at some point in the future, utopia came to be understood as something one could begin systematically working toward in the present. A slow drip rather than a great flood, for the actors on whom Allen's analysis focused, the "telos" of the utopian future became one of "ongoing action" in the everyday.[16]

In a number of respects, the left's growing interest in locality and the built environment can be considered as part of this shift into sustainable utopias. Resistance to the postwar destruction of what were deemed to be authentic urban lifeworlds and architectural forms had a long history in West Germany.[17] What initially had been a largely conservative movement intent on protecting traditional neighborhoods from the ravages of modernizing city planners became, over the course of the late 1970s, a broad-based coalition of groups who, albeit for very different reasons, sought to rescue German cities from capitalist development. In West Berlin, for example, groups of leftist neighborhood activists, Citizens Initiatives, progressive architects such as those associated with the journal *Arch+*, and members of the Evangelical Church came together under the auspices of the government-sponsored *Strategien für Kreuzberg* in early 1977 with the goal of developing new strategies for urban renewal in Kreuzberg, long considered to be one of West Germany's most "at-risk" neighborhoods.[18] The main work of the *Strategien* was conducted by the Project Commission, which was tasked with gathering and reviewing submissions for neighborhood improvement projects, ranging from suggestions for neighborhood centers to playgrounds to job training.[19] One project submission, for example, called for the creation of a neighborhood center that would both empower average citizens to solve problems and fight against unjust urban policies on their own and allow them to cultivate a sense of community through such activities as "eating, drinking, household management, craft work, organization of neighborhood assistance, making music, putting on plays, making films, continuing education, reading, presenting, writing, and printing books."[20]

In the months leading up to and immediately following the German Autumn, ever larger numbers of disillusioned antiauthoritarians began joining these initiatives to combat urban renewal. Leftist activists were intimately involved, for example, in the battle over the Feuerwache building in Kreuzberg, an old fire station that was occupied in May 1977 with the goal of creating a self-governed neighborhood center. Combining preservationist goals of protecting historic neighborhood structures with dialectical strategies for politicizing marginalized groups, the Feuerwache occupants demanded funds to renovate the existing structure, more citizen participation in neighborhood revitalization plans, and increased support for self-help projects. In addition to collectively renovating the building, which was set to be demolished to make room for a sports center, occupants and their allies created theater troupes, German-Turkish meeting groups, and an information center to help raise the consciousness and morale of "affected populations" (*Betroffene*) in the neighborhood such as immigrants, drug addicts, and unemployed youth. Despite an outpouring of support from surrounding residents and from progressive activists throughout the city, the occupants were evicted in June 1977. In a flyer published after the eviction, activists reaffirmed their commitment to combating the city's urban renewal programs and defending at-risk populations, writing: "We have seen, that a dialogue with the neighborhood administration is never possible. [. . .] They want those with problems to remain invisible and for the underdogs to suffer alone with their problems or be pushed into criminality so that that they can then be forcibly transported to Moabit [prison]. [. . .] We have nonetheless not come to the realization that we should give up. We

FIGURE 2.1. Cover image from "Stadtteilzentrum Feuerwache" (1977). Source: Papiertiger Archiv.

will keep on fighting but with other means."[21] As the flyer clearly indicates, the eviction of the Feuerwache did not result in a waning of enthusiasm for extralegal forms of urban activism but in a rising sense of frustration with city officials and with reformist strategies for change.

This was certainly the case, for example, with the Citizen's Initiative

SO36 (BI SO36), which was founded in late 1977 with the goal of developing projects to encourage more humane, "resident-oriented" forms of urban renewal in the SO36 neighborhood of Kreuzberg.[22] Members of the initiative advised renters in the neighborhood of their rights, advocated for the retention of older buildings, and published the *Südost Express*.[23] Faced with recalcitrant property owners and an unresponsive city administration, however, some of the activists in the BI SO36 also began to experiment with more creative action forms such as calls to illegally occupy some of the empty houses, a tactic that came to be known as *Instandbesetzungen*, a combination of the words "repair" (*instandsetzen*) and "occupation" (*Besetzung*). In February 1979, after months of failed legal battles, members of the BI SO36 occupied buildings on the Görlitzer and Lübbener streets in Kreuzberg to actively protest the destruction of living space and to draw attention to the failure of urban renewal policies.[24] Shortly thereafter they took part in the occupation of a building on the Cuvrystraße in Kreuzberg, which, like the earlier occupations, was only conducted after months of legal maneuvering to prevent demolition. Despite the fact that many members of the BI SO36 understood such occupations as last resort options, they proved to be incredibly effective forms of publicity, which not only generated support from left-leaning groups throughout the city but also galvanized others to follow suit. One group of squatters, for example, published an announcement in the *Südost Express* claiming that they had acted directly upon the suggestion of the BI SO36 by occupying an empty apartment building and were now prepared to offer advice to anyone else who might want to do something similar.[25] In the waning months of 1979, announcements of new occupations and invitations to join began appearing in alternative papers with increasing frequency. A new movement was taking shape.

Although similar in many respects to the politics of sustainable utopias, these early occupations also operated according to a number of additional temporal logics, some of which echoed the dialectical imaginaries of earlier generations of new leftists. For example, the squatters of the late 1970s often envisioned the occupations as dialectical tools that could advance broader revolutionary agendas by shining a critical light on the "politics of ghettoization" practiced by city officials and capitalist "speculators" (*Spekulanten*). Despite being less overtly radical than the antiauthoritarian practitioners of leftist dialectics from the previous decade, many of the organizers of these initial squatting actions nonetheless subscribed to similar progressive temporal logics in which capitalist modernity's negated others were operationalized as a means to fuel the liberatory momentum of dialectical progress.[26]

At the same time, however, the occupations also served as mechanisms for reproducing the feelings of progressive breakthrough into the new championed by West Germans in the immediate postwar and by some of the experimental groups of the 1970s, in which overcoming the traces of the past embedded in the bodies and the built environments of the postwar was seen as the necessary precondition for breaking through into the future. The BI SO36 and its leftist allies meticulously documented their DIY house repairs, for example, with a summer 1980 flyer from the Adalbertstraße 6 noting that "it is possible to repair living spaces with only very few means and bit of self-initiative," and juxtaposing images of painting supplies, brooms, and left-alternative activists working alongside neighborhood residents to collectively repair the houses with illustrations of demolished and desolate buildings.[27] In a number of respects the imagery conveyed in this flyer can be understood as a reenactment of the original scene of postwar futurity, in which narratives of building new lives and alternative futures necessarily played out against a backdrop of ruins. Progress, here, was premised on repeatedly overcoming the past. Hans and Susanne from the *Murderers Are among Us* would have felt right at home. The capacity of postwar domestic environments to serve as spaces where one could come into contact with the traces of the past, overcome these traces in a reenactment of postwar progress, *and* utilize them as the setting for dialectical activism made them into particularly resonant spaces for experimenting with new temporal logics in subsequent years.

While some leftist critics looked on these burgeoning shifts in revolutionary consciousness with horror, others began retooling dialectical logics to account for the experimental practices that were emerging in the left-alternative milieu. For example, while Wolfgang Kraushaar condemned the budding alternative movement as apolitical, self-centered, and out of touch with reality, the editors of *Autonomie: Neue Folge* argued that dialectical leftists could successfully incorporate the new youth cultures into radical political projects.[28] In the preface to the March 1980 edition of *Autonomie: Neue Folge*, for example, the editors wondered whether "behind the youth delinquency and the self-destructive behaviors, there might be the collective development of a line of resistance" that the left could take advantage of through a strategy of "sabotaging all forms of city planning and demanding the state relinquish the right to decide who can live where."[29] Dialectical leftists could thus envision ways to incorporate these new patterns of activism into the prescribed pathways of revolutionary dialectics. The burgeoning punk movement of the late 1970s, however, would prove much trickier.

∴

Emerging just as the events of the German Autumn were reaching a fevered pitch, the punk movement did not fit neatly into leftist political categories: whereas some viewed punks as potential revolutionaries, others saw them as unwelcome byproducts of capitalism.[30] The punks, for their part, viewed much of the West German left—especially its focus on nature, authenticity, and utopia—as an embarrassment. According to music critic and social theorist Greil Marcus, the punk movement, and particularly the Sex Pistols, captured the imagination of youth around the world due in no small part to its unapologetic rejection of almost everything. "Damning God and the state, work and leisure, home and family, sex and play, the audience and itself," Marcus argued, "the music briefly made it possible to experience all those things as if they were not natural facts but ideological constructs: things that had been made and therefore could be altered or done away with altogether."[31]

In part this rejection of the ideologies, practices, and aesthetics that suffused West German society mirrored the ideological positions of anti-authoritarian and alternative leftists, who also sought to negate contemporary society. For the punks, though, such acts of negation were not meant to contribute to dialectical temporal logics, nor were they envisioned as the necessary preconditions for entering an atemporal state of authenticity. Instead, punks imagined acts of negation as a way to open the future such that one could begin experimenting with new ways of being outside of what Anna Lowenhaupt Tsing has called the "handrails" of progress.[32] Unlike those who sought to freeze the dialectic in order to dwell in a timeless state of authentic negation, the punks developed strategies for increasing the tempo of progress to such an extent that it began careening out of control, becoming what some claimed it always already was: a spinning top on a road to nowhere. Beyond generating critical awareness about the ultimate lack of directionality within progressive temporal forms, though, the punks' goal was to hijack the transformative capacities of modernist-progressive time (both the dialectical and the reconstruction-era variants) in order to forge a mode of being that was not bound by any goals. In a sense, then, punk negation did have an overarching purpose: namely, to free individuals from all ideological and temporal logics. The motive was to destroy motives. As no-future futurists, the punks stoked a form of being as endless becoming, a carnival of negation that was both incredibly liberating and ultimately unsustainable.

Given its lowly beginnings at the intersection of provocationist art and urban vice, the punk movement's meteoric rise in the music charts, on the sidewalks, and in the clubs was nothing short of extraordinary. Whether it was Johnny Rotten's bloodcurdling proclamations that he was an anarchist/antichrist, Poly Styrene's shouts of "Oh Bondage, Up Yours," or Abwärts's menacing screams of "Stalingrad, Stalingrad, Germany is a catastrophic state," punk functioned as a call to arms that inspired an entire generation to tear down the social, cultural, and political infrastructure of society and replace it with something more dynamic, more creative, more alive. In cultural backwaters like Cleveland, Manchester, Wuppertal, and Basel, enterprising young people embraced the opportunity to experiment with new sounds, new aesthetics, and new ways of offending polite society. In the German-speaking world, alongside metropoles like Hamburg and West Berlin, smaller cities like Düsseldorf and Zurich emerged as the centers of punk experimentation. Johnny Rotten's spectacular and highly publicized transgressions may have officially sparked the movement, but in places like Düsseldorf and Zurich the scene had been set years before. Whereas the Zurich punks took their cues from an intellectual rediscovery of Dada and from youth activists' demands for independent music venues, the punk movement in Düsseldorf emerged at the intersection of the electronic music scene surrounding Kraftwerk and Neu! in the 1970s and the city's art academy, where Joseph Beuys was as, if not more, popular than Sid Vicious.[33] After his experiences as a soldier in the war, Beuys had turned to art, eventually becoming a professor at the Kunstakademie in Düsseldorf where he consistently agitated his colleagues by implementing anarchist pedagogical practices in the classroom, allying himself with protesting students, and engaging in controversial performances that explored, among other things, the legacies of fascism and the problems of communication. After his dismissal from the Kunstakademie in 1972, his reputation among leftist students and artists increased to the point that he became a sort of father figure for multiple generations of artists and provocateurs.

If Beuys helped to popularize the idea that anyone could be an artist and anything could be art, electronic groups like Kraftwerk and Neu! served as examples of how music could lend itself to critical ends. Unlike explicitly political bands such as West Berlin's Ton Steine Scherben that initially sought to directly translate leftist ideas into musical forms as a means of spreading the message of revolution (with Rio Reiser, the band's leader, sometimes even reading quotations from Mao's "Little Red Book" on stage), Kraftwerk, Neu!, and other so-called Krautrock groups tended toward more experimental, more nuanced forms of critique.[34] Aside from some periodic instances of clear antiestablishment messaging in their music—such as Neu!'s song "Hero," in which Klaus Dinger yells "Fuck your business, fuck the press, fuck the bourgeoisie"—most of their critiques were built on juxtapositions of discourses, ideas, and imagery that, under the modern regime of temporality, did not belong together. Faust, for example, whose name referenced both Goethe's masterwork of German literature and the raised first symbol used by the antiauthoritarian left, listed Hitler, the Heisenberg principle, antimatter, relativity, cybernetics, and game theory as their musical influences in a band manifesto they distributed while on tour in 1973. Similarly, Amon Düül referenced Himmler, Wagner, Mercedes, Krupp steel, Kant, and Disneyland's Germanic fairytale landscapes in their songs.[35] Beyond lyrics, their musical styles also evinced a marked tendency toward radical eclecticism. Faust, for example, shifted between pared down, motoric music and acid-washed folk rock, while Can paired modernist experimentation with the almost incomprehensible, Dada-inspired lyrics of lead singer Damo Suzuki. Whatever this was, it was certainly not politics as usual in the context of 1970s West Germany. Not only is it almost impossible to imagine these bands being successfully marketed by major music industry labels (though in some cases they were), it's also very difficult to fathom how leftist groups might even begin to go about incorporating such groups into the progressive logics of revolutionary dialectics.

Kraftwerk, perhaps the most famous group to emerge from this milieu, also engaged in these provocative and irreverent forms of citation.[36] They famously portrayed themselves as machines and mannequins (even going so far as to propose sending mannequins to stand in for band members during live performances), wove together imagery from the Nazi era and the Economic Miracle (perhaps most memorably in their hit song "Autobahn," which juxtaposed the Nazi-era mythology of the interstate system with its representations in the postwar period), melded references to Fritz Lang's *Metropolis* with descriptions of contemporary German cities, and pointed to the Nazi and later American scientist Werner von Braun as a role model while discussing the superiority of the "German mentality."[37] Whereas one could follow Uwe Schütte and interpret Kraftwerk and their contemporaries as engaging in "redemptive work" by attempting "to fulfil a potential that never had a chance to develop, cut short as it was by fascism," I would argue by contrast that they were less interested in redeeming progressive imaginaries from the German past than in cultivating a highly sophisticated set of anarchist-oriented aesthetic and sonic practices designed to show that the Nazi era was not safely contained in the past but had suffused every corner of West German life, and that the future was not a horizon somewhere off in the distance but an imaginative projection of the present.[38] As Ralf Hütter himself noted, Kraftwerk hoped to use their music to explore "the simultaneity of past, present, and future," and thus to undercut the linear fantasies of progress.[39]

Beyond critiques of progressive dreamworlds, though, these experimental practices were also citations of the temporal dynamics of progress. As I argued in the previous chapter, progressive time is premised on repeatedly enacting the separation of the past from the present, which generates feelings of momentum toward the future. By consistently incorporating references to the German past as well as to obsolete social, political, and technological forms, only to immediately employ experimental/futuristic sounds to move beyond them, these artists used their music to reproduce moments of breakthrough into the new. Although such techniques may have been meant as ironic citations of progressive time, they also sparked genuine feelings of excitement. This sentiment is clearly visible in a statement by Michael Rother, who in his reflections on why Neu! took its name, recalled: "We called ourselves Neu! [New!]. We didn't want to look at what was to the left or the right or to let ourselves be stopped. We wanted to break through all walls. Destroy borders. Fly."[40]

Drawing inspiration from Beuys—often by way of the actions and publications of his students such as Jürgen Kramer who, among other things, published the often outrageous art/punk journal *Die 8oer Jahre* and took part in avant-garde provocations with Der Plan—and from the experimental musical and aesthetic styles developed by groups like Neu! and Kraftwerk, the nascent punks in and around Düsseldorf began producing critical art by pirating and misusing symbols from surrounding media landscapes and from the built environment of West German cities. Milan Kunc and the AtaTak Gallery (which later gave birth to Der Plan), for example, organized a demonstration in Wuppertal in which participants carried banners with pictures of Coca-Cola bottles and hamburgers marked with Cyrillic script.[41] The idea that they could produce something both critical and new by creatively misusing existing aesthetic forms and ideological narratives was experienced as something of an epiphany. According to Detlef Diederichsen, "history was newly divided into a before and an after. [. . .] A new time had dawned, and everything was set back to zero, all systems newly tested."[42] The aesthetics and sounds of punk offered West German youth a way to reproduce the feeling of zero hour, of a new departure into the unknown, and it spread like wildfire.

This was certainly the case in cities such as Düsseldorf, Rodenkirchen, and Wuppertal, where punk groups emerged at a dizzying speed in the years between 1976 and 1980. One of the main reasons for this explosion of punk subcultures in the area was the existence of the Ratinger Hof, a small venue located near the Kunstakademie in Düsseldorf where experimental artists like Beuys, nascent punk groups, disaffected leftists, and even former Vienna Actionists rubbed shoulders in a small room with stark white walls and neon lights, which Gabi Delgado, the lead singer of Deutsch Amerikanische Freundschaft (German American Friendship), called "magic."⁴³ The scene at the Ratinger Hof was notoriously raucous with constant fights, performance art pieces run amok, and a general air of one-upmanship. According to Jürgen Engler, the sociabilities practiced at the Ratinger Hof could not be characterized as a form of "togetherness" (*Miteinander*) since "one had to prove oneself on a daily basis and constantly receive approval."⁴⁴ Given that, in its ideal form, punk implied an incessant transgression of social, cultural, and experiential boundaries, participants in the scene felt compelled to constantly define and defend their status as "real punks" by engaging in ever more radical actions. While this competitive atmosphere was anathema to the authentic warmth valued by the left-alternative scene, it *was* conducive to extraordinary levels of cultural and social innovation. It was a space in which people could be anything they wanted, where gender, style, and beliefs could be reinvented on a daily basis, where the only thing one was not encouraged to be was boring. Although eventually eclipsed by clubs in larger cities like Hamburg and West Berlin, for a brief moment in the late 1970s, the Ratinger Hof was the undisputed center of German punk.

Düsseldorf and surrounding cities were also home to some of the earliest punk fanzines. These DIY publications provided information on upcoming concerts and events, forged networks between geographically dispersed groups, and allowed teenagers to experiment with the boundaries of acceptable comportment. *Ostrich*, for example, was legendary less for the quality of its reporting than for its uncompromising assault on accepted values and for its commitment to destroying the boundaries between different times and different ideological systems. In addition to reporting on musical trends from London and New York, the pages of *Ostrich* were filled with images that remain shocking even today. Cover images of the magazine included a photograph of young punks holding a sign that read "Rodenkirchen is burning," and a collage featuring punk bands, Hitler, and a large swastika.⁴⁵ The content was similarly disturbing. One illustration, for example, featured a young punk giving a Hitler salute and proclaiming, "Eat Shit, Motherfuckers!"⁴⁶ An interview with the band MALE noted that their interests included "themselves, masturbating, fucking, pornos, suckling pig sandwiches, sun glasses, torn up clothing, and Coke."⁴⁷ A faux description of a Charlie's Girls concert described how the band members terrorized alternative leftists by publicly embracing Nazi aesthetics and then bombed the city Cologne, which they corroborated with a photograph taken after the actual bombardment of the city by American and British aircraft in WWII.⁴⁸ Perhaps ironically referencing the RAF's identification with the Soviet army and the Royal Air Force, the authors of this story claimed affinity with any and all perpetrators of violence, from American capitalists to Nazis.

All of these examples clearly indicate punk's obsession with provocation. Thomas Schwebel, a prolific member of the early West German punk scene, summarizes this sentiment: "Basically, it was all about [. . .] shock. It was possible to accomplish this with extremes. Either swastika or RAF machine gun. Both were available. Out on the streets both triggered the same reaction. Total disturbance."[49] As this statement and the previous examples from *Ostrich* suggest, one of the primary means by which punks attempted to shock polite, West German society was by mobilizing Nazi aesthetics. They wore swastikas and other fascist symbols on their clothes, included images of Nazis (often in direct proximity to other "stars" of the movement like Iggy Pop) in fanzines, and referenced fascist ideologies in their songs. At small punk venues in cities throughout West Germany, throngs of young people—some of whom were clad in leather jackets with safety pins and painted slogans reading "no future" and others in various outfits made from postindustrial waste—could, for example, watch Gabi Delgado gyrate violently on stage as he spat out lyrics such as: "Move your hips / and dance the Mussolini [. . .] and now the Adolf Hitler / and now the Jesus Christ." According to Delgado, "words like Mussolini are tabu [and thus] had an uncannily dangerous effect for young people."[50] Striking a similar tone, a 1978 collage created by Frank Fenstermacher used images of planes, ships, cars, and buses to overwhelm the visual field and to transform the scarcely perceptible human figures into objects among objects. The chaotic set of militaristic images is accompanied by the caption "DESIRE TO LIVE IN A STRONG NATIONALIST STATE SO AS NOT BE SO ALONE."[51] It is worth noting here how far removed this aesthetic was from the postrevolutionary politics that were emerging at the time. Indeed, it is nearly impossible to imagine the organizers of the TUNIX festival or participants in leftist therapy groups singing along to songs imploring them to dance the Mussolini.

Despite the fact that it has received the most attention in the literature on punk, fascism was far from the only ideology that punks misappropriated. They were also, for example, drawn to dystopian, nihilistic images of civilizational decline. Take, for example, the S.Y.P.H. song "Zurück zum Beton" in which they sing: "I must be dreaming, / I only see trees, / forests everywhere, / and then I suddenly notice that I'm like an animal here, / a fucking animal. // return to concrete, /return to concrete, / return to the subway, / return to concrete, / there where a person is still a person, / there were there is still love and happiness / [. . .] repulsive, repulsive, nature, nature, / I want pure concrete / [. . .] no birds, no fish, no plants, / I want in concrete to dance."[52] In the American context, the Talking Heads made a similar point, singing about how they missed the Dairy Queens, discount stores, and 7-11s and how "if this is paradise, [they] wished [they] had a lawnmower."

Others waxed enthusiastic about industrial spaces and impending civilizational collapse. According to Delgado, "We used to climb over fences at night and take pictures of industrial areas. [. . .] We felt like children of the factory."[53] Some were even more extreme in their admiration for the aesthetics of apocalypse. Jürgen Kramer, for example, juxtaposed pagan inspired phrases such as "joyful fire [*Freudenfeuer*]" with images of nuclear mushroom clouds in the sixth number of his magazine *Die 8oer Jahre*. The organizers of the 1981 Geniale Dilettanten festival in West Berlin called the event "the great Armageddon show."[54] Other bands named themselves after West German industrial concerns. The name of the band Die Krupps, for example, referenced not only themes of industrial decline but also, because of the company's actions during the war, the fascist legacy of German industrialism. Punks proudly carried plastic bags instead of hemp or cotton, wore vinyl and leather instead of self-knitted sweaters, wrote "no future" on their ripped jackets, put safety pins through their ears and cheeks, and rejected organic food in favor of cheap fast-food restaurants. The contrast between punk's embrace of civilizational decline and much of the alternative left's focus on authenticity as a way to prevent the coming apocalypse is really quite striking.

The highly sensationalized imagery surrounding the RAF and leftist radicalism more broadly also found its way into punk's citational maelstrom. According to Wolfgang Müller, Blixa Bargeld of Einstürzende Neubauten "transformed the pathetic-totalitarian gestures of the K-Gruppen that were dissolving at the end of the 1970s into art performances. Out of the aesthetic of the APO, he created an aesthetic of apocalypse."[55] Perhaps pointing to the media's tendency to spectacularize violence, Gabi Delgado quipped that his favorite shows as a kid were the British crime program *Mit Schirm, Charme und Melone* and sensationalist news reports on the activities of the RAF, who he called "the heroes of [his] youth just like Bruce Lee or [the soccer star] Wolfgang Overath."[56] Similarly, the early punk band S.Y.P.H. graced the cover of their album *Viel feind, viel ehr* with photographs lifted from tabloid newspapers of the baby carriage used in the RAF's abduction of Hanns Martin Schleyer. S.Y.P.H. also included sampled vocals from news reports on the events of the German Autumn in their song "klammheimlich," with the song title itself being a clear reference to the "Buback-Nachruf." The refrain of the song, "heldentum / eigentum / eigenheim / stammheim," which can be translated as "heroism / possessions / private home / prison," juxtaposed some of the most salient symbols the Economic Miracle (property and the single-family home) with the RAF's critiques of capitalism and state violence as well as their deaths in prison.⁵⁷

S.Y.P.H.'s suggestion that there was an analogy between the RAF's media presence and the spectacularized imagery of the Economic Miracle points to yet another dimension of punk's citational practices, namely its campy embrace of the aesthetics of consumer capitalism. One band from this period even named itself Wirtschaftswunder (Economic Miracle) and composed jarring tracks where, among other things, they sampled vocals from the popular West German television programs while chanting "television, television, television" and composed chaotic songs praising the benefits of the market economy. Others simply celebrated the small pleasures afforded by consumer society. In his memoir about the Punk and New Wave scenes, for example, Moritz R of Der Plan fondly remembered a trip to southern California where, upon eating at Taco Bell for breakfast, he felt for the first time in his life like he really belonged.⁵⁸ The group Freiwillige Selbstkontrolle (F.S.K.) made this point even clearer in their song "Moderne Welt," proclaiming simply "we say yes to the modern world." Bowing to punk taste for the ephemera of consumer society, the editors of the fanzine *Muzak* distributed a 1980 edition of the magazine wrapped in McDonald's packaging.

As some of these examples indicate, punk and New Wave artists did not restrict themselves to citing particular historical periods or distinct ideologies; they also engaged in what Guy Debord and the Situationists had earlier described as détournement, a form of activist provocation in which disparate forms of meaning are juxtaposed with each other to produce novelty or critical awareness. Musicians connected to early iterations of what would become Der Plan, for example, layered the dense philosophical texts of Hegel over simplistic electronic beats, thus simultaneously mixing high and low culture as well as the hallowed German past with the nonsensical beeps and boops of consumer society. Years later when Der Plan was faltering due to drug addictions and religious conversions among some of its members, Moritz suggested resuscitating the band by renaming it Katholisch Kitsch and playing only jam band versions of religious songs. The Swiss group Kleenex/LiLiPUT mixed references from fairytales and American pop culture while dressed in chaotic outfits composed of outmoded youth styles and various forms of consumer waste. Similarly, the visual art produced in the punk and New Wave milieus often juxtaposed images of advertisements, everyday consumer objects, scenes of apocalyptic destruction, and science-fiction style visions of the future.⁵⁹ A series of illustrations in the 1980 book *AMOK/KOMA. Ein Bericht zur Lage*, for example, depicted a character named Koma Kid donning X-ray glasses and a wry smile in various historical and futuristic settings. Koma Kid appeared as the face of an

Oscar award, hanging out with world leaders, holding up a newspaper reading "Tokio Bombed," having sex with a figure who had a computer as a head and who was using a hammer and sickle as an S-M prop, helping US soldiers plant a turkey (instead of a flag) at Iwo Jima, and so on. The sequence of images was interspersed with absurdist stories such as one that described a Nazi community in Paraguay where the residents spent most of their time yodeling in the beer garden.[60]

In what has since proved to be one of the most influential interpretations of the punk movement, Dick Hebdige argued in his 1979 book on subcultural style that punks, like subcultures more broadly, acted like bricoleurs who appropriated the symbolism of the dominant culture and recombined it for critical effect. Punk style, according to Hebdige, "reproduced the entire sartorial history of post-war working-class youth cultures in 'cut up' form, combining elements which had originally belonged to completely different epochs."[61] In critically appropriating the visual cues of industrial decline in Britain, the punks became visual signifiers of social contradictions who were then "forever condemned to act out alienation, to mime its imagined conditions, to manufacture a whole series of subjective correlatives for the official archetypes of the 'crisis of modern life.'"[62] Although such critical citations of domination presented a challenge to hegemonic cultural forms, they were unable to create a foundation for stable alternative subjectivities. Indeed, the punk subculture, according to Hebdige, remained "abstract, disembodied, decontextualized. Bereft of the necessary details—a name, a home, a history—it refused to make sense, to be grounded, 'read back' to its origins," and thus remained trapped in its role as a purveyor of "visual puns."[63]

To a certain extent, Hebdige's contention that punk should be understood as a strategy of critical appropriation and ironic citation adequately captures the essence of the movement. The combination of Nazi imagery, antiauthoritarian symbols, and pop cultural artifacts was undoubtedly meant to serve as a critical commentary on the continuities between the fascist past and the democratic present.[64] In this sense, punk could be viewed as a return to the provocative techniques of the antiauthoritarian left, which sought to shock the public into a greater awareness of the real conditions underlying their existence and thus encourage them to begin working toward revolutionary change. This is almost certainly part of what punk was about; however, their visions for revolutionary transformation tended to begin and end with facilitating creativity and personal autonomy for themselves. According to Peter Fischli: "It's precisely because these things were already in existence that the punk of the seventies was able to spread like wildfire. Because it had no history, but rather pieced lots of different stories together to create something new, like a cocktail shaker. [...] The notion of copyright was temporarily abolished, and copying was part of the game, as long as you used the mismatched pieces to tell your own story."[65] While punk shared the new left's assumption that negating the present could facilitate the new, it was much less concerned with the ultimate endpoint of such innovation. The goal was simply to leap repeatedly into the unknown.

In a sense, punks and their allies were putting into practice critical strategies of destruction and creation theorized in an earlier historical moment by Walter Benjamin. Writing on film and the transformation of perception, Benjamin argued: "Our taverns and our metropolitan streets, our offices and furnished rooms, our railroad stations and our factories appeared to have us locked up hopelessly. Then came the film and burst this prison-world asunder by the dynamite of the tenth of a second, so that now, in the midst of its far-flung ruins and debris, we calmly and adventurously go traveling."[66] According to Benjamin, the technologies of film and photography allowed artists to disaggregate objects, people, and experiences from their original contexts and to recombine them in new forms. Similarly, punk and New Wave artists made use of an eclectic array of media to shatter the narratives of postwar life and to create new worlds and new identities from the resulting debris. Destruction, in this case, was both the necessary precondition for and the primary substance of innovative creativity. Punk was built on the idea that one could joyfully engage in a perpetual movement to nowhere, a dialectical negation without end. The oft-repeated phrase "no future" was thus not only a reference to punk's apocalyptic dimensions but a description of the movement itself.

Punk-inspired artists were consumed with the desire to invent new modes of expression out of the fragments of existing cultural forms. According to Michael Kemner, "what counted, was a new way of thinking, a new style of creativity [...] The Motto was: fast! Play fast, come together fast, practice briefly, go public."[67] Similarly, authors writing for *Ostrich* transcribed popular song lyrics and guitar chords so that budding punk musicians could play along or, even better, remake the songs as their own. They also encouraged readers to embrace their own creativity, writing: "THE POWER IS IN OUR HANDS," and "do what you want, don't let yourself be commanded around!! Speak your mind."[68] Wolfgang Müller of the experimental group Die Tödliche Doris elevated this DIY ethos into a theory of art when he organized the Geniale Dilletanten festival in 1981, arguing that one should understand "mistakes in playing and writing [*Ver-spielen* and *Ver-schreiben*] as positive" because they offered the "possibility to find new forms of expression that have not yet been discovered." He went on to claim that "anyone who has correctly understood the idea of dilettantism can never become a serious musician. That would be death itself."[69] Beyond reiterating punk's widespread aversion to "selling out," Müller is also suggesting that creativity could only take flight through repeated acts of breaking free from dominant social, cultural, and temporal logics. Embracing dilettantism would thus not only make it harder for experimental artistic forms to be incorporated into capitalism, it would also fuel constant innovation and perpetual movement.

Given that many of them were trained artists, it should come as no surprise that participants in the punk and New Wave scenes mobilized a wide array of audiovisual techniques to experiment with and disassemble existing temporal structures. For example, they used strobe lighting at concerts, stop- and slow-motion film, and the electronic manipulation of sound to modify the basic rhythms and embodied temporalities governing everyday experience. According to Müller, the art produced by the experimental group Die Tödliche Doris had effects similar to that of a strobe light. "The effect of a strobe light consists of creating an optical illusion. [. . .] At regular temporal intervals, it sends flashes of light into a space. In a dark environment, the eye focuses on the illuminations. [. . .] The images that emerge appear to be chopped up [. . .] . Through the rhythm of the light, flowing movement disappears. The Tödliche Doris is absent presence. Doris appears through the permanent absence of her body."[70] Strobe lighting as well as related techniques such as slow-motion film fractured the "natural" flow of embodied time into myriad particle-like moments, which resulted both in the reenchantment of the everyday and in new forms of temporal perception.

These techniques were liberally employed in Super 8 films.[71] In a variety of short films produced between 1976 and 1980 and projected onto the walls of punk concerts and other scene events in Zurich, René Uhlmann, for example, made extensive use of stop- and slow-motion techniques to dissect and manipulate the passage of time and the tempo of bodily comportment. In a number of these films, Uhlmann manipulated the tempo of everyday social interactions within the punk movement by radically altering the projection speed of the film. In many of the film sequences, Uhlmann slows down the flow of bodily movement to such an extent that it is transformed into a series of interconnected poses. Each moment, these sequences suggest, represents a mysterious universe unto itself, a portal to different worlds. In other films, Uhlmann used stop-motion animation techniques to create visual collages that mixed images of everyday people, punk rock stars, Nazi soldiers, Coca-Cola advertisements, Mickey Mouse, plastic toys, and news headlines to create an effect of everything happening at once, of diverse objects, people, and ideas coming together to form new constellations of meaning.

When projected onto the walls of concerts, these short films must have had a very strange effect indeed. Concertgoers would have been confronted not only with the glitchy bodily movements associated with dancing at punk concerts but also with distorted images of themselves and of the mediatized images they consumed in their everyday lives being projected onto the walls, all while listening to the dissonant instrumentation and absurdist lyrics that characterized Swiss punk. Rooms full of people wearing leather and plastic clothing with slogans like "Zureich" ("too rich") written on them; strobe lighting cutting up already frenetic movement; images of oneself and Mickey Mouse moving at slow motion across the walls; dissonant rhythms; chanting from the stage: "the sad ones they will be slaughtered / the world becomes happy // the evil ones they will be slaughtered / the world becomes good // the idiots they will be slaughtered / the world becomes wise // the elderly they will be slaughtered / the world becomes young // I stand here and you stand there / and between us not even a word."[72] Using these and related audiovisual techniques, punk concerts functioned as interstitial spaces that both fractured the temporal and ideological structures of postwar lifeworlds and encouraged those in the audience to repeatedly form new selves in the debris.

Young artists in West Berlin shared this proclivity for modifying temporal rhythms through experimental film techniques. Whereas some filmmakers found it sufficient to capture people engaged in various forms of absurdity—such as the 1982 film "Hüpfen '82," in which two people engage in a variety of everyday activities like drinking tea while joyfully hopping—most relied on some form of technical manipulation to achieve their desired effects.[73] An early example of this comes from Walter Gramming's 1978 film "Hammer und Sichel," which combines disturbing images of a man rubbing a hammer and sickle over his body in a sexually suggestive fashion while radically sped up and slowed down versions of the Internationale play in the background. It is worth keeping in mind the broader context in which this film was produced: just as some of the activists at TUNIX were looking for ways to transform themselves into authentic opponents of capitalist modernity, Gramming was filming a man performing fellatio on the shafts of a hammer and a sickle as the Internationale dissolved into a menacing, apocalyptic drone.[74]

Two other films produced in West Berlin in this period—"E Dopo?" (1981/82) and "Ohne Liebe gibt es keinen Tod" (1980)—utilized similar techniques but shifted the focus from a critique of leftist ideology to one of body politics. In "Ohne Liebe gibt es keinen Tod," for example, we first see a woman dancing alone in an apartment. Very quickly, however, a triangle of light begins to isolate parts of her body, the objects in the room, and her movements thus destroying any sense of emplaced, authentic subjectivity. Similarly, "E Dopo?" destroys the unity of the subject by transforming fluid movements into collections of discrete moments. The film portrays a sexual encounter in which all sense of natural sexuality is destroyed by the focus on individual body parts. Further corroborating this message, the two actors periodically hold up photographs of shadows and abstractions.[75] Although perhaps a commentary on the increasing fetishization of sexuality, the film can also be read as a seething critique of the alternative left's obsession with embodied authenticity.

Just as artists used the manipulation of visual images to fracture the fluid flow of temporality, musicians experimented with time through the electronic manipulation of sound. In some instances, this program of temporal experimentation was overtly stated in band manifestos. The Swiss band HERTZ, for example, described themselves in the following way: "We construct tones. We construct feelings. Construction is a game. We play happy and sad music. [. . .] HERTZ, the voice of reason. Music destroys time. We are making hits, we are making free time. We change with the times. We believe today in tomorrow."[76] Playful experimentation with modes of temporal perception, they argued, was both an act of destruction and a mechanism for endless innovation. In a series of essays in the 1982 Merve volume *Geniale Dilletanten*, Nikolaus Untermöhlen of Die Tödliche Doris also explicitly referenced the role of musical experimentation in the destruction of narrative time. Whether through "primordial music," through the "rhythm of machines," or through "cultivated music," Untermöhlen argued, "music structures time."[77] Such temporal structurings, however, are far from permanent. Indeed, according to Untermöhlen, artists can manipulate sounds so as to unleash the creative forces that remain buried within these musical forms. "The music evaporates into noises. In the gas form all sense of order disappears. Every tonal element has its own specific individual movements, which cannot be anticipated in their connected form. The pieces collide in ever stronger movements. They jump their tracks and are hurled in new directions. The energy level increases [. . .] and the effects can no longer be predicted."[78] Although I lack the evidence to make this argument with any certainty, it seems here that Untermöhlen and his colleagues were calling for the creation of a musical version of Deleuze and Guattari's rhizome.

Members of Die Tödliche Doris put these ideas into practice on a number of occasions. In one series of concerts, for example, they taped themselves singing and then performed in front of a live crowd while pretending to play what was actually prerecorded music. They taped this performance, including the crowd's reaction, and then for the next concert played this tape while again acting as if they were playing live music. This went on for the next several concerts so that by the end they were simultaneously performing multiple different contextual moments layered on top of one another. As Thomas Groetz has argued, Tödliche Doris was less interested in producing music than in casting an "acoustic gaze at things themselves" and exploring "how one moves in time and space."[79]

Although punk and New Wave artists were primarily concerned with manipulating media for critical ends, they also used their own bodies as tools for fracturing established social forms. They accomplished this by transforming themselves into signifiers of abjection, which, according to Judith Butler, refers to "those 'unlivable' and 'uninhabitable' zones of social life which are nevertheless densely populated by those who do not enjoy the status of the subject."[80] In part, this performative embrace of abjection resembled the leftist fascination with negation as a necessary component of revolutionary politics. In the punk and New Wave movements, though, embracing the abject was disconnected from dialectical directionality, meaning that the goal was to destroy existing modes of being so as to freely reconstitute the self rather than to further a transcendental revolutionary project. In her memoir about punk life in West Berlin, for example, Eva Bude wrote: "I desperately needed to escape from the narrowness of my cage and my family, which took away my air for breathing like the noose around the neck of a hanged man. [Joining the punk milieu] was like a leap into cold water," where she was finally able to constitute her life as she saw fit.[81]

Although the primary goal of these collective acts of transgression was to destroy existing social structures so as to facilitate individual autonomy, they also served as the foundation for new modes of sociability. According to Bude, the punk milieu came to serve as her "new 'family.'" The movement was full of "people, that understood you. To whom you belonged. That took you seriously."[82] It was a space in which participants could be seen and accepted as they truly were, as damaged, imperfect, and angry, a space in which establishing new social relations depended on the active destruction of existing forms of social relationality. Unlike members of the left-alternative therapy groups that were exploding in popularity in these years, punks tended not to believe that meaningful social interactions necessitated healthy subjectivities. To the contrary, they suggested that real social bonds could only be formed between people who had fully embraced their own abnormalities.

Müller and Untermöhlen's 1979 film *Material für Nachkriegszeit* serves as a good example of the seemingly limitless possibilities for social interaction that emerged in the punk and New Wave milieus. To make the film,

FIGURE 2.2. Punks in front of the New Kreuzberg Center in Berlin Kreuzberg. Photo by Manfred Kraft. Source: Umbruch Bildarchiv.

they gathered various discarded photographs from photobooths around West Berlin and then organized them into a series of partially reconstructed images of people and abstract shapes. Describing the film, Müller noted: "Gradually a body arises from the multitude of anonymous people. It simultaneously consists of singularities and builds a unity. The absent body appears through photographic snapshots [*Abbildungen*]. It emerges out of abstraction, brokenness, and out of scars—all of which simultaneously connect themselves to a body in space. It is a vibrating space which takes leave of the mathematical time-space model. [The juxtaposition of the portraits] create forms of presence [*Präsenzen*]. These forms of presence become observable, they become perceptible through the absence of the unknown body and the presence of their intimacy."[83] Fractured, broken bodies, the film suggests, can be brought together to form intimate assemblages outside of the spatial and temporal frameworks of mainstream society. Like sounds and images, bodies could also be liberated from the alienating master narratives that governed life and meaning in capitalist societies.

Describing a moment of religious awakening while taking LSD at Disneyland, Moritz R of Der Plan observed: "Everything suddenly became one image: the American way of life, old Europe, my opinions about art. It was an initiation ritual into a new religion. [...] I saw an altar before my spiritual eyes, with ducks as angels and Walt Disney as God."[84] To a certain extent Moritz was surely playing the amusing iconoclast by speaking of cartoon ducks as catalysts for a new religion. At the same time, though, his mass cultural infused epiphany speaks to the nature of the punk and New Wave movements. Seeing the spectacularized representations of "old Europe" at Disneyland, Moritz not only came to the conclusion that old Europe was itself an ideological fantasy, but also that the act of unmasking the fantastical nature of the world could generate a quasi-religious feeling of creative freedom. In showing that nothing was true, punks claimed that everything was allowed.

Punk and New Wave artists became addicted to this vertiginous feeling of transcending the given order of things, and they wasted no opportunity to put it into practice in all areas of life. Utilizing aesthetics, style, bodily comportment, and forms of musical innovations that Jack Halberstam described as "the performance of sonic forms of chaos," they incessantly called dominant temporal logics into question by ironically citing them (as in Wirtschaftswunder's songs about television, *Muzak's* appropriation of McDonald's packaging, and the tendency of New Wave artists to wear absurd renditions of business attire) and by détourning them with repressed or negated elements (as Gabi Delgado did by encouraging people to dance the Adolf Hitler *and* the Jesus Christ).[85] This was certainly a form of critique, yet it was also much more than this. It was a mechanism for fragmenting the ideological unity of progressive time and thus opening the future. According to Hans-Christian Dany, punks evinced a desire to "run towards the black hole" of the yet-to-come.[86] As in Einstürzende Neubauten's sonic repurposing of the material remnants of the twentieth century, punks dwelled with the ghosts of the past in order to propel themselves, chaotically, into the new.[87]

While punk and New Wave artists clearly rejected the progressive teleologies of the leftist dialecticians and the postwar reconstructionists, they had not abandoned the commitment to novelty. To the contrary, the feeling of breaking through into new terrain was one of the hallmarks of the punk and New Wave movements. Punks sought to generate momentum toward the future by creatively misusing existing social, cultural, and political symbols, by "throw[ing] away and in some cases deform[ing] the old signs and hang[ing] the broken pieces around [their] neck[s]."[88] Without teleological guidelines, however, this process of constantly negating the present to break through into the future, of profaning all that is holy and melting everything solid into air, became unsustainable. Like the final scene of Jacques Tati's 1967 film *Playtime*, punk and New Wave artists were spinning in circles and doing so with ever greater speed. This is clearly visible in the stylistic changes of these years. Once leather jackets and mohawks became symbols of belonging rather than critique, they were replaced by outmoded business suits, then by neon, and so on without end. In its commitment to the ever new, punk remained ever the same.

Whereas some in the movement seemed to resent the necessity of constantly changing to outpace the "posers," others embraced it. In his 1981 essay "Neue Hinweise: Im Westeuropa Dämmerlicht" ("New Directions: In the Twilight of Western Europe"), for example, Thomas Meinecke of the band Freiwillige Selbstkontrolle (F.S.K.) and the journal *Mode & Verzweiflung* (*Fashion & Doubt*) uncompromisingly embraced modern life while rejecting the authenticity discourses of "the Hippies," which he associated both with the nature-romanticism of the left-alternative milieu and the machine-romanticism of New Wave. Against this romanticized fetishization of atemporal authenticity, Meinecke championed what he called the cybernetic principle, arguing: "We cybernetic thinkers constantly revise our modes of thinking and acting based on their applicability to the modern world, which is undergoing constant transformation. [...] Today Disco, tomorrow subversion, the day after tomorrow a country outing. We call this voluntary self-control."[89] Others, by contrast, simply called it emptiness.[90]

∴

In the wake of the German Autumn, much of the West German left lost faith in the ability of radical acts of violence to spark progressive change. Some even began to move away from modernist-progressive temporal imaginaries more broadly. Many participants in the left-alternative milieu, for example, sought to escape the future by transforming themselves into romanticized images of the nonmodern other. As this chapter has shown, however, not all left-alternative activists and members of left-leaning countercultures abandoned progressive temporal imaginaries in the late 1970s. Some began to experiment with a number of new techniques for generating progressive breakthroughs into the new. Drawing from Svetlana Boym, I suggest that we view these temporal experiments with progressive time in the late 1970s as instantiations of the "off-modern," modes of being and perceiving that both operated within and sought to move beyond modernist temporalities.[91] The off-modern is still part of the progressive time regime of modernity, it's just a bit off. As Boym describes it, the off-modern represents "a detour into the unexplored potentials of the modern project. [...] It opens into the modernity of 'what if'" rather than just rehashing, yet again, the established, exclusionary narratives of progress.[92]

Whereas many in the left-alternative milieu sought timeless alternatives to the present by freezing the dialectic and attempting to dwell indefinitely in a state of authentic negation, other groups such as the punks, the early squatting movement, and many of the "sustainable utopians" described by Allen, began to reconceptualize the logics of temporal change. Participants in the punk and New Wave movement, for example, embraced the transformational potential of dialectical negation while abandoning its inherent directionality. In their fascination with the traditional placeworlds of neighborhoods like Kreuzberg, the burgeoning squatting milieu shared with their more romantically oriented left-alternative peers the desire to find spaces of authenticity within which to build autonomous lives—yet, unlike these groups, they often sought to mobilize the material traces of the past as ways to launch themselves into the future. They also resembled the punks in that both groups sought to fragment progressive temporalities and construct new selves in the debris, with the primary difference being that the squatters were drawn to the built environment, while the punks gravitated toward the media. In all of these instances, activists began to engage in a radical reimagination of revolutionary time, and in so doing, they helped to lay the foundations for the emergence of postprogressive thought and practice.

As a new generation of leftist youth began losing patience with the methodical legal strategies championed by reform-oriented activist groups in the late 1970s, they increasingly looked to the practices being developed by off-modern activists for alternatives. They began squatting houses, attending punk and New Wave concerts, and joining groups focused on transforming local conditions in neighborhoods, schools, and workplaces, thus contributing to the increasing overlaps between the different forms of off-modern activism that had emerged in the years following the German Autumn. The coming together of these different activist practices and temporal imaginaries (for example punk's focus on directionless dialectics and the squatter's fascination with material traces of the past in the built environment) would prove to be extraordinarily explosive, eventually helping to jumpstart the urban youth revolts of 1980–81.

Echoing some of the ideas being developed by Michel de Certeau in his influential 1980 book *The Practice of Everyday Life*, the experimental author and punk ally Jürgen Ploog gestured toward some of the contours of this emerging spatiotemporal imaginary, when he implored his readers to "reject prescriptions about where the road leads [because] the rules of space mean that movement is adventure, that even a well-known path through a measured city can produce something unexpectedly startling."[93] Like Ploog, youth activists in the early 1980s had begun to imagine that the layered temporalities of place could be used to construct autonomous lives that were free from the prescribed paths of progress and thus open to the future. The following chapters trace the emergence and the spread of these postprogressive imaginaries of place in West Germany during the 1980s and 1990s, beginning with the outbreak of the youth revolts of 1980–81.

[CHAPTER THREE]

The Youth Revolts of 1980–81 and the Radical Potential of the Present

With the growing awareness that the era of high growth was coming to an end, that ecological crisis was looming on the horizon, and that the new left had largely failed in its attempt to fundamentally transform West German society, many began to lose faith in the progressive futures that had suffused almost all dimensions of postwar life. For some, this led to a resigned retreat into the self, something clearly evident in the youth heroin scene depicted in Christiane Felscherinow's 1978 autobiography, *Wir Kinder vom Bahnhof Zoo*.[1] Others, though, refused to give up on the feelings of momentum and breakthrough that had motivated so many of their predecessors. In an article in *Der Spiegel* documenting the wave of youth protests that coursed through Zurich in the summer of 1980, one of the participants, for example, described her frustrations with the slow pace of change in the late 1970s, noting: "When I came back from a trip around the world last Autumn, I suddenly noticed, how constricting and ancient Zurich is. The city and its residents seemed as if they were encased in concrete. And I suddenly had the desire to break out of the concrete. I wanted to find a vast openness which seemed not to exist in Switzerland."[2] She viewed the existing state of Swiss society as a suffocating imposition, a straitjacket preventing her from finding new paths forward, and she was far from alone in these feelings. As the decade dawned, young leftists in cities across Europe began exhibiting a marked desire for novelty, adventure, and change, a phenomenon that Michael Rutschky called "a hunger for experience," which neither the leftist establishment nor the pop cultural styles offered to youth at the time were in a position to satisfy.[3] Finding a new route into the new implied a rejection not only of tradition but also of the traditional forms of progress.

These burgeoning desires for novelty, adventure, and radical change dovetailed perfectly with the experimental cultural practices and aesthetic innovations that were being developed by the off-modern activists of the late 1970s, especially the visions of endless becoming and creative destruction coming out of the punk and New Wave milieus. Unlike progressive reformers in government and in left-leaning organizations like the *Strategien für Kreuzberg*, the practitioners of punk and New Wave posited that real change could only come by continuously negating the logics of postwar life. Many came to see punk-style negation as both a mechanism for destroying the violent and constricting power structures that dominated life in the late twentieth century and as a way to facilitate new forms of creativity. The chaotic models of creative destruction developed in these movements came to seem like viable strategies for reviving the feelings of futurity and progressive breakthroughs into the new that many leftist youth so desperately wanted in the late 1970s.

Chaos was indeed an essential component here. According to Blixa Bargeld, lead singer of the band Einstürzende Neubauten (Collapsing New Buildings): "Structures emerge from chaos and not the other way around. [...] In the Greek, philosophical, original sense, Chaos referred to: the condition of the universe before creation."[4] In a 1982 interview, Bargeld elaborated on this sentiment: "Old objects, meanings, buildings, and also music will be destroyed, all traces of the past are abandoned: only out of destruction can something really new be created."[5] William Levy made a similar point in his 1980 poem "Invocation of Chaos," writing: "Chaos is the same as the spirit of God / Chaos is the origin of the universe / Chaos is the basis of all progress: / [...] come here you gangsters of the sky. Wake up and gather together / terrorists are everywhere / terrorists are / full of fervor / terrorists are / godlike / [...] cower down and invoke the Chaos / *as the chaos overtakes us*."[6] Bargeld, Levy, and many others in and adjacent to the punk and New Wave movements, believed that one could spark such moments of original/originating chaos by further fracturing the smooth temporal facades of postwar life, which due to an array of factors were already reeling in the late 1970s. The collapse of dominant temporal frameworks was, according to these figures, not something to be feared, but something to be invoked since only collapse would liberate people from prescribed developmental paths and allow them to break through into the truly new.

Paradoxically, then, given their "no future" attitude, the punks offered an alternative way to pursue novelty and the feeling of breaking through into something different: destroy the narrative frameworks that structured the postwar order and create new worlds amid the ruins. The New Wave group Andreas Dorau und die Marinas made this point in musical form, cheerfully singing: "The world is horrible. Life is grand. Why is that so difficult to understand?" In the campy 1983 music video for the song, the "Marinas" grow cartoon angel wings and fly through the clouds, while Andreas Dorau dances with a skeleton through a landscape filled with images of Greek pillars, cacti, and gas station pumps. The video concludes with a group of people sitting arm-in-arm and warming themselves in front of an exploding mushroom cloud, as they sway to the music, joyfully singing "la-la-la-la-la-laaa-laa-laa."[7] The impending collapse of the world, this video suggests, offered a unique opportunity for renewal and reinvention. Bakunin, it seems, was making a comeback in the 1980s.

Throughout the late 1970s, participants in the punk and New Wave movements danced menacingly around the edge of the volcano in the safety of their clubs, their art studios, and their living rooms. While not in and of themselves a threat to public order, these semiprivate rehearsals of radical social and cultural regeneration circulated to ever wider audiences through albums, fanzines, concerts, and (increasingly) music videos.[8] Fed up with the glacial pace of political transformation in the late 1970s and early 1980s and pining for the feelings of movement and breakthrough that characterized much of the Red Decade and, for that matter, the postwar more broadly, disaffected leftists began to leave the therapy circles and the political working groups to pursue more extreme forms of regeneration. Slowly but surely, the apocalyptic aesthetics and experimental sociabilities of the punk and New Wave movements began to seep into the imaginations and the practices of leftist youth in West Germany. The result would be explosive.

According to Peter Glaser, "young people throughout Europe felt something begin to stir in their souls. Something pure, clear, hard, burning, angry had fallen into the world like a Meteor. [. . .] In a world full of coerced causation and craving for rationality, we sought the unexplained, undefined, uncharted territory. Areas that belonged to us."[9] Similarly, Jürgen Ploog lamented the reactionary conditions of the Federal Republic, writing: "A prisoner to its past, nearly excluded from the present, this country is drifting towards a hopeless future. Borders are everywhere, options nowhere in sight." Instead of simply drawing resigned attention to the hopelessness of the situation, though, he called for immediate, regenerative action by quoting Burroughs: "It's time that this monopoly is broken. [. . .] A cry rings through the city: 'Nothing is true and everything is allowed.'"[10] Ploog, along with many others in the early 1980s, began to envision a new wave of leftist resistance consisting of a fusion of the mythological dialectics of militant groups like the RAF and the punk-inspired principles of creative destruction and endless becoming. There would be a final showdown between the forces of order and those of negation, however it would not emerge from prescribed dialectical logics but from an anarchist explosion of creative negation in the present.

A good example of how radical leftist politics and punk aesthetics were merging in these years comes from a seemingly minor change in the sub-

FIGURE 3.1. Front cover of *Radikal* (Nr. 77, March/April 1980).
Source: International Institute of Social History, Amsterdam.

title of the March/April 1980 edition of *Radikal*, a radical leftist newspaper published in West Berlin that had largely rejected the post-1977 disavowal of leftist militance. Despite its commitment to confrontational politics, previous editions of *Radikal* sorely lacked creativity, a point that is clearly corroborated in the rather dry subtitle of the paper: "Socialist Paper for West

Berlin." Like others on the fringes of the left-alternative milieu who refused to accept the gradualist progressive temporalities and long-term strategic visions of the integrationist factions of the postrevolutionary left, the editors of *Radikal* were rebels without a cause, revolutionaries who desperately wanted to move forward but were unable to figure out how to free themselves from the ideological frameworks of the 1970s. The March/April 1980 edition, however, signaled that change was in the air. Rather than simply referring to itself as the socialist paper for West Berlin, the subtitle of this edition read "*Radikal*: Being Radical Means Tackling Issues at Their Roots," which was paired with an image of a hand shooting a rock with a slingshot along with a caption reading: "We don't have a chance, but we're going to use it."[11] Subsequent subtitles continued in this vein, with the May 1980 title "Paper for Freedom and Adventure" and the September 1980 title "Paper for Uncontrolled Movements in West Berlin and Elsewhere."[12] The tone of the articles shifted as well: instead of reports on revolutionary movements abroad and nostalgic essays on memories of militance past, the pages of these new editions were filled with stories of European youth awakening from their slumber to take control of their lives and engage in acts of direct resistance. The editors were mobilizing punk aesthetics and ideas as a way to revive the feelings of revolutionary momentum.

These discursive and rhetorical shifts were accompanied by a broader transformation in the aesthetic tone of the paper. The editions of *Radikal* published in the months and years following the March 1980 edition jettisoned the tried-and-true documentary-style images and the squared blocks of theory-heavy text for colorful illustrations and asymmetrical text collages. Countercultural youth, anti-imperialist revolutionaries, and oppositional figures from different historical eras all blended together in the pages of *Radikal*, united by their commitment to rebellion and creative destruction. The aesthetic and discursive shifts taking place in the pages of *Radikal* had parallels in other leftist publications as well. For example, Zurich's *Stilett*, a politically oriented punk fanzine which began publication in 1979, used subtitles such as "Drug-Addicted, Anarchist, People's Paper" and "Paper for Spray-Painters and Freeloaders" as well as off-kilter layouts and images to signal its opposition to the static state of politics and society.[13]

In addition to embracing the anarchist aesthetics and the destructive rhetoric of the punk and New Wave movements, disaffected leftists also began mimicking the social forms developed in the bars, the concerts, and the street corners of the European punk milieu. Unlike the warm sociabilities championed by much of the left-alternative milieu in the 1970s in which the overarching goal consisted of purifying oneself and one's immediate social environments to hasten the coming of the revolutionary future, punk-inspired sociability was premised on embodying ugliness, on collective acts of transgression, and on acts of creative destruction. In a 1981 poem, for example, a West Berlin squatter suggested that forms of oppositional sociability made squatters and youth activists dangerous, "because [they] will be able to show that things can be different and perhaps / the small house fire will become a neighborhood fire and then a city fire . . . / and then a world fire."[14] Instead of seeking to overcome her damaged self so as to facilitate the coming of the revolution or essentializing the lifeworlds of supposedly authentic negations of capitalist modernity to create utopian enclaves in the present, the author of this poem advocated for communities where people accepted each other as they were, damages and all, and who could thus set the world on fire.

Participants in the youth movements also borrowed from punk the idea that destruction and chaos could serve as catalysts for sparking new relationships between people, new forms of intimacy that were seen as superior to the modes of being together propagated by the left-alternative milieu, whose penchant for performative authenticity was seen as a hindrance to real engagement with others. In his memoir about the youth movements of the early 1980s, for example, Thomas Lecorte described a daydream he had while being arrested for taking part in a demonstration in West Berlin: "I scrambled to my feet, found myself in a foreign area but ran nonetheless down familiar streets. All around there was the smoke and noise of a riot, the banging and screaming, the car motors and the clanging of paving stones, the hissing gas and the crackling fire, and I ran aimlessly, climbed and fell and climbed again, and couldn't find a way out. Then I reached a high wall, and once I was at the top, I saw a squatted house, and on the wall was Anna, and [. . .] she just gave me a kiss [. . .] and I disappeared into the distance."[15] Taking an active part in the destruction of the given social order, this passage suggests, was increasingly seen as a necessary catalyst for developing new forms of intimacy.

Modifying the ubiquitous phrase *Gefühl und Härte* ("feelings and harshness"), we could perhaps say that the new sense of self that began to emerge in the youth movements of these years implied that genuine feelings only emerged *through* harshness. This sentiment comes through clearly in Jörg Buttergeit's 1984 documentary film *So war das S.O. 36: Ein Abend des Nostalgie*.[16] The film—which consists of a disorienting array of images and sounds, including scenes of Godzilla wreaking havoc on a Japanese city, punks passionately kissing at a West Berlin subway station, romanticized kitsch from German *Heimat* films, dissonant screaming, traditional *Schlager*-style songs, crowds affectionately throwing beer cans at a band, documentary footage of bombed-out buildings in Berlin, and interviews

FIGURE 3.2. At a demonstration in Berlin.
Photo by Manfred Kraft. Source: Umbruch Bildarchiv.

with participants in the youth movement—suggests that destroying the rules which governed postwar life could facilitate personal autonomy and meaningful social connections even as it furthered the dissolution of postwar order. While some still hoped to freeze the dialectic so as to remain safely ensconced in the unchanging spaces of authentic negation, others came to see constant upheaval and perpetual becoming as the only real way forward. This was clearly still an iteration of progressive breakthroughs into the new, but one that was almost entirely stripped of directionality.

This burgeoning anarchism within the texts and practices of the radical left was both constitutive and symptomatic of the increasing intensity of the youth revolts that spread throughout European cities in the spring and summer of 1980. Beginning with the March 1980 battle over the Vondelstraat squat in Amsterdam, groups of radical youth across West Germany, Switzerland, and the Netherlands came together in street protests, youth centers, and squatted houses to proclaim both their independence from established leftist practices and ideologies and their desire for the immediate transformation of European society. The 1981 Grauzone song "Wütendes Glas" clearly illustrates the new anarchistic subjectivities that emerged when radical leftists began dancing the destructive dances of the punk and New Wave milieu in the streets: "bursting glass / bloody face / fast life / artificial light / practiced movements / fondling hands / dancing bodies take leave of reason / [. . .] stand up and go / let yourself drift / listen to the laughter / feel how they perish / tense hands / beat against the wall / dancing bodies take leave of reason."[17] Intimacy, destruction, anarchy, dancing, chaos, and creation all merged in the streets, the squatted houses, the youth centers, and the concert venues of cities across Central Europe. These were spaces where existing forms of meaning could be critically cited, where acts of negation could be practiced in every aspect of life, and where logics could be de- and reterritorialized to create the ever new.

Although Amsterdam and surrounding Dutch cities had been home to numerous squats throughout the 1970s, most had been characterized by relatively apolitical attempts to find adequate living spaces. The combination of a severe housing shortage and the existence of a large number of empty buildings made cities like Amsterdam ideal venues for squatting. Asked about her reasons for illegally occupying a house, one squatter in Amsterdam simply responded "What should I say? I live here and that's it."[18] The situation quickly intensified, however, with the concerted efforts of squatters in the city to defend the occupied building at the Vondelstraat in early March 1980. This was the moment when the *Kraaker Bewegig* (Squatting Movement) in Amsterdam truly took off.[19] The radicalization of the movement in the wake of the Vondelstraat culminated just more than a month later in a massive riot during the Coronation of Queen Beatrix on April 30, 1980. While demonstrators successfully disrupted the ceremonies in the center of Amsterdam with violence and chants of "Geen Woning, Geen Kroning" (no homes, no coronation), they also managed to alienate many of their allies in the left-leaning public.[20] According to Lynn Owens, these events initiated a nascent split in the movement between those who championed radicalization and those who believed that such radicalization was counterproductive. Initially, though, the events of spring and summer 1980 in Amsterdam galvanized leftist activists in cities across northern and central Europe.

While the events in Amsterdam were indeed important initiators of the wave of European youth revolts in 1980–81, the youth movement in Zurich proved to be a more immediate catalyst for West German activists. After months of advocating for an independent concert venue at the Rote Fabrik building in Zurich, activists decided to stage a demonstration in front of the opera house on the night of May 30, 1980. The organizers of the demonstration hoped to use the action at the opera house to draw attention to the city's bias toward high cultural institutions. What they got instead was something altogether different. As the crowd of protesters swelled with revelers leaving the Bob Marley concert at the Hallenstadion—perhaps softly humming "Get Up, Stand Up" as they made their way through the winding wealthy shopping streets near the opera house—the protest action transformed into an all-out riot. Some of the participants in the riot who were interviewed for an article in *Der Spiegel* noted that they had simply been walking through the city on a Friday evening when they noticed that something was happening at the opera. "And there was something crazy going on, an incredibly good feeling at the opera house where hundreds of people had gathered. We felt eerily connected to one another." Another participant chimed in, telling the *Spiegel* reporter: "It was the same with me. That night gave me an uncannily freeing feeling: suddenly I experienced how hundreds of others shared the same feelings and desires as I did."[21] As youth threw stones at police and played music in the streets, they began to feel as if they were part of a new collective.

The riots that periodically swept through the city in the summer of 1980 were certainly significant, but it was the peculiar language and aesthetics employed by activists in the Swiss youth movement that really struck observers. They referred to themselves as the "cultural corpses of the city," to Swiss society as "a glacier," and to the movement itself as a form of heat that would melt the glacial ice that had enveloped Switzerland and thus unleash a new dynamism in the world. As seen in figure 3.3, the aesthetics developed in the movement were similarly fantastical, and often included a jumbled array of political slogans, punk lyrics, illustrations, and irreverent citations of the press, advertisements, and city politicians. The journalist Reto Hänny took note of the language and the aesthetics employed by the protesting youth, calling attention to its peculiar intensity and radical novelty, especially in relation to the more staid forms of leftist discourse in the late 1970s. Youth discourse, he noted, "explodes / bursts / pulverizes / gets things rolling / leads / towards laughter."[22] The acts of collective negation that characterized these movements sparked a feeling of breakthrough but not one that was geared toward any preconceived revolutionary ends; it was a breakthrough, as Hänny argued, into infinite, indefinite joy. One participant simply stated: "I go out into the streets to show that there are still people in this nation, people who can act irrationally."[23]

Such sentiments clearly unnerved the general public in West Germany and Switzerland. Reporters for *Der Spiegel*, for example, warned readers that they too might soon be confronted with "street fighters masked with El-Fatah bandanas who shoot steel balls from dark windows at police armed only with plastic shields," while those at the *Neue Zürcher Zeitung* argued that the riots were led by "professional agitators [who are working toward] the systematic subversion and destruction of our social order [*Ordnung*]."[24] Despite, or, given the general desire on the part of many youth protesters to oppose the forces of order, perhaps because of, such strong condemnations from the press and from city officials, the riots grew in intensity throughout

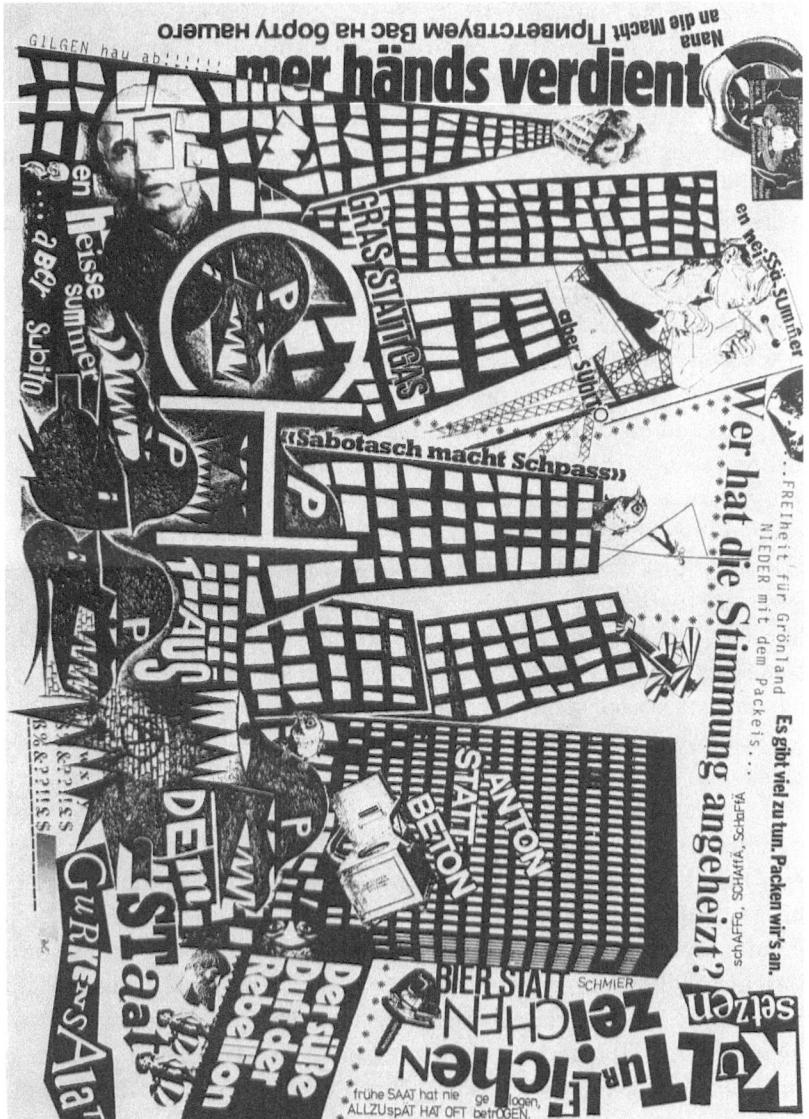

FIGURE 3.3. Image from *Subito* (Nr. Eis, 1980).
Source: International Institute of Social History, Amsterdam.

the summer of 1980, a period that activists began affectionately referring to as the hot summer (*heissa sommer*) that would free "Greenland from the Pack Ice" and radically overturn the existing social order.[25] Eventually, under constant pressure from youth protesters and their allies within the leftist scene, city officials consented to the opening of an autonomous youth center (AJZ) on the Limmatstrasse in late June 1980. The opening of the AJZ was not, however, to mark an end to the "youth unrest" in Zurich. Provided with a new base of operations, youth activists continued to organize disruptive protests throughout the summer. Following waves of critiques from conservatives in the city, the occupants of the youth center were evicted in September 1980. This further radicalized the protesters, whose neo-Dada flyers, films, and actions would come to exert a strong influence on urban activists in West Germany.

One of the most significant documents to come out of the youth revolts in Zurich was the widely circulated cult film *Züri brännt*, which was named after a Swiss punk song which was itself named after the Clash's influential hit "London's Burning." Documenting the emergence of the youth protests in Zurich and making use of a compelling array of experimental audiovisual techniques, the film galvanized thousands of young people in cities across German-speaking Europe to follow in the footsteps of Zurich's protest movement by embracing anarchist politics, subversive and experimental cultural production, and acts of creative destruction. In his 1983 novel about the youth revolts in West Berlin, for example, Michael Wildenhain described how a theater full of people watching the film were so inspired by its message that they collectively rushed out of the theater to take part in a demonstration against the eviction of the squat on the Winterfeldstrasse.[26]

The film opens with slow, ominous music as a line of text ticks across the screen: "Zurich burns. Sandstorm in the ice desert. [...] A hot year in a cold city." Viewers are then confronted with a series of black-and-white images of Zurich's picturesque yet empty old town, large office buildings, and freeways before a singsong, almost hysterically theatrical voice cuts through the deadeningly monotonous sequence of urban imagery to deliver one of the most memorable and quoted statements to come out of the youth movement: "Beneath, where the plaster begins to crumble, where bashful rivulets from Kleenex-cleaned asses flow together in stinking sewers, there the rats have lived for a long time, wild, rampant, and joyous. They speak a new language. And when this language breaks through into the daylight, it will be done, no longer said, black-and-white will no longer be clear, old and new will be one thing [...] and all of the dream dancers will converge to burn the fathers."[27] The film depicted the youth revolts as an outbreak of creative destruction in which young people from across the world would come together to overturn the power of the state and unleash the new. A clearer indication of the ways in which punk-style ideas and aesthetics were transforming leftist politics in these years would be difficult to envision.

Around two hours north of Zurich by car, the wealthy West German university city of Freiburg was heavily influenced by the protests and aesthetics surrounding the alternative youth center. Freiburg had been home to a number of squats throughout the 1970s, including the Hummelstraße in 1974, the Freiau in 1975, and the Dreisameck in 1977.[28] Similar to the squats organized by the BI SO36 in West Berlin, the Dreisameck was initially tolerated by the police and generally not considered a serious threat to public order. This situation shifted dramatically in March 1980 when it became clear that authorities planned to evict the squatters. Threatened with eviction, the residents of the Dreisameck became increasingly interested in occupations in other cities and welcomed leftist visitors and well-wishers from across Europe. In May, for example, the residents of the Dreisameck invited squatters from Amsterdam to give a talk on the defense strategies used at the Vondelstraat.[29] Dutch squatters were in high demand in these years due to the widespread media coverage of the militant protests surrounding squatting in Amsterdam, and the Dreisameck activists hoped to use the event to learn about their successes as well as to galvanize leftists in Freiburg.

In spite of their attempts to forge alliances with squatters from other cities, the residents of the Dreisameck were evicted on the morning of June 8 as more than a thousand police officers drawn from cities and towns surrounding Freiburg cordoned off a number of city blocks around the squat and forced the residents out of the building. Although these events marked the end of the Dreisameck, they also represented the beginning of Freiburg's very own "hot summer," which roiled the city for the next many months. This was a period in Freiburg marked by frequent, oftentimes violent protests, some of which drew up to ten thousand people.[30] In a particularly memorable demonstration on October 17, squatters and their supporters marched through the city in a "platoon of the dissatisfied," blasting punk music and defacing various office buildings with paint.[31] The revolution was now, they were its protagonists, and the strategy and ultimate goals were identical: autonomy through total negation.

The situation in the easygoing university city was tense as demonstrators roamed the streets breaking windows and writing graffiti such as "Freiburg—Police city" (*Freiburg—Polizeiburg*) while troops of heavily outfitted police beat demonstrators, arrested hundreds of people, and generally wasted no opportunity to make a strong showing of state power. The local papers were flooded with letters from citizens, some of whom expressed their dismay at the "fascist" displays of police violence and others who were disgusted by the demonstrators' apparent lack of proper decorum.[32] One particularly irate letter-writer expressed dismay that his taxes were being used to combat unruly students to whom he would then have to give more money later in life when they became his doctors and lawyers.[33]

On the final day of demonstrations, a speaker gave voice to the frustrations and anger driving the protests, proclaiming: "Our hunger for happiness, freedom and sensibility cannot be silenced by this society. They can only offer us perverted and crippled [versions] of our utopias."[34] This defiant speech in front of hundreds of demonstrators served as a call to arms, urging listeners to keep fighting for the realization of their dreams, for a society of intimacy and happiness free from the sociotemporal logics that structured postwar society. Some, it seems, were listening. Later that day, demonstrators occupied the Schwarzwaldhof, which would become Freiburg's most infamous squat.

While it had been highly active in the initial stages of the squatting movement, West Berlin was late to join the wave of youth revolts pulsing through European cities in the spring and summer of 1980. Throughout the summer and fall of 1980 there were minor skirmishes with city authorities, including one particular incident in which the police attempted to prevent a street theater troupe in front of the Adalberstraße squat from impersonating officers, which resulted in a heightened sense of tension within the city. There was nothing, though, that approached the intensity of the June riots in Zurich and Freiburg.[35] For many radical leftist commentators, the *Instandbesetzungen* of late 1979 and early 1980 were simply too tame and too cautious to generate much excitement. The outbreak of youth revolts in Amsterdam, Freiburg, and Zurich, however, began galvanizing West Berliners into action. As news of the revolts in these other cities found their way into the pages of brochures and newspapers in West Berlin, the radical factions within the postrevolutionary left—which, it should be remembered, were already being transformed by an infusion of punk and New Wave aesthetics—began gaining ground against their more cautious colleagues. For example, an October 1980 pamphlet titled "When the Enemy Fights Us It Is Good and Not Bad because It Means That We Have Really Affected Him" called for more radical forms of activist practice in West Berlin and cited movements in Amsterdam, Zurich, Bremen, and El Salvador as inspirations and potential allies.[36]

Another brochure from October featured images of crowds and burning barricades on the cover and described a demonstration on October 10 as an "awesome feeling" in which the police called for help as the paving stones "methodically knocked against the street."[37] It also reproduced a flyer from Zurich that proclaimed: "We have had enough—we want to live—and not be encased in concrete and destroyed. For that reason, thousands of autonomous activists have organized tiny cells with the goal of finally melting the pack ice."[38] Yet another example comes from the foreword to the October edition of *Radikal* in which the author provocatively argue that it is time for action, for "RESISTANCE: no longer printed, no longer in chains, I want to resist, scream, dance, fly—untamed!"[39] To claim that the activists in West Berlin were prepared for revolution is a serious understatement. They were positively consumed with the desire to join the excitement, to finally bring the volcanic dance of the punk and New Wave movements into the streets of the walled city.

They finally got their chance on December 12, 1980, when riots broke out following a police action meant to prevent the planned occupation of the apartment building at Fränkelufer 48. The night of December 12, which was to become legendary in the West German squatting movement, was filled with burning barricades, broken glass, violent confrontations with the police, plundering, and arrests the likes of which West Berlin had not witnessed since the student protests of the late 1960s. A reporter for the *Tageszeitung* who had been skeptical of the earlier squatting actions was totally entranced by the events, by the "feeling of the masses, of movement, of 'us.'"[40] Others were equally affected by the events of December 12 and by the mass demonstrations of the following weeks. For the most part, the mainstream press and establishment politicians reacted to the protests with a mixture of shock and disgust. A series of articles in the *Berliner Morgenpost*, for example, claimed that the preparations for the destructive protests had long been in the works and that, according to information received from the police, they were initiated by bands of outside agitators, most likely anarchists from cities like Amsterdam, Freiburg, and Zurich.[41] Many on the left, by contrast, judged the protests positively. In a *Tageszeitung* article, for example, Firiz Scheytan expressed sheer joy after taking part in the ten-thousand-person demonstration to protest the arrests of demonstrators, writing, "the dream of the Berlin Commune is by no means extinguished."[42] Netzwerk Selbsthilfe, the Alternative List, and even the Maoists of the Communist League of West Germany all expressed support for the protests and for the squatters' opposition to the capitalist "rent-profiteers" and bourgeois city officials who, they argued, were the real sources of violence.[43]

Whereas the establishment factions of the postrevolutionary left expressed a considerable degree of satisfaction with the turn of events in the city, the members of the radical left who had been pining for years for some sort of movement were positively overjoyed with the events of late December. As the cover image of a special issue of *Radikal* depicting an elderly woman stealing a lamp out of a plundered storefront with the caption "Internal Unrest: Berlin's Autonomous Activists Attack" ironically suggested, radical leftists believed that the riots represented an unleashing of revolutionary potential from a new generation of activists who were no longer bound by the outdated ideologies and action forms of the past. One author, for example, wrote that the violence on the streets represented "a cry for more air to breathe, the cry for our identity, the war cry of uncontrolled movements, which can no longer run backwards but only forwards."[44] Another urged the demonstrators to "ignore the priests who have been trying for the last twelve years to push you into integration. It's war in Kreuzberg. We didn't want it—and yet we have been waiting for it for a long time."[45] Others focused on the ways in which the protests were providing spaces for the cultivation of radical forms of autonomous intimacy outside of the chrononormative logics of the state. An untitled piece in the special December issue of *Radikal*, for example, depicted a series of abstract shapes and human forms along with text reading: "Ever more people are leaving work, school, and family and are straying through the streets searching for friendships."[46] The outbreak of youth riots, which emerged at the confluence of punk and New Wave aesthetics, the activism of the late 1970s squatting movement, and the radical leftist desire for immediate transformation, served as something of a siren song for the disaffected, calling them to escape from their humdrum everyday existence and finally take the plunge into a new life, one they might actually find worth living.

The call was answered as thousands of disaffected leftist youth hungering for novelty and adventure streamed into cities like Freiburg, Zurich, and West Berlin. Thomas Lecorte's autobiographical account of his time in the movement serves as an excellent example of this process. As a young person in the 1970s, Lecorte (a pseudonym) was not interested in politics, though he had a sense that something was wrong in the world. "There was the 'Third Reich.' [. . .] And hunger and disease, concentration camps and atom bombs, rape and torture, meanness and cruelty," all of which gnawed at his conscience but for which he had no adequate response.[47] After witnessing the riots of December 12, which he described as a "foreign land, a foreign time," a parallel universe of experience, Lecorte began to seriously think about the importance of militant opposition.[48] In March, he picked up his first stone: "There was screaming and rumbling in the air, the origin of which could not be determined. It filled the space along with the police sirens, the gas, the stones. It was no longer a space that I observed. The stone, the first stone, my stone had filled the space. I belonged to it. It was as if I was immersed, no the opposite: [as if I had] surfaced out of the gloomy, blurry, perception under the water into the clear and sharp air. Now it was finally clear, what was [actually] happening, where it belonged and where I belonged. The first thing the stone meant for me was that the police were brought to a standstill, [they] went from hunter to hunted. Out of fear became courage, out of powerlessness a euphoric strength."[49] The act of picking up a paving stone and hurling it through the window of a bank or into a crowd of police, Lecorte suggests, was thus much more than a violent assault against capitalism and the state, more than a straightforward attempt to "destroy what is trying to destroy you" (*macht kaputt, was euch kaputt macht*), as the popular leftist rallying cry from the 1970s would have it. It was also an act of subjective awakening, a moment of profane illumination in which collectively transgressing established social logics allowed one to glance behind the comforting fog of the known into the possibilities of a different world.[50]

∴

While a number of historians have mentioned the youth movements of these years in passing, only a few have sought to analyze them in their own right. One such author is Lukas Hezel, who has attributed the outbreak and the radicalization of the youth revolts to broader shifts in temporal consciousness associated with the end of the economic boom in the 1970s. Due to downturns in the economy and looming environmental catastrophe, youth in the late 1970s and early 1980s, Hezel argues, began losing faith in the possibilities of a brighter future, meaning that their only real option for happiness was to take what they wanted in the present. Beyond merely seeking to realize happiness in the present, however, Hezel also notes that youth activists in the early 1980s engaged in senseless acts of violence and destruction in order to keep the "threatening feelings of powerlessness in the face of the dark horizons of the future" momentarily at bay.[51] One could think here of Hans Ulrich Gumbrecht's argument that the feelings of alienation associated with life in "the broad present" tend to elicit countervailing practices meant to ground the self in the concrete. For Gumbrecht, these practices included tattooing and adrenaline sports; for Hezel, violent protests against governmental officials served similar ends.[52] In reading the youth revolts as a set of strategies for coming to terms with the "transitional phase of temporal orders after the boom," Hezel also echoes some of Frederic Jameson's arguments on postmodernism as the "cultural logic of late capitalism."[53] For Jameson, whose most famous essay on the subject appeared near the conclusion of the first wave of youth revolts in the 1980s, "postmodern" social, cultural, and aesthetic forms mirrored the underlying economic and temporal logics of late capitalism. In interpreting subcultural forms as superstructural iterations of underlying economic realities, as aesthetic maps of material change, this position downplays the productive dimensions of countercultural milieus, that is, their capacity to do more than simply reflect deep structural changes.

In part, Joachim Häberlen makes a similar argument in his book *The Emotional Politics of the Alternative Left*, noting that, for the youth activists of 1980–81, "only the brief moment of transgression mattered, but what came after this moment remained irrelevant. After all, the perspectives of the future were bleak anyway. If there was 'no future,' as a popular slogan put it, because the future meant only destruction anyway, then only today mattered, without hope also without fear about the future."[54] Häberlen does not, however, claim that the youth movement's penchant for presentism can be attributed to underlying transformations in temporal regimes. Instead, he argues that youth activists in the early 1980s radicalized the practices developed by earlier generations of leftists, which sought to produce feelings of irrationality and exuberance in order to counteract what they understood more broadly to be the oppressive emotional regimes of capitalism. They "longed for such moments when their stable and rational selves dissolved, believing that only then intense and otherwise oppressed feelings might surface. Rioting and dancing excessively could be emotionally productive practices, precisely because leftists expected them to do so."[55] For Häberlen, then, the outbreak of the youth revolts were not the result of deep structural shifts, but an intensification of existing leftist techniques for producing "moment[s] of extraordinary, exuberant feelings that broke through the constraints of the emotional regime of capitalism."[56]

Although convincing in many respects, neither of these interpretations fully takes into account the progressive temporal practices and beliefs within and against which youth activists were operating. Indeed, both Hezel's suggestion that the temporal practices of the youth movement reflected the broader collapse of futurity and Häberlen's arguments on the constitution of emotional strategies for overcoming capitalism gloss over the progressive temporal logics that had infused postwar life and within which youth activists were operating. Instead of viewing them as mere reflections of deeper shifts in the modernist time regime or as imaginative attempts to generate intense moments that would momentarily overcome the perceived emotional damage inflicted by capitalism, I interpret the youth movements within and against the corpus of progressive temporal practices that were developed throughout the postwar decades. Not only does this interpretation place the locus of changing regimes of temporality within the youth movements themselves, it also indicates that, rather than antimodernists who rejected postwar temporal forms in their entirety, youth activists should be understood as off-modern actors looking for ways to redeploy the temporal forms of the modern time regime so as to find new paths forward, novel strategies for breaking through into the genuinely new.

Throughout this book, I have focused on the diverse ways in which multiple generations of West Germans sought to embrace a future-oriented mode of being in time. Whereas Germans in the immediate postwar period looked to launch themselves into the future by erasing, containing, or otherwise overcoming the past, leftist activists worked feverishly to bring about the utopian future through multiple different iterations of dialectical progress. As both the reconstruction-era and the dialectical visions of progressive development lost some of their luster in the late 1970s, leftist youth found themselves without clear guidelines for establishing temporal momentum. While the integrationist iterations of progress may have worked for some, they left many others feeling melancholic.[57] The off-modern experiments with progressive time developed in the late 1970s, and especially the punk and New Wave movements, by contrast, offered new temporal techniques for breaking through into the new. In embracing some of these experimental temporalities and combining them with the universalizing desires of radical leftists to totally remake the world (rather than just oneself and one's immediate environment), the youth movements of 1980–81 sought to revive the feelings of futurity, momentum, and breakthrough that had motivated West Germans throughout the postwar period. In what remains of this chapter, I document some of the aesthetic and activist forms that emerged at the intersection of leftist ideas of radical revolution and the endless negation and perpetual becoming championed by the punk and New Wave movements.

As was also the case with their predecessors in the antiauthoritarian movements and the experimental musical milieus of the 1970s, participants in the squatting and youth movements of the early 1980s sought to uncover the violence that lay buried within the dreamworlds of postwar life. Many, for example, believed that engaging in acts of subversion and spectacular violence, whether through participating in street riots or illegal occupations of empty houses, would reveal the true character of consumer society and representative democracy. In an "Open Letter to the Citizens of Berlin!" following the September 1981 death of Klaus-Jürgen Rattay, for example, the Schöneberg Squatting Council called attention to various forms of state violence, writing: "You say that we are violent. But where does this violence come from? Did we systematically destroy this city through urban renewal projects? Did we build a highway through a residential area? Did we build living silos [*Wohnsilos*] that destroy people? Did we build this world of concrete and plastic where there is not even space for children?"[58] Another example comes from the "Paving Stone Ballad," a popular poem from the period that was often spray-painted on walls, cited in speeches, and, in one memorable instance, yelled from the top of a large apartment building in West Berlin.[59] The first line of the ballad reads: "They have raised you amidst concrete and today they complain that you, concrete child, have stones in your hands."[60] Militant opposition, whether in street riots, in leftist rhetoric, or in acts of destruction, was understood as a necessary response to the structural violence perpetrated by the agents of the state *and* as a mechanism for making such violence visible.

Many focused on more subtle forms of violence that lay just beneath the surface of the everyday and which could emerge at unexpected moments. One depiction of this more sinister form of violence comes from a brochure provocatively titled "The Plunderers—from the Movement, for the Movement," and opens with a description of a typical, if unpleasant, urban scene in which "the smell of piss and shit float through a sea of white cars, colorfully shimmering televisions, accompanied by the chemical smell of perfumes and creams, the Sunday roast of fat ducks with red cabbage and potatoes, and the vestal communion dresses, through artificial shopping streets." Amid this unsettling, if relatively innocuous, urban scene a middle-aged man sits on the subway, smiling pleasantly while musing upon his recent shopping triumphs. Suddenly, the tenor of the story drastically shifts as the brutality that lies hidden beneath the social order begins bubbling to the surface: the man on the subway becomes visibly nervous, starts to sweat profusely, and then dabs at the blood that has inexplicably begun running down his leg. The story then abruptly concludes: "Shadows of the past? Such small indispositions are completely normal in a world, which has not changed after Auschwitz, but which has Auschwitz behind it and nuclear war ahead."[61]

One gets a similar impression from a scene in the 1981 cult film *Paßt bloß auf!* which documents the squatting and youth movements in Freiburg. Here, the viewer is confronted with a number of middle-aged salespeople hawking an array of consumer goods, including an automated piano that allows anyone to produce catchy tunes from a variety of musical genres and a special teeth-whitening agent to cover up coffee and cigarette stains, to an avid group of consumers in a Freiburg department store.[62] Despite the fact that it depicts a seemingly normal shopping experience, the scene is filled with tense, nervous energy as the shoppers continually pause to peer anxiously at the camera, as if questioning their own complicity in some unknown crime. The film then shifts abruptly into a fast-paced, anxiety-inducing montage in which images of people walking down one of Freiburg's many pedestrian-zoned street are juxtaposed with smiling mannequins wearing designer fashions and stunned, vacant expressions. Propelled forward by a nervous, threatening, and rapidly intensifying drumbeat, the scene becomes increasingly frantic before finally culminating in the shattering of a department store display window. Echoing Fassbinder's arguments from

The Marriage of Maria Braun, the film suggests that the consumer dreamworlds of the postwar period were no longer able to contain the threats past or hasten the onset of the utopian future. Instead, they produced myopic consumers unable to imagine any alternatives. Unlike Fassbinder, however, the producers of *Paßt bloß auf!* viewed such prospects positively, for it was only from the shattered remains of postwar progress that youth felt that they might be able to construct something new. The temporal imaginaries that arose in these years conceptualized futurity as dependent on ruination.

Like their predecessors in the 1970s, the participants in the youth movements believed that the nightmares of the past haunted the present, that the murderers were still among them, lurking around every corner, behind polite smiles on the subway and friendly faces on the street. Echoing both the provocative tactics of groups like Kommune I and the sly détournements of the punks, youth activists sought to call attention to the manifold failures of progressive temporal regimes by highlighting objects and environments that had been excluded from the postwar order. Given that progressive temporalities are premised on removing or containing traces of the past in order to simulate a feeling of momentum toward the future, constantly uncovering the presence of the past (whether in the environment or in one's own person) served as a means by which one could explode the normative narratives of progressive time and build new worlds in the ensuing ruins. This calls to mind Walter Benjamin's analysis of "the time of the now" in which "moments of danger" allow new configurations of the past, present, and future to emerge. Freeing the past from its pastness, in other words, seemed to offer an opportunity to upend (and thus potentially overturn) the temporal mythology of the postwar state and in so doing to open up new avenues for collective becoming, a reorientation of being in time in which the future was opened through the liberation of the past. Whereas both the reconstruction-era and the dialectical visions of temporal progress sought to instrumentalize, erase, or contain the past so as to propel society into the future, participants in the youth movement embraced a set of temporal practices built on bringing the past into the present, not so as to collectively overcome it or to sublate it into prescribed futures, but to negate the present while also dwelling in a state of temporal indeterminacy. Uncovering the persistent presence of the past and, more broadly, that which had been deemed obsolete in the postwar order, was simultaneously a tool for scrambling progress and a catalyst for unleashing the unpredictably new.

The nature of this new approach to revolutionary transformation can clearly be seen in the language and the aesthetics employed by participants in the youth movements. In an illustration included in the magazine *Subito*, for example, a confusing jumble of arrows and illustrations is coupled with

FIGURE 3.4. Freizeit 81 flyer reproduced in *Die Plünderer* (1981). Source: Papiertiger Archiv.

a caption reading: "After long and meticulous research, we have finally succeeded in tracking down the international ring leaders' PLAN for the riots in Zurich, Bern and Basel."[63] The youth revolts, this illustration suggests, were not part of any sort of preconceived plan but a spontaneous outburst of destructive negation, one which united diverse activist and countercultural milieus in the service of radical change. An announcement that appeared in the *Instandbesetzerpost* struck a similar chord while also pointing to the centrality of apocalyptic imagery within the youth movements: "We have set ourselves up comfortably behind barbed wire and under neon tubes. We are all zombies in the admission wing and anxiously await the new Hiroshima 1984 [...] For us it's about more than just dwelling: Zyklon B for everyone. [...] All hail discordia."[64] Or take yet another example from the back cover of the brochure "The Plunderer," in which an image of troops storming a beach on Normandy is coupled with a caption reading: "HURRA, WE'RE LANDING ON THE WANNSEE [lake in Berlin]!!! [...] THE MASSES DO WELL TO DESTROY (THEMSELVES + OTHERS). THE DEPARTURE POINT FOR ANARCHY IS THE DESTRUCTION OF CIVILIZATION. I DON'T KNOW WHAT I WANT, BUT I KNOW HOW I CAN GET IT."[65] Alain Vidon, a participant in the Swiss punk scene, gave clear voice to the transhistorical imaginaries motivating the new youth movements, noting: "Much like the tribes in the dark ages, our Celtic ancestors, the Vikings, the Knights Templar, the prehistoric priests with their mythical oracles, we were the fleeting mercenaries of humor, we were the world bandits, driven by the wonderful essence of the unreal, drunk and living in the here and now."[66] This was not, however, an ahistorical temporal imaginary but one in which the collapse of clear divisions between the past and the present served both to overturn the chrononormative power of the state and to create a foundation for new forms of being in time that were unpredictable, undetermined, and thus ostensibly free.

The combination of the sublime, apocalyptic aesthetics developed by the punk and New Wave movements and the impatient, confrontational politics of the radical left sparked a new temporal imaginary in which leftists felt as if they were operating in a landscape that existed outside of dominant spatial, temporal, and logical frameworks, a radical nowness in which the presence of the past both fractured the facade of progress and opened the future. These moments of revolt and temporal transgression were akin to religious epiphanies, lightning strikes of clarity that not only facilitated a deeper knowledge of the surrounding profane world, but also gave participants the feeling that they were being transported into another dimension. According to some of the Dutch activists of the Agentur BILWET group, the street demonstrations of the early 1980s were "unique, local, ecstatic. In the event there occurs a compression of time. It is of such an intensity that it reduces the past and the future into nothing. It appears as an intrusion of the present into the stubborn advance of history."[67] Squatted houses were similar in that they represented "entryways into an ahistorical space," thresholds to an alternate, autonomous reality.[68] In the squatted houses "no

FIGURE 3.5. Front cover of *Die Plünderer* (1981). Source: Papiertiger Archiv.

one worried that the projects lacked perspective; what counted was the journey, the expanding space of one's own life rhythm—where this led to was of interest to no one. No future. It was an explosion, facilitated through the simple pleasure of the here and now."[69] Where exactly it led may indeed have not been of interest, but it *was* immensely important that it lead somewhere new. Indeed, the consistent references to an ahistorical here and now was actually not ahistorical at all—it was a cacophonous concert of distinct temporalities that had been forcefully liberated from the iron-cage logics of progress and that began flowing together in the energized spaces of the street protests and the squatted houses to create what Anna Lowenhaupt Tsing might call a "polyphonic assemblage."⁷⁰ Place was clearly an essential component in these new imaginaries, and I will return to it in depth below.

Such mystical pronouncements about transcending the physical limitations of time and space were not limited to a group of nostalgic activist-intellectuals from Amsterdam reminiscing about the warm, psychedelic glow of times long past; they were also evident within documents produced during the revolts. Take, for example, this report from a participant in the June riots in Zurich, who noted: "It was a wonderful feeling! [. . .] In battle you feel totally high, forget everything around you, don't perceive anything, yet you FEEL SOLIDARITY. [It was] a real adventure playground. Oh, the city began to come alive!"⁷¹ Or another, also from a participant in the June riots in Zurich: "One felt oneself again. It was a medicine for the heart and soul when a windowpane exploded. Joy, as if life had just begun."⁷² As the rioters took over city streets, filling them with music, joy, and destruction, objects and identities that had once seemed fixed began to lose their previous contextual meaning and to come alive, thus offering opportunities for adventure, novelty, and limitless transformation. The riots were moments in which the flow of time began to fracture, when the familiar contours of urban space melted into landscapes of fantasy, when the radical all-at-onceness of the present meant that the presence of the past ensured the openness of the future. In this sense, then, "no future" was definitively *not* a negation of the future but a radical opening of its horizons. The present was filled with multiple temporal rhythms, alternative pathways of becoming and being outside of the prescriptive pathways offered by postwar progress. One needed only to free them from the "pack ice."

As was also true in the punk and New Wave movements, such acts of radical negation were both constituted by and constitutive of extreme expressions of creativity. Many participants in the revolts directly connected such creativity with violent opposition to bourgeois society. In an interview conducted by the *Blatt* magazine in Munich, members of the radical group Freizeit 81 (Freetime 81) argued, with obvious reference to the aesthetics and practices of the punk and New Wave movements: "Destruction is also creative. One can justify destruction as an act of vengeance [but it also] includes the construction of something new." They continued, "everyone who can imagine doing something under the name of Freizeit '81 (no matter what) can and should conduct such actions under this name [which] is a symbol of dissatisfaction."[73] Another article vehemently denied the common critique that the youth movement had nothing to say, noting that youth expressed a "creative speechlessness of the [paving] stones [...] the non-normalized wordless cry of creativity [which] cannot be integrated into the circus of the State."[74] Not only were such expressions of creative destruction seen as dangerous for the logical coherence of the state, they also were understood as facilitating forms of "counter power" out of which new communities, aesthetics, and temporal logics could emerge.

A frequent theme in the literature produced by the movement was that one could creatively reuse the disembedded fragments of modern society to produce novel cultural forms.[75] An article in the second edition of *Subito*, for example, urged a depressed youth for whom consumer products were bringing no joy, to take control of the objects and recombine them into something novel, into a new, adventurous reality: "So, grab the objects from the stores, take the dresses and the dead dolls, build figures out of them, build fashionable brats [*Modefratzen*], sex idols, scarecrows, build managers, teachers, bosses, parents, police, cucumber planters. Then take TV sets, pinball boxes, gadgets and machines and build robots from them: monstrous, money eating, children eating, people eating, cucumber eating [robots], build giants, dwarves, witches [...] and then let all the people see your spectacle: Murder and manslaughter: monsters eating children, robots strangling sex idols, giants squash little teachers."[76] Such imagery, although perhaps shocking to many leftists, would have seemed familiar for youth who had been socialized in the punk and New Wave milieus of the late 1970s and for whom the ideas of creative destruction and radical pastiche were already well established.

These sentiments were put into practice on numerous occasions. Residents at the KuKuCK (Art and Culture Center of Kreuzberg) complex in Kreuzberg, for example, built massive structures from discarded consumer appliances to display, and at times ritually dance around, in the courtyard while squatters in Amsterdam reveled in the act of giving new life to obsolete objects by incorporating them into the everyday practices of autonomous life. According to the authors of *Bewegungslehre*, squatted houses "proved themselves to be magnets for things, that were not consumed but valued for their uniqueness. In every occupation, first the house had to be totally cleared, in order to then stuff it full of junk that one had found on the streets. Wooden ironing boards, ovens, kitchen sinks, a car door, warning lights, bed posts, neon lamps, mannequins."[77] In many instances, the houses themselves were transformed into works of art. In addition to its prominent trash sculptures, the KuKuCK, for example, was decorated with an enormous mural of a group of witches brewing bombs. Photographs taken

FIGURE 3.6. KuKuCK Fassade (1981). Photo by Manfred Kraft.
Source: Umbruch Bildarchiv.

inside the houses show walls that were totally covered in graffitied slogans such as "No Future" and "We want to live" as well as painted images depicting everything from large monsters to playing children.[78] Such creative art projects transformed squatted houses into preeminent locations for producing, displaying, and viewing oppositional works of art. Indeed, squats were not only places to live or locations for political activism, but they were also art galleries and performance spaces that generated extreme forms of artistic experimentation.

The squatters also integrated themselves into these jumbled montages of resignification. Much like the objects gathered inside the houses, squatters considered themselves to be discarded material. Inside the protective walls of the squatted houses residents created new configurations of meaning by collectively dwelling amid the objects and the environments that had been deemed obsolete by the logics of progress. They utilized unwanted materials to continually develop novel modes of communication, clothing styles, and social codes. The back page of the January 1981 edition of *Radikal* provides a good illustration of this process: "Everyone changes their name, place of residence and identity whenever they want, invents new conversation forms on a daily basis, new occupations, new forms of expression, new ceremonies, new perversions, new musical directions, new clothes, new words, new feelings, new family relationships, and new forms of sabotage and agitation."[79] Similarly, the authors of *Bewegungslehre* noted that squatters "had their own topology of secret signs: houses, cafés, junk shops, bike paths, streets and bridges, symbols, signals, posters, costumes and hairstyles. The smell of clammy leather jackets and houses without showers, cat piss, plastic bags with rearview mirrors from cars, removed traffic signals, meetings, demos, rallies, meeting points, telephone chains and fighting troops, illegible telephone jargon, first names and house numbers."[80] In the squatted houses and in street riots, young activists finally felt free to engage in radical acts of creative production, to escape from the confinement of established narratives of being and becoming. Their location on the edge of intelligibility made it possible to appropriate and critically redeploy common objects from the cosmos of consumer culture. Washing machines, TV sets, mannequins, toys, cartoon characters, and even, as Gabi Delgado illustrated, fascist fashion accessories served as totemic objects with which participants could create the new.

As noted above, these creative practices of destructive bricolage were coupled with the development of new forms of revolutionary intimacy, autonomous modes of "being-together" that were seen as the total inversion of the "the excruciating loneliness and emptiness of everyday" life in the dead cities of postwar Europe.[81] A nostalgic essay written in the twilight of the movement powerfully expresses the importance of these new intimacies that arose in the heat of battle: "Friends, where have you gone? You with whom I battled in the streets. [. . .] For a worthwhile future. What a feeling to feel that you are not alone with your fears, your weakness. What fascination shone from our eyes what an infectious enthusiasm, what a spontaneous joy in life flew out of us. Friends who I found in the nights, on the streets, don't let the fire go out. There is still so much there so many barriers to tear down, to break through to smash. Don't let the sun go down. Come on. Fight. Live."[82] Safely ensconced behind the protective walls of the squatted houses, no one worried about properly implementing plans for the utopian future or about politicizing the marginalized agents of revolution. Instead, the goal became to liberate the self from normative narratives of being and becoming so as to freely experiment with alternative forms of community.

One squatter, unconsciously channeling the sociology of Emile Durkheim, noted: "When you're in a group you have a feeling of 'us.' In the situation of living together with other people, you get a crazy good feeling which also gives you enormous strength."[83] A Swiss activist connected to the AJZ in Zurich made a similar point, writing: "We are connected through the experience of a world of uncontrolled borderlessness and an absolute trust."[84] J. C. Wartenberg, who had taken part in some of the earliest squats in West Berlin in 1979, remembered these early months of the youth movement very fondly, writing: "Every day was a new adventure. For me it was the best time in Kreuzberg. [. . .] All the people around me developed exceptional strength, bubbled over with a desire for life. Everyone was important."[85] As concrete spaces of radical openness the squats thus facilitated an environment in which everyone was welcome to participate. They were both grounded, localized spaces and borderless, decontextualized landscapes in which one could explore unknown dimensions, what the authors of *Bewegungslehre* described as a "space of perpetual metamorphosis," where everyone was welcome to constantly reinvent, and thus endlessly become, themselves.

Another example of these intimate relationships comes from *Paßt bloß auf!* The film is full of scenes juxtaposing the love, friendship, and community that arose amid the youth movements with the alienation of everyday life in mainstream society. A particularly poignant example of this comes in the final minutes. This sequence opens in what appears to be the alternative youth center in Freiburg, which was formed in the wake of the March 1981 eviction of the Schwarzwaldhof. Young punks clad in the typical attire of the subculture—leather jackets with "no future" painted on them, 3D glasses, ripped jeans—dance to a song with the catchy chorus: "Germany, Germany, it's all over." They speak to the camera about the future, growing vegetables with vodka, and finding true love all the while dancing and playfully interacting with the camera and with each other. The scene then abruptly shifts to an underground archive in the mountains where Germany's cultural heritage is protected from disasters, both natural and man-made. The camera follows the archivist deep beneath the mountains and pans over hundreds of identical capsules containing, so we learn, significant cultural objects such as the original plans for the Cologne Cathedral. The distinction here between the infectious vitality of the youth movement and what the filmmakers clearly saw as the cavernous emptiness of the nation's past serves as a striking example of the ways in which lived intimacy was counterposed to relations based on classification and hierarchy.

The occupations of empty buildings in derelict urban areas initially started as a form of postrevolutionary protest meant to draw attention to the destruction of authentic urban lifeworlds and the criminal practices of property developers. As radical leftist groups and countercultural activists began to take part in the occupations, however, they became centers of the youth revolt, expansive experiments in alternative living that facilitated novel temporal practices. In the early 1980s, the occupied houses came to be understood as environments of temporal transcendence, portals to a cosmic landscape of perpetual becoming and transgression. By dwelling amid the discarded objects, fractured utopias, and forgotten pasts of the squatted houses, youth were able to forge new connections outside of the logics of progress. Despite the fact, however, that the squatted houses were understood as liberated spaces that facilitated a seemingly limitless experiential expansion into the vast uncharted territories beyond the borders of established spatiotemporal logics, they were also localized, grounded landscapes, the subversive potential of which was premised on their contextual specificity, on their historically dissonant materiality, and on their embodiment of times and dreams long past. It is, after all, very difficult to envision such transgressive social and cultural practices emerging from the occupation of a suburban house built in the postwar period.

While I will hold off on discussing the ways in which squatters dealt with these contradictions between embedded, historically saturated spaces and transcendent subjectivities until the following chapters, it is worth noting at this point that the concrete, auratic nature of the squatted houses helped to make the youth movement legible for broad segments of the population. Whether on the right or the left, observers saw the houses as localized, bounded areas of difference and diversity, spaces of alterity where alternative modes of living were accepted and where the rules of normal society did not apply.[86] The squatters' belief that particular landscapes facilitated subjective freedom, in other words, eased their incorporation into mainstream iterations of urban nostalgia, which, as many historians have argued, were gaining traction in these years.[87]

This tendency to see the squatted houses as spaces of alterity that enabled one to immediately immerse oneself in a different reality was particularly attractive for left-alternative youth throughout Western Europe who wanted to take part in the movement. Joining the movement was simple: all one had to do was make the decision to move into an already squatted house or, for those who were more ambitious, gather a group of friends to squat their own house. In his 1983 thesis, Matthias Heisig, for example, described how he and a group of friends initially visited some of the squatted houses in Kreuzberg before making the fateful decision to squat a house of their own. They quickly began renovating the space, which they liked to think of as the 113th squatted house in West Berlin, and forging connections with their neighbors. He described life in the houses as a "search for a different lifestyle, which one could sense just by standing in the stairwell."[88] Despite some trouble with the punks who moved into the rear building, Heisig and his friends soon felt that they truly belonged, that the "'Block' became a real 'neighborhood.'"[89] As this example suggests, the deep symbolic connections between occupied houses and oppositional lifestyles meant that anyone could take part in the regenerative rituals of the squatting movement by simply dwelling for a short period in the transcendent environment of an illegally occupied house. It also meant, however, that one could just as easily leave the movement by moving out, by no means an uncommon occurrence.

A statement announcing the decision to form a Squatters' Council in Kreuzberg is indicative of the fact that many of the original activists in the movement initially approved of the rapid expansion of the milieu and the increasing number of squatted houses. The authors celebrated the fact that "the resistance against [. . .] the politics of the Senate and against the destruction of our neighborhoods is growing. Ever more people are turning to self-help, be it Citizen- and Renter-initiatives or the occupation and repair of the threatened houses."[90] Similarly, alternative newspapers like the *Instandbesetzerpost* kept tabs on the number of squatted houses in the city and enthusiastically reported on squats in cities throughout the nation. At least in the initial months, the success of the youth movement was believed to depend on the expansion of occupied spaces as well as on convincing ever larger numbers of average citizens that the squatters were engaged in a righteous battle against the forces of order.[91] The extraordinary numbers of self-introductions of new squats published in alternative papers in 1980–81 illustrates that numerous people eagerly embraced this opportunity to actively take part in the burgeoning resistance to urban renewal and to bourgeois lifestyles.[92]

Left-leaning members of the public sphere also viewed the squats as spaces of radical openness amid an otherwise alienating society. Take, for example, the following description of a squatted house in West Berlin, which was written by a leftist sympathizer who spent a few nights with the squatters in order to try and understand their lifestyle. While in the squatted house, the author was impressed both by the friendliness of the squatters and by the overwhelming, visceral fears involved with living illegally. On his first night, he wrote, "the paranoia of being evicted took hold of me, I kept waking up to listen to suspicious noises, in my nightmares a heavily armed policeman dragged me from my bed at least five different times."[93] Only upon leaving the house days later did these fears subside long enough for him to realize how truly strange and wonderful life in the houses actually was: "After a few days the heavy house door shut behind me, I realized with astonishment, that 'outside' everything was the same as it had always been. The commuter traffic was rolling along, the customers were still jockeying in the Supermarket, in the next street I could hear how the evening news had begun. I strolled to my house, passing porno bars and corner pubs. I want to listen to Bob Dylan and shut down."[94] Passing by the brightly colored houses with their provocative banners defying capitalism, the state, and bourgeois morality, left-leaning urbanites in cities like West

Berlin and Freiburg could imagine these spaces as modified reincarnations of their own antiauthoritarian years, as beacons of hope in an increasingly unwelcoming environment, and thus as legible, localizable spaces whose exceptional openness was balanced by its concrete materiality.[95] Squats could thus be incorporated into the logics of late twentieth century urban space, something that would facilitate their later utility for processes of gentrification.

∵

Describing the peculiar, mystical landscapes that emerged in the squatted houses and in the street demonstrations of the youth movements, the authors of *Bewegungslehre* noted: "In the middle of the city, amidst the concrete forms of everyday boredom, one entered a space of unending possibilities. It was not about creating something new but using the old to break through to somewhere else."[96] Unlike the dialectically inclined activists of the Red Decade, the anarchist youth of the early 1980s were not interested in channeling negation into established developmental pathways leading to a prescribed vision of the utopian future. Nor were they interested in politicizing the masses by lecturing them on their objective interests. Drawing from the transgressive sociabilities, the experimental artistic practices, and the apocalyptic aesthetics developed in the punk and New Wave movements, participants in the youth revolts of 1980–81 sought to negate the present by consistently uncovering the presence of the past. Not only would this contribute to the ongoing destabilization and fragmentation of the progressive temporalities that buttressed postwar power, it would also facilitate processes of liberated becoming, subjective practices in which the self could constantly be remade amid the proliferation of alternate temporalities. Indeed, no longer would the past be contained or sublated in order to fuel specific futures; instead, its proliferation would serve to create a space of endless becoming. The past was still necessary for constituting the future, but instead of attempting to overcome it as previous temporal practices demanded, the youth movements saw its persistent presence as the precondition of breaking through into the radically new. As was also the case in the punk and New Wave milieus, this was a process that required continuous acts of destruction. Creating a state of endless becoming meant that activists had to repeatedly blast the past out of the continuum of history. In the case of punk and New Wave, such destruction was primarily carried out in the realm of symbols. In the youth movements, by contrast, destruction took place in the symbolically laden built environments of urban (and particularly domestic) spaces. In order to keep the feeling of perpetual breakthrough alive, then, youth activists needed to engage in ever more radical acts of transgressive destruction and consistently widen the scope of negation. As the next chapter shows, this strategy proved very difficult to sustain.

[CHAPTER FOUR]

Perpetual Motion

Ritualization and Rebirth in the 1980s

In the youth revolts of 1980–81, urban activists, to quote the punk singer Nena, felt as if they were collectively "falling through space and time," as if they were on the verge of unleashing a wave of creative destruction that would definitively remake the world. By the early months of 1982, however, many began to worry that the movement had run its course, that the dream was over. The authors of a January 1982 article in *Schwarze Kanal* offered a particularly gloomy view of the situation, writing: "The cold hangs like a threatening immensity in the sky over the city, in which a frigid life threatens to spread. Not only is the movement itself freezing, but so are the relationships between the houses and between the people living in them. [. . .] '82 will in all respects not be rosy—'82 will be as gray as the dirty snow that falls in this city."[1] The September 1981 death of Klaus-Jürgen Rattay at a demonstration in West Berlin, the March 1981 eviction of the Schwarzwaldhof squatters in Freiburg, and the rampant heroin problems surrounding the AJZ in Zurich all signaled that the brief "hot summer" of 1980–81 was giving way to what was expected to be a long, cold winter.

And yet, the energies unleashed during the youth revolts refused to fade into obscurity. According to the Dutch authors of *Bewegungslehre*, the effervescent, ecstatic feelings of transcendence that emerged in the early months of the youth movement were, over the course of the 1980s, slowly subsumed into mediated images and normative codes for action. The movement, they argue, "is the memory of the event. It is [. . .] an image, a reflection or an interpretation of what came before."[2] What had originally been spontaneous outbreaks of creative destruction and temporal experimentation in the turbulent months of 1980–81 quickly settled into normative frameworks of behavior that echoed the feelings of the original transgressive "event." Whereas for the authors of *Bewegungslehre* such shifts from event into ritual signaled the youth movement's decline, they were also necessary for keeping the experimental social forms of these years from falling

FIGURE 4.1. Eviction of the Fränkelufer Squat in Kreuzberg on March 24, 1981. Photo by Michael Kipp. Source: Umbruch Bildarchiv.

into oblivion. Since the publication of Emile Durkheim's seminal work on the "elementary forms of religious life," social theorists have argued that the energies created in effervescent spaces of communal experience are necessarily translated into ritualized performances and symbols, into a diverse array of representations that are simultaneously derivative of the "original event" and constitutive of the consciousness, ideology, and practices that define social groups.[3] In the case of the 1980–81 youth movements, the original effervescent moments of temporal transgression generated an array of ritual objects, narratives, and behaviors, ranging from absurdist poetry, to trash sculptures, to musical genres, to rampages throughout the city, all of which functioned both to routinize the original acts of transgression and to make these practices more broadly accessible for audiences in West Germany and beyond. In other words, the experimental social, cultural, and aesthetic forms that emerged from the youth revolts of 1980–81 served as mechanisms for encoding the effervescent experiences of revolt into rituals and objects that could smoothly travel from one context to another, into transposable frameworks for being in time that allowed ever larger numbers of youth to consume and take part in the movement.

∴

As the authors of *Bewegungslehre* and numerous other autonomous activists from this period have argued, the media played a central role in defining the parameters and expanding the reach of the youth protest movements. Leftist and movement-specific newspapers such as the *Instandbesetzerpost*, which began publication in March of 1981 in West Berlin, were especially important in this regard. Circulated among squatted houses, participants in the movement, leftist sympathizers throughout the city, and neighborhood residents who were curious about what went on in the squats, the *Instandbesetzerpost* contained the latest news from the squatting movement in West Berlin, special reports on autonomous activism in other European cities, and first-person narratives about everyday life in the occupied houses. In addition to reading firsthand reports on the latest occupations, evictions, and political debates in the "Letters from the Front" segment, readers of the *Instandbesetzerpost* could also brush up on their home repair skills with instructional articles on repairing roofs, installing electrical systems, and fixing plumbing.[4] Furthermore, the articles in the *Instandbesetzerpost* gave readers privileged access to the internal dynamics of the squatted houses, including comical reportage on banal gossip from inside the scene. One article in this series, titled "The Best from the Rumor Kitchen," noted: "In the KuKuC (this is the correct way to write it) Susi, 8 weeks old, is said to have shit on the carpet in the café where dogs are no longer allowed. Is that true?"[5] From the casual tone to the inane content, this article exudes a sense of familiarity with the houses and their residents. The *Instandbesetzerpost* as well as similar papers like the *Kiez Depesche* also served as forums in which squatters could announce new occupations and introduce themselves to the larger community. Whereas in the early months of the movement such announcements had an aura of innovative transgression, by 1981 most of them conformed to a simple framework announcing the occupation, inviting guests to come visit, and calling for donations of furniture, food, and money.[6] The act of living illegally was being normalized.

By reprinting individual flyers and self-introduction letters, papers like the *Instandbesetzerpost* served as essential tools for centralizing the various messages coming out of the movement. At times they read like circulating bulletin boards in which flyers and announcements could be perused by a broad audience in the city and beyond.[7] For many, this centralization of information served as an indispensable guide for navigating the scene. One reader, for example, wrote a letter to the editors of the *Instandbesetzerpost* in which he expressed his hope that the paper would continue to be published, noting: "When I was a novice in the front city, the BP was the only source to find out what was going on in the scene."[8] Others, though, viewed the normalization of protest language with skepticism. In his novel on the squatting movement in West Berlin, for example, Michael Wildenhain depicted official protest language as an intrusion into the flow of everyday life by randomly inserting popular slogans and song lyrics into the narrative and setting them off with bold type.

Much like the alternative newspapers of the period, the mainstream press in cities throughout West Germany and Europe more broadly were also filled with sensationalist stories of squatted houses and youth protests. At times, these reports consisted of simple narratives of events within the movement.[9] Others, though, explicitly attempted to paint the youth movements in a negative light. An article in the *Berliner Morgenpost*, to give but one example, titled "Squatters—Contact to the 'Red Cells,'" recounted a government report on the connections between squatters and terrorists.[10] These articles gave readers the alarming impression that the youth movements were rapidly spreading across the continent and that anyone might fall victim to the sinister machinations of the masked "chaos makers" (*Chaoten*). Even leftist newspapers such as the *Tageszeitung* sometimes corroborated these impressions of the protesting youth as apolitical hordes driven by an irrational desire for violent confrontation and destruction. A November 1980 article, for example, highlighted statements by youth protesters in Hannover such as "we don't really think about too much, we get drunk and make actions, that's all."[11] By portraying the protests as drunken escapades conducted by bored urban youth, such articles contributed to the growing sense within some of the more established factions of the postrevolutionary leftist milieu that the youth movement was not to be taken seriously.

Although the vast majority of mainstream news articles on the squatters were negative, there were also numerous reports that sought to provide a more balanced examination of the youth revolts by exploring the larger context of their actions and their political demands. One article in the *Tageszeitung* provided an in-depth look at the exceptionally democratic political forms practiced in the movement by recounting a meeting of the Squatter Council (*Besetzerrat*) which took place at the KuKuCK in West Berlin in April 1981.[12] An article in the *Tagesspiegel* titled "What Squatters Think" attempted to define the ideology of the movement by interviewing fifty-seven squatters from twelve different houses. Obviously impressed with what they found, the authors noted: "This form of living together in the occupied houses with a great number of more or less familiar kindred spirits has no precedent."[13] An article in the *Süddeutsche Zeitung* described the dreams that had motivated the squatters, noting: "A few years ago they set out from quaint, clean-swept small cities in Münsterland, in the Black Forest, and in Bavaria, broke free from their parent's care, which they perceived as a corset, fled from the 'dream of dream partners, children, jobs, and televisions.' They came on the D-Train to Berlin and then the subway to Kreuzberg and began their search for a new freedom."[14] In translating the activities and ideologies of the protesting youth into easily consumable news stories, the mainstream media contributed to the emergence of a normative explanatory framework of the movement, a set of narratives and parameters that defined, and thus constrained, ecstatic experience.

As is evidenced by the large numbers of letters to the editor concerning the youth movements, the reading public was positively fascinated with stories of the protesting youth who dressed in strange costumes, illegally occupied houses, and marauded through city centers. Many of these letter-writers expressed their disdain for the movement by questioning the true motives of the protesters. In an angry letter to Bishop Kruse published in the October 18, 1981, edition of the *Tagesspiegel*, for example, Ursula Rehbein of Berlin chided the Bishop for his public defense of the squatters and pedantically informed him that nowhere in the Bible did it say that people should be lazy and live off the money of others.[15] Similarly, an FDP politician from Freiburg wrote in to the *Badische Zeitung*, arguing that the city had not worked so hard to "create the pedestrian paths so that demonstrators could rip out the paving stones and throw them at the windows of businesses or innocent citizens."[16] While most of the letters to the editor struck a critical tone, some expressed shock at what they viewed as excessive use of force by the police and support for the overarching goals of the youth activists.[17]

Much like the mainstream newspapers, film and television documentaries also helped to fashion a coherent narrative of the squatting movement in which average viewers throughout the nation could gain a better understanding of the goals and desires driving participants in the youth movement. Although many such television programs portrayed the protesting youth in a negative light as bands of spoiled children who were too lazy to work and too narcissistic to behave properly, some attempted to portray them in a more positive light. After watching one such program, titled "History of an old House," Erika Ebert from Stuttgart was so moved by what she saw that she decided to write the squatters of the Manteufelstraße 40 in Kreuzberg a letter, in which she noted: "If I was still young, I would pack up my things and come to help." The letter, which was also sent to the mayor of West Berlin, concluded by declaring: "You are the youth that we need [those who] develop fantasies, who are still living as a collective."[18] Whether positive or negative, the images that streamed into living rooms across the nation provided viewers with a concrete sense of what the houses and their occupants looked like, of the sorts of activities that they engaged in, and of the various headaches they caused for average citizens. Although they undoubtedly fanned the flames of hatred among more conservative audiences, it seems highly likely that these images also convinced disaffected youth in provincial towns throughout the nation to engage in similarly radical acts.

To give but one example, Gudrun Gut, who later became the lead singer of influential post-punk bands like Malaria!, was so enamored with the idea of West Berlin as a rebellious space filled with activists and countercultural experimentation that she decided to travel there herself, an experience that corroborated her feelings completely. Upon arriving in Kreuzberg she thought to herself: "Here is where freedom begins. In that moment it was clear to me that I had to leave the narrow enclosure of West Germany and live in this city."[19] As this example suggests, the images of protesting youth in cities like West Berlin that regularly appeared in mainstream newspapers and on television news programs throughout the country could serve as siren songs for the disaffected, calling them to abandon the humdrum existence of their everyday lives and take the leap into a different world.

While television reporting was certainly important for translating the squatting movement into narratives that could be consumed by a wide array of audiences throughout West Germany, documentary films produced by squatters and sympathizers were much more significant for leftist audiences. These films clearly illustrated the overarching goals, the aesthetics, and the forms of sociability that characterized the youth movement. The 1981 film *Wo die Angst ist Geht's Lang*, for example, offered viewers an unobstructed view of life in the houses by depicting scenes of alternative youth collectively engaged in repair work, DIY bicycle maintenance, collective dinners, outdoor bathing, political conversations, graffiti art, and demonstrations. In addition to providing viewers with an inside look into life in the squatted houses, the film also clearly illustrated one of the central ideological tenets of the movement by juxtaposing scenes of collectivity, revolutionary aesthetics, and ecstatic togetherness with images of empty houses, police searches, and wealthy speculators.[20] Other films focused on the relationship between squatters and their families. The 1982 film *Am Anfang war doch nicht der Pflasterstein* opens by juxtaposing images of isolation and loneliness in high-rise apartments with contrasting scenes of communal warmth in the squatted houses before shifting into a documentary-style investigation of a mother and father visiting their daughter in an occupied house on the Potsdamer Straße. Despite initially disapproving of their daughter's decision to live illegally in a squatted house, by the end of the film, the mother and father begin to evince sympathy for her lifestyle choices and to question their own commitment to the chrononormative frameworks of West Germany.[21] Protesting youth, it seems, were "good to think with."

As was also the case with previous generations of autonomous leftist activists, the participants in the youth movements of 1980–81 produced an extraordinary number of pamphlets, brochures, and flyers that were designed to make political demands, to invite others to take part in protest actions, and to provide justification for and explanations of their activism. Especially in regard to justifying and explaining their actions, these brochures served to further solidify an overarching narrative of the youth movements that proved palatable to broad segments of the left-leaning public. The November 1981 brochure produced by the squatters of the Winterfeldstraße 31 serves as a particularly good example here. The illustrated image on the cover of the brochure provided a view of the entire house in which, due to the absence of an exterior wall, the private actions taking place inside of the individual rooms were clearly visible. In one room, a group of squatters sat around the table under the graffitied slogan "emotions and harshness" (*Gefühl und Härte*); another was filled with building material accompanied by the phrase "do something" (*Tut Wat!*); while another contained two people sitting behind a table awaiting a group of elderly neighborhood residents who were stopping by for a visit.[22] A series of handwritten notes reproduced in the brochure also gave the reader the sense that they were privy to the inner environment and intimate details of the houses. One of the notes read: "The goal of washing dishes is to *clean* the dishes." In another, neighborhood children expressed their feelings about the squatters, writing: "We love you so much and we are really fond of you. We want you to stay."[23] The brochure also included a series of letters from some of the groups who were acting as sponsors (*Paten*) for the house in which they expressed their fondness for the squatting lifestyle, noting: "We wish for you: that you can wake up in peace and eat breakfast, clean the walls, smoke cigarettes, install windows, cook, fix the roof, chat, lay floors, play with the kids, renew the water pipes, write newspaper articles, take long baths, go to the squatter council, drink beer, snuggle, lay plumbing, sleep and dream."[24]

Given the importance of experimental art and music in generating the ecstatic energies of the youth movements in the first place, it should come as no surprise that these media also figured prominently in ritually codifying the revolutionary energies emerging from these milieus. The visual artists collectively known as the Neue Wilden, for example, emerged in conjunction with the squatting movement in West Berlin and went on to exhibit their impressionistic artwork throughout the world. In the foreword to a 1982 book on these artists, Wolfgang Stock argued that the peculiar conditions of West Berlin were essential for generating the vitalistic impressionism of the Neue Wilden, writing: "Here the problems are larger and the contradictions crasser than in other places and, on the other hand, the population is more colorful, life more intense, the atmosphere more open. Whether punks or political sects, alternative democrats or new wave groups: here one is always a step ahead of the rest of the country, and thus many think of Berlin as the capital of the new German art scene."[25]

A 1983 video produced by the experimental group Notorische Reflexe also pointed to the deep connections between contextually specific forms of transgression and artistic representations. The video consists of a series of overlapping scenes, including cars driving down crowded streets in West Berlin, people setting up an art installation, the Brandenburg gate, a man dancing in the nude, police in riot gear, and punk concerts. In one particularly memorable scene, an image of a hand playing a bass guitar is overlaid onto a group of protesters overturning and setting fire to a police car.[26] As the film illustrates, art and music functioned as resonant, transposable media with which to ritually reenact and aesthetically narrate the ecstatic energies of the youth movement. As such, they served as modes of representation that could communicate the effervescent immediacy of the youth movements to audiences throughout Germany and the world more broadly—me included.

Although most clearly evident in the yearly May Day parade in Berlin, the role of street demonstrations and festivals in ritually reenacting moments of original transgressions was already well established in the early 1980s. One of the clearest examples of this comes from the 1981 TUWAT festival in West Berlin that was intended to serve as a pan-European meeting of squatters and autonomous activists. In a video calling on activists to travel to West Berlin to take part in TUWAT, the viewer is treated to scenes of squatted buildings, of youth marching together, and of ritual destruction as the narrator implores all those who feel isolated and oppressed to come together to combat the state. Similarly, a flyer titled "TUWAT SPEKTAKEL IN BÄRLIN AB 25.8" called on activists to come to Berlin, "the fissured ass of the nation," to prevent the authorities from "exterminating our living space and our connections." It went on to note: "We will erect protected villages on all of the squares of Berlin, overflow the city with chaos makers [*Chaoten*], terrorists, punks, hippies, layabouts [*Gammler*], drunks, gays, anti-fascists, lesbians, squatters [*Kraaker*], AJZ fighters, the flipped out, etc. The city must stink and seethe."[27] In an interview with the *Tageszeitung* the organizers of the festival further corroborated this sentiment, noting: "It is important, that [TUWAT] brings together the diverse individual battles which are being fought all over—the battles against organized inhumanity."[28] Echoing a similar statement from the 1980 Swiss film *Züri brännt*, the authors of the TUWAT flyer downplayed the differences between these various marginalized groups in order to posit a transnational alliance united by acts of anarchist negation.

While the postrevolutionary leftists of the *Tageszeitung* expressed some trepidation that the festival could spiral into disorganized, regenerative forms of violence, many of West Berlin's city officials were entirely convinced that it would do so. They confiscated TUWAT flyers, railed against the mindless *Chaoten* in the press, and, in one instance, broke into the TUWAT central office to search for contraband.[29] Similarly alarmist critiques of the festival continued well after it had become clear that it would not produce the waves of destructive violence and chaotic rioting that West Berlin's city officials had initially feared. One of the most vocal critics of the TUWAT festival in this period was the very conservative Secretary of the Interior, Heinrich Lummer. Lummer, who was a particularly reviled figure among participants in the youth movements, went so far as to express his support for the foundation of a paramilitary group named Citizen Action against Chaos and called on his fellow Berliners to "do nothing for TUWAT but do everything for Berlin."[30]

Although the fears of West Berlin's conservative politicians were overblown, TUWAT was representative of the growing connections between youth activism in different cities. In the wake of the eviction of the Schwarzwaldhof in Freiburg, for example, radical youth from Amsterdam to West Berlin took to the streets to demonstrate their solidarity with activists in what many had taken to calling Polizeiburg. An announcement for a demonstration in West Berlin on Black Friday (March 13, 1981) in the week following the eviction of the Schwarzwaldhof noted: "Today the city should explode! In all corners, people need to realize that we're here, this cesspool of squatter and their sympathizers. [. . .] Decentralized actions of the Fun Guerillas [*Spaßguerilla*] in all of the neighborhoods, on land and in the sky. The governing shit birds [*Kackvögel*], the destruction-renovators [*Kaputtsanierer*], hostage takers, and master prison builders are not classified as protected monuments."[31] This passage reflects the sentiment that squatting and autonomous activism in cities throughout Europe were part of one central resistance movement engaged in a common struggle against "the state." Squatting was no longer merely an experimental temporal practice meant to facilitate limitless becoming; increasingly it was seen as a routinized catalyst of global revolution.

In addition to forging a sense of transnational unity between activists in different cities, these demonstrations also served as some of the most powerful initiation rituals of the youth revolts, as moments when diverse groups of otherwise uninvolved people could come together to show solidarity with one another, to clearly distinguish between "us" and "them," and to participate in the rush of collective effervescence. Take, for example, a report written by a participant in a demonstration in West Berlin on September 22, 1981, in which the author noted:

> I stood there on the corner as the demonstrators, in ghostly silence, tore down not just the construction sites, but the entire moral structure of the ruling society. The ghostly atmosphere, lit by the artificial neon lights, which had never been so absurd as in this moment, the uncanny roar that escorted the mass, the atmosphere stretched almost to the breaking point, it was something that words cannot describe, feelings that cannot be fully articulated. [...] I stood at the crossing, surrounded by inhuman concrete silos, unreal neon light, absurd electronic advertisements, the symbols of a false living space, and all my personal goals and problems seemed unimportant—here it was about much more than my own individual fate, it was a desperate, mute fight for a new life.[32]

Demonstrations acted as gateways into an alternate reality in which experience faded into a transcendent battle between power and its manifold discontents. As was also true at the height of the antiauthoritarian movements of the 1960s, these events allowed participants to feel the effervescent rush of being on the verge of the new. They were moments characterized by collective acts of negation and by a feeling of limitless possibilities.

According to many of the original participants in the youth revolts, over the course of the early 1980s mass demonstrations such as the one described above increasingly lost their spontaneous, contextually specific characteristics. As more people joined the marches, some activists began worrying that demonstrations had become self-referential exercises in simulating feelings of collective transgression, ends in and of themselves in which everyone could experience the emotional rush of revolution by throwing rocks at police, breaking store windows, and setting cars on fire.[33] They were venues in which anyone could "come out of their holes, make noise and ruckus, and fight against the establishment."[34] As the name of a demonstration in October 1980 in Freiburg clearly indicates, these were "marches of the dissatisfied," public expressions of collective absurdity in which everyone was welcome to lose and/or find themselves in the effervescent rush of mass protest.[35] In part, the unanchored, borderless quality of mass demonstrations facilitated the expansion of the youth movements into new venues. At the same time, though, this opening up of the revolutionary experience removed demonstrations from their auratic contexts. According to the Agentur BILWET group, this process of alienation was further facilitated by self-appointed groups of professional revolutionaries who monopolized

FIGURE 4.2. Aftermath of a demonstration during Ronald Reagan's 1982 visit to Berlin. Photo by Manfred Kraft. Source: Umbruch Bildarchiv.

insurrectionary authenticity. "The message of these groups was: You can't take part in actions like we do but you can mimic them, if you study our texts and find out how we did it. They legitimated their actions with the thought that 'ever more people are taking part' in order to then organize more actions of the same sort."[36] Transgressive acts of mass militance, they argued, had become simulacra of revolution, subjective posturing that had no connection to the surrounding environment.

As noted in the previous chapter, the materiality of the squatted houses also facilitated the ritual expansion of the movement. The symbolic power attributed to the squatted houses, their status as sacred spaces of the movement, meant that the effervescent energies of 1980–81 could be contained within spatially circumscribed areas of difference, which, depending on one's political position could either be interpreted as "free space" (*Freiraum*) or "lawless space" (*rechtsfreier Raum*). The squats also facilitated a shift toward more streamlined forms of activism through an increasing focus on the proper social and material forms of revolutionary dwelling. Take, for example, the brochure "What Is Being Done in the Squatted Houses?" produced by an architectural initiative in Schöneberg, in which the authors provided the public with a detailed account of the repair work that had gone into creating communal areas, kitchens, childcare facilities, and workshops, as well as descriptions of the liberated forms of sociability that were being cultivated in the houses. Such innovative dwelling forms, they went on to argue, "should be extended outside of the houses."[37] The squat thus came to represent a new, transposable model of urban dwelling that could easily be applied to a variety of contexts.

Another example of this codification of revolutionary practices comes from a 1982 brochure on the Regenbogenfabrik squat in which one of the occupants described everyday life in the putatively liberated zone as, in a number of respects, highly regimented. In addition to organizing cooking, cleaning, childcare, household repairs, and public outreach campaigns, the squatters of the Regenbogenfabrik/Lausitzer Straße also took part in periodic meetings (*Plenum*) that included "reports on committees, the Squatters Council, and other such things, discussions of legalization concepts, Vogel/Braun's complaints to the Senate and what it meant for us, the party on the coming Sunday, Karin's girlfriend moving in, some peoples' dissatisfaction with the eating group."[38] After the transgressive novelty of living outside the narrative frames of the postwar began to fade, the occupants of the squatted houses were confronted with the harsh and oftentimes entirely unexciting realities of organizing workable forms of communal living. Especially for those who envisioned their houses as projects that would last well into the future, such codifications of everyday life were a necessity even if they also often resulted in a dilution of the anarchist sensibilities of the movement.

∴

The transition from effervescent explosion into ritualized action was, on the one hand, highly beneficial for the youth movement as it allowed activists from different regions and from diverse political backgrounds to transcend their local contexts and come together under the shared banner of revolutionary negation. An article in *Stilett* points to this sense of a united leftist movement, noting: "Suddenly it was burning in all of the corners and ends of Europe. [...] The riots became the same everywhere," as they began to fight against a common enemy: "The enemy in the form of anodyne shop windows. The enemy in the form of deadly traffic. The enemy in the form of hostile concrete. The enemy in the form of empty houses. The enemy in the form of departing localities. The enemy in the form of saber-rattling politicians. The enemy in the form of bloodthirsty robots. The enemy, the pig! [...] Everywhere needs more oil in the fire, until the great party on the beach below takes off. So, people, listen to the signals and set off for ... what now ... oh right, for the (next) last battle!"[39] The increasing ritualization of the movement made it possible for a diverse array of youth activists to imagine themselves as part of a transnational revolution, one that shared a common enemy, common goals, and a common aesthetic. This sense of unity is concisely, if rather absurdly, summed up in a text from Denise, an 18-year-old participant in the youth protests in Zurich who argued that society was divided into two classes: "The robots and the animals. Robots are programmed automatons. Animals act according to instinct, desire, and feeing. It's obviously better to be an animal than a machine."[40] A clearer statement of the overwhelming feeling of "us" versus "them" that reigned supreme in the youth movement would be difficult to imagine.

This sense of unity in diversity was further solidified by the fact that activists involved in the squatting milieu often traveled to visit squats in other cities.[41] An amusing example of this comes from an illustrated story in which the French cartoon characters Asterix and Obelix are reimagined as traveling youth activists. After helping the residents of the Schwarzwaldhof in their battle against the evil speculators (here represented by the Romans), Asterix and Obelix take their leave in order to join the famed "tour de Crawall (Berlin-Hamburg-Bremen-Goettingen, Frankfurt, Freiburg, Basel, Zürich, Hintertupfingen)."[42] The early 1980s witnessed the creation of an increasingly interconnected network of activists who could seamlessly move from the AJZ in Zurich to the Schwarzwaldhof in Freiburg to the squatted houses in West Berlin. This is not to say, though, that all regional peculiarities were lost amid a translocal aesthetic of autonomous leftist values. In West Berlin, for example, residents of squatted houses constantly complained about the ever-present Swabians who, when it was their turn to cook dinner for the squat, inevitably evinced their provincialism by making cheese spaetzle.[43]

While undoubtedly beneficial as a mechanism for expanding the parameters of the movement, many youth activists were far from pleased with the shift toward ritualized behavior, and not just because they were tired of cheese spaetzle. Many experienced the transition from what they saw as original principles of revolutionary negation into ritualized forms of action as an unwelcome reversal of priorities. What had initially been conceived of as localized protests designed to realize a specific set of goals had become, they argued, a form of spectacle, a mode of action that abandoned local particularities and the authentic needs of the "Betroffene." An article in the *Instandbesetzerpost*, for example, decried the fact that the participants in the Squatter's Council had all but abandoned local concerns in favor of endless discussions about the next demonstration or the newest squatted house.[44] The situation was similar in Freiburg where, after the eviction of the Schwarzwaldhof squatters, many in the movement turned their attention entirely to actions designed to protest police tactics and the trials of activists.⁴⁵ While not denying the necessity of such actions, some participants warned that the movement was in danger, "as in the case of fashion," of becoming "the avant-garde of the next shopping season."⁴⁶

A particularly vicious critique of the ritualization of the movement comes from J. C. Wartenberg, who in his memoirs of life in Kreuzberg in the 1980s lamented the fact that activists from across Europe began to descend on Kreuzberg looking only for adventure and for the next big showdown with the police. "On the one hand," Wartenberg wrote, "it was great to experience how Kreuzberg was filled with colorful chaos, but on the other hand I often had the feeling that all of the trash [*Schrotties*] and adventure-seeking petit bourgeois from across Europe were coming to Kreuzberg, because it appeared to them that it was a great, lawless free space. Everyone who was looking to get out of their boring everyday lives, or were just itching for a fight, lolled about the empty houses and declared them occupied."⁴⁷ An article from Zurich made a similar point by referring to youth activists as "autonomous lemmings [. . .] who run from action to action, from demo to demo, and when we no longer know where to go, we make a new demand, that it is even bigger and better than all that came before."⁴⁸ While some blamed these developments on thrill-seekers within the movement, others argued that media representations were largely to blame. One article, for example, noted that "thousands of pictures form labyrinths, which the immobile [*Bewegungslosen*] wistfully follow, get lost and upon realizing this, are tempted into following a newly created image."⁴⁹ The movement was becoming spectacle, an unwitting imitation of consumer capitalism.

In contrast to those who decried the effects of ritual as fundamentally anathema to the movement, others seemed to have found the situation highly amusing, at least in retrospect. Take, for example, Sven Regener's novel *Der kleine Bruder*, which portrays the leftist scene as a theater of comic absurdity. The novel follows Frank Lehmann as he leaves his home in Bremen in search of his brother Manni who is working as an artist in Kreuzberg. Frank quickly runs into trouble, however, when he finds that Manni has since changed his name to Freddie and gone missing. The ensuing hunt for his lost brother leads Frank on a wild journey through the labyrinthine world of Kreuzberg's alternative milieu, a journey which is marked by a steady descent into increasingly absurd layers of theatrical representation. The novel constantly discredits authentic forms of subjectivity by depicting individuals as mere impersonations of types. Some play the role of punks attempting to convincingly exude a "no-future" attitude, others of left-alternative lifestyle radicals constantly turning conversations into plenums, and others of avant-garde artists in search of fame. Even Frank becomes mired in this vast web of misidentification by unwittingly impersonating his brother, Manni/Freddie, a situation that leads one of Freddie's acquaintances to proclaim: "Shit man, when Freddie comes back, then we will have him twice [...] it's totally confusing."[50] Upon entering a squatted house in the neighborhood, Frank finds that even this paragon of revolutionary authenticity is nothing more than an empty signifier, a "squatting simulation" in which a group of artists led by the faux punk singer P. Immel impersonate squatters in order to increase the value of their art, which, appropriately, consists mainly of repurposed trash that they plan on selling to art collectors in West Germany and New York.[51] As the narrative progresses, the revolutionary landscape of Kreuzberg is steadily transformed into a surreal stage of deception and misrecognition, in which the freedom to assume a new identity comically dissolves into a freedom from assuming any sort of fixed identity at all. While some blamed this state of affairs on the media and on the thrill-seekers, it seems more realistic to view it as a logical outgrowth of the youth movement's desire for endless becoming through constant negation, which, due to its defiant rejection of completion, directionality, and categorization was almost bound to end up spinning into nowhere.

Such comic representations of the descent into simulation, or simulated dissent, were, however, rather uncommon. Most participants fell into one of two camps. Those associated with what would come to be called the Müsli faction advocated for a negotiated end to the conflict in which the squatted houses would become quasi-legal spaces devoted to self-help, neighborhood social work, and the development of alternative visions of urban renewal. They sought to cultivate authentic connections to place and to social forms which many believed were being destroyed by the decontextualized practices of the protesting youth. Not willing to give up on the expansive inclusiveness and the chaotic energies of the youth movement, others remained committed to the creative-destructive practices forged in 1980–81. They hoped to push the borders of the movement into ever new territories until it consumed the world in flames. These so-called Mollis, also known as the non-negotiators, were certain that that the energies they had unleashed would not easily be put to rest, that if only they could keep dancing around the volcano, the great breakthrough into the posthistorical future would eventually come to pass. They misinterpreted endless becoming as an instantiation of leftist dialectics that had a natural endpoint in a final, apocalyptic overcoming of capitalist modernity.

Veterans of earlier leftist movements as well as the self-appointed experts on the youth revolts did not remain neutral in this burgeoning division within the youth movement. Many of the groups that supported the overarching goals of the protesters, and especially those that took part in the massive West German Parliamentary Commission designed to study the revolts, mobilized a set of social-psychological theories on "post-adolescence" to account for the sudden emergence and unfamiliar behavior of the protesting youth.[52] Due to a wide array of historical factors associated with the advent of late twentieth-century modernity the established academic theories of adolescent behavior were no longer believed to be entirely applicable. Rather than a short phase of rebelliousness and experimentation preceding the transition to stable adulthood, experts began to interpret adolescence as an extended period of liminality, characterized by existential doubt, a weak sense of purpose, and "an egotistical concentration on the self."[53]

While some commentators mobilized this paradigm to point to the psychological deficiencies of the protesters, others argued that postadolescent behavior was fundamentally progressive in its orientation. Postadolescent protest, these more supportive experts argued, was not only symptomatic of large-scale social, political, and environmental problems, it also offered a possible way out of the various impasses faced by European societies in the late twentieth century. In the Prognos report commissioned by the West German Parliamentary Commission, for example, the authors argued that the crises faced by postadolescent youth were not limited to certain age groups but represented "a mirror image of the entire society."[54] Due to their particular sensitivity to the contradictions and problems faced by contemporary society, they could serve as mediators between the present and the future, as pathfinders on the road to a better tomorrow. The Swiss authors of the pamphlet "Thesen zu den Jugendunruhen" made a similar point about the constructive dimensions of postadolescent protest, arguing: "It is positive that values which act as a corrective to the one-sided materialistic and technological development of our society are again coming to prominence." The authors went on to note that the oppositional social, cultural, and political forms that were being developed by the protesting youth offered contemporaries a blueprint "for a more humane future, if only the politicians would take it seriously."[55]

Such positive readings of postadolescent protest were not limited to state-funded panels of experts tasked with interpreting the new generation of rebellious youth but were widespread among leftist commentators as well. The psychologist Jörg Bopp, for example, echoed an argument that was often propagated by the activists themselves when he noted: "It is not the youth protests that are the central social and political problem but the dead-end politics that provoked their eruption."[56] In addition to viewing youth as the canaries in the coal mines of postindustrial society, leftist commentators also followed their colleagues in the state commissions by arguing that youth activism contained the blueprints for reform. Taking the *Kerngehäuse* complex in Kreuzberg as an example, Peter Schultz-Hageleit argued that squatters were cultivating models of authentic living that fulfilled the natural human desires for community and warmth so lacking in contemporary West German society.[57] Similarly, the sociologist Walter Hollstein claimed that youth protesters should be applauded for their rejection of "success, status symbols, careers, and consumption [in favor of] autonomy, self-realization, creativity, commonality, fulfilment, and happiness."[58]

Many activists who had been involved in the student movements and in the antiauthoritarian politics of the 1970s also viewed the youth movements in a largely favorable light. Dieter Kunzelmann, who since we last encountered him had renounced armed insurrection, argued that the "creativity and the fantasy of the squatters was breathtaking [. . .] and maybe even stronger than in the anti-authoritarian movement."[59] In a letter written from prison, the leftist author Peter-Paul Zahl gave a particularly rousing endorsement of the movement, arguing that the squatters represented Kreuzberg trying to defend itself from the speculators. He then went on to describe the movement in poetic prose: "The pack ice is becoming brittle. Through the streets of Kreuzberg and even West Berlin, an icebreaker is moving full speed ahead, colorfully painted, full-throated, festive; grass is breaking through the asphalt; fireworks are expertly blasting apart the apartment towers, fresh wind and sunshine are replacing the air-conditioners."[60] Although in significantly less flowery prose, Bernd Rabehl also expressed his somewhat circumscribed admiration for the squatters, noting "it is a movement without leaders, a movement without political form, in which every individual is engaged to the highest degree."[61] Despite being impressed by their thoroughly antiauthoritarian character, however, Rabehl also mobilized an argument that Habermas had originally used against the student movement, to claim that without any overarching political perspectives, the youth protesters faced the danger of slipping into protofascist forms of actionism. "In the fight against the police," Rabehl wrote, "they take the form of the police, in the fight against authority they themselves become authorities, in the fight against Lummer, they become Lummer. This happens because they have no principles, no analytical categories, because they just act based on 'feeling,' and 'feeling' is vague, susceptible to myth, to backwardness."[62] Much like the social-psychologists discussed above, veterans of the antiauthoritarian movements of the 1960s and 1970s both admired and feared the youth movement, believing that it offered a possibility for enacting radical social change but only if it was properly sublated into the established temporal patterns of progress.

Progressive Christian groups expressed similarly measured levels of support for the protesting youth. Left-leaning Christians had been among the first to raise their voices in opposition to the destructive urban renewal policies of the 1970s. Unlike the youth protesters of 1980–81, however, activists in the church were much more committed to a sustainable strategy of protecting authentic lifeworlds and slowly working toward the utopian future. Despite these differences, Christian groups such as the members of the Evangelical Church in West Berlin expressed admiration for the squatters' attempts to create a more welcoming, humane form of communal togetherness. In a speech at a church service held at the Schultheiss squat in the Zehlendorf neighborhood, Armin Waldschmidt pointed to a slogan reading "Don't sell your dreams," and argued that such sentiments were necessary to combat the alienation and suffering of contemporary society. Their dream, he went on, consisted of "sustainable, humane society, in which trust, warmth, tolerance, empathy, sympathy, and concern reign supreme. [. . .] It is the dream of a 'home,' a '*Heimat*,' that is built collectively."[63] They also supported the squatters' critiques of urban renewal policies in the city. Klaus Duntze's 1981 paper "Berlin Dwelling Politics, their Social Repercussions, and the Task of the Church," for example, directly called on the members of the Evangelical Church to support the squatters in their fight against callous urban politics, which, he argued, were destroying traditional lifeworlds in Berlin and contributing to a more alienated, unsatisfying society.[64] Members of the Evangelical Church also attempted to raise money for the squatters, offered their churches as meeting spaces for youth activists, and, in many cases, joined other "sponsors" (*Paten*) who took on the responsibility of supporting particular squatted houses.[65]

The *Paten* movement in West Berlin consisted of a diverse group of citizens who were, for one reason or another, sympathetic to the squatting movement and wanted to offer tangible assistance. For the most part, their work consisted of advocating for the legalization of the houses and attempting to convince their fellow citizens that the squats were actually beneficial to the city. A press release written by the "Paten against evictions—for a Housing-political Solution" group, for example, chided the Berlin Senate for fighting against the squatters while ignoring the larger issues resulting from a failed housing policy.[66] In some instances, the *Paten* visited "their" squatters to illustrate their solidarity, to prove to the public that the squats were not dangerous nests of terrorism but utopian projects populated by idealistic youth, and to try and prevent evictions. In December 1982, for example, Günter Grass visited the house for which he served as sponsor to read selections of his poetry. Despite the fact that most of the residents did not respond positively to his poems, Grass declared that he would never give another public reading in Berlin if the squatters were evicted.[67] When a number of houses were threatened with eviction in August 1981, the progressive theologian Helmut Gollwitzer joined other *Paten* of the threatened houses by publicly moving into one of the squats.⁶⁸ The photos documenting this incident show a very happy Gollwitzer carrying a large pillow as he enters the house. While the *Paten* were often able to galvanize public support for the squats, they also had their critics. Following Gollwitzer's solidarity action, for example, an anonymous letter-writer harshly chastised him for handing Berlin over to "the Reds and the Terrorists," before concluding: "Poor Germany, poor Berlin. God will punish you!"⁶⁹

Before moving on, one additional group of supporters deserves mention, namely the web of activists involved with organizations like Netzwerk, which Benny Härlin described as the "greatest *Paten* of the movement."⁷⁰ The activists involved in Netzwerk, which had initially emerged in the wave of left-alternative activism surrounding the TUNIX festival, along with similar organizations like Netzbau, SHIK, and the Society for Self-governed Dwelling tended to interpret the squatting movement through a vaguely dialectical lens as a somewhat misguided but ultimately valuable attempt to combat urban renewal policies and unsustainable economic development. The organizers of SHIK, for example, pointed to the unique forms of community being developed in the squatted houses to argue that the occupants were "trying to live and work 'differently.' [. . .] The diversity of the projects in a relatively small area and the at times exceptionally dense interconnections are [positively] transforming life in the neighborhood."⁷¹ By organizing negotiations between youth activists and government officials, developing models for legalizing the houses, and providing money to the squatters for the purposes of repair, groups such as Netzwerk sought to reintegrate the revolutionary energies of the youth movement into more acceptable forms of leftist politics. In a number of cases, they were successful in their attempts to legalize the squatted houses: by January of 1984, 59 squatted houses in West Berlin had received a lease agreement.⁷²

Despite such successes, however, the activists involved in these groups were more often than not extraordinarily frustrated in their interactions with the senate, the police, and other municipal offices concerned with developing responses to the squatting movement. In their December 1982 decision to dissolve Netzbau, for example, members cited the duplicity of the senate as one of their primary reasons, noting: "In this current political situation, we can no longer advise the squatters to negotiate with people who treat them as wild beasts [*Freiwild*]."⁷³ While some in the senate were certainly sincerely interested in developing peaceful solutions, others were determined to eradicate all traces of the squats from the city. The conservative West Berlin city government under Mayor Richard von Weizsäcker and Secretary of the Interior Heinrich Lummer was much more likely to clear squatted houses, which they depicted as refuges for criminals bent on destroying the nation, than to go through the arduous and politically dangerous process of negotiating long-term leases.[74] Heinrich Lummer, in particular, wasted no opportunity to denigrate the movement as one that was led by spoiled children, that destroyed rather than repaired the houses, that was filled with petty criminals, and that generally brought shame on West Berlin.[75] Others in the city administration were somewhat more strategic with their expressions of disdain. In an internal government memo from June 1983, for example, one Dr. Klaus noted: "In regard to the legalized houses, it will be reported that the criminal acts there have not diminished and that these houses are increasingly chosen as a living place by members of the hard core [of the movement], since these houses can no longer be searched." He went on to note: "In public we should use facts and negotiation overtures to elicit support."[76] Netzwerk and its allies, it seems, were not wrong in claiming that conservative factions within senate were not to be trusted.

Whereas established leftists tended to view the Müslis as heirs of the student movements, they looked on the Mollis with horror. According to Josef Huber, who was one of the founding members of Netzwerk, the "utopian element has somehow come to a standstill, become quiet, slowly but surely fallen under the table and what's left is simply this naked character of revolt and battle."[77] Such feelings of distrust were mutual. In a 1981 discussion with squatters from the 1970s, for example, one of the participants angrily responded to the suggestion that contemporary youth lacked political perspective by referring to the older generation as "arrogant" and claiming that he would rather "speak to some bourgeois asshole."[78] The disagreements between the radical Mollis and the older generation of leftist activists were undoubtedly intense, but the real fireworks came from conflicts within the youth movement itself between the Mollis and the Müslis. To a certain extent the split between the Müsli and the Molli factions came about as a result of fundamentally different opinions on whether the squatters should negotiate with representatives of the state in order to legalize the houses. For all but the most radical Mollis who rejected negotiation on principle, leases were deemed acceptable only if a number of conditions were met. First, they demanded some variety of a "total solution" (*Gesamtlösung*) to the squatting question in which all of the houses occupied before a certain date would be legalized, something that most of the Müslis and their supporters at least initially supported.[79] Second, they demanded an immediate amnesty for all those who had been arrested in connection to the street protests. Especially in the early months of the movement when demonstrators marched through the streets chanting "1-2-3, Let the people free!" and organized gatherings outside the prison walls, the calls for amnesty had a unifying function. Indeed, while the various factions of the youth movement might not have agreed on the ultimate goals of the protests, they could all unite in their opposition to its overt criminalization.

Whereas in the early months of the movement these demands were met with general agreement, the increasing threat of eviction as well as the rising level of violence led many in the Müsli faction to begin seeking individual leases, a decision that threatened to alienate them from their fellow activists even as it increased their chances of long-term survival. This choice to engage in individual negotiations with property owners and the city enraged a number of the more radical activists within the youth movement who equated such actions with treason and argued that it was a slap in the face to those who were serving jail sentences.[80] According to the anarchist group AG Grauwacke, the non-negotiators never "really thought so much about whether it would be possible to hold onto the houses without some sort of lease or without any negotiations. [. . .] But ultimately that really didn't matter, since the real point was to keep moving forward: 'standing still is the end of movement' was the warning cry that the movement theoreticians from the radical faction often used. [. . .] Holding together, the 'us' feeling of the movement, was more important than any tactical observations. Anyone who engaged in negotiations was putting the brakes on, preparing the end of, shutting himself off from [. . .] the movement."[81] Similarly, an article in the radical West Berlin paper *Schwarze Kanal* argued that employing the language of negotiations and leases meant that the squatters were "speaking [the state's] language, [. . .] conforming to bourgeois norms and values."[82] Given their commitment to a vision of the movement as an end in and of itself, an endless carnival of ecstatic negation that facilitated leaps into the unknown, the Mollis categorically rejected the idea of legalization.

If negotiations were considered treasonous attempts to stop the movement in its tracks, contextualization was seen as a fate worse than death. Given their proclivity for interpreting the youth revolts as fundamentally irrational outbreaks of creative destruction, the activists associated with the Molli faction vociferously resisted all attempts to incorporate the movement into broader narratives such as those that were developed by reform-minded politicians, academics, and activists. In his memoirs about his time in the autonomous movement, Thomas Lecorte argued that "the left, liberals, and the right were in agreement. It was not possible for there to actually be people who in full consciousness spoke the way we did. It had to reinterpreted, interpreted, twisted, it had to be pruned and digested by the dominant language until it reached a level that was acceptable for reality."[83] This resistance to forms of contextualization was readily apparent when a group

FIGURE 4.3. Dialogue with the youth on February 7, 1982. Photo by Michael Kipp. Source: Umbruch Bildarchiv.

of politicians and experts associated with the Parliamentary Commission tasked with studying the youth movement visited a squat in West Berlin to engage in a "dialogue with the youth." After having been assured by the Schöneberg Squatter Council that they would be treated fairly "according to the statutes of the Geneva Conference," the representatives entered the squatted house at Potsdamer Straße 157, only to be greeted by blaring music with the decidedly unwelcoming lyrics "Germany must die so that we can live." Some of the squatters repeatedly asked the visitors uncomfortable questions such as "how is your sex life?" and "how much money do you make per month?" as a parody of the social-scientific investigation into their own lives. Others were even more direct in their refusal to engage in rational dialogue and spent the evening in ski masks (which were seen as a symbol of violent street protests) screaming at the commission about the death of the "pig system."[84]

Although certainly among the most visible perpetrators of the crime of contextualizing the movement, the Parliamentary Commission was hardly the only guilty party. One article in the *Schwarze Kanal*, for example, titled "Uh Oh, We Are Being Analyzed," drew attention to the fact that groups of university students were trying to "shine light" on the movement by inquiring about the squatters' "opinions, language, feelings, and relationships. [...] In so doing the students are assuming a role in the 'illuminate-analyze-destroy' tactic that the state so readily employs."[85] The journalists of the

Tageszeitung were also accused of trying to destroy the movement by incorporating it into logical structures of meaning. In a March 1982 article in the *Schwarze Kanal*, which along with *Radikal* served as one of the primary mouthpieces for the Mollis, titled "Down with the TAZ Imperialism," the authors noted: "It makes us puke that the *taz* uses its wide circulation and its 'leftliberal' monopoly to [. . .] become opinion leaders—alternative integration politics!"[86] Whether in the form of lease negotiations, academic analyses, or political incorporation, the radicals of the Molli faction viewed attempts to contextualize the protests as fundamentally anathema to the ecstatic, irrational outbursts of anarchist effervescence and creative destruction, which they believed stood at the core of the youth movements.

While there were some notable exceptions, most conservative politicians and commentators tended to agree with this more radical interpretation of the youth movements which held that the protesters were a danger to the state who should not, and perhaps could not, be fully integrated into mainstream society.[87] In a response to the government-sponsored "Theses on the Youth Revolts" pamphlet, for example, Jeanne Hersch argued that inadequate education and overly permissive upbringings had led contemporary youth to lose their moral compass and even their ability to rationally address their own needs. They had thus turned to dangerous forms of nihilism and to ostensibly progressive, liberated projects such as the autonomous youth center, which, in reality, were merely spaces of "emptiness, capriciousness, and a resentful nothingness."[88] While they may have differed on the origins of such nihilism, conservatives tended to agree on the basic nefarious character of the youth revolts. They saw in the squatted houses underlying "structures of violence" and "lawless zones," which endangered the very foundations of the democratic state.[89] In West Berlin this sentiment was apparent from the very beginning of the protest movement, though it began gaining steam in the period following the July 1981 Grunewald demonstration, in which activists from Kreuzberg "visited the speculators" at their homes in the affluent Grunewald neighborhood. Following this demonstration, a number of local media outlets began comparing the protesters to the Nazi brownshirts who terrorized society in the interwar period. In a July 1981 article in the *Berliner Morgenpost* titled "They Called Themselves Psychoterrorists," for example, images of the phrase "Jews out!" (*Juden raus!*) were directly juxtaposed with images of a masked protester spray-painting the phrase "real estate agents out!" (*Makler raus!*) on a wall.[90]

Similarly, other commentators portrayed the protests as the work of wild criminal bands determined to destroy the city, the state, and quite possibly even West Germany itself. Jürgen Wohlrabe of the West Berlin CDU Party noted: "These people have finally taken off their masks. At the very latest during the Grunewald action, they have made it quite clear that for them it has nothing to do with the abolition of housing shortages [*Wohnungsnot*] but with the intimidation of individuals and the terrorization of entire neighborhoods."[91] Wohlrabe's claim that the squatters were not actually concerned with improving living conditions in the city was common throughout the early 1980s. An August 1982 article in the *Berliner Morgenpost*, for example, debunked the squatters' claims to be repairing the houses, arguing that the evictions had uncovered that the squatted houses were not "occupied for the purposes of repair [*instandbesetzt*]" but "occupied for the purposes of destruction [*kaputtbesetzt*]." The article went on: "Walls and floors were ripped out and ceilings broken through. Empty apartments are used as trash heaps or toilets." Rather than repairing the houses for the purposes of creating "living space," they were simply using them as "refuges [*Fluchtburgen*] for criminals and for the drug scene."[92] Youth protesters, according to these conservative commentators, were nothing but irrational perpetrators of senseless destruction.

In many instances average West Germans shared these sentiments. In a series of letters to conservative senators in West Berlin, for example, Fred Grätz complained about the squatters who were living in his building, noting that they were basically asocial dropouts who terrorized their neighbors and destroyed the houses. In addition to making fun of him for his job at the *Tagesspiegel* and peeing outside his door, he complained, some of them had even spray-painted the phrase "here is a fascist collective with bath and toilet—Heil Hitler" on the wall outside his apartment.[93] Following the death of Klaus-Jürgen Rattay in September 1981, Jörg Friedrich went through the streets of Charlottenburg soliciting opinions on the youth protests. One person noted that the youth should be given "forced labor! Work and more work. Just like we had to work when we were young." Another argued that under Hitler youth would never have gotten away with such behavior. Yet another referenced the bus that killed Rattay and suggested that police "should chase them with buses, run them over, finished."[94]

∵

Despite the Mollis' best efforts to prevent *Stillstand*, the years following 1980–81 were indeed something of a long, cold winter for the movement. The masses were no longer attending demonstrations, squatters were no longer coming to the aid of their comrades who were threatened with evictions, and people were no longer visiting or writing supportive letters to imprisoned activists. As illustrated by the image on the front cover of the

FIGURE 4.4. Front cover of *Schwarze Kanal* (Nr. 1, 1982). Source: Papiertiger Archiv.

February 1982 *Schwarze Kanal*, in which a man with his head entirely obscured sits slumped in a chair with a sign reading "I am still alive" lying dejectedly at his feet, the search for new life was thought to be exhausted; the dreams of 1980–81 were finished, destroyed by a mixture of ritualized overextension, exhaustion, infighting, and state repression. It was dead and yet, at the same time, not. Ritual, after all, may signal the death of spontaneity but it is also a means by which to overcome death, to keep the past in the present. In closing this chapter, I suggest that some in the movement continued to mobilize ritual as a means of keeping the energies of 1980–81 alive.

This attempt to keep the fires of endless negation burning with ritual was most evident in the case of Freiburg. Following the eviction of the Schwarzwaldhof squatters in May 1981, many of the former residents moved into an empty hospital rented by Netzwerk that came to be known, rather appropriately, as the Marian Tomb (*Mariengrab*). Buried alive in the graveyard of the movement, the Freiburg anarchists spent much of their time nostalgically reminiscing about what could have been. A poem from this period reflects the mood: "plastic bag faces / in the shopping streets / blind eyes / meet mechanically / my reflection in the window / departure without a greeting [...] with my dreams / I cover myself up / and yet / it's not warm enough [...] is it not our fears / our doubts / that prevent us from flying / and the lies / which we forget daily / so as to not get hurt."[95]

They also, however, refused to believe that the energies unleashed at the height of the youth movement were actually gone forever. Throughout these years, activists hatched increasingly grandiose plans designed to awaken the movement from its premature death. A March 1982 flyer titled "Horror in Polizeiburg," for example, lamented "We are lost," before triumphantly declaring that the dead would return. "Simple-minded idiots that you are, the earthquake—you can be certain—will shake you all. [...] The movement cannot be erased because it is invisible. And it is always ready to strike." "Run, run" they declared. "All of the youth that you offended, that you called Gammler [...] stand ready. They will destroy Polizeiburg. We will remain your children until the bitter end. We will continue to act just like you, for your peace of mind, imagined us to be: as *Chaoten*, plunderers, cannibals, drug addicts, epileptics, profligates."[96] A flyer titled "Sickness" chided city officials for failing to quarantine those afflicted by uncontrollable outbreaks of creative-destructive dancing when they had the chance since now the virus was infecting ever more of the population.[97]

In another brochure, the dispossessed anarchists of Freiburg dreamed of reconnecting with the parts of themselves that had initially been awakened in the heyday of the youth movement, writing:

> Walpurgis night—imagined as a demonic exorcism—finally once more that happy feeling—we all together—rhythmic drumming—prosecution and joy simultaneously—new maneuverability—the city lay at our feet— tingling feeling of power—the feasible so near—and yet so far! Our voices, our music—thundering orchestra—ghostly echo of the concrete

world—fear of our own power—can it be possible? [...] WE HAVE FELT OUR DEMONS [...] Our strength is in our maneuverability—versatility!—Walpurgis night lets us foresee where our possibilities lie—CONQUEST OF THE EVERYDAY—there where they aren't! Let us refuse—slyly slip through the net—and attack! APPROPRIATE! they have taken almost everything from us—let's take it back: culture, creativity, feelings, love, food, nature, the streets, the houses, the children, death, fantasy, desire... We will become unpredictable—appearing everywhere, and yet being nowhere—gnawing rats, who carry the plague ... AUTONOMY—many streams, rivulets, together a seething sea [...] let's free our demons!!![98]

Those who had taken part in the youth movement, they suggested, had become living symbols of opposition, bodies infused with revolutionary energy who held within themselves the power to revive the radical potential of 1980–81.

Activists in West Berlin were also not willing to give up on their dreams of radically remaking the world just because the size and intensity of the demonstrations was on the wane or because many of the occupants of legalized houses had put down the paving stones and turned inward. Much like their absurdist comrades in the Black Forest, the West Berliners believed that if they could only keep the dance going long enough, the world would soon catch fire again. For some this implied an intense focus on spectacular acts of symbolic violence. In a letter to the editor from the April 1982 edition of *Schwarze Kanal*, for example, the author criticized an article in the *Tageszeitung* for its outright rejection of violence, noting: "Perhaps you're right when you say that bombs are not arguments. The 'pigs' strike with clubs / bomb with bulldozers / poison with chemicals / contaminate with atoms / kill with prisons / you're right / bombs are not arguments / bombs are just the first hesitant attempts to articulate the language that they / understand. We still have a lot to say!"[99]

One of the main groups seeking to keep the anarchist visions of the youth movements alive was a loose affiliation of activists who came to be known as the *Autonomen*, who were less interested in combating actual housing policies in the city than in "permanently challenging and pushing against the discursive borders that constrained" leftist activism.[100] Whereas the *Autonomen* championed militance, others looked to culture and art as the most effective arenas in which to keep practicing the regenerative politics of the youth revolts. Throughout the mid-1980s politically engaged artists continued to produce experimental films and music that explicitly sought to revive the energies that had been unleashed in 1980–81. A 1982 statement by the group Didaktische Einheit, for example, noted: "Life plays itself out in a frenzy of liberation from the shortcomings of the everyday. Between the borders of insanity and death. That is directly where the music of 'didaktische Einheit,' which is created anew with each performance, has nested. It conjures up catastrophes, choking fits, quickened pulses, convulsions, and orgasms. In the course of this, the listener becomes a participant, a part of the didaktische Einheit. [...] The music of the 'didaktischen Einheit': grandiose sound spectacle music, which jumps off the stage, moves in its magic near the listener, and makes them dance—the self dances, the songs of the dead, the battle cries tear fallen gods from heaven, in order to wake them into a new life."[101] This statement is accompanied by a series of images, including one in which the band members wear masks as they huddle around an old-fashioned baby carriage, referencing perhaps the carriage that was used to divert Hanns Martin Schleyer's car before he was abducted by the RAF, or perhaps the S.Y.P.H. album cover featuring this image. While all of this might seem somewhat bombastic, the music and videos produced by the band do indeed give one the sensation of being part of some sinister rite of reanimation. In a live rendition of "Piety = decline," the singer screeches to repetitive yet steadily intensifying rhythmic waves of violins, drums, and guitars. If the "demonic exorcism" described by the evicted squatters of the Schwarzwaldhof had a soundtrack, this would certainly be it.

Another example of this increasingly sinister form of ritualized art comes from a 1982 film produced by the avant-garde group Tödliche Doris titled "Berliner Küchenmusik." The film opens in a rustic domestic interior where a woman goes about the tasks of setting the table, fixing the drapes, and preparing a meal. This relatively innocuous scene is suddenly interrupted by a voice that narrates the story of a young girl on a school trip to a museum in Dresden who (miraculously) goes into labor after seeing an image of the Virgin Mary. Drums and dissonant violins begin to build in the background as various people with bags over their heads enter the room and sit at the table. Accompanied by increasingly ear-piercing music, a voice intones: "I am guilty. You are guilty. [...] It is the guilt structure. [...] Guilty, guilty, guilty!" As if dancing to the music, the dinner guests all lock arms and begin enthusiastically swaying back and forth. The music then suddenly stops, the people cease their dancing, silently form a line, and leave the room as the host happily calls "Aufwiedersehen!"[102] Guilty of some undefined crime and wearing bags over their faces like condemned people on their way to the gallows, the guests nonetheless successfully form an intersubjective unit by locking arms and dancing—they embrace their alterity and their exclusion from grace to become a community of the damned, a demonic dinner party, toasting their imminent rebirth.

By no means the work of a few isolated individuals who had lost their grip on reality, these examples are representative of a new subculture that formed during the heyday of the youth movements and continued long after most of the squats had been cleared and the paving stones had ceased to fly through the windows of department stores and banks. In his book on life in West Berlin, Wolfgang Müller of Die Tödliche Doris described the lively nightlife and art scene in the city as an interconnected network of spaces where the former squatters, New Wave artists, anarchists, and even stars such as Tabea Blumenschein came together to socialize, to develop projects, and to keep the ecstatic practices of directionless dialectics alive.[103] Along with the small bands of *Autonomen*, these groups continued to dream of creative destruction, of endless negation, and of exploding the progressive temporal frameworks of the postwar.

The years following the youth revolts were thus not only characterized by a slow incorporation of antisystemic energies into established social, cultural, and political structures. For a number of people who had been indelibly marked by the ecstatic experiences of 1980–81 such reincorporation was simply not an option. They were also not content, however, to remain in the shadows forever. The goal was always to flood the world once more with waves of creative destruction. The issue, though, was how to accomplish this radical expansion of the movement without letting the practices of directionless dialectics turn into mere spectacle, into acts of negation that, like the logics of capitalism, ended up going nowhere. How, that is, could the unmoored dynamics of postprogressive becoming be channeled and contained without losing their radically transcendent qualities? The following chapters explore some of the ways that squatters utilized the unique temporal qualities of the built environment to confront these issues over the course of the 1980s.

[CHAPTER FIVE]

Insurgent Dwelling and the Cultivation of Place in Hamburg's Hafenstraße

In November 1984, an article in *Die Welt* jubilantly proclaimed: "Squatting is nothing but a memory."[1] Heinrich Lummer, the infamous Interior Secretary of West Berlin, joined the celebrations, triumphantly announcing that law-abiding Berliners could again hold their heads high. After all, "who could have proudly claimed to be a Berliner during those troubled times?"[2] Even those who supported the squatters began to evince a resigned acceptance that the movement was rapidly passing into the realm of collective memory. One such supporter, Hermann Münzel, wrote a letter imploring city officials to preserve the famous wall painting on the side of the KuKuCK in Kreuzberg, noting: "I do not want to drive by a white wall and have to tell the youth groups: look, here is a five-story symbol of cold-hearted intolerance."[3] Supporters, it seems, could no longer hope for anything more than preserving the physical traces of faded utopian dreams. Such memorialization was not, however, what the victorious forces of the state had in mind. In a defiant, snarky reply to Münzel, one Dr. Klaus wrote: "It was with sadness that I learned from your letter [. . .] that your understanding of Berlin's cultural offerings is restricted to a square meter of house wall. Perhaps it would indeed be better if the students visited Berlin with other supervisors."[4]

The situation in Amsterdam, Freiburg, and Zurich was no different: across Europe, the radical dreams of 1980–81 were fading fast, buried beneath the office towers, cafés, and traffic corridors of urban life. The Vondelstraat, the KuKuCK, the Schwarzwaldhof, the AJZ—everywhere one looked, it was abundantly clear that the youth movements of the early 1980s were finished. Everywhere, that is, except in Hamburg where a row of dilapidated houses on the Hafenstraße were slowly ascending to a dominant position within the symbolic landscape of the autonomous left. Indeed, as "the squatters' movement elsewhere suffered a series of defeats, the Hafenstraße's capability to remain intact made it a symbol of almost mythic proportions."[5] The houses, which were covered with striking murals that implored Hamburgers to show "Solidarity with the RAF" or simply to "Fuck Off," and which were home to various fringe groups, including mohawked punks, runaways, drug addicts, and masked anarchists, became something of a national obsession in the mid-1980s. One look at this colorful "House of Horrors" on the banks of the Elbe River would certainly have sufficed to counter the premature pronouncements of the movement's death.[6]

Especially when compared to the raucous squatting movements taking place concurrently in other cities, the Hafenstraße in Hamburg began rather inauspiciously in 1980 when the Siedlungs-Aktiengesellschaft Altona (SAGA), one of the city agencies responsible for housing, allowed members of Studentenwerk and the Sozialpädagogischen Forschungsgruppe (SoFoG), both of which were left-leaning organizations created in the wake of 1968, to inhabit a row of government-owned houses in a particularly run-down area of St. Pauli Süd, an area notorious for crime and vice along the Elbe River that gained international fame in the early 1960s as the home away from home of the Beatles. By allowing students, recovering addicts, and other at-risk social groups to occupy the houses for a nominal fee, SAGA hoped to ease the housing crunch among some of Hamburg's most disadvantaged populations.[7] Such short-term rental agreements also helped to facilitate urban renewal projects since they not only enabled the city to protect otherwise empty properties from squatting actions and from legal challenges stemming from a "misuse of living space" but also, when the time came, to easily terminate the leases prior to the building's demolition.[8]

In the case of the Hafenstraße, however, nothing went according to plan. During an inspection of the apartments in 1982, SAGA ascertained that many of the remaining apartments had been illegally squatted by transient youth.[9] SAGA's initial observation was soon corroborated by the squatters themselves, who went public with an open letter to Senator Volker Lange, informing him that the houses had been occupied as a protest against the steady expansion of luxury apartments in Hamburg's urban center, the usurpation of affordable living space, and the structural exclusion of "undesirables" from gentrifying areas.[10] Given the close relationship between explosive youth unrest and illegal occupations in other cities during this period, SAGA and the Hamburg Senate were determined to prevent the Hafenstraße from becoming a lightning rod for leftist opposition in the city. They were not, however, in a position to evict the occupants. Their inability to differentiate the legal from illegal residents coupled with the complex system of laws protecting West German renters from eviction and the challenge from the CDU in the looming city elections rendered the SPD-dominated senate largely incapable of taking decisive action.[11] Following some minor clashes, including a 1982 incident in which supporters of the

Hafenstraße walled in the entrance to SAGA's headquarters, the residents signed a set of leases with the city on November 30, 1983.[12] The agreement consisted of twenty-seven individual leases with residents that were set to last until December 31, 1986, and included stipulations for city assistance with much-needed repair work.[13]

This initial step toward legalization was not to have the palliative effect for which city officials had hoped. Instead, between 1983 and 1986, the Hafenstraße steadily developed into one of the city's premiere countercultural meeting points. Thomas Osterkorn, a journalist for the *Hamburger Abendblatt*, described the cast of characters who populated the Hafenstraße in this period as "punks and youth from broken homes, orphanages, and prisons, as well as militant left-extremists such as Spontis and anarchists"—in short, not the sorts of people the city wanted living without official supervision in what was deemed prime real estate along the Elbe River.[14] For city officials, who hoped to renovate the area in time for Hamburg's 1989 celebration of its eight hundredth birthday, the Hafenstraße represented an unacceptable and embarrassing eyesore (*Schandfleck*) that besmirched the regal appearance and the law-and-order reputation of Hamburg.[15] Something had to be done.

For some, the houses presented more than just an image problem for the city; they came to be seen a threat to the very existence of the *Rechtsstaat*, a dangerous "lawless zone" (*rechtsfreier Raum*) in the center of West Germany's wealthiest city that threatened to destabilize the entire legal system. The CDU opposition in city government consistently railed against SPD policies, which, they argued, naively tolerated these dangerous attacks on the social fabric.[16] Hamburg's police and city workers also tended to view the Hafenstraße as a fundamental threat to law and order, arguing that their inability to safely enter the houses for repair work or to conduct searches enabled "chaos makers" to commit crimes with impunity.[17] Some officials took the argument of lawless space even further by proclaiming that the squat was becoming a center of terrorism. Such accusations were strengthened when Christian Lochte, the leader of the Federal Office for the Protection of the Constitution (*Verfassungsschutz*), gave an interview in the *Tageszeitung* in October 1985, claiming that terrorists associated with the RAF had infiltrated the houses and were using it as a base of operations.[18] The residents responded with irony by painting "The RAF lives here" on their doors.

By early 1986, city officials began taking decisive steps to break some of the leases before their official termination at the end of the year. As had been the case prior to the signing of the November 1983 leases, these attempts were consistently thwarted by the realities on the ground. Not only did the common tendency to sublet apartments in the Hafenstraße without first informing SAGA further complicate an already Byzantine set of regulations for eviction, but the increasingly combative nature of the residents made it highly difficult, if not entirely impossible, for officials to enter the houses in the first place. In the few cases in which officials succeeded in obtaining the necessary legal documents for eviction they were met by hundreds of angry residents who were determined to prevent entry into the houses. In October 1986, SAGA officials, under massive police protection, forcibly entered the houses, threw furniture out the windows, and painted over a mural calling for solidarity with the RAF.[19] Although they succeeded in evicting residents from six apartments, a series of blunders enabled squatters to reoccupy the properties with relative impunity. In the wake of this fiasco, SAGA officials determined that it would be necessary to inspect the apartments every three to four weeks in order to guarantee police support for further evictions. However, due to a series of interagency miscommunications, coupled with what appears to have been a bit of misinformation provided by the Hafenstraße's lawyer, city officials failed to follow through with the required house visits, thus necessitating that they rely on court-ordered eviction proceedings (*Räumungsklage*) instead of direct police action.[20] For a space that was supposedly characterized by lawlessness, the residents proved particularly adept at wielding the letter of the law.

Throughout 1987, the houses remained headline news, prompting nearly everyone to take sides in what some were calling a civil war.[21] A number of celebrities publicly expressed their support for the project. Wolf Biermann, for example, noted: "Every time my kids and I ride by [the Hafenstraße] on our bikes, it makes me happy both that the residents are still there and that I don't have to live there. For me, my hometown of Hamburg remains tolerable when such odd people are allowed to remain. I think Hamburg has enough middle class hygiene."[22] Hamburg millionaire Jan Philipp Reemtsma and Green Alternative List (GAL) politician Michael Herrmann also got involved in the conflict, initially by forming an arbitration group (*Vermittlergruppe*) that was tasked with negotiating a solution between the squatters and the senate and then by suggesting an outright purchase of the houses by a private entity.[23] At one point Reemtsma and other members of the arbitration group even deemed it necessary to take a helicopter to the island of Sylt in order to discuss the situation with a vacationing Mayor Dohnanyi.[24] Finally, in November 1987, the public heaved a collective sigh of relief as the squatters removed the barricades and accepted Dohnanyi's compromise proposal to extend the lease.[25] Unlike the 1983 agreement which consisted of individual leases between SAGA and residents, Dohnanyi's compromise both nominally removed the city from the equation by naming the Laewetz Stiftung as the property owner and treated the residents as a collective entity represented by the Verein Hafenstraße.[26] Dohnanyi's success in averting what surely would have been a violent showdown between the thousands of autonomous activists camped out behind the Hafenstraße's barricades and the massive army of police, many of whom had been summoned from surrounding cities, came to be known as the "wonder of Hamburg."[27]

Even after Dohnanyi's "wonder of Hamburg" agreement, there were periodic conflicts between the Hafenstraße and the city. Especially after Voscherau replaced Dohnanyi as mayor, the city became much less well-disposed toward the complex.[28] Police observations and periodic raids into the houses continued to define everyday life in the Hafenstraße. In the spring of 1989, for example, the police raided a parking lot abutting the Hafenstraße where numerous people had set up an encampment consisting of cars, trailers, and tents sporting pirate flags.[29] Not without reason, the squatters interpreted this as a preliminary step in a renewed attempt to forcibly clear the houses and thus responded with intense resistance.[30] The press, for its part, continued to dutifully stir up fears of terrorism with periodic reports about violence and criminality in the houses, including one that claimed RAF terrorists in the Hafenstraße planned to murder Helmut Kohl.[31] These new accusations of terrorism led to a heated debate in the Bundestag on September 19, 1990, in which delegates, perhaps taking a needed break from discussing unification, accused Hamburg's administration of tolerating a lawless space in which terrorists could freely plot the subversion of the republic. Not to be outdone by national politicians, average Hamburgers also continued to voice their displeasure with the Hafenstraße. In July 1988, for example, there was a minor movement in which citizens, as well as some of the more outspoken CDU officials, refused to pay their parking tickets in protest over the senate's seeming unwillingness to confront the squatters.[32]

In 1990–91, *yet another* conflict over evictions in the Hafenstraße made its way into the headlines. Hafenrand, the organization that took over the management of the houses from the Laewetz Stiftung following a series of disagreements between the Laewetz board and the senate, attempted to evict some of the tenants of the houses who had been refusing to pay their rent and who they believed were engaging in criminal behaviors.[33] The bailiff (*Gerichtsvollzieher*) refused to serve the eviction notices, arguing that the language of the lease allowed him to evict the Verein Hafenstraße as a whole but not the individual renters, who had their own agreements with the Verein.[34] Following the court's decision to uphold the bailiff's position, Hafenrand was forced to consider more time-consuming legal strategies for ending the leases.[35] The situation of legal limbo continued until 1995, when the Patriotische Gesellschaft von 1765 organized a series of meetings between representatives of the Hafenstraße and the senate with the express goal of bringing the long-standing conflict to a peaceful and definitive conclusion. Initially, both sides rejected the solutions proposed by the Gesellschaft. Supporters of the Hafenstraße were unhappy with suggestions that the houses be privatized, while the senate felt that the agreement would not only be depicted as a surrender to the forces of disorder but would also leave the city with too many lingering connections to its longtime nemesis.[36] The situation was finally resolved in January 1996 with the decision to sell the houses to the Genossenschaft Alternativen am Elbufer, an organization with representatives from the city, the Hafenstraße, and other concerned groups of citizens.[37] After sixteen years of legal battles, street protests, and paranoia, the city of Hamburg finally cut its remaining ties to the Hafenstraße. Walking through the area today, one would hardly realize that they were standing in what not many years before had been the center of autonomous activism in Europe.

For almost two decades city officials in Hamburg mobilized all of the resources at their disposal, from constant police observation, to complicated rental agreements, to lengthy court cases, to contain the Hafenstraße within the legal frameworks of the *Rechtsstaat*. What they failed to realize, however, was that such attempts to pacify the houses through legalization were doomed from the outset. Unlike the reform-minded squatters associated with the Müsli faction of the youth revolts who happily signed leases in exchange for the long-term security of a place to live, the residents of the Hafenstraße were determined to forge a truly autonomous space, one in which the social codes and temporal imaginaries of postwar society held absolutely no sway. This did not mean, however, that occupants and supporters fully embraced the orthodox position of the Mollis, in which the infinite and unfettered expansion of radical negation implied a downplaying of local context. To the contrary, the Hafenstraße squatters insisted upon the importance of cultivating embedded connections to place even as they remained committed to directionless dialectical practices. In this chapter, I propose that the Hafenstraße was instrumental in honing a set of spatial and temporal practices that combined the youth movement's commitment to radical negation as an end in itself with a belief in the auratic, embedded dimensions of the place-world more common to the left-alternative milieu. Although nascent rumblings of this "third way" were clearly evident during the youth revolts, they tended to take a backseat to orthodox ideological positions which called either for endlessly expanding the movement in the hope of initiating an apocalyptic wave that would wash over and renew the world, or for using the unique historical aura of the squatted houses to dwell indefinitely in a state of frozen dialectical negation. The extraordinary duration of the conflict over the Hafenstraße, however, allowed this nascent ideology to develop into a fully fledged framework for engaging with urban space, one that wove together the postprogressive temporal forms championed in the youth movement with the historically layered qualities of the built environment.

∵

One of the central components of life in the Hafenstraße was the focus on creating spaces that facilitated individual autonomy. Relying heavily on the rhetoric developed by earlier generations of squatters, the occupants and supporters of the Hafenstraße sought to draw clear distinctions between liberated life inside of the walls of the squat and the alienating, disciplined existence that they believed had infused all dimensions of life on the outside. One resident described the experience of eating in the *Volksküche* (the Hafenstraße's communal dining area) as the diametrical opposite of the bourgeois dining experience: "Sometimes you cooked, sometimes others cooked, and some days there was no dinner at all because everyone felt like being alone."[38] In his pop ethnography of the squat, Carl-Heinz Mallet reminisced about his time in the Hafenstraße, writing: "I could speak or stay silent, daydream, forget myself in the music, or look out the window. I could stretch out my legs as far as I wanted, sit or stand on the podium, loll about with Josef or take a nap, like Olaf once did. I could dress however I liked, have a beard or a shaved head. I could get up and leave without any explanation and without saying goodbye, and no one would ask where I was going. No matter what I might do, no one would stare at me. Where else in the entire world can one conduct oneself with so little compulsion?"[39] As in earlier occupations, the unique spatiotemporal qualities of the Hafenstraße were seen as particularly conducive to cultivating liberated subjectivities. It was as if the chrononormative dimensions of late twentieth-century West Germany were somehow unable to penetrate the painted walls and the barricaded doors of the occupied houses.

Anne Reiche, who had spent time in prison for her participation in the June 2nd Movement, also described life in the Hafenstraße as one characterized by extraordinary levels of subjective freedom, noting that although the residents came from all different walks of life and were free to pursue their own desires, such diversity was part of the strength of the squat since it allowed them to forge new connections and alliances across difference.[40] As these reflections indicate, the focus on radically autonomous individualism in the Hafenstraße was not understood as antithetical to community and social warmth. In addition to living according to their own wishes and desires, squatters shared the responsibilities for cooking, cleaning, and childcare. Residents also sought to abolish alienation by designing spaces that encouraged communal exchange and the free movement of objects: internal doors were removed, and food and other possessions were often shared in common among the residents. According to one occupant: "Here everything is much opener. I wanted to borrow a filter full of coffee from a stupid rental building next door. The woman just looked at me. 'Coffee? We don't have any.' And bang, she shut the door. They don't let anything leave their own four walls."[41] As was true of many squatted houses, the Hafenstraße was conceptualized as an open space in which people and their possessions could freely circulate, thus enabling residents to develop forms of sociability not mediated by capitalism or by the normative judgments that determined social interactions in the outside world. It was a space where, as one squatter put it, "there is room for people to actualize themselves, where communication can be supported through space."[42] The houses were thought to enable a form of community where people engaged with each other as liberated, autonomous individuals rather than as social types, where they knew "almost everyone by their first name, but almost never by their last name."[43]

Although the internal layout of the houses was seen as an essential component in the creation of liberated subjects, acts of transgressive negation were also central. Occupants consistently drew attention to the dominant social forms they hoped to destroy. One 1987 pamphlet, for example, noted: "The Hafenstraße does not want to be licked clean, sanitized, conventional and bourgeois." Rather they want to aggravate "the wormy, assimilated" bourgeoisie, which has "only etiquette books [. . .] in their heads."[44] Other authors took a more militant tone, imploring readers: "No peace with the eviction terrorists! [. . .] No peace with the manor houses! No peace with capitalist normality!"[45] Another resident discussed his feelings toward West German society at length, noting: "When you want to destroy the state, you have to begin by refusing to pay your rent. I want to be finished with this pig system. Do you know where all they have tried to stick me? In psychiatric wards, in prison, in special schools, in a home for those with behavioral problems. And do you know why? Because I am too strong. [. . .] I no longer want to be a German. I don't want the judges to pass sentences in my name which make me want to puke. In the name of the people! Without me. Becoming stateless is an impossibility unless another state takes me. But what state would want to take me?"[46] Staying true to the punk idea that authentic modes of being could only emerge through the active negation of power, residents of the Hafenstraße conceived of their own freedom as interwoven with the destruction of the state and its manifold forms of disciplinary and temporal normalization. It was only in negating or transgressing normalized modes of comportment that residents of the Hafenstraße felt they could break through into a new life. Reiche was clearly aware of this dimension of life in the Hafenstraße when she lamented the 1987 agreement that led residents and their supporters to take down the barricades. Having spent so much of her life in the militant anarchist milieus of the early 1970s, she was well aware that opposition to state power was a necessary component in the cultivation of liberated lives.

Perhaps unsurprisingly, punk bands playing at the houses were among the most vocal in aggressively rejecting all dimensions of West German society. Some called attention to the state's involvement in international violence with lyrics such as: "you take their freedom / what's your permission / and as the corpses pile / you nod with pride."[47] Many of the Hafenstraße's more sympathetic neighbors, however, were also vocal in their denunciations of state violence, especially at the height of the conflict in 1987 when large swaths of the neighborhood were cordoned off, helicopters circled the houses at all hours of the day, and thousands of heavily armed police marched through the streets. Although these critiques were primarily conducted in the deadly serious tones of impending social breakdown, there were times when comedy was seen as the only valid response. In one particular instance, some of the residents of St. Pauli Süd began publicly questioning which one of their neighbors had suddenly decided to purchase a large tank and park it in the street.[48]

Drawing from a long tradition within the New Left, the Hafenstraße squatters also called attention to the continuities between West Germany and the Nazi regime.[49] A 1989 pamphlet pointed to the German government's racist double standard evident in the fact that it allowed 650,000 German immigrants to enter the country, yet somehow could not find enough room for 1,500 Sinti and Roma.[50] Allegations of fascist continuity also surfaced in descriptions of police actions against the Hafenstraße. An October 1986 pamphlet described how the police trashed apartments "with fascist treachery."[51] Another implicitly referenced Nazi urban policies by calling attention to the city's "social-hygienic dream" of "a clean, crime-free, tourist friendly, profit-oriented harbor area."[52] Following the violent eviction of six of the Hafenstraße houses in 1986, the squatters distributed a flyer in which they narrated the vindictive, brutal tactics of the police, which included the destruction of houseplants, musical instruments, pictures, and "everything that expresses life."[53] While not explicitly involved in the eviction procedures, other city agencies were also deemed fascist by the residents of the houses. Some flyers, for example, called attention to the Nazi origins of the Hamburgisch Electricitäts-Werke and depicted its workers as storm troopers.⁵⁴

In addition to exposing the fascist qualities of the state, residents of the Hafenstraße also mobilized arguments developed by urban activists in the 1970s to draw attention to the city's role in the destruction of authentic social forms and auratic places, arguing, for example, that Hamburg's urban renewal strategies sacrificed equitable housing for architectural simulacra and exchanged real forms of community for mere façades of neighborliness.⁵⁵ A 1983 flyer accused the city of planning "deep garage—shopping center—video store—single home—toilet—constructions" in the area occupied by the Hafenstraße houses. "Even this beautiful area," they lamented "is set to become a concrete wasteland."⁵⁶ A 1987 pamphlet titled "Zussamen Wohnen Zussamen Kämpfen" featured an image of people defending themselves on the roof of a house and railed against the city for supporting new housing projects that were "too valuable for poor devils, the jobless, foreigners, and the unruly." These areas, the flyer charged, were set to be cleared of "unhappy elements" and "unmanageable courtyards" to make room for an "endless cemetery of quiet and order."⁵⁷

Mobilizing phrases such as "We won't let our lives be prescribed. Period," the residents of the Hafenstraße exerted considerable energy to demarcate life inside the houses from the violence, oppression, and alienation which they believed characterized postwar society.⁵⁸ Such demarcations of liberated spaces could not, of course, proceed only along the lines of critique. It was also necessary to physically protect the houses against incursions from the outside world. One of the most basic forms of defense was to remove all name markers from the houses. Because city officials, be they bailiffs serving court orders of eviction, police looking for criminals, or even HEW workers trying to make residents pay their electricity bill, required names in order to carry out their duties, removing such markers was an easy and effective way to defend the houses against the forces of law and order. These strategies proved to be extraordinarily successful. Indeed, the archives are full of frustrated reports from city officials who were unable to gain access to the buildings. In one such report, the bailiff noted: "Whether at the building entrance or at the individual apartment doors, one cannot find name tags. Doorbells are absolutely nonexistent. There are also no mailboxes, merely a so-called collective mailbox at some of the houses. [...] These collective mailboxes also have no name designations."⁵⁹ Another report, this time from the police, lamented: "The living situation in the house is not like a normal apartment building since the residents often change, visitors are sometimes taken in—the milieu is not easily manageable."⁶⁰

The houses might have been difficult to manage—that is, difficult to incorporate into the established legal and conceptual frameworks of the postwar order—but the city administration certainly cannot be faulted for lack of effort. The sheer number of diagrams, photos, and detailed sketches they collected is truly astounding. They took pictures of the doors and windows of the houses, made detailed notes about who was coming and going, and pored over existing blueprints to try and ascertain what sort of defensive modifications the squatters may have made to the houses. What is especially interesting to note here is the extent to which these images, diagrams, and reports focused on the material qualities of the houses themselves. Looking at the hundreds of images of doors taken by police surveillance teams, it seems clear that officials conceived of the houses themselves as sinister, inscrutable, crime-generating vortexes operating in the middle of the city. Much of the press dutifully followed suit, with the *Frankfurter Allgemeine Zeitung*, for example, comparing the entryways of the houses to "dark dangerous caves" filled with unknown horrors.[61] The built environment itself came to serve as a primary protagonist in the ongoing conflict.

At the height of the conflict from late 1986 to the signing of the leases in 1987 autonomous activists from cities throughout West Germany as well as from Amsterdam, Copenhagen, London and Zurich repeatedly traveled to the Hafenstraße to people the barricades and defend what they saw as autonomous territory against the international forces of order. The barricades themselves, however, were only a first line of defense in the increasingly fortified houses. As early as October 1986, an article in the *Hamburger Abendblatt* noted with alarm that the residents were stockpiling weapons and were transforming the houses into an "unconquerable fortress."[62] Throughout these years, the battle over the Hafenstraße served as a rallying point for autonomist activists throughout Europe. Responding to the eviction of six apartments in October 1986, for example, activists in Berlin, Lübeck, and Copenhagen engaged in retaliatory acts of violence, including the destruction of property at the Goethe Institute in Copenhagen, which increased the paranoia among officials that the Hafenstraße was a nodal point in some sort of sinister international network of leftist terrorism.[63] As the conflict increasingly spread beyond the walls of the houses and even beyond the borders of the city and the nation more broadly, worried citizens and officials could no longer take solace in the belief that the threats to the democratic order were being contained within an easily monitored space. The houses were transcending their spatial context, spreading across the nation.

Unsurprisingly, Hamburg officials and the regional press depicted these attempts to demarcate a liberated zone in the middle of Hamburg, as well

FIGURE 5.1. Front cover of *10 Meter Ohne Kopf* (1987).
Source: International Institute of Social History, Amsterdam.

as the open "provocation of order and good manners," in an unfavorable light.[64] One of the most common reactions was to interpret the houses as a lawless zone that bred violence and terrorism. According to Hartmut Perschau, leader of Hamburg's CDU: "As long as the squatters live there, there can be no peace. [. . .] The houses have always been the starting point for criminal acts. Cars were broken into, radios stolen, people attacked, workers shot at, and the city overtaken by violence and terror."[65] At another point, Perschau directly compared the activists supporting the Hafenstraße to Nazi agitators, arguing that "one should not overlook the fact that the residents of the Hafenstraße want to destroy the democratic *Rechtsstaat* [. . .] We must not repeat the same mistakes of the Weimar Republic."[66]

Christian Lochte made a similarly alarmist argument, noting that the Hafenstraße was "no alternative living project, no idyllic island in the midst of capitalism," but part of a "structure of violence," which threatened to spread throughout the city.[67] This notion that squatted spaces were equivalent to "structures of violence" that not only offered sanctuary to criminals but actually generated criminality was increasingly common in the mid-1980s. What, for the squatters and their supporters, was a radical spatial experiment meant to facilitate autonomous lifeworlds, was terrorism, licentiousness, and corrosive lawlessness in the eyes of conservatives. The solution, as far as the West German right was concerned, was exceedingly simple: "This law-free realm must be removed immediately."[68] Whereas Hamburg's SPD politicians, especially those surrounding Mayor Dohnanyi, tended to pursue vaguely dialectical-reformist strategies by seeking to incorporate the Hafenstraße into the legal and conceptual frameworks of the postwar order, conservative factions in the senate and especially rightwing voices in the press interpreted the houses as an unacceptable and fundamentally dangerous law-free zone that had to be cleared of residents and then torn down. Simply evicting the squatters was inadequate; the houses themselves had to be eradicated.

For residents and supporters, the Hafenstraße represented a "Free Space" (*Freiraum*) in which one could cultivate autonomous lifeworlds by actively negating the social forms, legal frameworks, and progressive myths of the postwar. As was also the case in the punk and New Wave movements as well as in the youth revolts of 1980–81, for the occupants of the Hafenstraße, creation and becoming were premised on destruction and negation. Conservatives in the senate and in the media largely agreed with the squatters' interpretation of the houses as spaces of radical alterity. However, what for the youth protesters and squatters was a "free space," was a "lawless space" for the defenders of order. Both groups thus viewed the houses on the Hafenstraße as spaces of autonomy that were set apart from dominant spatiotemporal logics. As the conflict slowly unfolded over the course of the 1980s, the moderate left position of the SPD, which held that the state was large enough to incorporate a wide variety of different social, spatial, and even temporal logics, was consistently pushed out of the conversation in favor of ideological extremes. With the dialectical strategies of the moderate left out of the picture, the residents of the Hafenstraße and their conservative opponents were free to collectively reimagine the occupied houses as spaces of radical negation that transcended their spatiotemporal context even as they remained in place.

The residents of the Hafenstraße came to be seen (and to see themselves) as the absolute negation of the modern, democratic order whose very existence threatened the future of the nation. In addition to authenticating themselves as autonomous actors by constantly negating the given social order, they also came to view the concrete, auratic qualities of the houses as a necessary component of their activism. The extraordinary duration of the conflict thus helped to solidify a new spatiotemporal imaginary, in which transcendence and endless negation came to be paired with emplacement and aura. This was already nascent in the youth movements of the early 1980s but only came fully into its own in spaces such as the Hafenstraße, where the length of the occupation facilitated the development of deeper connections to place. In the remainder of this chapter, I explore the nature of this experimental spatiotemporal framework by exploring how the Hafenstraße positioned itself as both transcendent and emplaced—or, to use the language employed by the residents and supporters, how it managed to be "everywhere" even as it "remained."[69]

∴

As we have seen in the previous chapters, many radical leftists in the late 1970s and early 1980s were positively consumed with the desire to liberate themselves from what they understood to be the oppressive fetters of mainstream social, cultural, and spatiotemporal logics. Uncompromising declarations of existential liberation from the surrounding world were a central theme in the manifold coming of age narratives produced in the period. In Leonie Ossowski's 1982 novel *Wilhelm Meister's Abschied*, to give but one example, Wilhelm makes the fateful decision to leave the comfortable bourgeois environment of his family home in Lichterfelde for a squat in Kreuzberg. In an imagined speech to his father, which he theatrically reenacts with the assistance of his new family in the squat, Wilhelm proclaims his freedom: "I am not your monument. I have a right to my own life about which I will decide. My experiences are my own. Can you not understand that yours do not interest me? The world that you made remains your world and does not concern me."[70] Like Wilhelm, many young leftists viewed life in West Germany as indelibly marked by capitalist alienation and by the restrictive narrative logics of progressive time. Echoing the practices of creative destruction developed in the punk and New Wave movements,

Wilhelm, like many other youth activists, suggested that genuine change emerged not from a strategic reification of preconceived utopian futures (whether of the liberal-capitalist or the leftist dialectical varieties), but through processes of endlessly negating the present and building an autonomous life from the debris. As evidenced by Wilhelm's reenactment of the speech to his father with his new family in the squat, many activists came to see the squatted houses as ideal spaces in which to reconstruct a new life, as spaces where they could reengage with the objects and environments of postwar life and turn them into weapons of liberation.

Although the street protests received the most attention during the height of the youth revolts, the squatted houses were also important venues for cultivating postprogressive sensibilities. In both instances, transgressive acts of destructive negation facilitated a seemingly limitless form of becoming, a mode of breaking through into the new that was not determined by preordained narrative logics. As was the case with squatted houses in other cities, the Hafenstraße was understood as a demarcated space of radical possibility in which residents were able to transgress the constitutive norms of the postwar order and experiment with new forms of subjectivity, sociability, and temporality. It was like a street riot but contained within the walls of domestic space, a form of what I am calling insurgent dwelling. Dwelling in what were understood to be spaces of perpetual negation not only allowed squatters to continually reconstitute themselves; it also enabled them to forge connections with a wide array of off- and anti-modern forms of being in time. As Anna Lowenhaupt Tsing has argued: "Unencumbered by the simplification of progress narratives, the knots and pulses of patchiness are there to explore"—"knots and patchiness," I would add, that were particularly resonant in the layered temporalities of place.[71]

In a certain sense, then, locations such as the Hafenstraße were indeed "everywhere." Collapsing spatiotemporal contexts (or, in the words of Blixa Bargeld, "new buildings") opened a chaotic field of possibilities, a polyphony of alternatives with which one could begin reconstituting oneself and one's relationship to the world. As a large slogan painted on the exterior wall of the Hafenstraße proclaimed, the goal was for the "criminals of all countries [to] unite!" I would suggest that we interpret criminals, here, to refer to those who find themselves outside the chrononormative, disciplinary status of modern subjects, and unity as something based not on any preconceived futures or common pasts but on a shared opposition to the hegemonic spatial and temporal logics of late twentieth-century capitalist modernity.

As disaffected youth withdrew behind the walls of the Hafenstraße, they increasingly came to see themselves as part of an international network of opposition, a budding counterpower united in its desire for creative destruction. Countless flyers, for example, made the connection between the squatters' battles against the senate and international liberation movements. On the occasion of Prince Charles's visit to Hamburg, the squatters hung signs that read: "Smash the H-Block! Victory to the IRA!" Explaining these actions, Radio Hafenstraße reported: "What binds us with the colleagues in Northern Ireland, is that we are both resisting the antihuman system that built such torture chambers. This is international solidarity."[72] One flyer claimed that the Hafenstraße belonged "to those in the world that struggle against the Deutsche Bank, whether it's because they support the racist system in South Africa and earn billions on the hunger and blood of those forced into perpetual underdevelopment, or because they press the Senate to remove us."[73] Another made the case for a relationship between the Hafenstraße and international struggles by referencing the forces of globalization, noting: "Internationalism for us implies that we understand the system which we are fighting against to be global. The worldwide economic system and NATO are the causes of our daily oppression. [. . .] We want to learn from [these] movements."[74] Residents pointed out that the Hafenstraße had "developed connections" in its fight "against the pig system—against brokdorf, contra-terror in Nicaragua, apartheid murder, US terror in Libya."[75] Even the press took notice of the Hafenstraße's catchall approach to revolution, noting that Radio Hafenstraße played "a confused mixture of Palestinian freedom songs, hardcore punk, [and] communist fighting songs."[76]

To a certain extent, then, the residents of the Hafenstraße had reembedded themselves into an international network of opposition, which transcended the spatiotemporal contexts of the houses. In this sense, they were operating within the parameters laid out by the Molli factions of the youth revolts which also tended to posit radical negation as an expansive strategy that could unite diverse groups across the world in a collective movement that would overthrow capitalist modernity. In the case of the Hafenstraße, though, such diverse forms of dissent were not meant to be sublated into any overarching revolutionary narratives, but incorporated into loose insurgent networks that contested the exercise of state power in all areas.[77] It was a network of dissent destined to constantly change based on the exigencies of the moment. In this sense, it was very much like the forms of anarchist relationality envisioned by theorists such as Bakunin, Goldman, and Kropotkin.

The residents of the Hafenstraße did not restrict themselves to forging international connections but found comrades in history as well. Some authors, for example, explicitly allied themselves with Klaus Störtebeker, Hamburg's own Robin Hood who was executed for piracy in the early fifteenth century. His popularity among the squatters was unrivaled: not only did they name an antifascist information and communication center after him, but one pamphlet even proclaimed him to be mayor of the Hafenstraße.[78] The murals told a similar story. Whereas some of these murals proclaimed solidarity with earlier forms of international labor activism, others sought to draw connections between late twentieth-century imperialist violence and colonial projects of the past.[79] Unlike left-alternative romantics, however, they were not looking to co-opt these groups as authentic negations of capitalist modernity that one could use to freeze the dialectic and dwell indefinitely in a space of authentic otherness, but to create networks of resistance, novel configurations of multiperspectival opposition that contributed to the further fragmentation of progress while also sparking acts of postprogressive becoming. The relationship between the Hafenstraße squatters and other forms of resistance came to be thought of as one that was based on structural analogy rather than outright equation. Unlike the visions of revolution propagated by large numbers of leftists in the Red Decade, differential forms of resistance and negation were not normalized according to overarching temporal logics. Instead, they were understood as diverse iterations of radical asynchrony all caught in the empty, homogeneous time-web of the present.[80]

Unsurprisingly, given the tendency of the far left and the far right to converge on such matters, the press and conservative politicians tended to reinforce the notion that the squatters were structurally affiliated with historical and international forms of opposition. At times, politicians and journalists described the squatters in language that had once been used to dehumanize Jews in the 1930s. During a senate meeting on the topic of the Hafenstraße, Herr Müller referred to the squatters as vermin (*Gesindel*), a comment that was followed by Senator Wagner's cautious reminder about what happened in the past when "people were called vermin and scum."[81] Others in the press and rightwing parties depicted the residents of the Hafenstraße as dirty, immoral, and basically un-German. The decidedly centrist magazine *Der Spiegel*, for example, relied on terms of uncleanliness, such as "muck" (*Schmuddel*) when describing the squatters and their houses.[82] Another article in *Der Spiegel* described the houses of the Hafenstraße as representing an "outright un-Hanseatic scene."[83] While many liberals avoided such loaded language, they still described the occupants of the houses as structurally equivalent to others who had been excluded from postwar society. Michael Sachs, the state's representative to the Verein Hafenstraße, for example, depicted the residents as a "typical form of contemporary youth fringe group. People who have family problems, problems in school and at work, those who can't find jobs, who have had difficulties in their childhood and who have been thrown out of bourgeois normality. It is a tough clientele."[84]

The mythology of the Hafenstraße also found its way into popular culture. For example, Jan Guillou's crime novel *Der demokratische Terrorist*, which was originally published in Swedish but very quickly translated into German, narrates the story of an undercover detective who is tasked with tracking down a dangerous group of international terrorists bent on destroying the democratic order in West Germany. Upon infiltrating the anarchist milieu at the Hafenstraße, the detective discovers an entire network of RAF-affiliated terrorism which eventually leads him to arms dealers in the Middle East and international militant groups plotting the assassination of Western leaders.[85] The brightly painted walls of the squatted buildings and the anarchism of the residents were, the novel suggests, nothing more than a countercultural facade hiding a parallel universe of terrorists, drug lords, and weapons dealers. Although admittedly a bit far-fetched (it is, after all, a popular crime novel), Guillou's narrative does succinctly point to the ways in which the squatted houses like the Hafenstraße were increasingly interpreted as vortexes of criminality, nodal points in an international and transhistorical network of subversion. For many of the more paranoid figures on the right, such a scenario would have appeared quite plausible. They seemed convinced that behind the heavily defended doors of the Hafenstraße, one would find not a group of youth engaged in countercultural experimentation, but a nest of terrorists plotting to destroy society. Conservatives claimed, not without reason, that the Hafenstraße had burst its contextual borders, that it was "überall."

In addition to the ubiquity of the phrase "Hafenstraße überall," residents of Hamburg and other West German cities were also consistently confronted with the slogan "Hafenstraße bleibt," or "Hafenstraße remains," which appeared on the walls of the squat, on pamphlets, and in graffiti scrawled throughout the city. Although on the surface this was simply a statement of the squatters' commitment to resisting eviction, I would like to suggest that it was also more than this, that the phrase reflects the significance of the auratic built environment for grounding postprogressive imaginaries. The squatted houses on the Hafenstraße, this phrase suggests, were not empty spaces of transcendental negation, but concrete localities, symbolically loaded landscapes with deep historical roots. One of the most striking expressions of this position came from a squatter who vehemently rejected the notion that residents of the Hafenstraße could end the conflict by simply putting down their weapons and quietly moving into the country to form a commune, noting: "Old houses are full. Full of work, full of history, their history, the history that they embody; of the people that have lived there and how they have lived. Our life, our ten years of a hundred, in which the walls with their cracks leave traces. our walls, our traces. '*Hafen bleibt.*'"[86] The Hafenstraße itself had a history and a future. It had memories etched into its walls. It was haunted by the ghosts of the past who could guide its occupants into a different future. The Hafenstraße, in other words, was no mere *space* but a *place*, a location rife with memories, with unique references, with its own embedded temporalities. It was a "memory of itself—a place where time reflects back upon itself."[87]

In the punk and New Wave movements as well as in the youth revolts of the early 1980s, participants sought to produce feelings of progressive breakthrough into the new by consistently negating existing social, cultural, political, and aesthetic forms. Drawing on strategies developed by avant-garde performance groups like the Actionists, by experimental music acts like Kraftwerk, and even by pop cultural bands like the Beatles, one of the most common ways to accomplish this was by bringing "the past" (or anything that had been deemed obsolete or repressed by capitalist modernity) into the present and thus unsettling the smooth temporal logics of progress. Think, for example, of Gabi Delgado's attempts to disrupt West Germany's conception of itself by encouraging youth to "dance the Mussolini." In the case of punk and New Wave artists as well as the more radical factions of the youth revolts, this process was by its nature expansive and highly volatile. Like the models of capitalist value creation that it subversively, though in some cases perhaps unintentionally, cited, this technique for generating progressive momentum was forced to consistently jump from one context to the next in order to maintain the dynamic feelings associated with creation through destruction. Movement was premised on perpetual negation and on never standing still.

Occupied houses, however, offered a way to engage in acts of constant negation while also remaining in place. As repositories for obsolete objects, bodies, and aesthetics, the squats served as bounded areas of radical difference, spaces in which paraphernalia from toppled totalitarian regimes, broken pinball machines, and disco balls, among other things, could coexist in a durational state of temporal indeterminacy.[88] Dwelling amid these objects, residents of squatted houses could disrupt the temporal logics of progressive modernity and perpetually reinvent themselves just by going about their everyday lives. In the squats, dwelling amid ruins became a form of insurgency. One could simultaneously destroy ascendant temporal logics, embrace perpetual movement into the new, and build a life with meaning, memories, and duration. One could dwell, in short, with momentum.

The squatted buildings were not, though, just buildings; they were also homes, and as such represented a particularly resonant form of place, especially in the context of postwar Germany. As I argued in the first chapter of this book, normal West German subjectivities, intelligible, postfascist selves, were forged at least in part in the newly aestheticized spaces of the postwar home. Along with shopping districts, office buildings, and outdoor leisure areas, domestic spaces served as preeminent venues within which pasts were mastered and the dreamworlds of progress were materially constituted. On the one hand, homes facilitated new forms of subjectivity by offering postwar Germans a refuge, a reconstituted version of *Heimat*, which "came to embody the political and social community that could be salvaged from the Nazi ruins."[89] They served as a counterweight to the exhausting tempo and disorienting futurity of postwar capitalism by grounding everyday experience in auratic, contextually specific environments that evoked a simpler past and the comforts of temporal continuity. On the other hand, though, these domestic interiors also served as environments in which a diverse array of bodies and objects could be chrononormatively reconfigured into vehicles for the reification of progressive time. Whether through bucolic *Heimat* films from the 1950s, through the barrage of advertising images proclaiming the necessity of the nuclear family, or through the numerous housing exhibits that marked the postwar period, West Germans were taught that the home represented an ideal space within which to reconstitute meaningful forms of being in time, a space in which to contain the past and reach toward the future.[90] The postwar home, that is, functioned as a space in which the unsettling, ghostly fragments of the past were woven into new narratives of progress, providing postwar Germans with concrete mechanisms for grounding themselves in time and serving as active agents of the future.

Despite its utility as a disciplinary technique for reifying postwar temporalities and regimes of power, domesticity has also been interpreted as posing a potential threat to the stability of such regimes of normalization. In his work *The Production of Space*, for example, the French theorist Henri Lefebvre argued that spaces of acceptable deviation from the norm, spaces, like the home, in which one could momentarily escape from the overwhelming logics of capitalism, show "where the vulnerable areas and potential breaking-points are."[91] Writing just as the wave of youth revolts was washing over European cities, Michel de Certeau made a similar point in his influential book *The Practice of Everyday Life*. According to de Certeau, built environments retain traces of past lifeworlds and can thus serve as passageways into alternative realities. The home thus "remains believable, still open for a certain time to legends, still full of shadows."[92] Invoking the spirits that lay dormant in the shadows of the home, "the accumulated times that can be unfolded" in the present, according to de Certeau, offers the possibility of "invert[ing] the schema of the *Panopticon*."⁹³ As mediators between the past, present, and future, postwar homes were filled with traces of alternative lifeworlds, pasts that had only partially been incorporated into the logics of postwar progress, and which thus held the possibility for temporally unsettling the present. Scholars of ruins have made similar arguments about outmoded spaces.⁹⁴ Summarizing some of this scholarship, Caitlin DeSilvey and Tim Edensor note: "As sites characterized by multiple temporalities, ruins offer opportunities for constructing alternative versions of the past, and for recouping untold and marginalized stories."⁹⁵

Viewing the postwar home as a pluritemporal environment that contained the traces of the partially mastered past helps to shed light on why the squats came to be such significant sites for the cultivation of postprogressive practices. On the one hand, occupying these sites allowed squatters to uncover the partially buried traces of the past in the present and wield them as tools for destabilizing the narratives of postwar progress. On the other hand, though, beyond unleashing uncanny pasts as catalysts for directionless dialectical negation, the occupation of domestic spaces also put squatters in control of one of the central, chrononormative-disciplinary mechanisms of postwar power. These were the spaces, after all, in which postwar regimes sought to forge what Judith Butler has called "bodies that matter," spaces where postwar Germans acquired meaningful subjectivities by enacting narratives of progress. According to Butler, it is possible to disrupt such regimes of normalization by "citing" them. "This is citation, not as enslavement or simple reiteration of the original, but as an insubordination that appears to take place within the very terms of the original, and which calls into the question the power of origination."⁹⁶ Building on these theories, I propose that we think of the acts of domestic insubordination carried out on a daily basis in squatted houses like the Hafenstraße not only as attempts to liberate the traces of the past in order to negate and potentially explode progressive time (which they were), but also as militant occupations of the disciplinary, subject-generating spaces of the home. The integrative potential of domestic space in the postwar, its role in generating intelligible "bodies that matter," enabled the squatters of the Hafenstraße to incorporate the outmoded and the excluded into the auratic, subject-generating space of the home.

In some cases, it appeared as if the residents' desire to cultivate auratic forms of belonging within the walls of the Hafenstraße might result in their falling victim to a romantic longing for the vanished landscapes and the authentic social forms of the German *Heimat*, similar to what literary theorist Svetlana Boym has called "restorative nostalgia."⁹⁷ One pamphlet from 1993, for example, provided a detailed description of the squatter's plans for the construction of a new housing facility in the vicinity of the Hafenstraße, which on the surface resembled conservative attempts to counteract the alienating effects of modernity through a resuscitation of traditional forms of community.[98] In keeping with the practices of insurgent dwelling, however, such romantic evocations of vanished communal spaces and the lost art of *Gemeinschaft* almost always sought to incorporate modes of being that had been excluded from postwar modernity. The aforementioned plan, for example, included stipulations for bathrooms and sleeping areas for the homeless. The goal here was thus not to romantically reconstruct the German past in the present, but to subversively occupy the integrative, subject-generating space of the home for more radical ends.

Some of the literature explicitly narrated how populations that had been excluded in the postwar period found a home and a welcoming community in the Hafenstraße. The authors of the 1984 "Open Letter," for example, argued that the Hafenstraße was squatted to provide a home for those who had no place to go in the system.[99] One squatter reminisced about the crazy dogs, the noisy kids, and the open windows. It was a place with "more sense for justice than for law," a "tranquil" spot in which "the foreign [*Fremde*] found a home [*Heimat*]." "Like weeds in dog shit," the houses grew out of tainted society to provide a place in which one could "live together without strangeness [*Fremdheit*]."[100] Another clearly stated: "It doesn't matter how you feel about yourself, here you are at home, here you can be human."[101] In a set of letters reproduced in *St. Pauli Einschnitt*, two residents from the former GDR expressed gratitude that the Hafenstraße had offered them a place where they could finally feel at home again. In the first letter, Hans-Jürgen Neumann began abruptly with "I know who I am again! Since I visited you, I know who I am again. One from below, just like it was in the DDR." He went on to note: "I am no longer homeless, and I know that we can only live in this *Heimat* collectively."[102] As Neumann's comments clearly indicate, the insurgent home was explicitly designed to offer excluded subjects the chance to become "bodies that mattered."

In addition to offering a space in which abjected populations could feel at home without being subjected to forced normalization, the residents of the Hafenstraße also sought to bring together imagery of leftist resistance with that of belonging. The massive murals and the irreverent graffiti that covered the houses, for example, clearly illustrated these connections. The walls of the Hafenstraße were covered with representations of resistance, including an image of Martin Schleyer with a symbol for LSD (supposedly to show that politicians needed to take more drugs); a black cat symbolizing the workers' struggle in the United States; a Palestinian woman engaged in resistance with the words "shit state, let's fight for our rights"; Disney characters with guns; a large phrase reading "It's not us who have failed, but those who are responsible for homelessness and war [. . .] for the destruction of nature and life. We will still be dancing when no one even remembers Voscherau and Lochte"; and the tongue-in-cheek claim that if the city attempted to evict the squatters, they would "call the Russians."[103] In and of themselves, these images would have been shocking to many passersby, but their location on the façades of older houses made them doubly subversive. Traditional buildings, and houses in particular, had long served as some of the primary sites on which German national identity was inscribed. Covering them with images of international forms of leftist resistance was thus not only a challenge to the city government but to the essentializing logics of the nation.

Similarly, the pamphlets and flyers produced in support of the Hafenstraße also wove together imagery of resistance with that of domesticity. In one brochure, for example, a group of photos collected under the caption "Inside" juxtapose images of a squatter changing a baby's diaper with an anarchist plenum and a punk concert.[104] A similarly disruptive image depicted squatters in ski masks engaged in a variety of domestic chores like vacuuming and hanging laundry out to dry. One particularly clever illustration détourned the RAF symbol, which consisted of a star with a machine gun, by replacing the machine gun with a power drill, thus suggesting that seemingly benign acts of home repair could themselves be revolutionary.[105] Another pamphlet juxtaposed a quote from an elderly woman in the neighborhood describing how the squatters helped carry her groceries up the stairs of her apartment, with images of masked defenders defiantly flying a pirate flag above the barricaded houses.[106] To a certain extent such imagery, which was ubiquitous in the material produced by the squatters and their supporters, was meant to differentiate the supposedly dangerous but actually quite harmless activities of the squatters from the very real violence of the state. But they were also, I would like to suggest, attempts to portray the occupied houses as centers of insurgent dwelling, spaces where one could ground the self in place while also negating existing social conditions.

Throughout the long conflict over the Hafenstraße, squatters and their supporters produced a number of videos to supplement their pamphlets and murals. The audiovisual format allowed them to clearly enunciate the Hafenstraße's commitment to insurgent forms of dwelling. One video counterpoised squatters cooking dinner with an official voice declaring them terrorists. Others wove images of police brutality into scenes of domestic life. One of the most powerful juxtapositions included the camera panning over seemingly harmless images of domestic life inside the houses with the sound militant drumming.[107] This was not only a cinematic technique

FIGURE 5.2. Image from *10 Meter Ohne Kopf* (1987).
Source: International Institute of Social History, Amsterdam.

designed to produce some sort of audiovisual dissonance on the part of the viewer, but a concise portrayal of the Hafenstraße's radicalism. The battle over this row of houses was not simply a conflict between "chaos makers" and "the system," it was a battle over the possibility of being a revolutionary subject, one in which domestic practices challenged the structural foundations of the state. By citing the dominant discourses surrounding the home, the squatters mobilized domesticity's extraordinary powers of integration to transform a diverse array of excluded and oppositional subjects into "bodies that mattered," whose presence both disrupted the chrononormative temporalities of the postwar and provided a model of radical living in which one could dwell in negation.

The German media also took notice of these ideological claims and oftentimes sought to undercut the squatters' claims to domesticity and homeliness. One article, for example, described the disorder of the houses: "Next to a couple of intact tables and chairs there were lorries full of junk, which as described by the police 'stunk and looked like a rat's ass.' This trash is, however, useful for the Hafenstraße since it can be thrown out of windows."[108] A 1986 article in the notoriously reactionary *Bild* newspaper made a similar point, noting: "Chaos houses: Street fight with the police. New terror in the St. Pauli Hafenstraße: from the chaos houses there droned a deafening music. The police measured the music to be 90 decibels—the music was as loud as a jackhammer. Then suddenly it was quiet. Then 25 left radical *Chaoten* stormed out of the house (including punks with yellow hair, ripped pants)."[109] Another article from *Bild* included an illustration of the houses with the caption "Dr. Terror's House of Horrors." The image provided an explanation of how the rooms functioned in the houses, including the attic for the production of illegal radio programs, the kitchen, which was known to serve as a meeting point for the "scene," the barbed-wire windows, the steel doors, and the bedroom where they make Molotov Cocktails.[110] In these articles, everyday customs were transformed into signs of chaos and terror. "Stones are not used in this world for building, only for throwing; leather clothing is not seen as practical or as a fashionable accessory, but as the armor of chaos; bandannas are only used as masks; colored hair is only a sign of the diabolical and music is only an atavistic ritual."[111] Many in the press were clearly unsettled by ways in which the residents of the Hafenstraße occupied not just space, but the highly symbolic space of the German home, and used it as a refuge for the uncanny elements which it had been designed to exclude.

∴

Reflecting on the embattled history of the Hafenstraße, one resident wrote:

> For us it's about the people, about giving any and every one the possibility to change themselves, rather than simply pushing them aside as 'disruptive elements' with hundreds of police, with forced deprivations

[*Zwangsentzug*], eviction proceedings, psychiatry, and prison. It's about a life without fear, guilt, and punishment. [...] A system like this one which cannot satisfy the existential needs of the people has no future other than in violence. [...] We will stand against it. And therein lies our opportunity to engage more directly with all of those who are rising up. Indeed, the battle for our lives here is also a battle [...] for the lives of all.[112]

The Hafenstraße was not an empty space in which countercultural youth were free to follow their desires regardless of the consequences. It was a liberating, autonomous, and transcendent space precisely because it was an embedded place-world, a subject-generating landscape within which the excluded subjects of capitalist modernity could leave traces, have families and friends, and take pride in their lives. By occupying the temporally layered and highly symbolic environment of the traditional home, activists both embraced the contextual specificity, the innate revolutionary aura, of the space *and* gained the ability to transcend their spatial and temporal contexts by connecting to oppositional populations around the world and by endlessly negating dominant social logics. The houses on the Hafenstraße were fixed locations that constantly referenced landscapes and experiences that reached far beyond their spatial and temporal frameworks. As such the Hafenstraße came to function almost like a religious shrine for the late twentieth century autonomous left, as a rooted landscape of perpetual becoming, a portal to different worlds and different times in which one could constantly transcend the self by forging connections with (rather than controlling, objectifying, or otherwise subsuming) the excluded others of modernity, where one could dwell radically amid the manifold ruins of progress. Although unique in many respects, the Hafenstraße came to serve as a model for autonomous spaces throughout European cities. Confirming the fears of conservative commentators throughout the country, the Hafenstraße became a symbolically rich nodal point in a vast network of insurgent dwelling.

[CHAPTER SIX]

Carnival Time and Creative Destruction in the New Berlin

In the late 1980s, radical leftist protest in West Germany crystallized around a few ongoing campaigns such as the anti-apartheid movement, anti-nuclear power activism, and the relatively small-scale antigentrification battles being waged by groups like *Volxsport* in West Berlin.[1] Large-scale events such as the militant defense of the houses on the Hafenstraße generated widespread excitement among activists from across the ideological spectrum of the left. As noted in the previous chapter, the squatted houses on the Elbe River in Hamburg–St. Pauli captured the imagination of autonomous activists throughout West Germany and Europe more broadly, with many squatted centers in West German cities explicitly claiming the Hafenstraße as their main inspiration.[2] The battles surrounding the houses, which peaked in late April 1987, mobilized thousands of supporters, including ordinary citizens who marched through the streets of Hamburg to protest state violence and urban reconstruction, and autonomous activists throughout Europe who attacked symbols of power in cities like Amsterdam, Copenhagen, and London.[3] The mass demonstrations of late April 1987 in Hamburg were followed by large-scale riots in West Berlin, which broke out on May 1.[4] What began as a street festival in Kreuzberg to celebrate May Day quickly transformed into a scene of mass chaos after a group of activists overturned a police car, most likely in retaliation for a police raid on the offices of the anti-census movement that morning. Events quickly escalated as individuals from across the city descended on Kreuzberg to take part in the conflagrations. The situation was made even more chaotic by the widespread participation of neighborhood residents in the looting and destruction. By the end of the night, a Bolle supermarket was burned to the ground, countless shops were plundered, and hundreds of people were injured.

On the one hand, the events of late April and early May 1987 generated a serious backlash against leftist violence. Rather unsurprisingly, many conservative commentators harshly critiqued the riot as an unacceptable act of political terrorism, with the speaker for the Berlin Senate, for example, mobilizing a long-standing trope by referring to the rioters as Anti-Berliner.[5] A journalist for the *Westfallenblatt* called for a "clear and powerful crackdown" in order to bring the area and the radical left more broadly under control.[6] Conservatives were not, however, alone in voicing their dismay at the autonomous left's increasing willingness to engage in mass acts of vandalism and violence. An article in the increasingly integrationist but still decidedly left-leaning paper *Die Tageszeitung*, for example, urged activists to remember that Kreuzberg was not a stage on which to act out revolutionary fantasies against the state but a neighborhood in which people lived, worked, and raised children.[7] Along similar lines, a journalist for the *Volksblatt* called attention to the fact that many of the rioters in Kreuzberg were only short-term residents, looking for adventure. Young people, the author noted, "come from the provinces, have their 'Kreuzberg-phase' and then go back to their bourgeois or petit-bourgeois environments. [...] It's a mark of pride [*Es schmückt*] to have lived there for a while." Such behavior, he went on to suggest, was destroying the unique spatiotemporal qualities of the *Kiez*.[8] For these left-leaning critics acts of violence such as the May 1st riots were nothing more than spectacles of revolt conducted by bored, misguided adolescents.[9]

Many activists involved in West Germany's burgeoning *Autonomen* movement, by contrast, evinced significantly more enthusiasm for the outbreaks of rioting and violence, which they interpreted as a potential revival of earlier forms of large-scale leftist activism. Two short films from 1987, *Hönkelrausch* and *Blau ist Rot*, illustrate this growing fascination with irreverent forms of violence, especially when it involved international symbols of power. In *Hönkelrausch*, an artistic rendition of Reagan's head is submitted to various acts of desecration: It is covered with sauce and eaten, covered with bread and pecked by pigeons, and taken to the zoo and offered to the animals as a snack. The militant tone of the film is further intensified by images of activists with painted faces swinging flaming torches to the steady beat of a drum. Equally forthright in its advocacy of violent uprising, *Blau ist Rot* spliced together scenes of historical and contemporary rioting in order to present an image of transhistorical joy in destruction.[10] Throughout the late 1980s, radical groups such as *Volxsport* in West Berlin further radicalized the shift toward violence by desecrating trendy (*Schicki-Micki*) storefronts, destroying pornography shops, attacking upscale restaurants, and heckling politicians, all of which hearkened back to the youth movements of the early 1980s.

Writing in the wake of the May 1 celebrations in 1989, an author in the radical leftist paper *Interim* provided an explicit justification for violent confrontation with the state, noting: "Fighting your way out of situations in which you are defenseless and lack perspective is always right even if it's only for your own self-esteem."[11] Although many leftist activists tended to reject such sentiments, West Germany's *Autonomen* increasingly viewed violent confrontation as not only acceptable but necessary. Given the overwhelming power of their stated opponents—capitalism, fascism, patriarchy, the state—the tendency toward violent, highly symbolic forms of action is not at all surprising. Much like the militant groups of the Red Decade, the *Autonomen* of the mid to late 1980s sought to use violence both as a way to illustrate their own revolutionary credentials and as a catalyst for sparking a more widespread revolt. Unlike their predecessors in the 1970s, however, the *Autonomen* of the mid-1980s were less concerned with ensuring that their actions fit into dialectical visions of historical change than in the acts of radical negation themselves. Little did they know, events taking place on the other side of the Berlin Wall would fundamentally alter their perspective.

The events leading up to the fall of the Berlin Wall in 1989 and German unification in October 1990 are far too complex to adequately reconstruct in the space of this chapter.[12] There are, however, two important points on which I would like to briefly touch. First, without discounting the significance of economic and geopolitical factors in the fall of communism in East Germany, it is important to keep in mind the centrality of the East German opposition, both in the political events of 1989–90 and in the subsequent wave of squatting and urban activism. Emerging from the protective space offered by East German churches, this opposition encompassed artists, punks, environmentalists, leftist Christians, and others who hoped to liberalize the regime without necessarily abandoning socialism. They formed groups such as the New Forum, Democracy Now, Democratic Awakening, and the Initiative for Peace and Human Rights as well as "Round Table" groups that served as public forums for negotiating with the SED regime.[13] Although politically unsuccessful, the practices and ideologies of the East German dissidents left an enduring legacy of humanitarianism, ground-level democracy, passive resistance, and social justice that continued to influence much of the German left both during the period of the *Wende* and well after reunification.

The second point to which I wish to draw attention is that the failure of these oppositional groups to stem the growing nationalist tide, coupled with the truly astounding tempo of social, political, and spatial transformation during the *Wende*, left many on the left deeply disenchanted. The rising tide of neo-Nazi violence against minorities, skyrocketing income disparities and unemployment, and urban restructuring projects geared toward the needs of corporations and the rich shattered the dreams of the socialist revolutionaries.[14] The feelings of horror on September 4, 1989, when protesters emerged from the *Nikolaikirche* in Leipzig chanting "we want out," were significantly amplified over the course of the following months.[15] Not only had socialism collapsed, but as the March 1990 elections and the October 1990 unification celebrations indicated, an invigorated form of German nationalism had begun to take its place. Oppositional intellectuals in East Germany were not the only ones who watched the unfolding dramas of unification with disbelief. Western intellectuals and public figures also suffered from an acute case of historical and political vertigo.[16] In his essay "What Am I Talking For? Is Anybody Still Listening?" Günter Grass, for example, bemoaned the loss of a critical public sphere in Germany and sharply criticized his fellow citizens for their headlong rush into unity.[17] Deemed the culmination of German history by some, reunification was for many others a nightmare from which they were unable to wake.

Joy and triumphalism on the part of pro-unification German officials was not, of course, a sufficient blueprint for the very challenging task of creating a united German state, not to mention a nation. Politicians quickly realized that they would have to take immediate steps to integrate East and West Germans, who, unsurprisingly, had drifted rather far apart over the course of the previous forty years. Always a subject of rancorous debate, Berlin's landscape again came to occupy a central position in the discussions over how to forge a shared identity in the wake of unification. Reconstructing the symbolic landscape of Berlin, however, posed serious problems. According to Wolfgang Kaschuba, postunification Berlin represented "an urban landscape whose public spaces and orders are more open, undefined, transitory and whose symbolic topography seems to be based on diverse maps and organized in various dimensions."[18] Following unification, Berlin struggled to find a "common symbolic grammar" that could unite East and West Germans.[19] What, for example, was to be done with the remnants of the Berlin Wall, with the countless Lenin statues dotting the landscape of East Berlin, or with the ruins at Potsdamer Platz, which in the early twentieth century had been widely considered an epicenter of urban modernity? Even more complicated than the legacies of communism were the legacies of the Nazi past which marked the urban landscape. Would this past be memorialized or, as many on the right initially advocated, quietly swept under the rug?

From Peter Eisenman's Memorial to the Murdered Jews of Europe and Daniel Libeskind's postmodern Jewish Museum to the corporate-funded developments at the Potsdamer Platz and the demolition of the Palace of the Republic, the history of postunification Berlin is filled with controversial construction projects that were widely understood to be material interventions into German national identity.[20] That is, by modifying the urban landscape, officials, planners, and others in the place marketing industry believed that they could not only transform Berlin into a "global city" but also into a potent symbol of national renewal. As Claire Colomb has convincingly argued, this modification of the urban landscape in the "new Berlin" should be understood within the context both of the reinvention of a "normalized" Germany identity and the global embrace of place marketing strategies in which politicians and teams of experts fervently sought to attract international flows of capital by rebranding urban centers.[21] Some sites such as Friedrichstraße and the yet-to-be-constructed Palace would create tangible links to Berlin's past glories while others such as Potsdamer Platz, the new government buildings surrounding the Reichstag, and even the construction sites themselves were meant to illustrate Germany's technological prowess and its embrace of modernity.[22] Other locations, including the preserved section of the Wall and the Memorial to the Murdered Jews of Europe, explicitly referenced the horrors of the past but framed it as something with which Germans were successfully coming to terms in their long march back to civilization.[23] In other words, Berlin was to be reconstructed as a preeminent site of progress in which the past was safely contained in monuments and museums and the German people, whether from the East or the West, could come together to collectively move forward into the bright future.

Although often accompanied by rancorous debates in Parliament and in the newspapers, these rebuilding projects and the discussions surrounding them were at least partially successful in creating a new identity for Germany and especially Berlin. While they failed to attract the levels of global capital to the city that they had hoped, the purveyors of place marketing did manage to lay the material and ideological foundations for a new national public sphere in reunited Germany, one in which the past and future seemed to be safely anchored in the urban landscape.

Throughout the early 1990s, leftist groups associated with the East German opposition movement, the more radical factions within the Green Party, the West German *Autonomen*, antiracist activists, and the vast array of countercultural groups that made up the so-called alternative milieu, many of whom lived in West Berlin neighborhoods like Kreuzberg, joined forces to combat the emergence of the new Germany. They pointed to the destructive effects of capitalist consumer culture in the former GDR, the rise in rightwing violence against minorities, the rapid gentrification of neighborhoods like Mitte and Prenzlauer Berg, the exploding rates of unemployment and homelessness, and the shrinking space for public debate. Although they may have been disenchanted by the trajectory of historical events, they were far from admitting defeat. The explosive proliferation of squatting and neighborhood activism in Berlin provided a space in which these oppositional groups could come together, if only briefly, into a critical counterpublic sphere where the creation of a different Germany was more than fleeting fantasy and where the dream of a unified leftist opposition again seemed possible. The urban landscape of the New Berlin was thus not only the setting for nationalist narratives. It was also the space within which oppositional movements sought to concretize narratives of another Germany, one in which the past had not been prematurely silenced and the future had not been predetermined by the interests of neoliberal capitalism. Postprogressive spatial and temporal practices would prove to be highly useful tools in this conflict. This chapter shows how the resurgence of postprogressive temporal practices both assisted activists in their battle for the soul of the new Germany and sparked a carnival of negation and creative destruction that transformed Berlin into one of the capitals of youth culture in the early twenty-first century.

∴

The third wave of German squatting was initiated by occupations carried out by East German activists. Despite the fact that West German leftists had significantly more experience with overtly political forms of squatting, including the occupation of several houses directly preceding the fall of the Berlin Wall in 1989, it was the activities of the East German opposition that most directly sparked the third major wave of German squatting.[24] In December 1989, a group of activists from the East squatted the house at Schönhauser Allee 20 in Prenzlauer Berg and subsequently published a flyer claiming that they were working for the "preservation of the old Berlin cityscape."[25] Shortly thereafter, another East German group squatted a house at Scheinerstrasse 4 and noted: "As of Christmas 1989 the GDR is open for plundering. Thus, we find it necessary, to protect the assets that are accessible to us from abandonment." They went on to assure readers that surviving Stalinism prepared them well for navigating the "dictatorship of world capitalism."[26] Throughout the early months of 1990, many activists from West Berlin began moving into the vast number of abandoned turn-of-the-century buildings in the eastern sections of the city.[27] According to an article in *Interim*, the initial impetus for this migration of radical leftists from the West into East Berlin came from activists in the East who desperately wanted to protect older buildings from demolition yet, given the huge number of such structures, needed assistance in order to do so.[28]

Western leftist groups were more than happy to oblige the request. The Mainzer Straße squat in Friedrichshain, to which I devote significant attention in the following pages, began in just such a way. In late April 1989, East German activists placed an ad in *Telegraph*, calling on West Berliners to help them squat a number of houses in Friedrichshain, which they feared would otherwise be demolished as part of a citywide urban restructuring plan. Interested parties met at the Kirche von Unten on April 29 to plan what would eventually become one of the most well-known squats to emerge in these years.[29] By the end of May, there were more than two hundred fifty squatters from multiple countries living in the *Gründerzeit*-era houses near the showcase socialist project at Karl-Marx-Allee.

While Western activists were happy to help their counterparts in the East defend older housing stock from capitalism and the wrecking ball, they were also drawn to the houses because of the opportunities such spaces offered for breaking free from the ideological torpor of the late 1980s—the chance, that is, to revive the momentum of 1980–81 or to follow the Hafenstraße in creating their very own spaces of insurgent dwelling. According to the author of an article in *Interim*: "A rapid politicization process began for many people. Primarily this can be traced back to people breaking free from individualization and resignation, [activities] for which the houses offered ideal conditions. Dozens of new connections arose in this way. [. . .] For many people here occupation means [. . .] going on the offensive again and changing the conditions in this city ourselves. It's not just the really overworked *Antifa* who will have noticed that it's us rather than the fascist kids who control the streets of Friedrichshain now."[30] As this passage indicates, Western activists viewed the occupied houses in the East as something of a catchall solution to their problems. Not only would the houses allow them to forge new connections with leftist and countercultural groups in the GDR and wage a more effective battle against the resurgent forces of nationalist order, but they would also facilitate a rapprochement within the West German left, a return to the days when leftists from across the ideological spectrum felt a common sense of purpose. As in 1980–81, postprogressive practices served as particularly useful mechanisms for bridging divides within the broader left.

Due in part to the influence exerted by antifascist *Autonomen*, early squatters were especially concerned with protecting themselves and others against the rising threat of fascism, which, given the rapid resurgence of neo-Nazi groups in East Berlin, was hardly unreasonable. Especially in neighborhoods like Friedrichshain, squatters erected intricate defensive ramparts at the doors and windows of their houses in order to guard against potential fascist attacks. Those living in the Mainzer Straße as well as other squats in Friedrichshain were particularly vigilant due to the close proximity of their houses to the fascist squat on the Weitlingstraße in Lichtenberg.

The 1991 film *Sag niemals nie* documents some of the conflicts between the Mainzer Straße squatters and the residents of the Weitlingstraße, which took place in the days surrounding Pentecost in 1990, showing, for example, young fascists marching through the Mainzer Straße breaking windows and yelling as the squatters chant "Nazis get out," as well as the leftist counterdemonstration in which squatters marched to the Weitlingstraße to confront the residents, many of whom stood on the roof yelling insults, throwing rocks, and giving Hitler salutes.[31] On the one hand, neo-Nazi groups did indeed pose a serious threat to leftists as well as to minority groups in Germany. On the other hand, though, the squatters' fascination with these conflicts, which one squatter at the Mainzer Straße referred to as "a fetish," points to the fact that these historical reenactments of the often-violent battles between Nazis and communists that took place in the streets of interwar Berlin were, in some sense at least, existentially constitutive acts for the movement, just as they had been for groups like the RAF.[32]

For many squatters and their supporters, the revival of German fascism was impossible to separate from the nationalist euphoria sweeping the country. The 1990 film *Petra Pan und Arumukha: Der Traum von ordentlichen Anarchisten* made this connection between nationalism and far-right violence explicit by splicing footage of Nazi salutes into images of the unification celebrations in October 1990.[33] Leftist protesters made a similar point when they marched through the city during the unification festivities, chanting "Never again Germany" and holding signs reading: "Germany, shut up—that's enough!!!"[34] In one of the many texts associated with this demonstration, the authors called on the "living contradictions" within the new system, by which they meant radical leftists and anyone else who found themselves excluded from the new Germany, to take to the streets thereby becoming symbols of opposition both for "ourselves and for everyone around the world who is confronted with the blood-sucking, genocidal Germans." The article concluded with a rousing call for leftists to take part in the demonstration against reunification and for a "re-breakdown" (*Wiederzusammenbruch*).[35] Such practices, which clearly call to mind many of the dialectical strategies of the 1970s, are indicative of the influence exerted on the early squatting movement by many of the radical leftist groups who remained committed to the position of total revolution through negation.

Squatters and their supporters also spent considerable time and energy demonstrating their opposition to bourgeois norms and values, which they interpreted as imbued with racism and sexism. The back cover of the August 4, 1990, edition of the *Besetzerinnenzeitung*, for example, advertised a festival to be held at the Mainzer Straße, "a festival with women and men from all parts of the world, who despite the misanthropic chauvinism, do not

FIGURE 6.1. Front cover of *BesetzerInnen Zeitung* (Nr. 6, September 25, 1990). Source: International Institute of Social History, Amsterdam.

allow their solidarity with each other to be taken away [and] in which everyday sexism against women and macho images have no place."[36] Activists also attempted to openly subvert bourgeois social norms by engaging in behaviors such as dressing in drag, eating breakfast in the middle of the streets, dyeing their hair bright colors, blasting punk music, and painting phrases such as "Germany, perish" and "We shit on the Fatherland" on the houses. Such attempts to aggravate the surrounding population tended to be quite successful. The Mainzer Straße "queer house" (*Tuntenhaus*), perhaps unsurprisingly, managed to elicit some of the harshest critiques from surrounding neighbors. A certain Herr W. from the Bürgerinitiative Mainzer Straße, an organization created to combat the squat, expressed his displeasure at public displays of homosexual affection, bemoaning the "open presentation on the street . . . Children have to see that. I find it unpleasant when lesbian women caress each other or gay men march about the street to showcase coitus."[37] Frau F., another member of the Bürgerinitiative, complained that the squatters had sofas in the street, had painted garish murals and offensive slogans on the walls of the houses, and even refused to officially register with the police.[38] She went on to note that they engaged in such behavior in order to provoke the surrounding neighbors: "We have nothing against this sort of lifestyle, but it should take place within their own four walls, thank you very much."[39] Some residents made more radical suggestions for dealing with the squatters. One resident of the neighborhood, for example, suggested "forced labor; work them till they drop."[40]

Echoing the ideas of creation through destruction that had suffused the youth movements, squatters in 1989–90 sought to demonstrate their opposition to dominant norms and values in an attempt to open up the possibility of an alternative future for Germany. They also sought to develop communal forms, which unlike those built on nationalist principles, were expressly open to difference. The open-ended inclusivity of the squatting movement that emerged in the houses of East Berlin in 1989–90 is clearly demonstrated in a number of statements made by residents of the Mainzer Straße. One person, for example, compared life in a small apartment to life on the Mainzer, noting: "[When] I live with 300 people in a street, then I might randomly end up in any sort of situation with someone with whom I can develop good ideas and engage in some sort of action."[41] Another resident mused: "For me the most important experience from my half year in the Mainzer Straße was a new openness and tolerance. [. . .] Hippies, anti-imperialists, kids, stoners, Ossis, autonomen, punks, women, gays, Wessis, lesbians, pacifists, men, and a thousand other compartmentalized identities melted together and became the Mainzer."[42] The sense of endless possibility achieved through this concentrated multitude is summed up quite succinctly by yet another resident who noted: "You know what, in the Mainzer, all you had to do was go out the door and say I want to do something and then immediately two people were standing there saying: alright, let's do it then. It was brilliant."[43] Although the resurgence of nationalism added a new sense of urgency to the situation, in imagining that one could forge a

FIGURE 6.2. Squatted house on Mainzer Straße in Berlin (1990). Photo by Kappa/Umbruch Bildarchiv. Source: Umbruch Bildarchiv.

liberated space in which acts of negation facilitated radically undefined and expansive forms of community, the squatters in East Berlin were echoing ideas and practices of grounded negation and insurgent dwelling developed in the Hafenstraße.

Cafés, street festivals, concerts, demonstrations, and the ever growing network of squatted houses all helped to produce a network of autonomous spaces where one could encounter difference and embrace the unknown.[44] Virtually every squat had some sort of café, many with telling names like Café Subversiv or Café Anal, where residents had the chance to mingle with neighbors, discuss current events, develop common projects, or listen to lectures on everything from Stalinism to firsthand accounts of antifascist resistance in the 1930s. The performances at the Mainzer Straße Tuntenhaus, in particular, were exceptionally popular affairs. One attendee described them as "simply unforgettable highlights, great moments in the culture. There were Quiz programs, pop song competitions, and various dance festivities. Do you know 'Der grosse Preis'? They had 'Der grosse Scheiss,' complete with acts by pop singers, guests from the audience, and prizes to win."[45] Here, the squatters were employing tried-and-true techniques of building subcultural community by appropriating and critically redeploying dominant social codes, but with the added twist that these events were not limited to members of a well-defined scene but were open for almost everyone. In addition to cafés, there were bookstores, movie theaters, children's playgrounds, and public kitchens in which children and the elderly could eat for free. The Tuntenhaus on the Mainzer Straße ran the Max-Hoelz Antiquariat for DDR Literature in which visitors could stop in to peruse material from the GDR.[46] Film screenings were also quite popular. The Kino Anschlag's weekly lineup for late September 1990, for example, included Polanski's *Macbeth*, a film on the Hafenstraße, a documentary film titled *Vaters Land*, and, to round it out, Mel Brooks's *Spaceballs*.[47]

All of these functionally specific locales were vital to the formation of an open, counterpublic network, yet they were all dependent on the existence of the actual squatted houses themselves, of which there an astounding number in the early months and years after the fall of the Wall. Squatters mobilized a wide array of mediums ranging from flyers to articles in leftist newspapers to video documentaries to announce new squats. Relatively formulaic, these "self-introductions" tended to open with an announcement that a group of people from diverse backgrounds have squatted a house at such-and-such an address in order to protest the activities of the new German/German government. Take, for example, the widely circulated text "Hausbesetzer. Selbstdarstellungen von 16 Projekten aus Friedrichshain Mitte und Prenzlauer Berg," in which the authors claimed that their goal was to "break through the customary structures of isolated living, build an autonomous neighborhood culture, and prevent the destruction and vacancy of inhabitable houses." The authors went on to note: "Don't look away—fantasy against violence! Don't isolate yourselves—build projects in your own neighborhoods."[48] The remainder of the document is taken up by descriptions of each of the individual houses, the people who lived in them, the projects they were developing, and expressions of their desires to forge new connections in the scene. The only thing that is atypical about this pamphlet is that it combines the descriptions of multiple houses in a single document. There are hundreds of similar self-introductions in the archives, all of which contributed to the sense that the movement was on the move again.

This fundamentally open form of community may have been anchored in specific spaces, even if the contiguity and extensiveness of such spaces was largely imagined, but it was also highly mobile. One of the primary mechanisms for circulating counterpublic discourses and values among members of the public was through flyers, brochures, and alternative newspapers such as the *Besetzerinnenzeitung*, *Interim*, and *Telegraph*, which called on people to come to demonstrations, introduced new squatted houses, provided information on alternative cultural offerings, reported fascist attacks throughout the city, and discussed leftist revolutionary strategy.[49] In some cases, activists openly debated the purpose of such publications. For example, the 00 edition of the *Besetzerinnenzeitung* opened with a series of articles debating the organization and overarching goals of the paper, with some hoping to create an "internal squatters' info paper as a forum for organizing the movement, for guaranteeing a steady flow of information [among members of the scene], for self-introductions, and for conceptual debates," and others expressing their preference for an "open house paper [*Häuserzeitung*] directed at the 'broad masses' for the representation and illustration of our ideas and life forms, for political education, and publicity work [*Öffentlichkeitsarbeit*] more generally."[50] Although the paper ultimately ended up serving both as an internal information exchange and as a way to represent alternative lifestyles for the broader public, the debate itself is quite telling. As members of an oppositional counterpublic, the organizers of the *Besetzerinnenzeitung* were forced to grapple with tough conceptual problems such as how best to produce knowledge without setting dominant norms, how to create connections among diverse populations of activists, many of whom did not know each other, and how to balance coherent representations of the movement with internal diversity and autonomy—in short, the same types of questions with which the squatting and youth movements had been grappling since the early 1980s.

In addition to printed texts, images and videos were also important forms of communication for the movement. One of the most popular forms of entertainment at the squats was screening films depicting other squats, especially films about the Hafenstraße, of which there are an astounding number.[51] The proliferation of films about the Hafenstraße represented a growing trend among German leftists to produce and consume documentary films about themselves. In Berlin, no group was more prolific in this regard than AK Kraak, an organization that produced periodic video magazines that reported on pressing issues in the movement. In AK Kraak's *Video Magazin 2* from September 1990, for example, a woman faces the camera and employs a theatrical news anchor voice to catch viewers up on the latest developments in the scene, including the negotiations between squatters and city officials, the threat of evictions, and updates from the meeting of the "Lease Forum" (*Vertragsgremium*). There was also a report on the eviction of a petting zoo and self-help project in Berlin-Wedding, interviews with squatters, and segments introducing new squats.[52]

One of the repercussions of this open circulation of counterpublic discourse was that it sometimes resulted in formulaic reproductions of oppositional modes of dwelling, both in Berlin and in cities throughout Germany. Take, for example, the "Report from Greifswald," in which activists from Greifswald, a small city about two hours' drive north of Berlin, reported on the alternative scene in their town.⁵³ The radical leftist scene, they noted, was rather small in Greifswald, an observation confirmed by the fact that although they had a Hafenstraße it lacked any squatted houses. Nonetheless, they proudly recounted instances when they stood up to neo-Nazis and the forces of order by unrolling a sign at the Greifswald vs. St. Pauli football match reading "Solidarity with the FC St. Pauli and the Hafenstr" and defacing the Commerzbank.⁵⁴ The oppositional practices being developed in Berlin could thus be replicated in diverse locales.

As was true throughout the 1980s, such codifications of anarchist practices were thought to pose a threat to the spontaneity and the directionless acts of negation that were so highly valued by many in the movement. At the same time, however, refusing to codify radical practice meant that the squatters could lose their edge in the battle against state authorities. Take for example a letter sent to neighbors of the squatted house at the Scharnweberstraße 38, which was reproduced in the *Besetzerinnenzeitung*. The commentary accompanying the form letter noted: "This flyer for surrounding neighbors can be used as a foundation for anyone who has (for whatever reason) not yet been able to make contact with their neighbors." Such contact, the author noted, was necessary for breaking down the "interpersonal walls" that prevented engagement with the broader community.⁵⁵ While many squatters fell in line with these normative frameworks, others began to question whether using a form letter to create authentic connections might itself be a problem.

In many instances, such attempts at instituting centralized forms of behavior generated strong resistance. The discussions surrounding the "Squatter Council" and the *Vertragsgremium*, both of which functioned as nonbinding decision-making bodies for the squatted houses, are a case in point. For some, these organizations represented a necessary mechanism by which the diverse factions of the movement could work together toward common political goals.⁵⁶ For others, however, these organizations created unwelcome hierarchies. An article in *Telegraph*, for example, noted: "What's truly unbelievable [about the push for centralization] is that these demands come primarily from West Berliners, despite the fact that they are working from autonomous positions, that is decentralized, self-controlled, self-organized forms of life and activism." For many who grew up in the East, the author went on to note, such forms of hierarchy were simply not acceptable.⁵⁷

Activists in these years often disagreed about the overarching goals of the movement. For some, the occupied landscape represented an open, inclusive space where a diverse array of individuals, everyone from drag queens, to punks, to East German intellectuals, to elderly neighborhood residents, could come together to formulate new modes of sociability and belonging outside the narrative logics of national progress. As was also case during the youth movements of the 1980s and especially during the conflict over the Hafenstraße, such postprogressive imaginaries depended on the palimpsestic qualities of the urban landscape, in which traces of the past exploded the temporal continuum of progress and allowed autonomous subjectivities and sociabilities to flourish in its ruins. This vision was particularly well suited to the environments of post-Wall East Berlin, the fragmented nature of which were thought to enable endless breakthroughs into the ever new. Others, though, were much less interested in cultivating the transgressive openness of the squatted landscape than in dialectically redirecting it toward more properly revolutionary ends. Endless becoming, they feared, was nothing more than a countercultural veneer covering the expansion of capitalism. Still others worried that the carnival of negation and becoming that characterized life in and around the squatted houses in 1989–90 threatened to overwhelm auratic connections to place. Initially, at least, these differences remained on the back burner as leftists collectively threw themselves into the breathtaking expansion of the movement. As the new city government began cracking down on the squats, however, the tensions rose to the surface, and the movement fractured in a number of different directions. The following section documents the feelings of exuberance that united leftists in the early months of the movement as well as some of the conditions leading to the movement's collapse and its legacies in the New Berlin.

∴

The months following the fall of the Wall were an exciting time for the radical left: tens of thousands of protesters took to the streets in colorful costumes, new houses were squatted daily, and activists from East and West Germany came together to collectively enact alternative futures. This sense of unbounded optimism is clearly evident in one of the opening scenes from the film *Sag niemals nie* (*Never Say Never*), in which the viewer is initially confronted with a ruined landscape of crumbling buildings in East Berlin. Dramatic ambient music intensifies the feeling of postapocalyptic dread as the camera pans across the ruined landscape. Suddenly, an upbeat guitar riff cuts through the gloom as a whimsical Peter Pan figure skips across the screen. The scene then quickly shifts to one of joyful exuberance and infinite possibility in which crowds of people fill the streets, masked figures repel down the front façades of crumbling buildings, and groups of activists begin collectively repairing the houses. In *Petra Pan und Arumukha: Der*

Traum von ordentlichen Anarchisten (*Petra Pan and Arumukha: The Dream of Orderly Anarchists*), the same Peter/Petra Pan figure appears again, nonchalantly skipping through the landscape and stopping periodically to spray-paint a number on a house wall. At one point we even see Petra spray-paint the number 1000, indicating the belief that this time around the movement was an unstoppable force, that the anarchist energies emerging in the interstitial, asynchronous spaces of East Berlin would finally fulfill their potential by completely remaking the world.[58] Beyond the parallels between these scenes of leftist exuberance during the *Wende* and those from the youth revolts of 1980–81, they also bore a striking resemblance to the early postwar period, in which ruined spaces seemed to offer an extraordinary opportunity for renewal.

Upon crossing the increasingly porous border between East and West Berlin, Western activists consistently expressed their amazement at the city's "anomalous" temporal qualities. Writing about his experiences at clubs and in squatted houses in Mitte in 1989–90, Anton Waldt, for example, noted: "You just walked over—and suddenly you were in the Zone! Museum village East Berlin: a forlorn area, sparsely settled, the stock of abandoned apartments. [...] The temporary anomaly of East Berlin was not just endlessly exciting, but also obviously part of something much bigger. A crazy person [who lived in one of the squatted houses] developed a theory that the TV tower at Alexanderplatz was a the center of a particle accelerator for time travel." He wrote that everyone had been transported into some sort of parallel universe in which the past was always present and the future was always open.[59] Similarly, in describing the house and techno club in the basement of the squatted art complex known as the Tacheles, Ulrich Gutmaier wrote: "A laser beam crossed through the club from left to right. Like a finger pointing to the future, which touched a history that seemed to have stopped in 1945 when Berliners spent their nights in the air raid shelters waiting on the Red Army."[60] He went on to refer to the Tacheles in particular and Mitte more broadly as an "open wound," a wormhole that "catapulted you into the immediate postwar period."[61] Reminiscing about an incident in which squatters in Mitte found mummified corpses in one of the houses and then brought them into the living room, Gutmaier wrote: "Even the dead were for a brief moment part of the everyday. They dwelled in the same space as the living. It was a Carnival where the low and the high switched places. One did not need to have mummies in the living room in order to see the death and the destruction of the city. One was reminded of it in front of every door. East Berlin was full of remains. Every stroll through the streets took you by ruins, wastelands, faded inscriptions that advertised products and stores that haven't existed in fifty years. Their owners were all long dead."⁶² In keeping with the postprogressive temporal imaginaries developed during the 1980s, activists in the months surrounding the *Wende* viewed these traces of the past as tools with which to spark the new, uncanny asynchronicities that disrupted the present and opened the future.

Whereas in the late 1970s and early 1980s, countercultural activists and experimental artists sought to uncover traces of the past in order to explode the temporal logics of progress and ride the debris into unknown landscapes of the future, in East Berlin such residual traces of alternative temporalities, which were similar to what Shannon Dawdy has called "patina,"⁶³ were simply impossible to avoid. Walter Benjamin's fantastical "time of the now," in which multiple different pasts and futures overlapped in the space of the present, had in a number of respects become the norm. Whereas for theorists like François Hartog, such conditions of presentism are seen as a problem, for activists in the early 1990s, they were immensely exhilarating. As the temporal frameworks of the Cold War crumbled, they left behind a diverse array of discarded, disconnected fragments in the form of Lenin statues, army uniforms, abandoned houses, consumer goods, advertisements, sections of the Berlin Wall, and furniture, which activists from Kreuzberg, Hamburg, Freiburg, Amsterdam, London, New York, and Tokyo could collect and reconfigure into powerful tools for negating the present and thus radically opening the future. In navigating the fractured temporal landscape of unification-era Berlin, activists mobilized many of the techniques developed by youth protesters in the early 1980s. The sheer volume of such asynchronous objects, however, shifted the focus from negation to creation. The world of the modern time regime, it seems, was already crumbling, meaning that activists felt free to experiment with the possibility of creating new modes of dwelling in the liminal, interstitial spaces between temporal logics.

Perhaps a few examples are in order here. In a particularly outrageous performance at the Mainzer Straße Tuntenhaus, a notoriously kitschy locale replete with "flowers in the window and any number of pretty pictures on the walls, and frilly candle holders and pink Chiffon around the lamps," a group of men, many of whom were dressed in drag, donned Free German Youth (FDJ) uniforms as they sang socialist songs and waved the East German flag in front of a raucous and very appreciative crowd.⁶⁴ Now, one might reasonably look on this episode merely as an indication of the autonomous left's terrible taste level and their inability to recognize that the collapse of Cold War logics was experienced by many as a catastrophe, but it's difficult to deny the truly astonishing nature of the performance. Indeed, here is a group of Western autonomous activists in drag, wearing uniforms from an East German youth organization, all the while illegally occupying a

FIGURE 6.3. Street festival on the Mainzer Straße (September 8, 1990). Photo by Umbruch Bildarchiv. Source: Umbruch Bildarchiv.

house in the heart of East Berlin, which at that point was still the capital of the GDR.[65] In the chaotic temporal environments of post-Wall East Berlin, activists and artists continued the punk tradition of creating new worlds out of the ruins of the old. And like the youth activists of the early 1980s and the Hafenstraße squatters, they also refused to reintegrate these temporal fragments into coherent narrative of progress, something which cannot be said for the neoliberal logics that would soon take root in Berlin. They sought to transform infinite becoming into a mode of being in time, to make it possible to dwell indefinitely in fragments and ruins. Although in principle not that different from the anarchist practices the 1980s, the activist forms that emerged in East Berlin in 1989–90 took on a particularly intense hue due in part to the profusion of asynchronicities in the built environment.

Incorporating the material traces of the socialist past into everyday life was common practice in these years. Some used the abandoned objects of socialism as fashion accessories. Marco Bölke, for example, remembered taking protective helmets and masks from an abandoned factory to create clubbing costumes.[66] Similarly, Ulrich Gutmaier recounted a particular instance in which a group of squatters were thrilled to find a box of hats from the East German children's circus with which they could adorn themselves.[67] Others took furniture to decorate their clubs, bars, homes, and art galleries. Bastian Maris happily remembered how he and his friends drove by the Humboldt University every Wednesday to pick through the refuse of "forty years of GDR history in the form of scientific equipment," which they then installed as art pieces at the Glowing Pickle, one of a number of experimental art galleries that opened in the Scheunenviertel in the early 1990s.[68] The group of artist provocateurs connected to the Mutoid Waste Company took this proclivity for exhibiting the abandoned objects from the socialist past to new heights when they displayed abandoned tanks and jets throughout the city. Juxtaposing objects and environments from multiple different pasts, activists sought both to further the collapse of twentieth-century progressive dreamworlds and to create new worlds from the ensuing fragments. They joyfully took part in a carnival of negation and becoming, an endless process of reinvention through creative destruction.

In another example, again from the Mainzer Straße, autonomous activists scrambled the legacy of the West German Left by gathering for a dinner party at which the attendees, most of whom were completely naked save for their ski masks, sat down for coffee and cake at the famous table from Kommune I, which they had previously stolen from the offices of the *Tageszeitung*.[69] In a flyer announcing the fact that the table was stolen, titled "Be Wild and Do Awesome Things!" and signed by the "Central Committee of the Roving Hash Rebels," they wrote: "This table is a social-revolutionary relic and has for a long time had no business being with you. You have nothing to do with social or revolution."[70] The editors of the *Tageszeitung* promptly responded in an article with the comparatively underwhelming title "Give the Table Back!" in which they angrily wrote: "The table has served the antiauthoritarian and leftist movements over the past 21 years ten times more than it will a group of West-squatters in an East Berlin house."[71] In conducting this action, the Mainzer Straße squatters sought not only to undercut the self-congratulatory, progress-oriented narratives of the West German left, but also to forge new networks of unmoored relationality by removing a symbolic object from what they viewed as the overly restrictive narrative logics of leftist history and inserting it in new, undefined configurations of meaning. The goal was not to reincorporate the table into an alternative narrative logic, but to gather symbols from multiple different ideologies in a durational state of productive abeyance, which offered the possibility of boundless freedom.

There are countless additional examples of such anarchist temporal activism in the period, including one instance in which various squatters held a press conference where they theatrically reenacted well-established patterns of leftist publicity work, except for their costumes: they conducted the interview in animal masks and dresses.[72] Or another in which Daniel Pflumm transformed the name and the damaged aesthetic of the sign on the electrical shop he squatted into the label "Elektro," which he then put on T-shirts, on records, and on advertisements for his events. Incorporating traces of the past into the squatted landscape was quite common in this period. Other locales such as Farben, Friseur, Obst & Gemüse, and WMF also retained the names of the buildings in East Berlin that they had illegally occupied. Pointing to the allure of such practices, Gutmaier called them a "stroke of genius" since a "damaged logo is more seductive than one that is intact because it provides a sense of ephemerality." He went on to argue that the logo brilliantly managed to "compress a particular time and a particular place into one sign."[73] The peculiar "seduction" of such practices emerged, I contend, from the sense of subjective freedom they elicited. Refusing to abide by established temporal frameworks, the activists of this period felt as if they were on the borders of space and time, at the marginal edges of meaning. Unlike postwar iterations of progress, the postprogressive anarchists of these years did not want to reincorporate these traces of the past into settled narratives of being and becoming. They included a diverse array of obsolete objects in the everyday environments of squatted life so as to construct a world with disruption and chaos as its foundation. Though, in the case of using asynchronous traces of the past as logos, it also becomes clear that this form of temporal anarchy could easily align with capitalist practices of value creation.

Techno clubs such as the famed Tresor also served as spaces in which to develop the anarchist temporal practices associated with ruin dwelling.[74] After taking part in experimental music scenes like the Geniale Dilettanten in Kreuzberg in the early 1980s, Dmitri Hegemann traveled to American cities such as Chicago and Detroit where he came into contact with house music and the Afrofuturist techno being produced by artists like Drexciya. When the Wall fell in 1989, Hegemann and his colleagues created the Tresor in part as a way to bring this music to Berlin. The first incarnation of the Tresor was located in the underground vault of the bombed-out building in Mitte that had housed the Wertheim department store before its forced Aryanization in the 1930s. Locations such as the Wertheim vault, Hegemann noted, produced "a sense of astonishment at the real history of the building [that] went hand in hand with the pleasure of appropriating the locations. [. . .] History had washed up this space at your feet, and now it was a matter of making it your own somehow."[75] Feeling as if "the walls were talking to [him]," he couldn't help but think "about the life stories behind them, about the joyful moments and the family tragedies."[76] Describing his feeling upon first entering the vault, Johnie Stieler, an East Berliner and one of the club's founders, made a similar point, noting: "None of us could even speak. We just walked around silently with our lighters."[77] The historical aura of these sites, coupled with the experimental musical acts that played in them, allowed visitors to constantly reinvent themselves in the interstices of temporal logics.

Located in an old industrial building near the River Spree, the Berghain offered similarly exceptional affective experiences. Described as the "birthplace of memories, the Heimat for Drag-Queens, the shelter for the insane, and the residence of atmosphere," the Berghain was unforgettable. "There was this spirit that was palpable in the entire Berghain that here everything was possible. [. . .] The moments in the Berghain were always enormous. The feelings were too intensive to be real. You didn't know whether you had landed in the middle of hell or heaven. You just constantly transgressed your own boundaries and when you finally came out into the old world, you needed days to work through everything that you had done, seen and heard in these 20 hours."[78] At times, these dance floor ecstasies spilled out into the streets. Writing about the Love Parade in Berlin, for example, Slavko Stefanoski noted that "it was a movement, a philosophy of life. We were living at the center of the world."[79] It also increasingly spilled out into the virtual world. After the Elektro club was evicted from its space in Mitte for stealing electricity in 1994, for example, its founder Daniel Pflumm made the decision to take his art and music to the Internet.[80]

The repetitive beats and irreverent sampling associated with techno proved to be a particularly useful tool for fragmenting established temporal logics and for forging new subjectivities and sociabilities in the interstitial spaces opened up therein.[81] Music, according to the theorist Simon Frith, is exceptionally well suited for experimenting with time: it "enables us to experience time aesthetically, intellectually, *and* physically in new ways. [. . .] Music, to put this another way, allows us to stop time, while we consider how it passes."[82] Writing about sampling, Simon Reynolds makes a similar argument: as "ghosts you can control," recorded music "is pretty freaky, then, if you think about it. But sampling doubles its inherent supernaturalism. Woven out of looped moments that are each like portals to far-flung times and places, the sample collage creates a musical event that never happened; a mixture of time-travel and séance."[83] As a musical form that consists of rhythmic distortion and sampled quotations from other musical genres and from everyday life, techno fits these descriptions well. It enabled dancers and musicians to reorganize and weave together the rhythms of the body and of the historically resonant environment into a collective algorithm for experiencing and experimenting with space and time, a soundtrack for dwelling asynchronously.

Although techno clubs were certainly among the most popular locations for experiencing the uniquely expansive subjectivities and the anarchist temporal practices associated with ruin dwelling, they were far from the only such venues. Describing a peculiar bar named Sniper, for example, Andreas Busche wrote: "The Sniper knows no beginning and no end: a loop that one can enter and leave like a video installation in a museum. The club as temporal medium. [. . .] On a screen in the back of the shop the most bizarre video collages were running every evening [. . .], everything cut together, chopped up, superimposed, reassembled, looped, stretched into eternity." These loops "put the audience into a debilitated trance like state." Added to all of this was a "nerve inducing sound [. . .] an unrelenting muzak" made up of diverse musical genres as well as samples from the media, which the author admiringly described as form of "plunderphonics."[84]

Berlin's burgeoning ruin dwellers were not above poking fun at the mystical pretensions of their own activist practices. In a flyer titled "Germaneninfo Nr. 1" from August 1990, for example, the authors initially conformed to the established patterns of a formulaic self-introduction. They began by noting that they were a group of Westphalians who wanted to convey their ideas to the public. These ideas, however, were far from typical. They included: "the retention of archaic shamanism [. . .] the conservation and protection of magical places of worship and hallucinogenic plants [. . .] complete information against collective stultification [*Verdummung*] and the creation of a creative chaos—using all media from computers to telepathy."[85] This same group also submitted a rather long self-introduction to AK Kraak, which opened in a wilderness setting with people in leather jackets and black jeans methodically building a shrine atop a rock formation. After a few minutes a naked man emerges from the nearby pond and begins drinking from a skull while discussing the politics of squatting, the healing power of the sun, and the fascist misappropriation of mysticism. Contributing yet another layer of absurdity to the scene, a cat scrambles to remain perched on the speaker's naked body, eliciting breaks in the mystical soliloquy as well as peals of laughter from the camera crew.[86] In another instance, which took place in Mitte years later, a group of artists connected to the formerly squatted house on the Auguststraße 10, better known as the Culture and Life Project, or KuLe, painted slogans outside of the house reading "Destroy what," "Resistance requires," and "are pigs," all of which are comically incomplete versions of popular political slogans from the squatting movement.[87] Even the legacies of the early 1980s youth movements, it seems, were ripe for creative misuse and became part of the citational maelstrom.

This carnival of anarchist negation and creative destruction met a serious roadblock with the brutal eviction of the Mainzer Straße. The chain of events leading to the eviction of the Mainzer Straße commenced on the

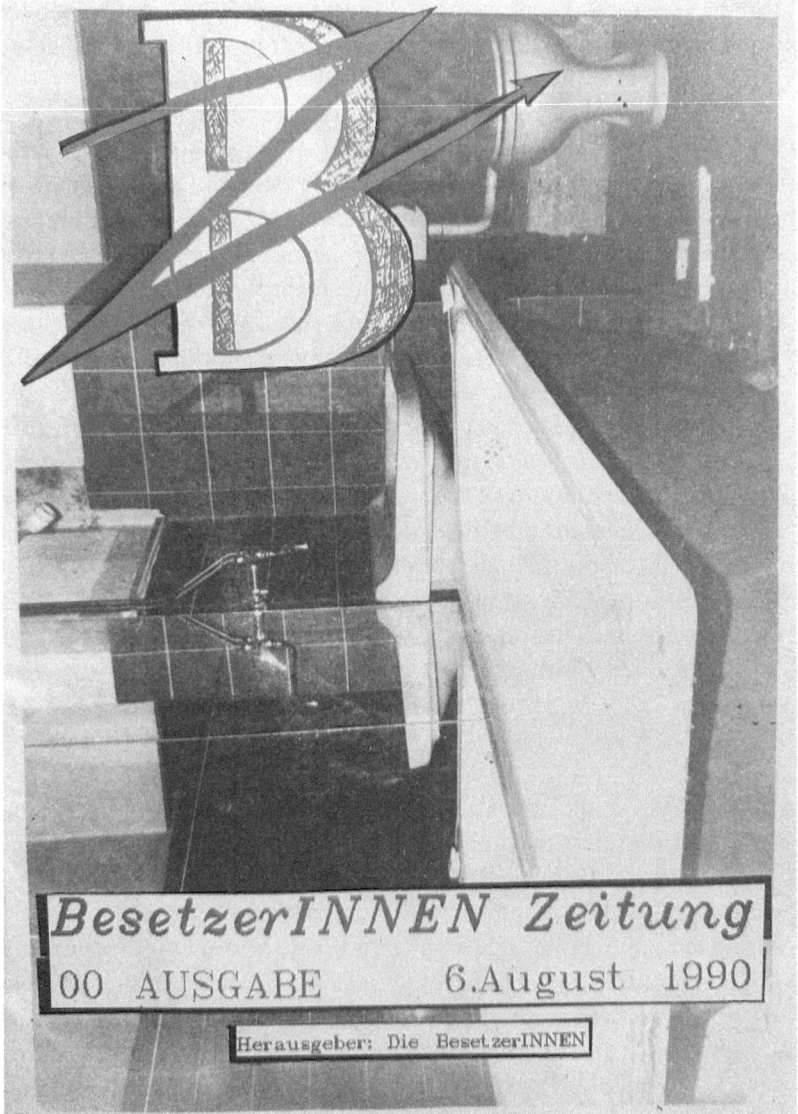

FIGURE 6.4. Front cover of *BesetzerInnen Zeitung* (Nr. 00, August 6, 1990). Source: International Institute of Social History, Amsterdam.

November 12, 1990, as activists gathered to protest the clearance of the Pfarrstraße 112 and the Cotheniusstraße 16.[88] The situation quickly escalated over the following days as masked *Autonomen* from across northern Europe, and, if the authorities are to be believed, especially from the Hafenstraße in Hamburg, built barricades in the streets, threw rocks and Molotov

Cocktails from rooftops, and refused to vacate the area. Thousands of police officers moved in on the morning of the fourteenth and, after many hours of violent conflict with the squatters and their supporters, successfully took control of the street. In the wake of the eviction, in which numerous people were injured and almost three hundred fifty arrested, many reacted with anger, sadness, and disbelief.[89] Whereas conservative city officials depicted the events as "riots [that] have nothing to do with social or political protest but are simply violent criminality of the worst sort" and argued that the Mainzer Straße residents "manifested an appalling rejection of all the peaceful values that constitute our society," others harshly critiqued police violence and the astounding duplicity of city authorities.[90] An editorial in *Telegraph*, for example, mused that the clearance of the Mainzer Straße was primarily meant to break the opposition to urban renewal.[91] An article in the *Besetzerinnenzeitung* suspected more than urban renewal was at the root of the violence, noting: "The fact that leftist and antifascist literature was destroyed, reminds us of bygone times and throws a large shadow on your supposed 'understanding of democracy.'"[92] Many neighbors joined the critical chorus with some claiming that the police actions reminded them of fascist times and others simply lamenting that, after the squatters' eviction, the Mainzer Straße was once again "damned gloomy."[93]

⁂

In the wake of the Mainzer Straße eviction, the boundless optimism and negationist carnivals of 1989–90 began receding into the background. Many activists, echoing the reformist Müsli strategies of the mid-1980s, shifted their focus toward developing alternative lifestyles within the houses and securing long-term rental agreements. At times the overtures for peaceful negotiation came from progressive city officials who wanted both to secure space for alternative lifestyles and avoid the disruptions and violence of the Mainzer Straße eviction. In a November 16th letter from the Residential Property Developer in Prenzlauer Berg to the Besetzerrat Prenzlauer Berg, for example, officials reiterated their strong desire to negotiate rental agreements for the majority of the houses in their jurisdiction.[94] The lengthy and oftentimes Byzantine negotiations between the various official organizations in charge of housing issues and the Prenzlauer Berg Besetzerrat eventually led to an agreement on November 1, 1991, commonly known as the Prenzlauer Line.[95] Squatters in other neighborhoods such as Mitte and Friedrichshain worked for similarly wide-ranging agreements, although with much less success.[96] Activists in Mitte even looked into the possibility of securing sponsors in the hopes that, if nothing else, the houses could "remain as cultural and social food for thought," monuments to moments of alternative temporal imaginaries.[97]

While many squatters seemed content with the prospect of integrating themselves into the landscape of the New Berlin as social and cultural "food for thought," others had no such intention. In the wake of the Mainzer Straße evictions, many autonomous leftists renewed their commitment to decontextualized modes of violent opposition. In the Volxsport declaration "Klarheit für Berlin" the authors noted that they had "de-glassed" the SPD offices and desecrated those of the Alternative List. They then reproduced statements of solidarity from cities throughout Germany and Europe. One statement from Hannover seethed: "Our hate is immeasurable. We know that it is not just about Berlin but about all of the squatted houses and centers, and about all those who are involved in the fight."[98] A solidarity declaration from Italy titled "A Fire Unites Us" noted: "A line of fire and revolt against the ruling classes has erupted, against their banks, their cities and their decisions. It is a fire that leaves marks, a fire that unites us and above all our indestructible joy and anger to fight, to destroy the linchpins of the imperial society, to weave a network of oppositional forces and to work our way along the path of liberation."[99] Another article in *Interim* encouraged readers to resist the trend toward privatization. Gesturing toward the mystical anarchist philosophies of Hakim Bey, they argued that the squats represented "fields of experimentation, nests, refuge castles, robbers caves and pirate ships. They are freed spaces. They have a power which is often only recognized after its gone" and thus must be defended at all costs.[100] For these activists, then, a retreat into private spaces and the comforts of local contexts was never a real possibility. Reviving the rhetoric of the Mollis, they argued that the battle must be taken to new heights, that Berlin represented one small theater in the increasingly global conflict between us and them. It is safe to assume, I think, that many of these activists subsequently shifted to the antiglobalization movements of the 1990s, perhaps taking part in events like the 1999 Carnival against Capitalism, the anti-G8 protests in Genoa in 2011, and the so-called Blockupy movement in Frankfurt.[101]

In the months and years following the eviction of the Mainzer Straße, the dreams of an expansive leftist counterpublic sphere motivated by postprogressive forms of infinite becoming and a network of those engaged in insurgent forms of dwellings faded somewhat. History seemed to be repeating itself: the movement had failed once again. And yet, as was also the case in the wake of the youth revolts of 1980–81, things had changed. Not only did the explosion of activism in the streets and squatted buildings of East Berlin rejuvenate members of the autonomous left who, after their defeat at the Mainzer Straße, set off on international adventures to combat a newly reinvigorated form of global capitalism. It also left its mark on the people, the places, and the culture of Berlin. More than just memorials to difference, traces of the postprogressive practices of 1989–90 remained apparent throughout the city, often becoming myths that would draw countless visitors.

According to Anton Waldt, for example, techno clubs such as Tresor bore "striking similarities" to the "energy, intensity, [and] brutal pathos" of the three day long battle over the Mainzer Straße and thus allowed a wide range of people to experience the affective qualities of 1989–90.[102] Similarly, as Daniela Sandler and Alexander Vasudevan have both argued, the squatting movement in Berlin fundamentally changed the city's urban practices, initiating what Sandler has called "a critical way of thinking about history and the city."[103] Historian Briana Smith has pointed to the ways in which art milieus in Berlin continued to promote alternative visions of the city well into the twenty-first century. According to Smith the egalitarian and creative "impulses" developed by leftist and countercultural artists "live on in contemporary Berlin: fueling artists' resolve to work outside of the market and organize in solidarity, and residents' vigorous defense of green spaces, affordable housing, and collectivist projects from capitalist incursions."[104] The maximalist dreams of these years may have faded, but the movement left traces that clung to the walls, the streets, and the sounds of the city, calling on people to look beyond the smooth veneer of the everyday and see the structures of capitalism and modernity "as the illusory dream images they always were," to tear down these structures of domination, and to build new worlds in the ruins.[105] In the end, then, some of the spaces of concrete negation developed during the heyday of the movement did become "food for thought," representational spaces of transgression and opposition made for public consumption—but if, as Vasudevan writes, such spaces "insist on the very possibility of a radically different understanding of what it means to think about and inhabit cities," then this seems like a victory.[106]

Epilogue

Reminiscing about his experiences in the squatting movement that roiled Berlin during the *Wende*, David Wagner wrote:

> Once upon a time, Berlin-Mitte was a wish-fulfilment zone [. . .] . Mitte was a frenzy of repurposing. The magic phrase was "temporary use." Jet fighters abandoned by a retreating superpower managed to become monuments in the very heart of the city. [. . .] Empty streets, crumbling façades—was the war still on? Or had it perhaps not even taken place here? Didn't everything look like the 1920s, didn't it all look like a film set? [. . .] It was so easy to be amazed. Mitte had dropped out of time— and was stuck in several different pasts at once. Pre-war and pre-pre-war, partly GDR and partly some strange inbetween-era where once again Germany had ceased to exist, but its new version hadn't actually come about yet. Mitte was in a gap. It became the magic city of the inbetween. It became a wish-fulfillment zone, everything was possible. There was dancing. There was dancing and drinking. And the eyes of the ruin-dwellers sparkled with the happiness of those who are in the right place at the right time [. . .] . It was tremendous in the rubble, it was a gigantic playground.[1]

A more poignant description of the ecstatic temporal forms and the radical sensibilities that reigned in the months surrounding reunification would be difficult to envision.

The surfeit of asynchronous objects and spaces in unification-era Berlin sparked a carnival of anarchist creativity in which the postprogressive practices that had developed over the course of the 1980s reached a new level of intensity. Just as they had in the youth movements of 1980–81, the uncanny traces of outmoded social, political, and economic forms still served as tools with which to fracture the narrative logics of progress and to construct experimental forms of being in time. In 1989–90, however, acts of outright negation came to take a back seat to acts of creative becoming. In interstitial spaces like Tresor, Tacheles, and the Mainzer Straße, anarchist youth sought to dwell among the manifold fragments of collapsing temporal logics and experiment with new forms of subjectivity and sociability outside of what Anna Lowenhaupt Tsing has called the "handrails" of progress.[2] Unlike the progressive temporal regimes that had infused much of postwar German life which sought to erase, contain, or narratively subsume traces of the past in order to generate feelings of momentum toward the future, squatters and other ruin dwellers largely refused to reintegrate these fragments of outmoded pasts into new structures of meaning. Categorically refusing to engage in acts of narrative closure allowed activists to cultivate a new mode of being in time in which the past remained present and the future remained open. Not only did these postprogressive modes of temporal practice facilitate acts of negation and endless becoming, they also helped to forge spaces of insurgent dwelling and belonging. The ruin dwellers of late twentieth-century Germany would likely have agreed with Michel de Certeau's suggestion that haunting was a prerequisite for dwelling authentically.[3]

Many activists, however, remained deeply skeptical of these practices. In some cases, the extraordinarily rapid expansion of the movement in 1989–90 coupled with the increasingly carnivalesque atmosphere it engendered elicited questions about the value and the viability of these postprogressive forms of being in time. Some wondered, not without reason, whether the focus on constant negation and endless becoming was leading to a worrisome erasure of lived experience and whether the exhilarating feeling of transcending space and time meant that many of the practitioners of postprogressive politics were disappearing into a haze of unmoored spectacle.[4] They worried, in other words, that postprogressive forms of being in time served the interests of capitalist value creation in which everything solid was melted into air.

In some cases, artists designed performances that sought to directly interrogate these issues. In a December 1990 performance, for example, a group of artists organized a fake occupation and invited visitors to attend. Upon passing through the human chain that had been formed to prevent the police from evicting the "squat," visitors entered the house through a small hole in the wall and then passed through a dark room with a voice intoning: "This is a new occupation. The new occupation is art. Art is not political." Visitors then proceeded upstairs to find an exhibition depicting the very real occupation and November 1990 eviction of the Mainzer Straße squat. The exhibit text is worth quoting at length: "You find yourself in an art exhibit. Everything that transpires in the space of this exhibit is simulated. The pictures that you see are deceptively similar reproductions of reality. [. . .] The police are playing the role of the police and you are playing the role of the exhibit visitors. The house is playing the role of an empty house being occupied. [. . .] The exhibit is an occupation. [. . .] You will experience the effect of police violence on your retinas, more exciting than in the movies, more vividly than on television. [. . .] Enjoy the adventure of a new occupation. One of the last adventures in our society."[5] In a commentary on the performance in the popular squatting newspaper the *Besetzerinnenzeitung*, the author expressed her lingering sense of confusion about the event, writing: "Somehow, I still don't quite understand whether this was some sort of film or not. Although I was actually present for the entire event, it still seems completely unreal."[6]

In an article in *Die Tageszeitung* reacting to a similar performance which took place many years later at the KuLe in which artists hung signs with comically incomplete versions of popular political slogans from the squatting movement on the walls of the building, Uwe Rada seemed simultaneously amused and perturbed by the performance, wondering: "Where does the space of self-irony end, and where does seriousness begin?"[7] As was true for many dialectically inclined leftists, Rada interpreted this refusal to reintegrate acts of negation into established narratives of revolutionary change as basically apolitical. The author of another article accompanying Rada's piece was much less ambivalent, acerbically noting: "The Tacheles [another well-known art/squat project in Berlin-Mitte] is now nothing but a ruin of its former self and simply waits to be cleared. There are hardly any more political impulses coming from the squatted houses." The only thing remaining of the squatting movement in Berlin, the author concluded, was "art, commerce, fashion."[8]

Although these critiques were leveled at artistic installations, they could just as easily have applied to many of the carnivalesque, postprogressive practices developed by the multiple generations of activists described in this book. Joining a long and illustrious line of leftist critics in West Germany, ranging from Jürgen Habermas and Rudi Dutschke to Wolfgang Kraushaar and Bernd Rabehl, these commentators dismissed the anarchist practices of the postprogressive left as apolitical, unreflexive genuflections to capitalism. Just as earlier generations of activists had dismissed the unruly, off-modern edges of the antiauthoritarian left, so again did leftist critics in the 1990s deride the irrational performances and the ecstatic temporal imaginaries that characterized postprogressive activist milieus as counterproductive, narcissistic harbingers of gentrification and commerce. Postprogressive temporal practices, in this reading, were not tools of liberation and renewal but a capitulation to state power and an unwitting reiteration of capitalism's static temporal logics in which the promises of the always new were in actuality always just more of the same.

To a certain extent, these critics have a point. The former centers of postprogressive activism have indeed often developed into hip locales with booming art and fashion scenes as well as exorbitant rent prices, areas to which artists, musicians, and alternative tourists flock for inspiration and adventure. This is certainly the case, for example, in many areas of contemporary Berlin, where the graffiti that once signaled an anarchist rejection of mainstream aesthetics and a desire to create radical new forms of being in time is now more often than not interpreted as a symbol of "up-and-coming" neighborhoods, well suited for young "creatives."[9] The popularity of these former sites of anarchist experimentation has not escaped the notice of place marketers within the city who have sought to capitalize on Berlin's particular appeal for the global youth market by explicitly championing the city's clubs, nightlife, and art scene.[10] A 2009 brochure from the Berlin Partner's marketing group noted: "Here you can be whatever you want [because] Berlin is the place to be for individuality."[11] Nor has it escaped the notice of property developers throughout the city who have attempted to capitalize on Berlin's reputation for hipness by radically increasing property values.[12] The alternative spaces and anarchist practices of Berlin are, so it seems, slowly being incorporated into the urban landscape as the unique and desirable quirks of a creative city on the rise.

Similarly, as the organizers of the Mainzer Straße exhibit suggested, postprogressive temporal practices have also become increasingly unmoored from the concrete concerns of embedded placeworlds. In many instances, these practices have morphed into transposable modes of being in time, which individuals and corporations across the globe can mobilize to generate cultural capital. In this sense, postprogressive practices serve as tools in the service of capitalist value creation in which the feelings of transcendent becoming generated by asynchronous objects and environments are subsumed into consumerist narratives of self-creation. Rather than radical mechanisms for upending chrononormative modes of being in time, they have become signifiers of hipness that represent no danger to dominant forms of power. Historian Joe Perry has made similar arguments in regard to the legacies of techno, the early radicalism of which, he claims, quickly dissipated as it fell victim to capitalism's tendency to appropriate, commodify, and thus domesticate all forms of difference. The story of techno in Berlin, Perry writes, "reveals the quicksilver mutation of subversive behaviors and identities into accepted and even profitable aspects of officially promoted 'underground' urban scenes. And it shows the ineluctable gobbling-up of potentially transgressive cultural forms by insatiable commercial and political interests."[13] This is clearly happening on a broad scale in Berlin and in capitalist societies across the globe, but it is not, I would like to suggest in closing, the inevitable outcome of postprogressive temporal imaginaries.

Recent years have witnessed a profusion of academic voices calling for a more wide-ranging and more critical interrogation of the temporal logics of progress.[14] For some, progress, modernity, and historicism represent fundamentally exclusionary forms of temporal consciousness that denigrate and even erase alternative temporalities. To counteract this state of affairs, they propose cultivating critical forms of academic analysis and ways of knowing that offer a more robust engagement with diverse temporal logics.[15] Others have focused on the ways in which identities and environments that have been deemed obsolete by the disciplinary, chrononormative dimensions of the modern time regime have developed alternative modes of being in time that have the potential to disrupt and potentially overturn contemporary forms of domination.[16] As Elizabeth Freeman, among others, has argued, these groups are engaged in a process of "inventing possibilities for moving through and with time, speculating futures, and interpenetrating the two in ways that counter the common sense of the present tense."[17] They serve as "interruptions" and as "points of resistance" to the temporal logics of modernity, and as such they "propose other possibilities for living in relation to indeterminately past, present, and future others: that is, of living historically."[18] Gary Wilder makes a similar point in his discussion of "concrete utopianism," writing that in its many different iterations, this practice "seeks to *render* everyday life subversively uncanny and untimely. It makes the familiar strange and the strange familiar. It makes pasts present and it anticipates, or conjures, futures now."[19]

Postprogressive forms of temporal disruption, these authors suggest, might offer a new route forward, a way to continue breaking through into the new, but one shorn of progressive modernity's tendency to subsume and eradicate difference. The future toward which these practitioners of temporal dissonance strive must be one that is not conceived as "the terminus of progress but as a redemption of the oppressed," as "chronopolitical rebellions against capitalism and its attendant narratives of progress."[20] One might reasonably counter such claims by noting that contemporary capitalism seems already to be engaged in processes of disruption and fragmentation and that such strategies thus run the risk of furthering these destructive trends under the guise of rebellion. As Joe Perry and many others have argued, capitalism has always been particularly adept at incorporating alternative temporal logics, and especially those built around forms of disruption, into its ever-expanding maelstrom of creative destruction.

According to the theorists associated with the French anarchist collective known as the Invisible Committee, however, this is not a reason to throw up one's hands in despair. The increasing fragmentation of our world, they claim, "can also give rise to an intensification and pluralization *of the bonds that constitute us*." Fragmentation, then, "doesn't [only] signify separation," it also represents "a shimmering of the world," a possibility to redeem the past and to forge new connections and new futures amid the rapidly proliferating fragments of our present.[21] Unlike earlier social movements, they go on to claim, the goal here is not to create a new social contract that, like the progressive temporal forms of the modern time regime, forcibly unites all of these fragments into a new system of meaning, but a "new strategic composition of worlds."[22]

Perhaps, then, in these times of collapse and fragmentation as well as neofascist attempts to counteract these trajectories with increasingly violent and exclusionary visions centered around nationalist restoration, we can look to the manifold practices developed by postprogressive activists in late twentieth-century Germany as well as the *many* other groups who have engaged in similar practices for ways to forge a new path forward. Dwelling amid an array of increasingly unmoored objects, environments, and bodies, can, to quote the authors of *Bewegungslehre* one last time, serve as "steppingstones to 'another reality.'"[23] Following in the footsteps of the ruin dwellers of the late twentieth century, we might all be on the lookout for objects and places, through which, to quote Vladimir Nabokov, "the past shines."[24]

Acknowledgments

This book would not have been possible were it not for the extraordinary levels of support I have received over the past many years from a wide range of people and institutions. I would like to thank the institutions that financially supported this work, including the Berlin Program for Advanced European Studies at the Freie Universität in Berlin, the history departments at Colorado College and the University of Chicago, and the Dean's Office and Crown Center at Colorado College; Douglas Fix, my advisor at Reed College, whose subaltern studies course helped to spark my interest in history; Leora Auslander, Michael Geyer, Moishe Postone, and Tara Zahra, my mentors at the University of Chicago, who believed in me even when I didn't and from whom I have learned an immeasurable amount; friends whom I met in my time at Chicago, including Misha Appeltova, Jake Betz, Sarah Miller-Davenport, Susannah Engstrom, Joachim Häberlen, Phillip Henry, Patrick Houlihan, Ke-Chin Hsia, Reha Kadakal, Semyon Khokhlov, Michael Kozakowski, Sam Lebovic, Emily Lord Fransee, Emily Marker, Katya Motyl, Sarah Panzer, Eleanor Rivera, Peter Simons, Lauren Stokes, Andrew Tompkins, Emily Weaver, and Michael Williams; my colleagues at the Berlin Program for European Studies, including Adam Bisno, Nicole Eaton, Lisa Haegele, Erika Hughes, Ryan Johnson, Akasemi Newsome, Alicia VandeVusse, Allison Vos, William Waltz, and Karin Goihl; my colleagues in the history department at Colorado College, Amy Kohout, Bryan Rommel-Ruiz, Carol Neel, Danielle Sanchez, Doug Monroy, Jamal Ratchford, Jane Murphy, Jennifer Golightly, John Williams, Paul Adlerstein, Peter Blasenheim, Purvi Mehta, Susan Ashley, and Tip Ragan; the staff at the University of Chicago Press, including Dylan Montanari, Fabiola Enríquez Flores, Mary Al-Sayed, and Tamara Ghattas, as well as Rosina Busse Grove, who copyedited the manuscript on behalf of the press, all of whom provided help without which I would have been utterly lost; the brilliant students I've had the pleasure of teaching at the University of Chicago and Colorado College; my research assistants Star Goudriaan and Jolie Curran; the many readers of draft versions of my manuscript, including the anonymous readers from the press as well as Jennifer Allen, Monica Black, Alice Goff, and Claudia Verhoeven; my extended family in Arkansas and Connecticut; my parents Tom and Bonnie and my sisters Alex and Suni; John Troyer and Barbara Sanders, who I wish could have seen this project through to its completion; Gwyn, Griffin, and Zara, who were always there when I needed them; the amazing archivists in Amsterdam, Berlin, Freiburg, Hamburg, and Zurich; and finally, the activists and artists whose courage and creativity inspired me throughout the writing of this book.

Notes

INTRODUCTION

1. Benny Härlin, "Von Haus zu Haus—Berliner Bewegungsstudien," *Kursbuch* 65 (1981): 1–28.

2. Although I will occasionally reference squatting and youth movements in other Western European cities such as Amsterdam and Zurich, I primarily focus on the youth movements in West Germany.

3. Gerd Koenen, *Das rote Jahrzehnt: Unsere kleine deutsche Kulturrevolution, 1967–1977* (Cologne: Kiepenhauer & Witsche, 2001). On leftist protest in 1960s West Germany, see among others: Timothy Scott Brown and Lorena Anton, eds., *Between the Avant-Garde and the Everyday: Subversive Politics in Europe from 1957 to the Present* (New York: Berghahn Books, 2011); Tilman Fichter and Siegward Lönnendonker, *Kleine Geschichte des SDS* (Essen: Klartext, 2007); Robert Gildea, James Mark, and Anette Warring, eds., *Europe's 1968: Voices of Revolt* (Oxford: Oxford University Press, 2013); Ingrid Giltcher-Holtey, *Die 68er Bewegung: Deutschland, Westeuropa, USA* (Munich: CH Beck, 2001); Martin Klimke, *The Other Alliance: Student Protest in West Germany and the United States in the Global Sixties* (Princeton, NJ: Princeton University Press, 2010); Martin Klimke and Joachim Scharloth, eds., *1968: Handbuch zur Kultur- und Mediengeschichte der Studentenbewegung* (Stuttgart: J.B. Metzler, 2007); Quinn Slobodian, *Foreign Front: Third World Politics in Sixties West Germany* (Durham: Duke University Press, 2012); and Sabine von Dirke, *All Power to the Imagination! The West German Counterculture from the Student Movement to the Greens* (Lincoln: University of Nebraska Press, 1996). On squatting and related movements, see, among others, Claudio Cattaneo and Miguel Martinez, eds., *The Squatters' Movement in Europe: Commons and Autonomy as Alternatives to Capitalism* (London: Pluto, 2014); Joachim Häberlen and Jake P. Smith, "Struggling for Feelings: The Politics of Emotions in the Radical New Left in West Germany, c. 1968–84," *Contemporary European History* 23, no. 4 (November 2014): 615–37, https://doi.org/10.1017/S0960777314000344; Armin Kuhn, *Vom Häuserkampf zur neoliberalen Stadt: Besetzungsbewegungen und Stadterneuerung in Berlin und Barcelona* (Münster: Westfälisches Dampfboot, 2014); Lynn Owens, *Cracking Under Pressure: Narrating the Decline of the Amsterdam Squatters' Movement* (University Park: Pennsylvania State University Press, 2009); Squatting Europe Kollective, *Squatting in Europe: Radical Spaces, Urban Struggles* (New York: Minor Compositions, 2013); Bart van der Steen and Ask Katzeff, eds., *The City Is Ours: Squatting and Autonomous Movements in Europe from the 1970s to the Present* (Oakland: PM Press, 2014); Bart van

der Steen and Knud Andresen, eds., *A European Youth Revolt: European Perspectives on Youth Protest and Social Movements in the 1980s* (New York: Palgrave, 2016); Andreas Suttner, *"Beton brennt": Hausbesetzer und Selbstverwaltung im Berlin, Wien und Zürich der 8oer Jahre* (Vienna: Lit, 2011); and Alexander Vasudevan, *Metropolitan Preoccupations: The Spatial Politics of Squatting in Berlin* (Malden: Wiley Blackwell, 2015).

4. Härlin, "Von Haus zu Haus," 11.

5. Härlin, "Von Haus zu Haus," 11.

6. For an overview of the new left's use of militancy in the 1970s, see Luca Provenzano, "'Power Is in the Streets': Protest and Militancy in France, Italy, and West Germany, 1968–1979," *Contemporary European History* (2023): 1–18, https://doi.org/10.1017/S096077732300022X.

7. Although certainly an important dimension of antiauthoritarian activism in the 1960s, it was not until the 1970s that these ideas of power and everyday life became truly ubiquitous within West German leftist milieus. In part, this was surely a result of the growing popularity of poststructuralist thinkers like Michel Foucault, but it was also due to the analyses of power developed by activists in the Women's Movement. On the West German Women's Movement and its relationship to the New Left, see Christina von Hodenberg, *The Other '68: A Social History of West Germany's Revolt* (Oxford: Oxford University Press, 2024).

8. On some of the larger ideological patterns within anarchist politics, see David Graeber, *Direct Action: An Ethnography* (Oakland: AK Press, 2009).

9. Härlin, "Von Haus zu Haus," 24.

10. Terence Renaud, *New Lefts: The Making of a Radical Tradition* (Princeton, NJ: Princeton University Press, 2021).

11. Härlin, "Von Haus zu Haus," 25.

12. Härlin, "Von Haus zu Haus," 15.

13. Härlin, "Von Haus zu Haus," 7.

14. Härlin, "Von Haus zu Haus," 24–25.

15. In this sense, the youth activists of the 1980s were reviving anarchist ideas from the late nineteenth and early twentieth centuries, which also sought to undermine the validity of progressive timelines and representational politics. This shift toward anarchist thought was also apparent within some segments of the antiauthoritarian left of the 1960s, though in most cases they tended to temper such anarchist ideas with more orthodox Marxist positions. For a particularly radical example of this, see Daniel Cohn-Bendit and Gabriel Cohn-Bendit, *Obsolete Communism: The Left-Wing Alternative* (Oakland: AK Press, 2001 [1968]).

16. On the alternative milieu see Sven Reichardt, *Authentizität und Gemeinschaft: Linksalternatives Leben in den siebziger und frühen achtziger Jahren* (Berlin: Suhrkamp, 2014); and Sven Reichardt and Detlef Siegfried, eds., *Das Alternative Milieu: Antibürgerlicher Lebensstil und linke Politik in der Bundesrepublik Deutschland und Europa, 1968–1983* (Göttingen: Wallstein Verlag, 2010).

17. Fehlfarben, "Ein Jahr (es geht voran)," track 8 on *Monarchie und Alltag* (EMI Studios, 1980).

18. See in particular Gilles Deleuze and Félix Guattari, *A Thousand Plateaus: Capitalism and Schizophrenia* (Minneapolis: University of Minnesota Press, 1987).

19. This tended to be true even in the way that the youth activists of the 1980s engaged with the legacies of earlier leftist movements. Ritualistic disavowals of the 1960s New Left were almost always paired with attempts to resuscitate the aesthetic practices and ideas of manifold new lefts.

20. Härlin, "Von Haus zu Haus," 12–13.

21. Härlin, "Von Haus zu Haus," 26.

22. Härlin, "Von Haus zu Haus," 6.

23. Walter Benjamin, "Theses on the Philosophy of History," in *Illuminations: Essays and Reflections*, ed. Hannah Arendt (New York: Schocken, 1968), 261.

24. François Hartog, *Regimes of Historicity: Presentism and Experiences of Time*, trans. Saskia Brown (New York: Columbia University Press, 2015), xv.

25. Hartog, *Regimes of Historicity*, 149. On historical tourism and heritage sites in German-speaking Europe, see Valentin Groebner, *Retroland: Geschichtstourismus und die Sehnsucht nach dem Authentischen* (Frankfurt: Fischer, 2018).

26. Hans Ulrich Gumbrecht, *Our Broad Present: Time and Contemporary Culture* (New York: Columbia University Press, 2014), xiii. See also Andreas Huyssen, *Twilight Memories: Marking Time in a Culture of Amnesia* (New York: Routledge, 1995).

27. Fredric Jameson, "Postmodernism, or the Cultural Logic of Late Capitalism," *New Left Review* 1/146 (July/August 1984).

28. See Aleida Assmann, *Is Time out of Joint? On the Rise and Fall of the Modern Time Regime* (Ithaca: Cornell University Press, 2020); Lou Cornum, "Seizing the Alterity of Futures: Toward a Philosophy of History across Afrofuturism and Indigenous Futurism," *History of the Present* 13, no. 2 (October 2023): 166–91, https://doi.org/10.1215/21599785-10630116; Elizabeth Freeman, *Time Binds: Queer Temporalities, Queer Histories* (Durham: Duke University Press, 2010); Chris Lorenz and Berber Bevernage, eds., *Breaking up Time: Negotiating the Borders Between Past, Present and Future* (Göttingen: Vandenhoek & Ruprecht, 2013); José Esteban Muñoz, *Cruising Utopia: The Then and There of Queer Futurity* (New York: New York University Press, 2009); Marek Tamm and Laurent Olivier, eds., *Rethinking Historical Time: New Approaches to Presentism* (New York: Bloomsbury, 2019); Massimiliano Tomba, *Insurgent Universality: An Alternative Legacy of Modernity* (Oxford: Oxford University Press, 2019); and Gary Wilder, *Concrete Utopianism: The Politics of Temporality and Solidarity* (New York: Fordham University Press, 2022).

29. The phrase is taken from Kristin Ross's extraordinary book *May '68 and Its Afterlives* (Chicago: University of Chicago Press, 2002). My ideas here are also indebted to Ross's work on the Paris Commune in her book *Communal Luxury: The Political Imaginary of the Paris Commune* (London: Verso, 2015).

30. Konrad Jarausch, *After Hitler: Recivilizing Germans, 1945–1995*, trans. Brandon Hunziker (Oxford: Oxford University Press, 2006).

31. See Pascal Eitler and Jens Elberfeld, eds., *Zeitgeschichte des Selbst: Therapeutisierung, Politisierung, Emotionalisierung* (Bielefeld: Transcript, 2015); Moritz Föllmer, "Cities of Choice: Elective Affinities and the Transformation of Western European

Urbanity from the Mid-1950s to the Early 1980s," *Contemporary European History* 24, no. 4 (2015): 577–96, https://doi.org/10.1017/S096077731500034X; Sabine Maasen, Jens Elberfeld, Pascal Eitler, and Maik Tändler, eds., *Das beratene Selbst: zur Genealogie der Therapeutisierung in den 'langen' Siebzigern* (Bielefeld: Transcript, 2011); Reichardt, *Authentizität und Gemeinschaft*; Isabel Richter, "Psychonauts and Seekers: West German Entanglements in the Spiritual Turn of the Global 1960s and 1970s," *Contemporary European History* 33, no. 1 (2024): 250–66, https://doi.org/10.1017/S0960777322000121; Alexander Sedlmaier, *Consumption and Violence: Radical Protest in Cold-War West Germany* (Ann Arbor: University of Michigan Press, 2014); Detlef Siegfried, *Time Is on My Side: Konsum und Politik in der Westdeutschen Jugendkultur der 60er Jahre* (Göttingen: Wallstein Verlag, 2006); and many of the essays in Reichardt and Siegfried, eds., *Das Alternative Milieu*.

32. On the role played by the Nazi past in West German new lefts, see Timothy Scott Brown, *West Germany and the Global Sixties: The Antiauthoritarian Revolts, 1962–1978* (Cambridge: Cambridge University Press, 2013); Hans Kundani, *Utopia or Auschwitz? Germany's 1968 Generation and the Holocaust* (New York: Columbia University Press, 2009); A. Dirk Moses, *German Intellectuals and the Nazi Past* (Cambridge: Cambridge University Press, 2007); and Jeremy Varon, *Bringing the War Home: The Weather Underground, the Red Army Faction, and Revolutionary Violence in the Sixties and Seventies* (Berkeley: University of California Press, 2004). On the relationship between leftist practice and shifting ideas of the future, see Jennifer Allen, *Sustainable Utopias: The Art and Politics of Hope in Germany* (Cambridge, MA: Harvard University Press, 2022); Frank Biess, *Republik der Angst: Eine Andere Geschichte der Bundesrepublik* (Reinbeck bei Hamburg: Rowohlt, 2019); and Silke Mende, "Das 'Momo'-Syndrom: Zeitvorstellungen im alternativen Milieu und in den 'neuen' Protestbewegungen," in *Zeitenwandel: Transformationen Geschichtlicher Zeitlichkeit nach dem Boom*, ed. Fernando Esposito (Göttingen: Vandenhoeck & Ruprecht, 2017), 153–92. On temporality in the 1980s youth movements, see Lukas Hezel, "'Was gibt es zu verlieren, wo es kein Morgen gibt?' Chronopolitik und Radikalisierung in der Jugendrevolte 1980/81 und bei den Autonomen," in *Zeitenwandel: Transformationen Geschichtlicher Zeitlichkeit nach dem Boom*, ed. Fernando Esposito (Göttingen: Vandenhoeck & Ruprecht, 2017), 119–52; Joachim Häberlen, *The Emotional Politics of the Alternative Left: West Germany, 1968–1984* (Cambridge: Cambridge University Press, 2018), Joachim Häberlen, "(Not) Narrating the History of the Federal Republic: Reflections on the Place of the New Left in West German History and Historiography," *Central European History* 52, no. 1 (2019): 107–24, https://doi.org/10.1017/S0008938919000074; and Joachim Häberlen, "Heterochronias: Reflections on the Temporal Exceptionality of Revolts," *European Review of History* 28, no. 4 (2021): 531–48, https://doi.org/10.1080/13507486.2021.1897530.

33. The scholars I engage with on these topics include Aleida Assmann, Tobias Becker, Svetlana Boym, Fernando Esposito, François Hartog, Reinhart Koselleck, Chris Lorenz, Pierre Nora, and Claudia Verhoeven.

34. See, for example, Timothy Scott Brown, "1968 Underground: West German Radicals Between Subculture and Revolution," in *Subcultures, Popular Music and Social Change*, ed. William Osgerby (Newcastle: Cambridge Scholars Publishing, 2014), 219–34; Klimke and Scharloth, "Maos Rote Garden?"; Detlef Siegfried, *Sound der Revolte: Studien zur Kulturrevolution um 1968* (Munich: Weinheim, 2008); and Briana Smith, *Free Berlin: Art, Urban Politics, and Everyday Life* (Cambridge, MA: MIT Press, 2022).

35. On this point, see Philipp Felsch, *Der lange Sommer der Theorie: Geschichte einer Revolte, 1960–1990* (Munich: C.H. Beck, 2015).

36. Hal Foster, "Outmoded Spaces, 1993," in *Memory*, ed. Ian Farr (Cambridge, MA: MIT Press, 2012), 49–59.

37. Michel de Certeau, *The Practice of Everyday Life* (Berkeley: University of California Press, 1984), 108.

38. Christina Sharpe, *In the Wake: On Blackness and Being* (Durham: Duke University Press, 2016), 22.

39. On haunting, see Mark Fisher, *Ghosts of My Life: Writings on Depression, Hauntology and Lost Futures*, 2nd ed. (Winchester, UK: Zero Books, 2022); Avery Gordon, *Ghostly Matters: Haunting and the Sociological Imagination* (Minneapolis: University of Minnesota Press, 2008); and María del Pilar Blanco and Esther Peeren, eds., *The Spectralities Reader: Ghosts and Haunting in Contemporary Cultural Theory* (London: Bloomsbury, 2013).

40. Examples include the proto-anarchist communities that emerged in the "Russian Colonies" of late nineteenth-century Zurich and the Afrofuturist experimentation of 1980s Detroit. On anarchist communities in Zurich, see Faith Hillis, *Utopia's Discontents: Russian Emigres and the Quest for Freedom, 1830s–1930s* (Oxford: Oxford University Press, 2022). On Afrofuturist experimentation, see William Sites, *Sun Ra's Chicago: Afrofuturism and the City* (Chicago: University of Chicago Press, 2020), and Ytasha Womack, *Afrofuturism: The World of Black Sci-Fi and Fantasy Culture* (Chicago: Lawrence Hill, 2013).

41. Benjamin, "Theses on the Philosophy of History," 263. Some of the authors I engage with on this issue include Svetlana Boym, Shannon Dawdy, Hal Foster, Jack Halberstam, Greil Marcus, Christina Sharpe, and Anna Tsing.

42. Ben Lerner, *10:04* (New York: Faber and Faber, 2015), 19.

43. Svetlana Boym, *The Off-Modern* (New York: Bloomsbury, 2017), 5.

44. Boym, *The Off-Modern*, 40.

CHAPTER ONE

1. Amos Elon, quoted in Till van Rahden, "Clumsy Democrats: Moral Passions in the Federal Republic," *German History* 29, no. 3 (September 2011): 497, https://doi.org/10.1093/gerhis/ghr050.

2. There is a large body of literature on the continuities between the Nazi and the postwar periods. Some representative examples include Jeffrey Herf, *Divided Memory: The Nazi Past in the Two Germanys* (Cambridge, MA: Harvard University Press, 1999); Charles Maier, *The Unmasterable Past: History, Holocaust, and German National Identity* (Cambridge, MA: Harvard University Press, 1988); and Moses, *German Intellectuals and the Nazi Past*.

3. On the Nazi temporal imagination, see Alon Confino, *A World Without Jews: The Nazi Imagination from Persecution to Genocide* (New Haven: Yale University Press, 2014).

4. Anonymous, *A Woman in Berlin: Eight Weeks in the Conquered City* (New York: Picador, 2000), 201.

5. *Die Mörder sind unter uns*, directed by Wolfgang Staudte (1946, Deutsche Film).

6. On the Economic Miracle, see, among others: Monica Black, "Miracles in the Shadow of the Economic Miracle: The 'Supernatural '50s' in West Germany," *The Journal of Modern History* 84, no. 4 (2012): 833–60, https://doi.org/10.1086/667597; Erica Carter, *How German Is She? Postwar West German Reconstruction and the Consuming Woman* (Ann Arbor: University of Michigan Press, 1997); Hanna Schissler, ed., *The Miracle Years: A Cultural History of West Germany, 1949–1968* (Princeton, NJ: Princeton University Press, 2001); and S. Jonathan Wiesen, "Miracles for Sale: Consumer Displays and Advertising in Postwar West Germany, in *Consuming Germany in the Cold War*, ed. David Crew (New York: Berg, 2003), 151–78.

7. Philipp Felsch and Frank Witzel, *BRD Noir* (Berlin: Mathes & Seitz, 2016).

8. Assmann, *Is Time out of Joint?*

9. Harry Harootunian, *Marx after Marx: History and Time in the Expansion of Capitalism* (New York: Columbia University Press, 2016), 20. See also Luc Boltanski and Ève Chiapello, *The New Spirit of Capitalism*, rev. ed., trans. Gregory Elliott (London: Verso, 2018); Moishe Postone, *Time, Labor, and Social Domination: A Reinterpretation of Marx's Critical Theory* (Cambridge: Cambridge University Press, 1993); and Gary Wilder, *Concrete Utopianism*.

10. See Dan Edelstein, Stefanos Geroulanos, and Natasha Wheatley, "Chronocenosis: An Introduction to Power and Time," in *Power and Time: Temporalities and Conflict in the Making of History*, ed. Dan Edelstein, Stefanos Geroulanos, and Natasha Wheatley (Chicago: University of Chicago Press, 2020), 1–50; and Fernando Esposito and Tobias Becker, "The Time of Politics, the Politics of Time, and Politicized Time: An Introduction to Chronopolitics," *History and Theory* 62, no. 4 (2023): 3–23, https://doi.org/10.1111/hith.12324. On the related idea of "chronoferences," see Achim Landwehr, "Nostalgia and the Turbulence of Times," *History and Theory* 57, no. 2 (June 2018): 251–68, https://doi.org/10.1111/hith.12060. For a cogent critique of the idea of singular forms of temporal consciousness, see Chris Lorenz, "Out of Time? Some Critical Reflections on François Hartog's Presentism," in *Rethinking Historical Time: New Approaches to Presentism*, ed. Marek Tamm and Laurent Oliver (New York: Bloomsbury, 2019), 23–42.

11. Freeman, *Time Binds*, 3.

12. Hartog, *Regimes of Historicity*, 108.

13. On the trials, denazification, and questions of German guilt, see Monica Black, *A Demon-Haunted Land: Witches, Wonder Doctors, and the Ghosts of the Past in Post-WWII Germany* (New York: Metropolitan Books, 2020); Donald Bloxham, *Genocide on Trial: War Crimes Trials and the Formation of Holocaust History* (Oxford: Oxford University Press, 2003); and Jeffrey Olick, *In the House of the Hangman: The Agonies of German Defeat, 1943–1949* (Chicago: University of Chicago Press, 2005).

14. See Sean Forner, *German Intellectuals and the Challenge of Democratic Renewal: Culture and Politics after 1945* (Cambridge: Cambridge University Press, 2014); Daniel Fulda, Stefan-Ludwig Hoffmann, and Till van Rahden, eds., *Demokratie im Schatten der Gewalt. Geschichten des Privaten im deutschen Nachkrieg* (Göttingen: Wallstein, 2010); Udi Greenberg, *The Weimar Century: German Emigres and the Ideological Foundations of the Cold War* (Princeton, NJ: Princeton University Press, 2014); Jarausch, *After Hitler*; and Moses, *German Intellectuals and the Nazi Past*.

15. Rita Chin and Heide Fehrenbach, "German Democracy and the Question of Difference, 1945–1995," in *After the Nazi Racial State: Difference and Democracy in Germany and Europe*, ed. Rita Chin, Heide Fehrenbach, Geoff Eley, and Atina Grossman (Ann Arbor: University of Michigan Press, 2009), 106. See also Carter, *How German Is She?*

16. On the importance assigned to free choice for postwar Germany see Föllmer, "Cities of Choice."

17. The proclivity of nationalist regimes to highlight or in some cases invent national traditions as a counterweight to their futurist aspirations has been noted by many scholars. A classic interpretation of how this process played out in postcolonial regimes is Partha Chatterjee, *The Nation and Its Fragments: Colonial and Postcolonial Histories* (Princeton, NJ: Princeton University Press, 1993).

18. Susan Stewart, *On Longing: Narratives of the Miniature, the Gigantic, the Souvenir, the Collection* (Durham: Duke University Press, 1993).

19. Wiesen, "Miracles for Sale," 156.

20. Wiesen, "Miracles for Sale," 168.

21. *Kings of the Road*, directed by Wim Wenders (1976; Westdeutscher Rundfunk). The original German title of the film is *Im Lauf der Zeit*, literally "in the course of time."

22. On postwar domesticity, see Paul Betts, *The Authority of Everyday Objects: A Cultural History of West German Industrial Design* (Berkeley: University of California Press, 2004); Carter, *How German Is She?*; Greg Castillo, *Cold War on the Home Front: The Soft Power of Midcentury Design* (Minneapolis: University of Minnesota Press, 2010); David Crew, ed., *Consuming Germany in the Cold War* (New York: Berg, 2003); David Crowley and Jane Pavitt, eds., *Cold War Modern: Design, 1945–1970* (London: V&A Publishing, 2008); Dagmar Herzog, *Sexuality in Europe: A Twentieth-Century History* (Cambridge: Cambridge University Press, 2011); Eli Rubin, *Amnesiopolis: Modernity, Space, and Memory in East Germany* (Oxford: Oxford University Press, 2016); Johannes von Moltke, *No Place Like Home: Locations of Heimat in German Cinema* (Berkeley: University of California Press, 2005); and Ruth Oldenziel and Karin Zachmann, eds., *Cold War Kitchen: Americanization, Technology, and European Users* (Cambridge, MA: MIT Press, 2009).

23. Paul Betts and David Crowley, "Introduction," in "Domestic Dreamworlds: Notions of Home in Post-1945 Europe," special issue, *Journal of Contemporary History* 40, no. 2 (2005), 230.

24. Greg Castillo, "Domesticating the Cold War: Household Consumption as Propaganda in Marshall Plan Germany," in "Domestic Dreamworlds: Notions of Home in Post-1945 Europe," special issue, *Journal of Contemporary History* 40, no. 2 (2005): 261–88, https://doi.org/10.1177/0022009405051553. See also Castillo's book on the subject, *Cold War on the Home Front*, and the discussion of housing exhibits in Berlin in Sandra Wagner-Conzelmann, *Die Interbau 1957 in Berlin. Stadt von Heute—Stadt von Morgen. Städtebau und Gesellschaftskritik der 50er Jahre* (Petersberg: Michael Imhof Verlag, 2007).

25. Greg Castillo, "Marshall Plan Modernism in Divided Germany," in *Cold War Modern: Design, 1945–1970*, ed. David Crowley and Jane Pavitt (London: V&A Publishing, 2008), 65.

26. Quoted in Jane Pavitt, "Design and the Democratic Ideal," in *Cold War Modern: Design, 1945–1970*, ed. David Crowley and Jane Pavitt (London: V&A Publishing, 2008), 85.

27. Letter from Siegfried Kracauer to Leo Löwenthal (October 27, 1956). Quoted in van Rahden, "Clumsy Democrats," 502.

28. Frank Biess and Astrid Eckert, "Introduction: Why Do We Need New Narratives for the History of the Federal Republic?" *Central European History* 52, no. 1 (2019): 13, https://doi.org/10.1017/S0008938919000013. See also Biess, *Republik der Angst*; Black, *A Demon-Haunted Land*; Michael Geyer, "Cold War Angst: The Case of West-German Opposition to Rearmament and Nuclear Weapons," in *The Miracle Years: A Cultural History of West Germany, 1949–1968*, ed. Hannah Schissler (Princeton, NJ: Princeton University Press, 2001); and van Rahden, "Clumsy Democrats."

29. Natalie Scholz, "Ghosts and Miracles: The Volkswagen as Imperial Debris in Postwar West Germany," *Comparative Studies in Society and History* 62, no. 3 (2020): 493, https://doi.org/10.1017/S0010417520000158.

30. See Theodor Adorno, *Minima Moralia: Reflections from a Damaged Life* (London: Verso, 1978; Frankfurt: Suhrkamp Verlag, 1951); Herbert Marcuse, *Eros and Civilization: A Philosophical Inquiry into Freud* (New York: Vintage Books, 1955); Herbert Marcuse, *One-Dimensional Man* (Boston: Beacon Press, 1964); Max Horkheimer and Theodor Adorno, *Dialectic of Enlightenment* (Stanford: Stanford University Press, 2007); and Alexander Mitscherlich and Margarete Mitscherlich, *Die Unfähigkeit zu trauern. Grundlagen kollektiven Verhaltens* (Munich: Piper, 1967).

31. Miriam Hansen, "Spaces of History, Language of Time: Kluge's *Yesterday Girl* (1966)," in *German Film and Literature: Adaptations and Transformations*, ed. Eric Rentschler (New York: Methuen, 1986), 202.

32. Letter from Adorno to Leo Löwenthal, quoted in Felsch, *Der lange Sommer der Theorie*, 32.

33. On the emergence of these youth cultures, see Thomas Grotum, *Die Halbstarken: zur Geschichte einer Jugendkultur der 50er Jahre* (Frankfurt: Campus, 1994); Kaspar Maase, *BRAVO Amerika. Erkundungen zur Jugendkultur der Bundesrepublik in den fünfziger Jahren* (Hamburg: Junius, 1992); Bodo Mrozek, *Jugend—Pop—Kultur: Eine transnationale Geschichte* (Frankfurt: Suhrkamp, 2019); and Uta Poiger, *Jazz, Rock, and Rebels: Cold War Politics and American Culture in a Divided Germany* (Berkeley: University of California Press, 2000).

34. See Axel Schildt, Detlef Siegfried, and Karl Christian Lammers, eds., *Dynamische Zeiten. Die 60er Jahre in den beiden deutschen Gesellschaften* (Hamburg: Christians, 2003).

35. Julia Sneeringer, "Sites of Corruption, Sites of Liberation: Hamburg-St. Pauli and the Contested Spaces of Early Rock 'n' Roll," *Contemporary European History* 26, no. 2 (2017): 315, https://doi.org/10.1017/S0960777316000588. See also Julia Sneeringer, *A Social History of Early Rock 'n' Roll in Germany: Hamburg from Burlesque to the Beatles, 1956–69* (London: Bloomsbury, 2018).

36. For an analysis of the peculiar appeal of the Beatles in the early 1960s, see Devin McKinney, *Magic Circles: The Beatles in Dream and History* (Cambridge, MA: Harvard University Press, 2004).

37. Dieter Kunzelmann, *Leisten Sie keinen Widerstand! Bilder aus meinem Leben* (Berlin: Transit, 1998), 37.

38. Bommi Baumann, *How It All Began* (Vancouver: Pulp Press, 1977).

39. Siegfried, *Time Is on My Side*, 405.

40. On the spatial logics of the student movements, see Timothy Scott Brown, *West Germany and the Global Sixties*.

41. On the role of "impatience" in an earlier radical milieu, see Claudia Verhoeven, "Time of Terror, Terror of Time: On the Impatience of Russian Revolutionary Terrorism (Early 1860s–Early 1880s)," *Jahrbücher Für Geschichte Osteuropas* 58, no. 2 (2010): 254–73, https://www.jstor.org/stable/41052430.

42. Herbert Marcuse, *Eros and Civilization: A Philosophical Inquiry into Freud*, 2nd ed. (Boston: Beacon Press, 1966), xvi.

43. In addition to attempting to revolutionize countercultural youth, activists also looked to the economically disadvantaged, to immigrants, and, in the case of the Sozialistische Patientenkollektiv in Heidelberg, to the mentally ill as potential revolutionary subjects. See, for example, Franz-Werner Kerstin, "Juvenile Left-Wing Radicalism, Fringe Groups, and Anti-psychiatry in West Germany," in *Between Marx and Coca-Cola: Youth Cultures in Changing European Societies, 1960–1980*, ed. Axel Schildt and Detlef Siegfried (New York: Berghahn, 2006).

44. Reiche and Gänge quoted in Siegfried, *Time Is on My Side*, 489.

45. For an illuminating analysis of the festival in the broader context of the West German New Left, see the chapter on "Sound" in Timothy Scott Brown's book *West Germany and the Global Sixties*.

46. On Subversive Aktion, see Frank Böckelmann and Herbert Nagel, eds., *Subversive Aktion: der Sinn der Organisation ist ihr Scheitern* (Frankfurt am Main: Neue Kritik, 2002); Alexander Holmig, "Die aktionistischen Wurzeln der Studentenbewegung: Subversive Aktion, Kommune I und die Neudefinition des Politischen," in *1968: Handbuch zur Kultur- und Mediengeschichte der Studentenbewegung*, ed. Martin Klimke and Joachim Scharloth (Stuttgart: J.B. Metzler, 2007); and Kunzelmann, *Leisten Sie keinen Widerstand!* On the Provo movement, see Richard Kempton, *Provo: Amsterdam's Anarchist Revolt* (Brooklyn: Autonomedia, 2007).

47. Kommune I, "Wann brennen die Berliner Kaufhäuser?" (May 25, 1967). Reproduced in Kunzelmann, *Leisten Sie keinen Widerstand!*, 79.

48. For an analysis of this series of events, see Sara Hakemi, *Anschlag und Spektakel: Flugblätter der Kommune I, Erklärungen von Ensslin/Baader und den frühen RAF* (Bochum: Posth, 2008); Mia Lee, *Utopia and Dissent in West Germany: The Resurgence of the Politics of Everyday Life in the Long 1960s* (New York: Routledge, 2019); Wilfried Mausbach, "'Burn, ware-house, burn!' Modernity, Counterculture, and the Vietnam War in West Germany," in *Between Marx and Coca-Cola: Youth Cultures in Changing European Societies, 1960–1980*, ed. Axel Schildt and Detlef Siegfried (New York: Berghahn, 2006); and Joachim Scharloth, "Ritualkritik und Rituale des Protests: Die Entdeckung des Performativen in der Studentenbewegung der 1960er Jahre," in *1968: Handbuch zur Kultur- und Mediengeschichte der Studentenbewegung*, ed. Martin Klimke and Joachim Scharloth (Stuttgart: J.B. Metzler, 2007).

49. Siegfried, *Sound der Revolte*, 146–47.

50. Peter Schneider, *Rebellion und Wahn* (Cologne: Kiepenheuer & Witsch, 2010), 13.

51. Schneider, *Rebellion und Wahn*, 141. Similar feelings emerged in the "May Movement" in France. For a discussion of these events, see Renaud, *New Lefts*.

52. Schneider, *Rebellion und Wahn*, 142.

53. Susan Buck-Morss, *Dreamworld and Catastrophe: The Passing of Mass Utopia in East and West* (Cambridge, MA: MIT Press, 2002), 150.

54. Ross, *Communal Luxury*, 6.

55. Quoted in Koenen, *Das rote Jahrzehnt*, 183.

56. Werner Olles, "Kiff und Revolution," *Agit 883*, August 21, 1969, quoted in Brown, *West Germany and the Global Sixties*, 258.

57. For a transnational analysis of leftist experimentation and radicalism in the 1970s, see Michael Hardt, *The Subversive Seventies* (Oxford: Oxford University Press, 2023).

58. For a description of this event, see Kazuo Kandutsch, "The Event *Kunst und Revolution*," in *Vienna Actionism: Art and Upheaval in 1960s Vienna*, ed. Eva Badura-Triska and Hubert Klocker (Cologne: Walther König. 2012).

59. Eva Badura-Triska and Hubert Klocker, "Vienna Actionism and its Context," *Vienna Actionism: Art and Upheaval in 1960s Vienna*, ed. Eva Badura-Triska and Hubert Klocker (Cologne: Walther König. 2012), 11.

60. Schneider, *Rebellion und Wahn*, 194.

61. Schneider, *Rebellion und Wahn*, 194.

62. Dagmar Herzog offers a highly compelling analysis of this movement in her book *Sex after Fascism: Memory and Morality in Twentieth-Century Germany* (Princeton, NJ: Princeton University Press, 2005).

63. Michel Foucault, "Preface" in *Anti-Oedipus: Capitalism and Schizophrenia*, Gilles Deleuze and Félix Guattari (New York: Penguin Classics, 2009), xiii.

64. Foucault, "Preface" in *Anti-Oedipus*, xiii–xiv.

65. Häberlen, *The Emotional Politics of the New Left*, 170.

66. Reichardt, *Authentizität und Gemeinschaft*, 222.

67. Koenen, *Das rote Jahrzehnt*, 46.

68. On this point see Varon, *Bringing the War Home*.

69. Slobodian, *Foreign Front*, 77.

70. For an overview of these groups, see Wolfgang Kraushaar, "Berliner Subkultur: Blues, Haschrebellen, Tupamaros und Bewegung 2. Juni," in *1968: Handbuch zur Kultur- und Mediengeschichte der Studentenbewegung*, edited by Martin Klimke and Joachim Scharloth (Stuttgart: J.B. Metzler, 2007).

71. Kraushaar, "Berliner Subkultur," 265.

72. Baumann, *How It All Began*, 41.

73. On the RAF, see, among many others, Stefan Aust, *Der Baader-Meinhof Komplex* (Hamburg: Hoffmann und Campe, 2008); Karrin Hanshew, *Terror and Democracy in West Germany* (Cambridge: Cambridge University Press, 2012); Wolfgang Kraushaar,

Die RAF und linke Terrorismus (Hamburg: Hamburger Edition, 2006); Michael Sontheimer, *"Natürlich kann geschossen werden": eine kurze Geschichte der Roten Armee Fraktion* (Munich: Deutsche Verlags-Anstalt, 2010).

74. Margit Schiller, quoted in Koenen, *Das rote Jahrzehnt*, 376.

75. Gudrun Ensslin, quoted in Koenen, *Das rote Jahrzehnt*, 371.

76. Varon, *Bringing the War Home*, 13.

77. Although I do not have the space here to go into detail, the parallels between the "impatient" temporal imaginaries of the RAF and those of the late nineteenth-century Russian terrorists analyzed by Verhoeven are really quite extraordinary. Verhoeven, "Time of Terror."

78. On the Frankfurt Spontis, see Paul Hockenos, *Joschka Fischer and the Making of the Berlin Republic: An Alternative History of Postwar Germany* (Oxford: Oxford University Press, 2007); Sebastian Kasper, *Spontis: Eine Geschichte antiautoritärer Linker im roten Jahrzehnt* (Münster: Edition Assemblage, 2019); and Wolfgang Kraushaar, *Fischer in Frankfurt: Karriere eines Aussenseiters* (Hamburg: Hamburger Edition, 2001).

79. On postwar housing policy and its early discontents, see Harald Bodenschatz, Volker Heise, and Jochen Korfmacher, *Schluss mit der Zerstörung? Stadterneuerung und städtische Opposition in West-Berlin, Amsterdam und London* (Giessen: Anabas, 1983); Laura Bowie, *The Streets Echoed with Chants: The Urban Experience of Post-war Berlin* (Oxford: Peter Lang, 2022); Sarah Jacobson, "Redefining Urban Citizenship: Italian Migrants and Housing Occupations in 1970s Frankfurt am Main," *Contemporary European History* 33, no. 2 (2024): 634–50, https://doi.org/10.1017/S0960777322000662; and Adelheid von Saldern, *Häuserleben: zur Geschichte städtischen Arbeiterwohnens vom Kaiserreich bis heute* (Bonn: JHW Dietz, 1995).

80. Although the *Häuserkampf* in Frankfurt was the most well-known squatting movement in this period, it is important to note that it was not alone. In West Berlin, for example, groups of youth occupied the Bethanien Hospital in December 1971 while in Hamburg activists occupied the house at Ekhofstraße 39 in spring 1973.

81. ASTA Häuserrat, *Häuserkampf-info*, January 1, 1974.

82. "Wohnungskämpfe in Frankfurt. Ursachen und Hintergründe des sozialen Konflikts und wie SPD und bürgerliche Parteien ihn mit Gewalt zu lösen versuchen," in *Frankfurt. Zerstörung. Terror, Folter. Im Namen des Gesetzes*, Axel Wenzel, Jürgen Roth, and Häuserrat Frankfurt (Frankfurt: Megapress, 1974), 26.

83. Götz Aly, *Unser Kampf: 1968—ein irritierter Blick zurück* (Frankfurt: Fischer, 2007), 79.

84. On the fears induced by the past's tendency to cling to the postwar present, see Biess, *Republik der Angst*.

85. For alternative interpretations of the processes of radicalization in 1960s leftist milieus see Renaud, *New Lefts*; and Benedikt Sepp, *Das Prinzip Bewegung. Theorie, Praxis, und Radikalisierung in der West Berliner Linken 1961–1972* (Göttingen: Wallstein, 2023).

86. For an in-depth analysis of these events and their repercussions, see Hanshew, *Terror and Democracy in West Germany*.

CHAPTER TWO

1. This document, which was subsequently reprinted in countless student newspapers across West Germany, elicited both an outpouring of support among leftist groups as well as a strong wave of condemnation within the mainstream press. See also Hans-Joachim Klein, *Rückkehr in die Menschlichkeit: Appell eines ausgestiegenen Terorristen* (Reinbeck bei Hamburg: Rowohlt, 1979).

2. *Deutschland im Herbst* (*Germany in Autumn*), directed by Rainer Werner Fassbinder, et al. (West Germany: ABS Filmproduktion, 1978).

3. Bruno Gmünder, quoted in Michael März, *Linker Protest nach dem Deutschen Herbst. Eine Geschichte des linken Spektrums in Schatten des 'starken Staates', 1977–1979* (Bielefeld: Transcript, 2012), 204.

4. : See Karrin Hanshew, "Daring More Democracy? Internal Security and the Social Democratic Fight against West German Terrorism," *Central European History* 43, no. 1 (2010): 117–47, http://www.jstor.org/stable/40601021; and Karrin Hanshew, *Terror and Democracy in West Germany*. On the West German Green Party, see Jennifer Allen, *Sustainable Utopias*; Silke Mende, "Von der 'Anti-Parteien-Partei' zur 'ökologischen Reformpartei'. Die Grünen und der Wandel des Politischen," *Archiv für Sozialgeschichte* 52 (2012): 273–315; and Ludger Volmer, *Die Grünen: von der Protestbewegung zur etablierten Partei. Eine Bilanz* (Munich: Bertelsmann, 2009).

5. Meinrad Rohner, "Wir Kinder der Tertiasierung" quoted in Kasper, *Spontis*, 151.

6. On TUNIX, see Dieter Hoffmann-Axthelm, Otto Kallscheuer, and Eberhard Knödler-Bunte, *Zwei Kulturen. TUNIX, Mescalero und die Folgen* (Berlin: Verlag Ästhetik und Kommunikation, 1978), and Von Dirke, *All Power to the Imagination!*

7. Quoted in März, *Linker Protest nach dem Deutschen Herbst*, 212.

8. See, for example, Biess, *Republik der Angst*; Mende, "Das 'Momo'-Syndrom"; Stephen Milder, *Greening Democracy: The Anti-nuclear Movement and Political Environmentalism in West Germany and Beyond, 1968–1983* (Cambridge: Cambridge University Press, 2017); and Andrew Tompkins, *Better Active than Radioactive! Anti-nuclear Protest in 1970s France and West Germany* (Oxford: Oxford University Press, 2016).

9. Mende, "Das 'Momo'-Syndrom," 168.

10. Fernando Esposito, "Von *no future* bis Posthistoire: Der Wandel des temporalen Imaginariums nach dem Boom," in *Vorgeschichte der Gegenwart: Dimensionen des Strukturbruchs nach dem Boom*, ed. Anselm Doering-Manteuffel, Lutz Raphael, and Thomas Schlemmer (Göttingen: Vandenhoeck and Ruprecht, 2016), 410. See also Eva Horn, *The Future as Catastrophe: Imagining Disaster in the Modern Age* (New York: Columbia University Press, 2018).

11. "Council of the Tribes of the Berlin Mescaleros" (1978), quoted in Brown, *West Germany and the Global Sixties*, 359.

12. Häberlen, *The Emotional Politics of the Alternative Left*, 78.

13. See, for example, Thomas Schmid, "Autonomie von der Entwicklung—doch in der Entwicklung," in *Zwei Kulturen. TUNIX, Mescalero und die Folgen*, ed. Dieter Hoffmann-Axthelm, Otto Kallscheuer, and Eberhard Knödler-Bunte (Berlin: Verlag Ästhetik und Kommunikation, 1978).

14. See, for example, Joschka Fischer, "Vorstoss in 'Primitiven' Zeiten," *Autonomie* 5 (1977); and Herbert Röttgen, "Mythology in Revolution?" *Semiotext(e): The German Issue* 4, no. 2 (1982): 192–98.

15. Hans Peter Dürr, "Savage Ethnology," *Semiotext(e): The German Issue* 4, no. 2 (1982): 203–4.

16. Allen, *Sustainable Utopias*, 17.

17. See Bodenschatz, Heise, and Korfmacher, *Schluss mit der Zerstörung?* and Rudy Koshar, *From Monuments to Traces: Artifacts of German Memory, 1870–1990* (Berkeley: University of California Press, 2000).

18. "SOS für SO36," *Der Spiegel*, March 21, 1977.

19. For information on the organization of the Project Commission, see Lutz Böttcher, et al., "'Strategien für Kreuzberg.' Bericht der Vorprüfergruppe über den Wettbewerb," *ARCH+* 37 (1978): 63–73; and *Strategien für Kreuzberg* (Berlin: Senator für Bau- und Wohnungswesen, 1979).

20. "Stadtteilzentrum Kreuzberg" Projektentwurf der Projektgruppe 47 (January 25, 1978), 36 [Kreuzbergmuseum, Inv. Nr. 2010/27, Lfd. Nr. 27]. For a description of some of the projects, see Peter Borngesser et al., "Aktive Gruppen in Berlin—SO36 und Öffentlichkeit Endbericht der Projektgruppe 10 im Projekt 'Strategien für Kreuzberg'" (January 1978) [Kreuzbergmuseum, Inv. Nr. 2010/27, Lfd. Nr. 27]. Eventually, city officials decided to fund some of the winning projects. On city funding for projects, see "Vorlage—Zur Beschlußfassung—über das Projekt 'Strategien für Kreuzberg,'" Abgeordnetenhaus von Berlin Drucksache 8/126 (September 7, 1979) [Kreuzbergmuseum, Inv. Nr. 2010/27, Lfd. Nr. 27].

21. "Wir haben dazugelernt. Wir machen weiter" in *Stadtteilzentrum Feuerwache* (1977), 13–14 [Papiertiger Archiv, Brochures].

22. The BI SO36 is not to be confused with the Verein SO36, an official organization that received 50,000 Marks from the city to continue the work of the *Strategien*.

23. Like the *Tageszeitung*, the *Südost Express* was designed to serve both as a mouthpiece and as a resource for those affected by urban renewal policies in which interested parties could voice their concerns and learn about local issues such as the planned construction of a senior center or the activities of public housing companies like BeWoGe. See, for example, the articles: "Seniorzentrum Bethanien: Ein Platz für Rentner?" (March 1978); "Berlin 1985" (March 1978); and "Neuen Sanierungsträger in SO36?" (January 1979).

24. "Instandsbesetzungsaktion in Berliner Pressespiegel," *Südost Express* (March 1979).

25. "Wir machen ein Hausgemeinschaft," *Südost Express* (June 1979).

26. Mieterinitiative Chamissoplatz, "Instandbesetzung" (Summer 1980) [Papiertiger Archiv, Flugblätter bis 1988].

27. "Drei Wochen Instandbesetzung in der Adalbertstr. 6" (June 1980) [Papiertiger Archiv, Flugblätter bis 1988].

28. Wolfgang Kraushaar, "Thesen zum Verhältnis von Alternativ- und Fluchtbewegung. Am Beispiel der frankfurter scene," in *Autonomie oder Getto? Kontroversen*

über die Alternativbewegung, ed. Wolfgang Kraushaar (Frankfurt: Verlag Neue Kritik, 1978), 36.

29. "Zu Diesem Heft," *Autonomie: Neue Folge* 3 (1980): 3.

30. On punk in German-speaking countries, see Lurker Grand, ed., *Hot Love: Swiss Punk & Wave, 1976–1980* (Zurich: Edition Patrick Frey, 2007); Thomas Groetz, *Kunst-Musik: deutscher Punk und New Wave in der Nachbarschaft von Joseph Beuys* (Berlin: Martin Schmitz Verlag, 2002); Ulrike Groos and Peter Gorschlüter, eds., *Zurück zum Beton: die Anfänge von Punk und New Wave in Deutschland 1977–82. Kunsthalle Düsseldorf, 7. Juli—15. September 2002* (Cologne: König, 2002); Mirko Hall, Seth Howes, and Cyrus Shahan, eds., *Beyond No Future: Cultures of German Punk* (New York: Bloomsbury, 2016); Jeff Hayton, *Culture from the Slums: Punk Rock in East and West Germany* (Oxford: Oxford University Press, 2022); Frank Apunkt Schneider, *Als die Welt noch Unterging: Von Punk zu NDW* (Mainz: Ventil, 2006); Cyrus Shahan, *Punk Rock and German Crisis: Adaptation and Resistance after 1977* (New York: Palgrave, 2013); and Jürgen Teipel, *Verschwende deine Jugend: Ein Doku-Roman über den deutschen Punk und New Wave* (Frankfurt: Suhrkamp, 2001).

31. Greil Marcus, *Lipstick Traces: A Secret History of the Twentieth Century* (Cambridge, MA: Harvard University Press, 1989), 6.

32. Anna Lowenhaupt Tsing, *The Mushroom at the End of the World: On the Possibility of Life in Capitalist Ruins* (Princeton, NJ: Princeton University Press, 2015).

33. For a discussion of the relationship between art and the punk movement, see Groetz, *Kunst-Musik*; and Bert Papenfuß, "Kunsterziehung durch Punk," in *Lieber zu viel als zu wenig: Kunst, Musik, Aktionen zwischen Hedonismus und Nihilismus (1976–1985)* (Berlin: Vice Versa, 2003); and Schneider, *Als die Welt noch Unterging*, 62–70.

34. Members of Ton Steine Scherben also grappled with the issues of how artistic expression and political ideas could coexist. For an analysis of this process, see Timothy Scott Brown's chapter "Sound" in his book *West Germany and the Global Sixties*.

35. For a more wide-ranging analysis of some of these songs, see Ulrich Adelt, *Krautrock: German Music in the Seventies* (Ann Arbor: University of Michigan Press, 2016).

36. On Kraftwerk, see Uwe Schütte, *Kraftwerk: Future Music from Germany* (London: Penguin, 2020), and the collected essays in Uwe Schütte, ed., *Mensch—Maschinen—Musik: Das Gesamtkunstwerk Kraftwerk* (Düsseldorf: C.W. Leske Verlag, 2018).

37. See Melanie Schiller, "Wie klingt die Bundesrepublik? Kraftwerk, *Autobahn* und die suche nach der eigenen Identität," in *Mensch—Maschinen—Musik: Das Gesamtkunstwerk Kraftwerk*, ed. Uwe Schütte (Düsseldorf: C.W. Leske Verlag, 2018).

38. Schütte, *Kraftwerk*, 144.

39. Klaus Hütter, quoted in Schütte, *Kraftwerk*, 120.

40. Michael Rother, quoted in Rüdiger Esch, *Electri_City: The Düsseldorf School of Electronic Music* (London: Omnibus Press, 2016), 61.

41. See Che Seibert's descriptions of these events in Sven-Andre Dreyer, Michael Wenzel, and Thomas Stelzmann, eds., *Keine Atempause: Musik aus Düsseldorf* (Düsseldorf: Droste Verlag, 2018).

42. Detlef Diederichsen, "Wie ich mal meine Jugend verschwendete," in Groos and Gorschlüter, *Zurück zum Beton*, 111.

43. Gabi Delgado quoted in Esch, *Electri_City*, 215.

44. Jürgen Engler, quoted in Teipel, *Verschwende deine Jugend*, 107.

45. Cover images from *Ostrich* 4 (September/October 1977); *Ostrich* 5 (November/December 1977); and *Ostrich* 3 (July/August 1977).

46. *Ostrich* 3 (July/August 1977).

47. *Ostrich* 3 (July/August 1977): 40–41. The name of the band as well as their list of interests are indicative of the masculine orientation of the early punk movement.

48. *Ostrich* 5 (November/December 1977): 9.

49. Quoted in Teipel, *Verschwende deine Jugend*, 51.

50. Gabi Delgado, quoted in Esch, *Electri_City*, 305.

51. Reproduced in Groos and Gorschlüter, *Zurück zum Beton*, 16.

52. Reproduced in Groos and Gorschlüter, *Zurück zum Beton*, 6.

53. Quoted in Teipel, *Verschwende deine Jugend*, 79.

54. See Wolfgang Müller and Martin Schmitz, eds., *Die Tödliche Doris—Kunst* (Berlin: Martin Schmitz Verlag, 1999).

55. Wolfgang Müller, *Subkultur Westberlin 1979–1989. Freizeit* (Hamburg: Philo Fine Arts, 2013), 222–23.

56. Gabi Delgado, quoted in Esch, *Electri_City*, 185.

57. On the complex symbolism of this the song, see Cyrus Shahan, "The Sounds of Terror: Punk, Post-Punk and the RAF after 1977," *Popular Music and Sound* 34, no. 3 (July 2011): 369–86, https://doi.org/10.1080/03007761003726258; and Shahan, *Punk Rock and German Crisis*.

58. Moritz R, *Der Plan: Glanz und Elend der Neuen Deutschen Welle. Die Geschichte einer deutschen Band* (Kassel: Verlag Martin Schmitz, 1993).

59. See various collage images reproduced in Groos and Gorschlüter, *Zurück zum Beton*.

60. "The Koma Kid Smiles," in *AMOK/KOMA. Ein Bericht zur Lage*, ed. Jürgen Ploog, Paciao, and W. Hartmann (Bonn: Expanded Media Editions, 1980).

61. Dick Hebdige, *Subculture. The Meaning of Style* (New York: Methuen, 1979), 26.

62. Hebdige, *Subculture*, 65.

63. Hebdige, *Subculture*, 121.

64. While West German and British bands certainly exhibited this behavior it was perhaps most pronounced in the California cult band The Residents, whose fusion of bubblegum pop and Nazi imagery was clearly meant to illustrate the underlying similarities between consumer capitalism and fascism. See, for example, their 1976 album *The Third Reich 'n Roll*.

65. Peter Fischli, quoted in Silvano Cerutti, "Man bediente sich einfach bei dem was herumlag. Die Moral der hässlichkeit," in *Hot Love. Swiss Punk & Wave, 1976–1980*, ed. Lurker Grand (Zurich: Edition Patrick Frey, 2007), 112. Especially in his many collaborations with David Weiss, Fischli went on to become a highly celebrated artist.

66. Walter Benjamin, "The Work of Art in the Age of Mechanical Reproduction," in *Illuminations: Essays and Reflections*, ed. Hannah Arendt (New York: Schocken Books, 1968), 236.

67. Quoted in Teipel, *Verschwende deine Jugend*, 131.

68. Mary Lou Monroe, "Hey, ya ostrich readin' arsehole!" *Ostrich* 5 (November/ December 1977).

69. Wolfgang Müller, "Die wahren Dilletanten," in *Geniale Dilletanten*, ed. Wolfgang Müller (Berlin: Merve, 1982), 10–14.

70. Müller, *Subkultur Westberlin*, 60.

71. Super 8 presented the movement with a cheap, easy-to-use medium with which to create art and document their lives. Lacking audio capabilities, they also allowed artists to creatively combine music and video. See Petra Reichensperger, "Schlau sein—dabei sein," in *Lieber zu viel als zu wenig: Kunst, Musik, Aktionen zwischen Hedonismus und Nihilismus (1976–1985)* (Berlin: Vice Versa, 2003).

72. The lyrics are from the 1981 song "Schlachtet!" by the Swiss punk group Grauzone. The films, which are all untitled, are collected on René Uhlmann, *Punk Cocktail. Zurich Scene, 1976–1980* (2006).

73. Rolf Wolkenstein and Horst Markgraf, "Hüpfen '82," in *Berlin Super 80: Music & Film Underground West Berlin, 1978–1984* (Berlin: Monitorpop Entertainment, 2005).

74. Walter Gramming, "Hammer und Sichel" (1978) in *Berlin Super 80*.

75. Anette Maschmann and Axel Brand, "E Dopo?" (1981/82), and Ingrid Maye and Volker Rendschmidt, "Ohne Liebe gibt es keinen Tod" (1980), in *Berlin Super 80*.

76. HERTZ, "Das Manifest," in *Hot Love. Swiss Punk & Wave, 1976–1980*, ed. Lurker Grand (Zurich: Edition Patrick Frey, 2007), 164.

77. Nikolaus Untermöhlen, "Doris als Musikerin," in *Geniale Dilletanten*, ed. Wolfgang Müller (Berlin: Merve, 1982), 71.

78. Nicki Vermöhlen [Nikolaus Untermöhlen], "Grundlagen zur Molekularstruktur der Musik in den verschiedenen Zuständen," in *Geniale Dilletanten*, ed. Wolfgang Müller (Berlin: Merve, 1982), 60.

79. Thomas Groetz, *Doris als Musikerin. Die Tödliche Doris, Band 2* (Berlin: Martin Schmitz Verlag, 1999), 190.

80. Judith Butler, *Bodies That Matter: On the Discursive Limits of "Sex"* (New York: Routledge, 1993), 3.

81. Eva Bude, *Verpisst euch! Sex and Drugs and Hardcore-Punk* (Hamburg: Europa Verlag, 2005), 8.

82. Bude, *Verpisst euch!*, 177.

83. Müller, *Subkultur Westberlin 1979–1989*, 54.

84. Moritz R, *Der Plan*, 34–35.

85. Jack Halberstam, "Going Gaga: Anarchy, Chaos, and the Wild," *Social Text* 31, no. 3 (116) (Fall 2013): 128, https://doi.org/10.1215/01642472-2152873.

86. Hans-Christian Dany, "Im Kohlenkeller eines neuen Dekadenzbewußtseins," in *Lieber zu viel als zu wenig: Kunst, Musik, Aktionen zwischen Hedonismus und Nihilismus (1976–1985)* (Berlin: Vice Versa, 2003), 45.

87. See Klaus Laufer, "Eingeschlossene Bergleute machen sich zum Beispiel durch Klofzeichen bemerkbar," in *Geniale Dilletanten*, ed. Wolfgang Müller (Berlin: Merve, 1982), 21.

88. Schneider, *Als die Welt noch Unterging*, 110.

89. Thomas Meinecke, "Neue Hinweise: Im Westeuropa Dämmerlicht (1981)" in *Mode & Verzweiflung*, ed. Thomas Meinecke (Frankfurt: Suhrkamp, 1986), 36. For an in-depth discussion of F.S.K. and Meinecke's writing, see Nina Möntmann, "Die treibende Kraft der mobilen Anpassung," in *Lieber zu viel als zu wenig: Kunst, Musik, Aktionen zwischen Hedonismus und Nihilismus (1976–1985)* (Berlin: Vice Versa, 2003); and Shahan, *Punk Rock and German Crisis*.

90. *Die Düsseldorfer Leere* (1979): 3.

91. Boym, *The Off-Modern*.

92. Boym, *The Off-Modern*, 3.

93. Jürgen Ploog, "Showdown des Okzidents," in *AMOK/KOMA. Ein Bericht zur Lage*, ed. Jürgen Ploog, Paciao, and W. Hartmann (Bonn: Expanded Media Editions, 1980), 4.

CHAPTER THREE

1. On this scene, see Paul Hockenos, *Berlin Calling: A Story of Anarchy, Music, the Wall, and the Birth of the New Berlin* (New York: The New Press, 2017).

2. "Ich hab' ein unheimlich befreiendes Gefühl," *Der Spiegel* 52 (1980): 38.

3. Michael Rutschky, *Erfahrungshunger: ein Essay über die siebziger Jahre* (Cologne: Kiepenhauer & Witsch, 1980).

4. Blixa Bargeld, quoted in Max Dax, *Dreissig Gespräche* (Frankfurt: Suhrkamp, 2008), 127.

5. Blixa Bargeld, quoted in Hockenos, *Berlin Calling*, 89.

6. William Levy, "Aufruf zum Chaos," in *AMOK/KOMA: Ein Bericht zur Lage*, ed. Jürgen Ploog, Paciao, and W. Hartmann (Bonn: Expanded Media Editions, 1980), 243.

7. Similar changes were taking place in the intellectual milieu surrounding Merve Verlag, where left-leaning academics had replaced Adorno with Baudrillard and had begun reviving the mystical, antimodernist thought of figures like Nietzsche. The back cover of the 1978 Merve volume *Das Schillern der Revolte* (*The Shimmer of Revolt*), for example, argued that "it is high time to try out new incommensurable forms of overcoming or more precisely interrupting power, for example unorthodox thinking, inverting the rules of the game, making oneself unknowable, singing the praises of laughter, planning with the left hand, [...] exploiting contradictions, path breaking, listening to the music of the future." In addition to the 1978 Merve volume edited by Frank Böckelmann, Dietmar Kampfer, Ellen Künzel, Michael Makroupoulos, Robert Müller, Ulricht Raulff, and Walter Seitter, see also Phillip Felsch's discussion of these conceptual shifts in his excellent book on the intellectual history of the postwar West German left, *Der lange Sommer der Theorie*.

8. Although they had been in existence for a number of years, music videos were popularized by MTV in the early 1980s and became an essential medium for various New Wave movements.

9. Peter Glaser, "Geschichte wird Gemacht," in *Zurück zum Beton. Die Anfänge von Punk und New Wave in Deutschland, 1977–1982. Kunsthalle Düsseldorf, 7. Juli—15. September 2002*, ed. Ulrike Groos and Peter Gorschlüter (Cologne: König, 2002), 122–23.

10. Jürgen Ploog, "Showdown des Okzidents," 5–7.

11. *Radikal* 77 (March/April 1980): cover.

12. *Radikal* 78 (May 1980) and *Radikal* 81 (September 1980).

13. *Stilett* 51 (1979) and *Stilett* 53 (November/December 1979).

14. Corinna, "Du musst schon noch träumen können," reproduced in *Was wird in den besetzten Häusern gemacht? Eine Dokumentation am Beispiel von. 13. Besetzten Häusern* (Architekteninitiative Schöneberger Planung, 1981), 25.

15. Thomas Lecorte, *Wir tanzen bis zum Ende. Die Geschichte eines Autonomen* (Hamburg: Verlag am Galgenberg, 1992), 32.

16. Buttergeit later achieved cult status with his 1987 film *Nekromantik*, which told the story of a couple whose sexual attraction to dead bodies ended up destroying their relationship.

17. Grauzone, "Wütendes Glas" (1981).

18. "'Wonen is een Recht' Gespräch mit Kraakern in Amsterdam," *Tageszeitung*, July 18, 1980.

19. See "'Wonen is een Recht' Gespräch mit Kraakern in Amsterdam" and "Amsterdamer Impressionen," both in *Tageszeitung*, July 18, 1980. For an overview of the squatting movement in Amsterdam see Eric Duivenvoorden, *Een voet tussen de deur: Geschiedenis van de kraakbeweging (1964–1999)* (Amsterdam: De Arbeiderspers, 2000); Nazima Kadir, "Myth and Reality in the Amsterdam Squatters' Movement, 1975–2012," in *The City Is Ours: Squatting and Autonomous Movements in Europe from the 1970s to the Present*, ed. Bart van der Steen and Ask Katzeff (Oakland: PM Press, 2014); Owens, *Cracking Under Pressure*; and Agentur BILWET, *Bewegungslehre: Botschaften aus einer autonomen Wirklichkeit* (Amsterdam: Edition ID Archiv, 1991).

20. These events were chronicled in the fantastic documentary *De Stad was van ons* (1996), directed by Joost Seelen.

21. "Ich hab' ein unheimlich befreiendes Gefühl," *Der Spiegel* 52 (1980): 33.

22. Reto Hänny, "Freedom for Greenland—Melt the Pack Ice," *Semiotext(e): The German Issue* 4, no. 2 (1982): 290–92.

23. Christian Jordi, quoted in "Aus Unbehagen, Angst—für eine Gegenwelt," *Tagesanzeiger*, July 2, 1980.

24. "'Da packt dich irgendwann 'ne Wut,'" *Der Spiegel* 52 (1980): 23. See also Klaus Ammann, "Krawall und Massenmedien," *Neue Zürcher Zeitung*, June 20, 1980.

25. On the language that emerged in the Zurich youth movement, see Reto Hänny, *Zürich, Anfang September* (Frankfurt: Suhrkamp, 1981).

26. Michael Wildenhain, *zum beispiel k* (Berlin: Rotbuch, 1983), 62.

27. *Züri brännt*, directed by Markus Sieber, Ronnie Wahli, Marcel Müller, and Thomas Krempke (Zurich: Videoladen Zürich, 1980).

28. See Wolfgang Prosinger, "Krieg im Frieden: Die Gewaltsame Räumung des Dreisamecks in Freiburg," in *Besetzung—Weil das Wünschen nicht geholfen hat*, ed. Ingrid Müller-Münch, et al. (Reinbeck bei Hamburg: Rowohlt Taschenbuch Verlag, 1981).

29. "Veranstaltung mit den Kraakern im Dreisameck am Freitag 30.5" (May 1980) [ASBF, 14.3.2 II].

30. Excellent footage of the demonstrations can be found in *Freiburg—Polizeiburg* (Medienwerkstatt Freiburg, 1980).

31. See "Aufruf zum Zug der Unzufrieden am 17. Okt" and "Unsere Stellungnahme zur Demonstration vom 17.10 und ihre Nachwehen" [ASBF, 14.3.3.0 I].

32. Jutta Diefenbacher, "Nicht anpassen," *Badische Zeitung*, June 11, 1980; Karl-Ernst Friedrich, "Ich schäme mich," *Badische Zeitung*, June 11, 1980; and Wolfgang Heterich, "Heruntergespielt," *Badische Zeitung*, June 12, 1980.

33. Erich Biniossek, "Ich muß doppelt zahlen," *Badische Zeitung*, June 12, 1980.

34. "Rede auf der Abschlußkundgebüng am Dreisameck am Freitag, 13. Juni 1980," 3 [ASBF, 14.3.2 III].

35. On the street theater skirmish see "Augenzeugenbericht von den Krawallen in Kreuzberg: Statt Straßentheater gab es eine Straßenschlacht," *Der Abend*, September 2, 1980.

36. "Wenn der Feind uns bekämpft ist das Gut und nicht schlecht, weil das heisst, dass wir ihn richtig getroffen haben" (October 1980) [Papiertiger Archiv—Häuserkampf Berlin/W, September—November 1980].

37. "Die Schlacht! Now or Never," *Akut und Praktisch* (October 1980): 2. The demonstration on October 10 was the concluding event of the "Action Week" organized by the Squatting Council K36 (*Besetzerrat K36*). Around two thousand people took part in the march, which resulted in a few isolated skirmishes with the police and broken windows.

38. "N schönen gruß von d'bewegig orientierung, betrifft: feuer und flamme für diese stadt," *Akut und Praktisch* (October 1980): 8.

39. "Foreword," *Radikal* 83 (October 1980).

40. Gitti Hentschel, "Wenn die Munition verschossen ist," in *Sachschaden: Häuser und andere Kämpfe*, ed. Gudrun Grundmann (Frankfurt: Verlag die Tageszeitung, 1981), 15.

41. "Vorbereitungen auf den Straßenkampf lange bekannt," *Berliner Morgenpost*, December 18, 1980; "Polizei: Hintermänner der Besetzer wollen den Staat treffen," *Berliner Morgenpost*, December 17, 1980.

42. Firiz Scheytan, "Das ist der Kern einer sozialen Bewegung," *Tageszeitung*, December 24, 1980.

43. Netzwerk Selbsthilfe & Alternative Liste, *Extrablatt Berlin* (December 1980) [Papiertiger Archiv, Häuserkampf Berlin/W., 12/1980]; "Keine Räumung der besetzten Häuser!" *Kommunistische Volkszeitung*, December 19, 1980.

44. Harry Ticker, "Die Ereignisse werfen Schatten," *Radikal extrablatt* (December 1980): 2.

45. "Die Kunst der Provokation, den Staat der Lächerlichkeit preisgeben, die Ebene der nackten Konfrontation meiden, das Unabsehbare genießen," *Radikal extrablatt* (December 1980): 4.

46. Untitled, *Radikal extrablatt* (December 1980): 4.

47. Lecorte, *Wir tanzen bis zum Ende*, 39.

48. Lecorte, *Wir tanzen bis zum Ende*, 57.

49. Lecorte, *Wir tanzen bis zum Ende*, 78.

50. On this point, see Joachim Häberlen, "Sekunden der Freiheit: Zum Verhältnis von Gefühlen, Macht und Zeit in Ausnahmesituationen am Beispiel der Revolte 1980/81 in Berlin," in *Ausnahmezustände: Entgrenzungen und Regulierungen in Europa während des Kalten Krieges*, ed. Dirk Schumann and Cornelia Rau (Göttingen: Wallstein, 2015).

51. Hezel, "'Was gibt es zu verlieren, wo es kein Morgen gibt?'" 152.

52. Gumbrecht, *Our Broad Present*, 21.

53. Hezel, "'Was gibt es zu verlieren, wo es kein Morgen gibt?'" 125. Jameson, "Postmodernism, or the Cultural Logic of Late Capitalism."

54. Häberlen, *The Emotional Politics of the Alternative Left*, 258.

55. Häberlen, *The Emotional Politics of the Alternative Left*, 214.

56. Häberlen, *The Emotional Politics of the Alternative Left*, 211.

57. On leftist melancholia, see Enzo Traverso, *Left-Wing Melancholia: Marxism, History, and Memory* (New York: Columbia University Press, 2017).

58. Schöneberger Besetzerrat, "Offener Brief an die Bürger Berlins!" in Ermittlungsauschuss im Mehringhof, *Abgeräumt? Häuser geräumt . . . Klaus-Jürgen Rattay tot. Ermittlungsausschuss. Eine Dokumentation* (Berlin: Ermittlungsausschuss, 1981), 7 [Landesarchiv Berlin, Brep, 002, 38292].

59. *Paßt bloß auf!* (Medienwerkstatt Freiburg, 1981).

60. "Pflasterstein-Ballade," reproduced in *Bewegung in Freiburg—Narrenfreiheit für die Bullen?* (Freiburg, 1981) [ASBF—Brochures].

61. "Der Ansprechspartner," *Die Plünderer. Von der Bewegung—Für die Bewegung* (undated, likely Fall 1981), 6.

62. *Paßt bloß auf! Ein Film aus der Kultur von unten.* (Freiburg: Medienwerkstatt, 1981).

63. "Der PLAN," *Subito Nr. eis* (June 1980): 13.

64. "Hotel Honka," *Instandbesetzerpost* 3 (March 1981): 7.

65. Back cover, *Die Plünderer. Von der Bewegung—Für die Bewegung* (undated, likely Fall 1981). The brochure seems to have been produced by the radical group Freizeit '81.

66. Alain Vidon, "Der Tag, an dem Calvin ausflippte," in *Hot Love: Swiss Punk & Wave, 1976–1980*, ed. Lurker Grand (Zurich: Edition Patrick Frey, 2007), 305.

67. Agentur BILWET, *Bewegungslehre*, 168–69.

68. Agentur BILWET, *Bewegungslehre*, 14.

69. Agentur BILWET, *Bewegungslehre*, 17.

70. Tsing, *The Mushroom at the End of the World*, 24.

71. "A Night at the Opera," *Stilett* 56 (June/July 1980): unpaginated.

72. "En heissä summer aber subito," *Stilett* 56 (June/July 1980): unpaginated.

73. "Freizeit 81. Gefühl und Härte," *Radikal* 98 (October 1981).

74. "Von der Sprachlosigkeit," *Radikal* 88 (February 1981): 12.

75. This practice of creative pastiche was also, of course, a major part of the punk movement. See Hebdige, *Subculture*.

76. "An meine Schwester, oder alle die es werden wollen," *Subito* 2 (August 1980).

77. Agentur BILWET, *Bewegungslehre*, 22.

78. See, for example, Vera Isler and Michael Haller, *Die Kunst der Verweigerung: Wandmalereien in den Autonomen Jugendzentren der Schweiz* (Zurich: Pro Juventue, 1982).

79. Back page, *Radikal* 86 (January 1981). See also the interview with Roland Heer in *Wir wollen alles, und zwar subito! Die Achtziger Jugendunruhen in der Schweiz und ihre Folgen*, ed. Heinz Nigg (Zurich: Limmat Verlag, 2001), 125. There is a notable similarity here between these practices and what the Manson Family called "magical mystery touring." See, for example, Claudia Verhoeven, "'Now Is the Time for Helter Skelter': Terror, Temporality, and the Manson Family," in *Power and Time: Temporalities in Conflict and the Making of History*, ed. Dan Edelstein, Stefanos Geroulanos, and Natasha Wheatley (Chicago: University of Chicago Press, 2020).

80. Agentur BILWET, *Bewegungslehre*, 16.

81. Schöneberger Besetzerrat, "Offener Brief an die Bürger Berlins!" (November 5, 1981) [Landesarchiv Berlin, Brep, 002, 38292].

82. *Die Entfesselung des Begehrens. Bewegungsdiskussion in Babylon und anderswo.* This pamphlet is an undated collection of flyers and articles from the youth movement in Switzerland and West Germany. In the interest of providing a clear translation, I slightly changed the format of the poem.

83. Quoted in Reichardt, *Authentizität und Gemeinschaft*, 541.

84. "Ines: Wir spüren Körperwärme," in *Paranoia City oder Zürich ist überall*, ed. Manfred Züfle and Jürg Meier (Reinbeck bei Hamburg: Rowohlt Taschenbuch, 1982), 30. She went on to note that such feelings take time to cultivate.

85. J. C. Wartenberg, *Kreuzberg K36. Leben in [der] Bewegung. Kreuzberg inside bis zum Fall der Mauer* (Berlin: self-published), 146.

86. According to contemporary Marxist critics like David Harvey, this tendency to view bounded spaces of difference as innately revolutionary fails to account for the incorporative spatial logics of capitalism. Such oppositional groups, Harvey has noted, run the risk of being incorporated into postindustrial capitalism, since in "clinging, often of necessity, to a place-bound identity, [they] become part of the very fragmentation which a mobile capitalism and flexible accumulation can feed upon" (David Harvey, *The Conditions of Postmodernity* [Oxford: Wiley-Blackwell, 1990], 303).

87. Tobias Becker, "The Meaning of Nostalgia: Genealogy and Critique," *History and Theory* 57, no. 2 (June 2018): 234–50, https://doi.org/10.1111/hith.12059; Svetlana Boym, *The Future of Nostalgia* (New York: Basic Books, 2002); Rudy Koshar, *Germany's Transient Pasts: Preservation and National Memory in the Twentieth Century* (Chapel Hill: University of North Carolina Press, 1998); Landwehr, "Nostalgia and the Turbulence of Times."

88. Matthias Heisig, "Das Politikum der Hausbesetzungen am Beispiel der Berliner Ereignisse 1980–1983," Diplomarbeit: Freie Universität Berlin, 1983, 35.

89. Heisig, "Das Politikum der Hausbesetzungen," 36.

90. Presseerklärung, Besetzerrat K36 (June 12, 1980), reproduced in Kuno Haberbusch, *Berliner Linie gegen Instandbesetzer: Die "Vernunft schlägt immer wieder zu!"* (Berlin: N.p., 1981), 7.

91. This attempt to convince neighbors that the squats were actually beneficial resulted in the production of numerous brochures aimed at providing information on the positive work being done by the squatters. See, for example, Jutta and Stefan, *Wird Zeit, Dass Wir Leben! Wohnungsbaupolitik und Instandbesetzungen* (June 1981) and Architekteninitiative Schöneberger Planung, "Was wird in den besetzten Häusern gemacht? Eine Dokumentation am Beispiel von 13. Besetzten Häusern."

92. According to an official report, 1981 witnessed 237 squatting attempts in West Berlin, of which 44 were prevented and 22 were evicted. (Senator für Inneres, Pressemitteilung Nr. 14 b/82, 31.8.1982. In Bezirksamt Kreuzberg von Berlin, Büro des Bezirksbürgermeisters, *Hausbesetzungen—Teil 1*, October 1982.)

93. "Mann nimmt letztlich in Kauf, daß ein Bulle krepiert—man selbst geht ja auch das Risiko ein, dabei draufzugehen. Eine Reportage," in *Paßt bloß auf! Was will die neue Jugendbewegung?* ed. Jürgen Bacia and Klaus-Jürgen Scherer (Berlin: Olle und Wolter, 1981), 14.

94. "Mann nimmt letztlich in Kauf, daß ein Bulle krepiert," 16.

95. This sentiment is also clearly evident in another article from the same volume in which the author described the youth protesters as a necessary corrective to the overly politicized path taken by the New Left, noting: "The fight for a humane society can only be successful on the basis of our deep individual desires for a different, more peaceful, more satisfying and thus more sensible life." ("Was wir wollen, das kriegen wir nicht—was wir kriegen, wollen wir nicht. Von den 68ern zu den 81ern. Schafft zwei, drei, viele Kulturen," in *Paßt bloß auf! Was will die neue Jugendbewegung?* ed. Jürgen Bacia and Klaus-Jürgen Scherer [Berlin: Olle und Wolter, 1981], 22.)

96. Agentur BILWET, *Bewegungslehre*, 13.

CHAPTER FOUR

1. "Eiszeit '82," *Schwarze Kanal* (January 1982): 6.

2. Agentur BILWET, *Bewegungslehre*, 175.

3. See Emile Durkheim, *The Elementary forms of Religious Life* (New York: Free Press, 1995); and Bernhard Giesen, "Performing the Sacred: A Durkheimian perspective on the performative turn in the social sciences," in *Social Performance: Symbolic Action, Cultural Pragmatics, and Ritual*, ed. Jeffrey Alexander, Bernhard Giesen, and Jason Mast (Cambridge: Cambridge University Press, 2006).

4. See, for example, "Post von der Front: Schwarzer Freitag—Grauer Samstag," *Instandbesetzerpost* 2 (March 17, 1981): 3.

5. "Das Feinste aus der Gerüchteküche und so," *Instandbesetzerpost* 00 (March 2, 1981): unpaginated.

6. See, for example, the flyer announcing the occupation of the Fraenkelufer 30 reprinted in *Instandbesetzerpost* 5 (April 9, 1981).

7. See, for example, the announcements of new cafés, workshops, and occupations in *Instandbesetzerpost* 6 (Easter 1981).

8. Bernd, "Nicht aufhören," *Instandbesetzerpost* 30 (November 21, 1981): 4.

9. See, for example, "Die Schlacht vor dem Rathaus," *Berliner Morgenpost*, June 26, 1981; "Demonstrationen gegen Hausräumungen," *Tagesspiegel*, November 7, 1982.

10. "Hausbesetzer—Kontakt zu 'Roten Zellen,'" *Berliner Morgenpost*, June 19, 1982. See also "'Guerilla diffusa'—der breit gefächerte Angriff auf den Staat," *Frankfurter Allgemeine Zeitung*, June 17, 1982.

11. "Kopf und Faust eine Einheit!" *Tageszeitung*, November 7, 1980.

12. "Der Spaltung fand nicht statt," *Tageszeitung*, April 7, 1981.

13. Dorothea Hilgenberg and Uwe Schlicht, "Was Hausbesetzer denken," *Tagesspiegel*, October 10, 1981.

14. Volker Skierka, "Berlin: Das Ende der Hausbesetzungen," *Süddeutsche Zeitung*, August 25, 1984.

15. Ursula Rehbein, Letter to the editor, *Tagespiegel*, October 18, 1981.

16. Eugen Martin, "Geht nach Hause," *Badische Zeitung*, June 12, 1980.

17. See, for example, the letters from Jutta Diefenbacher and Karl-Ernst Friedrich in *Badische Zeitung*, June 11, 1980.

18. Letter from Erika Ebert to the Squatters of the Manteufelstr. 40 in Berlin-Kreuzberg (July 19, 1982) [Landesarchiv Berlin—Brep 002, 16498].

19. Gudrun Gut, "Von alleine läuft gar nichts," in *Nachtleben Berlin. 1975 bis heute*, ed. Wolfgang Farkas, Stefanie Seidl, and Heiko Zwirner (Berlin: Metrolit, 2013), 73.

20. Tamara Cybulski, Bettina van Nes, and Gottlieb Renz, dirs., *Wo die Angst ist Geht's Lang* (Berlin: dffb, 1981) [Autofocus Archiv, Berlin]. Another film, *Das Zögern ist Vorbei* (Berlin: MOB, 1981), makes very similar points though it also includes interviews with people on the street about Klaus-Jürgen Rattay's death.

21. Jens-Peter Behrendt and Bernd Liebner, *Am Anfang war doch nicht der Pflasterstein* (Vorhang auf, Film ab!, 1982).

22. "Die Instandbesetzer der Winterfeldtstr. 31" (November 1981): cover page [Papiertiger Archiv, Berlin].

23. "Die Instandbesetzer der Winterfeldtstr. 31" (November 1981): 29–30 [Papiertiger Archiv, Berlin].

24. "Die Instandbesetzer der Winterfeldtstr. 31" (November 1981): 24 [Papiertiger Archiv, Berlin].

25. Wolfgang Jean Stock, "Vorwort," in *Gefühl und Härte. Neuen Kunst aus Berlin, 8. Oktober bis 14. November 1982, Kunstverein München*, ed. Ursula Prinz (Munich: Kunstverein München, 1982), 7. As an article in the April 1982 edition of *Schwarze Kanal* titled "Freie Berliner Kunstaustellung—was soll'n das?" indicated, however, many in the movement did not approve of being made the subject of art. The authors disdainfully noted that in using paving stones to make art or taking pictures of punks on the streets, the artists were "breaking the movement into countless exhibition pieces." See "Freie Berliner Kunstaustellung—Was soll'n das?" *Schwarze Kanal* 3 (April 1982): 29.

26. Notorische Reflexe, *"Fragment Video"* (1983), in *Berlin Super 80: Music & Film Underground West Berlin, 1978–1984* (Berlin: Monitorpop Entertainment, 2005).

27. "TUWAT SPEKTAKEL IN BÄRLIN AB 25.8" (August 1981).

28. "Interview mit der Initiatoren von TUWAT: Ein Kongreß für die gesamte Linke," *Tageszeitung*, August 7, 1981.

29. See "Kreuzberger 'Tuwat'—Zentrale nach Überfall auf Zivilbeamte durchsucht," *Tagesspiegel*, August 11, 1981; and "Überfall! Chaoten schlugen mit Knüpeln auf einer Polizisten ein," *Berliner Zeitung*, August 11, 1981. See also the letter titled "TUWAT" from an unnamed person at Der Senator für Inneres. Landesamt für Verfassungschutz to den Regierenden Bürgermeister von Berlin—Senatskanzlei- z.H. Herrn Senatsdirektor Dr. Schierbaum (August 21, 1981) [Landesarchiv Berlin, Brep 002, 6429].

30. See "Lummer sagt wieder ab. Eine 'Bürgeraktion gegen Chaos' wurde gegründet," *Volksblatt*, August 26, 1981; "Lummer: Tu nix für Tuwat, tu alles für Berlin!" *Berliner Zeitung*, August 27, 1981; and Presseerklärung des Bürgermeisters und Senators für Inneres Lummer, "Tu nix für TUWAT, tu alles für Berlin" (August 26, 1981) [Landeskirchliches Archiv 55.5./1889].

31. Black Friday Demonstration Flyer (March 13, 1981), reproduced in Habersbusch, *Berliner Linie gegen Instandbesetzer*, 21. Conservative city officials in West Berlin were particularly enraged by the fact that activists from other cities traveled to West Berlin to take part in the demonstrations. Heinrich Lummer, for example, often called attention to this phenomenon in order to suggest that the squatters were actually not West Berliners but terrorists from places like Amsterdam and Zurich. See "Viele Hausbesetzer sind erst seit kurzem in der Stadt: Lummer legte Statistik über 1000 Personen aus der 'Szene,'" *Tagesspiegel*, August 17, 1981. Such sentiments were often countered by critics of the conservative city administration. In an open letter to Lummer, Oliver Schruoffeneger of the Alternative Liste noted that two-thirds of the Senators in Berlin's city government were not from West Berlin and that many people traveled to the city to take part in conservative demonstrations as well. He went on to ironically suggest that the CDU and their supporters might actually consist of "professional revolutionaries who travel from demonstration to demonstration throughout the country." Oliver Schruoffeneger, "Offener Brief an Innensenator Lummer" (August 17, 1981) [Landeskirchliche Archiv 55.5/1889].

32. "Augenzeugenbericht vom Abend des 22.9," in Ermittlungsauschuss im Mehringhof, *Abgeräumt? Häuser geräumt . . . Klaus-Jürgen Rattay tot. Ermittlungsausschuss. Eine Dokumentation* (Berlin: Ermittlungsauschuss, 1981), 60–61.

33. See, for example, the discussion of the protests during US Secretary of State Alexander Haig's visit in Häberlen and Smith, "Struggling for Feelings."

34. "Über Panks . . . ," *Egal* (December 1980): unpaginated [ASBF, 14.3.0 I.].

35. See "Aufruf zum Zug der Unzufrieden am 17. Okt" (October 1980) [ASBF, 14.3.0 I.].

36. Agentur BILWET, *Bewegungslehre*, 68.

37. "Was wird in den besetzten Häusern gemacht? Eine Dokumentation am Beispiel von 13. Besetzten Häusern," 21.

38. "Berichte zum kleinkrieg gegen die Spekulanten Vogel/Braun" (Berlin: Regenbogenfabrik & Lausitzer Str. 23, 1982), 10–11 [Papiertiger Archiv, Mieten-Politik, Widerstand, Stadtteil Politik, Berlin].

39. "AUSLAND. KURZNACHRICHTEN," *Stilett* 56 (June/July 1980): unpaginated.

40. Denise, "Pank statt Bank," in *Paranoia City oder Zürich ist überall*, ed. Manfred Züfle and Jürg Meier (Reinbeck bei Hamburg: Rowohlt Taschenbuch, 1982), 132.

41. On the issue of activist travel networks, see Axel Schildt, "Across the Border: West German Youth Travel to Western Europe," in *Between Marx and Coca-Cola: Youth Cultures in Changing European Societies, 1960–1980*, ed. Axel Schildt and Detlef Siegfried (New York: Berghahn Books, 2006); and Linus Owens et al., "At Home in the Movement: Constructing an Oppositional Identity through Activist Travel across European Squats," in *Understanding European Movements: New Social Movements, Global Justice Struggles, Anti-austerity Protest*, ed. Cristina Flesher Fominaya and Laurence Cox (London: Routledge, 2013).

42. "Asterix im Schwarzwaldhof" (1981) [ASBF, Brochures].

43. In her memoirs about life in West Berlin, Eva Bude expressed particular frustration at the customs of the Swabians. See Bude, *Verpisst euch!*

44. "Frontpost," *Instandbesetzerpost* 4 (April 1, 1981): 4.

45. See, for example, Aktionsgruppe Paula Panther/Karl Krallmich, "Manchmal fällt auf uns der Frost: Dokumentation zur kriminalisierung in Freiburg" (July 1981) [ASBF, Brochures].

46. "Thesen zur Diskussion. Was ist 'Bewegung'? Eine Notwendige Provokation," 13 [ASBF, Brochures].

47. Wartenberg, *Kreuzberg K36*, 185.

48. Markus Rüegg, "Die autonome Lemminge," *KAMIKAZE* 1 (May 1981).

49. "Öffentlichkeit—Der Tanz ums Goldene Kalb," *Die Plünderer. Von der Bewegung—Für die Bewegung*, 7. The authors of *Bewegungslehre* also tended to blame the media for the movement's descent into spectacle. See Agentur BILWET, "Spezielle Bewegungslehre: Besetzten jenseits der Medien," in *Bewegungslehre*.

50. Sven Regener, *Der kleine Bruder* (Frankfurt: Eichborn Berlin, 2008), 82.

51. The parallels to the Neue Wilden movement discussed above are hard to ignore.

52. For a detailed analysis of "post-adolescence" see A. G. Prognos, "Jugendprotest: Einstellungen und Motive von Jugendlichen in 8 ausgewählten Gruppen," in *Jugendprotest im demokratischen Staat. Enquete-Kommission des Deutschen Bundestages*, ed. Matthias Wissmann and Rudolf Hauck (Stuttgart: Edition Weitbrecht, 1983).

53. "Bericht der Enquete-Kommission," in *Jugendprotest im demokratischen Staat. Enquete-Kommission des Deutschen Bundestages*, ed. Matthias Wissmann and Rudolf Hauck (Stuttgart: Edition Weitbrecht, 1983), 37. As is clear from a letter sent by the Schöneberger Squatter Council to the Enquete Commission, the youth activists rejected this explanation of their behavior, noting: "You can't make the youth into patients when it is the system that is sick" (quoted in "Bericht der Enquete-Kommission," 34).

54. Prognos, "Jugendprotest: Einstellungen und Motive von Jugendlichen in 8 ausgewählten Gruppen," 115.

55. Kommission für Jugendfragen, *Thesen zu den Jugendunruhen* (Bern: Bundesamt für Kulturpflege, 1980), 21.

56. Jörg Bopp, "Trauer-Power. Zur Jugendrevolte 1981," *Kursbuch* 65 (1981): 163. For similar arguments, see the essays in Uwe Schlicht, ed., *Trotz und Träume: Jugend lehnt sich auf* (Berlin: Severin und Siedler, 1982); as well as Hans-Jürgen Wirth, *Die Schär-*

fung der Sinne: Jugendprotest als persönliche und kulturelle Chance (Frankfurt: Syndikat, 1984).

57. Peter Schulz-Hageleit, "Auf der Suche nach neuen Formen des gemeinsamen Lebens," *Frankfurter Rundschau*, July 15, 1981. See also Peter Schulz-Hageleit, ed., *Lieber instandbesetzten als kaputtbesitzen! Unterrichts Materialien zur Wohnungspolitik* (Berlin: Basis Verlag, 1981). It is worth noting at this point that arguments positing a close correlation between constrictive social environments and youth unrest had a long history in Germany. See, for example, Curt Bondy, *Jugendliche stören die Ordnung: Bericht und Stellungnahme zu d. Halbstarkenkrawallen* (Munich: Juventa-Verlag, 1957). Thanks to Joachim Häberlen for pointing this out.

58. Walter Hollstein, "Autonome Lebensformen. Über die transbürgerliche Perspektive der Jugendbewegung," in *Aussteigen oder rebellieren. Jugendliche gegen Staat und Gesellschaft*, ed. Michael Haller (Reinbeck bei Hamburg: Rowohlt, 1981), 212.

59. Kunzelmann, *Leisten Sie keinen Widerstand!* 149.

60. Peter-Paul Zahl, "Eisbrecher, Mitten in den Strassen, Volldampf Voraus," in *Instandbesetzer Bilderbuch*, ed. Wolfgang Krolow (Berlin: Lit Pol, 1981), unpaginated.

61. Bernd Rabehl, "Im Kampf gegen die Polizei werden sie die Gestalt der Polizei annehmen. Eine Einschätzung des aktuellen Jugendprotests. Gespräch mit Bernd Rabehl," in *Paßt bloß auf! Was will die neue Jugendbewegung?* ed. Jürgen Bacia and Klaus-Jürgen Sherer (Berlin: Olle und Wolter, 1981), 76.

62. Rabehl, "Im Kampf gegen die Polizei werden sie die Gestalt der Polizei annehmen," 81. See also "Von der Müsli- zur Molli-Fraktion . . . Über das Verhältnis der Alternativbewegungen zur neuen Jugendrevolte. Ein Gespräch mit Josef Huber," in the same volume.

63. Armin Waldschmidt, "Leben geht vor Eigentum," Redebeitrag anläßlich des Gottesdienstes in der Shultheiss-Niederlage am 1. Juli 1981" [Landeskirchliche Archiv, 55.5/1889].

64. This paper also generated a significant amount of dissent within the Evangelical community. See, for example, "West-Berliner Synode führte Debatte über Hausbesetzer," *epd Landesdienst Berlin* 91 (May 21, 1981). See also the letter from Bishop Kruse to the church community (March 1981) in *Kirche und Hausbesetzungen in Berlin (West)* (Berlin: Gemeindeberatung im Kirchenkreis Kreuzberg, 1983).

65. On fundraising efforts, see, among others, *Dokumentation: Kunst & Kulturcentrum Kreuzberg* (Berlin: Bauausstellung Berlin GMBH, 1984). On the church as meeting space, see, for example, "Alle oder keiner," *Tageszeitung*, July 13, 1982, which detailed a meeting of around 150 squatters held at the Apostel Paulus Kirche to discuss use agreements (*Nutzungsverträge*).

66. "Pressemitteilung, Paten gegen Räumung der besetzten Häuser—Für eine Wohnungspolitische Lösung" [Landeskirchliche Archiv, 55.5/1889].

67. "Günter Grass bei seinen Paten Kindern," *Volksblatt*, December 16, 1982.

68. On Gollwitzer's involvement in the *Paten* movement, see Helmut Gollwitzer, "Erklärung bei der Pressekonferenz der Solidaritätsaktion von Berliner Hochschullehrern, Künstlern, Schriftstellern, Pfarren u.a. für die Instandbesetzer" (June 22, 1981) [Evangelisches Zentralarchiv, Berlin, 686/7831].

69. Undated letter to Helmut Gollwitzer [Evangelisches Zentralarchiv, Berlin, 686/730].

70. "Netzwerk und die Hausbesetzer. Benny Härlin beschreibt eine 'Beziehungskiste,'" *Netzwerk Rundbrief* 23 (December 16, 1983): 72. On SHIK (Selbstverwaltete Häuser in Kreuzberg), see *"Wir wollen niemals auseinandergehen . . ."* (Berlin: SHIK, August 1983). Given that both groups emerged in the wave of postrevolutionary activism after the German Autumn, it should come as no surprise that Netzwerk shared goals and sometimes personnel with political parties like the Alternative List. In a speech in the Berlin Abgeordnetenhaus in July 1981, AL politician Klaus-Jürgen Schmidt posited a series of arguments that directly echoed those being made by the members of Netzwerk. In this speech, Schmidt declared that the real source of violence was the terrible housing policies of the city. "As long as this violence exists," he argued, "then there will be this sort of resistance to injustice" (Klaus-Jürgen Schmidt, "Rede der Alternativen Liste in der Aktuellen Stunden des Abgeordnetenhauses am 2.7.1981," 3 [Landeskirchliche Archiv 55.5/1889]).

71. "Kiez-träger oder Besetzer-Träger?" (January 1983), 11 [Papiertiger Archiv, Brochures].

72. Dr. Grüneberg, "Zur Senatssitzung am 10. Januar 1984" (January 5, 1984) [Landesarchiv Berlin, BRep 002, 27780 "Protokollen zu Senatssitzungen: Wohnungspolitik Hausbesetzungen]. See Senator für Inneres, "Pressemitteilung Nr. 14 n/82, 31.8.1982," in *Hausbesetzung—Teil 1, Bezirksamt Kreuzberg von Berlin, Büro des Bezirksbürgermeisters* (October 1982).

73. "Antrag auf Auflösung der Netzbau GmbH," Beschlußvorlage des Vorstandes für die Mitgliedversammlung der Netzwerk-Selbsthilfe, e.V. am 11. Dezember 82, 10:30 Uhr, Gemeindehaus Nostizstraße [Landesarchiv Berlin, Brep 002, 17127]. See also "Gespräch mit einer, der um besetzte Häuser verhandelt," *Tageszeitung*, October 19, 1982; "Senat lehnt Nutzungsverträge für geräumte Häuser ab," *Tagesspiegel*, November 6, 1982; and the November 5, 1982, letter from Netzbau, the Verein zur Förderung selbstverwalteten Wohnens (FsW), and Kiezträger SHIK to Mayor Weizsäcker [Landesarchiv Berlin, Brep 002, 17127].

74. See, for example, "Lummer fordert Reizgas gegen Chaoten in Berlin," *Berliner Morgenpost*, June 13, 1982; "Zwei vor der Legalisierung stehende NH-Häuser als 'Kriminelle Fluchtburgen'geräumt," *Tageszeitung*, November 2, 1982; and Dr. Rupert Scholz, Senator für Justiz, "Diskussionspapier zur Hausbesetzerfrage" (July 8, 1982) [Landesarchiv Berlin, Brep002, 16495].

75. "Viele Hausbesetzer haben eine Wohnung," *Morgenpost*, December 1, 1982; "Innensenator Lummer spricht von einer 'Kaputtbesetzung,'" *Tagesspiegel*, April 27, 1982; "Lummer fordert Reizgas gegen Chaoten in Berlin," *Berliner Morgenpost*, June 13, 1982; and "Lummer zur Lösung des Hausbesetzerproblems," Der Senator für Inneres Pressestelle 121/84 (November 8, 1984) [Landesarchiv Berlin, Brep 002, 17125].

76. Dr. Klaus, "Vermerk, Betr: Räumungen am 27. Jun 1983," 5–6 [Landesarchiv Berlin, Brep 002, 17128].

77. "Von der Müsli- zur Molli-Fraktion . . . Über das Verhältnis der Alternativebewegungen zur neuen Jugendrevolte. Ein Gespräch mit Josef Huber," in Bacia and Sherer, *Paßt bloß auf! Was will die neue Jugendbewegung?* 69.

78. See "Frankfurter Szenen: Stein und Bewußtsein," in Grundmann, *Sachschaden: Häuser und andere Kämpfe*, 50.

79. Even some progressive politicians supported this solution. See, for example, Frau Brunn's speech at the Berlin House of Representatives on September 23, 1982 (Abgeordnetenhaus von Berlin—9. Wahlperiod, 28. Sitzung vom 23. September 1982). See also Pressedienst, SPD Berlin (Nr. 1/80, 25.9.1981) [Landesarchiv Berlin, Brep002, 17124]. Most politicians, however, were opposed to such a total solution. In a statement in March 1982, for example, Construction Senator Rastemborski argued that while the city government was working toward developing new models for housing politics "such models cannot have as their goal a so-called 'total solution' but should in suitable cases help young people who want to practice alternative forms of living but are also willing to live within the legal order, by allowing them to help themselves." See "Ein Versuch zu neuen Wegen in der Stadterneuerung," Landespressedienst aus dem Senat (March 19, 1982) [Landesarchiv Berlin, Brep 002, 16497].

80. "Gedanken zur Räumung," *Schwarze Kanal* 1 (February 1982).

81. AG Grauwacke, "Verhandler? Vergisses," in *Autonome in Bewegung: aus den ersten 23 Jahren* (Berlin: Assoziation A, 2003), 45.

82. "Spielen—Verspielen—Handeln—Verhandeln," *Schwarze Kanal* 2 (February 1982): 9.

83. Lecorte, *Wir tanzen bis zum Ende*, 141.

84. See "Der Dialog hört nicht mehr auf!" *Schwarze Kanal* 00 (January 1982); and "Jugend-Enquete-Kommission traf sich mit Berliner Besetzern," *Tageszeitung*, February 9, 1982.

85. "Hoppla, wir werden analysiert! Uni-Dozenten wollen die 'Jugendrevolte' analysieren," *Schwarze Kanal* 1 (February 1982): 22. Other parties deemed guilty of such violent acts of contextualization included the *Paten*, Netzerk, and the journalists of the *Tageszeitung*—in other words, the members of the postrevolutionary left who were trying to help save the squats from the wrecking ball.

86. "Nieder mit dem TAZ Imperialismus," *Schwarze Kanal* 2 (March 1982): 11. Another article in the same issue detailed how thirty activists visited the offices of the *Tageszeitung* to see what sort of treachery they were engaged in ("TAZ-Tango").

87. One of the major exceptions to this position of absolute alterity comes from a speech made by Helmut Kohl at the Bundestag on March 19, 1981, in which he argued that the youth were pointing to real problems in modern society that went well beyond a mere shortage of affordable housing. Indeed, the youth were protesting "against the bleak perspectives of a technologically managed society, an anonymous and ever colder inhumane world for which the soulless machines for living of our concrete civilization have become the most galling symbol." Despite the fact that he believed they were pointing to real issues, however, Kohl also argued that youth had responded to these issues in unacceptable ways and with totally untenable solutions. Indeed, their actions threatened to produce a dangerous "lawless zone" that posed a serious threat to democracy. (Helmut Kohl, Speech at the 26. Sitzung des 9. Deutschen Bundestages [March 19, 1981], quoted in Bacia and Sherer, *Paßt bloß auf! Was will die neue Jugendbewegung?* 65–68).

88. Jeanne Hersche, *Antithesen zu den "Thesen zu den Jugendunruhen 1980" der Eidgenössischen Kommission für Jugendfragen: der Feind heisst Nihilismus* (Schaffhausen: Verlag Peter Meili, 1982), 11.

89. For an overview of press reactions to the squatting movement in West Berlin in the early 1980s see Rolf Amann, *Der moralische Aufschrei: Presse und abweichendes Verhalten am Beispiel der Hausbesetzungen in Berlin* (Frankfurt: Campus Verlag, 1985). According to Amann, the press created a moral panic surrounding the squatting movement and in so doing acted as an institution of social control (36).

90. "Sie nannten sich selbst 'Psychoterroristen,'" *Berliner Morgenpost*, July 14, 1981. See also Hans Heigert, "Ein anderer Judenstern," *Süddeutsche Zeitung*, July 15, 1981.

91. "Die Chaoten und Scharmachern wollen unsere Stadt ruinieren!" *Berliner Zeitung*, August 7, 1981.

92. "Viele geräumte Häuser waren beschädigt und verwüstet," *Berliner Morgenpost*, August 22, 1982.

93. Fred Grätz, Letters to Various Senators (January 1, 1982) [Landesarchiv Berlin, Brep 002, 16496].

94. "Volksstimmen nach dem 22.9.1981," in *Alles Plastik. Theaterstück für Menschen ab 14 von Volker Ludwig und Detlef Michel*, 109–10.

95. Udo Lang, "Zeitgedichte zur herbstlichen Stimmung zwischen Dreisameck Schwarzwaldhof und Mariengrab" (undated, likely 1982) [ASBF, Brochures].

96. E. Steinberg, "Schrecken in Polizeiburg" (March 1982) in "Die große Freiheit" [ASBF, 14.3.0 XIII].

97. "Die Krankheit" (undated, likely March 1982) in "Die große Freiheit" [ASBF, 14.3.0 XIII].

98. "Wirklichkeit durch Chaos," *Bewegung in Freiburg* (Freiburg, 1981).

99. Leserbrief, "Betrifft: taz—Kommentar 'Bombenstimmung in Berlin' v. Montag, 5.4.82," *Schwarze Kanal* 3 (April 1982): 2.

100. Freia Anders, "Wohnraum, Freiraum, Widerstand. Die Formierung der Autonomen in den Konflikten um Hausbesetzungen Anfang der achtziger Jahre," in *Das Alternative Milieu: Antibürgerlicher Lebensstil und linke Politik in der Bundesrepublik Deutschland und Europa, 1968–1983*, ed. Sven Reichardt and Detlef Siegfried (Göttingen: Wallstein Verlag, 2010), 498.

101. "Didaktische einheit," *Schwarze Kanal* 2 (April 1982): 27.

102. Die Tödliche Doris, "Berliner Küchenmusik" (1982), in *Berlin Super 80: Music & Film Underground West Berlin, 1978–1984* (Berlin: Monitorpop Entertainment, 2005).

103. Wolfgang Müller, *Subkultur Westberlin 1979–1989*.

CHAPTER FIVE

1. "Hausbesetzungen sind nur noch Erinnerung," *Die Welt*, November 13, 1984.

2. Heinrich Lummer, "Hausbesetzungen—Probleme und Lösungen" (November 8, 1984) [Landesarchiv Berlin, BRep 002, 17125].

3. Letter from Hermann Münzel to Eberhard Diepgen (May 24, 1985) [Landesarchiv Berlin, BRep 002, 17125].

4. Letter from Dr. Klaus to Hermann Münzel (June 3, 1985) [Landesarchiv Berlin, BRep 002, 17125].

5. Georgy Katsiaficas, *The Subversion of Politics: European Autonomous Social Movements and the Decolonization of Everyday Life* (Amherst: Humanities Press International, 1997), 128.

6. "Dr. Terror's House of Horrors," *Bild*, November 15, 1987, reproduced in *10 Meter Ohne Kopf*, 44 [Rote Flora, Box 09.400, HH Hafenstraße I].

7. Carl-Heinz Mallet, *Die Leute von der Hafenstraße: Über eine andere Art zu leben* (Hamburg: Lutz Schulenburg, 2000), 176. See also Bürgerschaft Drucksache 10/56 (July 13, 1982), Abgeordneten Klimke (CDU) [Staatsarchiv Hamburg, 136-1, 4927].

8. The "misuse of living space," or *Zweckentfremdung von Wohnraum*, was illegal in West Germany. See Heiko Artkämpfer, *Hausbesetzer, Hausbesitzer, Hausfriedensbruch* (Berlin: Springer Verlag, 1995).

9. Bürgerschaft Drucksache 13/2799, "Bericht des Parlamentarischen Untersuchungsausschusses 'Hafenstraße'" (December 22, 1988) [Staatsarchiv Hamburg, 136-1, 4924].

10. "Open Letter to Senator Volker Lange from the Residents of the Hafenstraße," reproduced in *Hafenstraße: Chronologie Eines Konfliktes* (Hamburg: Initiativkreis für den Erhalt der Hafenstraße), 1.

11. Bürgerschaft Drucksache 13/2799, "Bericht des Parlamentarischen Untersuchungsausschusses 'Hafenstraße'" (December 22, 1988) [Staatsarchiv Hamburg, 136-1, 4924].

12. *Hafenstraße: Chronologie Eines Konfliktes*, 2.

13. Bürgerschaft Drucksache 13/2799, "Bericht des Parlamentarischen Untersuchungsausschusses 'Hafenstraße'" (December 22, 1988) [Staatsarchiv Hamburg, 136-1, 4924].

14. Thomas Osterkorn, "Hafenstraße: Senat legt die Glacehandschuhe ab," *Hamburger Abendblatt*, August 10, 1985.

15. "Feuer und Flamme für diesen Staat," *Der Spiegel*, December 29, 1986. See also "Pressekonferenz der CDU—Bürgerschaftsfraktion am 15. Dezember 1986" [Staatsarchiv Hamburg, 136-1, 4926].

16. See "Fragen zum Verhältnis Polizei und Hafenstraße" [Staatsarchiv Hamburg, 331-1 II, Ablieferung 41, 20.37-3].

17. See Grosskreutz "Vermerk" (September 3, 1986) [Staatsarchiv Hamburg, 136-1, 4927].

18. *Wortprotokoll des Leiters für Verfassungsschutz Christian Lochte vor den PUA Hafenstraße* (1988). See also Behörde für Inneres, "Vermerk: Darstellung der Situation der Häuser Hafenstraße 106 bis 126 sowie Bernhard-Nocht-Str. 16 bis 24" (November 11, 1986) [Staatsarchiv Hamburg, 136-1, 4926].

19. "Hafenstrassen OHNE ENDE" (1986), reproduced in *Hafenstraße: Chronologie Eines Konfliktes*, 29.

20. On this series of events see the exchange of letters between Blohm, Pawelczyk, and Curilla [Staatsarchiv Hamburg, 136–1, 4926].

21. Hans-Joachim Lenger, "Die Quelle des Chaos," in *"Hafenstraße" Chronik und Analysen eines Konflikts*, ed. Michael Herrmann et al. (Hamburg: Verlag am Galgenberg, 1987), 90.

22. "Hamburger Prominente fordern vom Senat: Hände weg von der Hafenstraße," *Hamburger Rundschau*, December 18, 1986.

23. "Dickens klassisch: Der Millionär Jan Philipp Reemtsma bietet Hamburger Schmuddelkindern ein Zuhause," *Der Spiegel*, June 8, 1987. See also Bürgerschaft Drucksache 13/2799, "Bericht des Parlamentarischen Untersuchungsausschusses 'Hafenstraße'" (December 22, 1988) [Staatsarchiv Hamburg, 136–1, 4924].

24. Wagner, "Vermerk" (July 17, 1987) [Staatsarchiv Hamburg, 136–1, 4925].

25. "Wunder oder Illusion: Hamburg, Hafenstraße, Hafenstraßenbild," *Der Spiegel*, November 23, 1987.

26. Bürgerschaft Drucksache 13/2799, "Bericht des Parlamentarischen Untersuchungsausschusses 'Hafenstraße'" (December 22, 1988) [Staatsarchiv Hamburg, 136–1, 4924]. Although the Laewetz Stiftung was given ownership of the Hafenstraße houses, the city remained intensely involved in the daily operations of the property. This involvement in the day-to-day operation of the houses was in part enacted through the participation of city officials on the Laewetz board.

27. Mallet, *Die Leute von der Hafenstraße*, 180. Mallet estimates the number of law enforcement officers at five thousand.

28. "Hafenstraße: Geballte Faust," *Der Spiegel*, November 30, 1987. City officials such as Senators Wagner and Lange had never accepted Dohnanyi's agreement.

29. "Hafenstraße: Guter Zugriff," *Der Spiegel*, May 15, 1989.

30. "Hafenstraße Verteidigen Jetzt Erst Recht" [Rote Flora, Hafenstraße Flugblätter 88–89].

31. "Im Fadenkreuz der RAF," *Stern*, September 13, 1990; and "Das Nest des Terrors," *Hamburger Abendblatt*, September 12, 1990.

32. "Hamburg-Hafenstraße: Aus dem Herzen," *Der Spiegel*, February 8, 1988. See also Letter from Prof. Dr. Claus-Peter Kedenburg (Abg. CDU) to Senator Volker Lange (September 3, 1987) [Staatsarchiv Hamburg, 136–1, 4927].

33. Landgericht Hamburg, Geschäfts—Nr. 110, 121/89 (August 2, 1989) [Staatsarchiv Hamburg, 331–1 II, Ablieferung 41, 20.37–3].

34. Letter from H. Lorenz, Gerichtsvollzieher, to Rae Dr. Weiland (January 14, 1991) [Staatsarchiv Hamburg, 331–1 II, A41, 20.37–3].

35. See "Räumung der Hafenstraße . . . Alptraum oder Fata Morgana?" *Interne Information Polizei Hamburg*, 170 (November 23, 1990) [Staatsarchiv Hamburg, 331–1 II, A41, 20.37–3].

36. "Entscheidung Verschoben," *Hamburger Abendblatt*, January 21, 1995; "Privatisierung schmeckt gar nicht," *Frankfurter Rundschau*, February 10, 1995.

37. "Hafenstraße: Der Weg ist Frei. Bürgerschaft stimmt Kaufvertrag zu," *Hamburger Abendblatt*, January 18, 1996. See also Bürgerschaft Drucksache 15/4649 (De-

cember 19, 1995) Mitteilung des Senats and die Bürgerschaft [Staatsarchiv Hamburg, 331-1 II, Ablieferung 41, 20.37-3].

38. Annette, "Was halt mich hier bloß?" *St. Pauli Einschnitt* (Hamburg: Hafenrand verein für selbstbestimmtes Leben und Wohnen in St. Pauli e.V., 2000), 13.

39. Mallet, *Die Leute von der Hafenstraße*, 172–73.

40. Anne Reiche, *Auf der Spur* (Edition Cimarron, 2019).

41. "Rote Ernte," *Wiener*, February 1, 1987.

42. "Bauen," *St. Pauli Einschnitt*, 22.

43. Dorit van Aken, Monika Bischoff-Gombert, Martin Schirmacher, Simone Borgstede, Claus Petersen, Mathias Böge, Martin Junk, and Annette, "Annäherung," *St. Pauli Einschnitt*, 17.

44. "Hafenstraße" (August 1987) [Rote Flora, Hafenstrasse Flügblätter, 82–87].

45. "Kein Friede Mit Den Räumungsterroristen" (1986) [Rote Flora, Hafenstrasse Flügblätter, 82–87].

46. "Rote Ernte," *Wiener*, February 1, 1987.

47. Reproduced in *10 Meter Ohne Kopf*, 6. Lyrics are in English.

48. "Bedroht fühlen wir uns nur durch die Polizei," *Hamburger Rundschau*, December 4, 1986.

49. Some authors such as Joist Grolle have posited that the radical escalations of the conflicts surrounding the houses can be primarily attributed to the legacies of Nazism. See Joist Grolle, "Der Hamburger Hafenstraßenkonflikt und der Geisterkrieg um die Vergangenheit," *Zeitschrift des Vereins für Hamburgisch Geschichte* 91 (2005): 133–58.

50. "Deutsche Bank und deutsches Geld morden mit in aller Welt" (November 1989), reproduced in *StaatsTerrorismus Hat Kontinuität/ Lever Dot as Slav* (1990), 15 [Rote Flora, Box 09.400 HH Hafenstraße I].

51. "Hafenstrassen OHNE ENDE" (October 1986), reproduced in *Hafenstraße: Chronologie Eines Konfliktes*, 29.

52. "Hafenstraße braucht der Mensch!" (Decemeber 1986), reproduced in *Hafenstraße: Chronologie Eines Konfliktes*, 26.

53. "Hafenstraße" (June 1987), reproduced in *Hafenstraße: Chronologie Eines Konfliktes*, 42.

54. "HEW Klaut Strom. Senat Gegen Den Rest Der Welt, Oder: Das Imperium Schlägt Zurück," reproduced in *Hafenstraße: Chronologie Eines Konfliktes*, 20; "HEW in ungebrochener Nazi-Tradition" (1988) [Rote Flora, Hafenstraße Flugblätter 88–89].

55. Herrmann et al., eds., *"Hafenstraße" Chronik und Analysen eines Konflikts*, 26.

56. *Tageszeitung*, May 6, 1983, reproduced in *"Hafenstraße" Chronik und Analysen eines Konflikts*, ed. Herrmann et al., 23.

57. "Zussamen Wohnen Zusammen Kämpfen" (1987) [Rote Flora, Hafenstrasse Flügblätter, 82–87].

58. *10 Meter Ohne Kopf*, 14.

59. "Vermerk, Groskreutz (Der Leiter der Verwaltungsstelle für Gerichtsvollzieherangelegenheiten) 3.9.86," 2 [Hamburg Staatsarchiv, 136-1, 4927].

60. "Police Report FD721, Durchsuchungs-und Ermittlungsbericht" (November 20, 1987), 3. Attached to "Letter from Johann Klarmann (PUA) to Volker Lange" (May 11, 1988) [Staatsarchiv Hamburg, 136–1, 4924].

61. "Traurige Visitenkarte einer Weltstadt," *Frankfurter Allgemeine Zeitung*, April 26, 1985.

62. Thomas Ruhmöller, "Hafenstraße: Peinliche Polizei-Panne," *Hamburger Abendblatt*, October 13, 1986.

63. See "Solidaritätsaktionen in anderen Städten" [Staatsarchiv Hamburg, 136–1, 4926] and "Brandanschlag nach Teilräumung in der Hamburger Hafenstraße," *Frankfurter Allgemeine Zeitung*, October 30, 1986.

64. "Offener Brief," reproduced in *Gewalt Gegen Frauen*.

65. *Hamburger Abendblatt*, October 6, 1987, reproduced in *"Hafenstraße" Chronik und Analysen eines Konflikts*, ed. Herrmann et al., 9.

66. Quoted in "Hafenstraße Hamburg: Vertrage Unterschreiben; Reaktionäre Kreise Halten an Räumungsabsichten Fest" (Bund Westdeutscher Kommunisten, 1987) [Rote Flora, Hafenstrasse Flügblätter, 82–87].

67. "Wortprotokoll des Leiters für Verfassungsschutz Christian Lochte vor den PUA Hafenstraße" (May 1988) and "Wie gefährlich sind die Besetzter der Häuser in der Hafenstraße?" *Welt am Sonntag*, October 20, 1985.

68. "Das sagen die Parteien," *Hamburger Morgenpost*, September 12, 1990, reproduced in *Mord Pläne Gegen Kohl* [Rote Flora, Box 09.400 HH Hafenstraße I].

69. The phrases "Hafenstraße überall" and "Hafenstraße bleibt" were spray-painted on walls throughout West Germany and appeared in countless leftist documents in the period.

70. Leonie Ossowski, *Wilhelm Meister's Abschied* (Weinheim und Basel: Beltz Verlag, 1982), 123.

71. Tsing, *The Mushroom at the end of the World*, 6.

72. Radio broadcast (June 11, 1987), reproduced in *Hier Spricht Radio Hafenstraße*, 19. Signs in English.

73. "Deutsche Bank und deutsches Geld morden mit in aller Welt" (November 1989), reproduced in *StaatsTerrorismus Hat Kontinuität. Lever Dot as Slav* (1990), 15 [Rote Flora, Box 09.400 HH Hafenstraße I].

74. "No Future for the System" (1984) [Rote Flora, Hafenstraße Flugblätter, 82–87].

75. "Hafenstrasse OHNE ENDE" (1986), reproduced in *Hafenstraße: Chronologie Eines Konflikts*, 29.

76. "Hönkel, Grummel, Hönkel, Grummel: Der illegal Sender 'Radio Hafenstraße,'" *Der Spiegel*, November 23, 1987.

77. For a wide-ranging analysis of this mode of insurgent activism, see Tomba, *Insurgent Universality*.

78. "Unser Bürgermeister heisst Klaus Störtebeker" [Rote Flora, Hafenstrasse Flugblätter 88–89].

79. For an excellent collection of these murals, see Monika Sigmund and Marily Stroux, *Zu bunt: Wandbilder in der Hafenstraße* (Hamburg: St. Pauli Archiv, 1996).

80. Lou Cornum makes a similar point in regard to the relationship between indigenous and Afrofuturism. See Cornum, "Seizing the Alterity of Futures."

81. Senate meeting (September 24, 1986), quoted in Hermann, "Die Blitzaktion: Hintergründe eines Polizeieinsatzes," in *"Hafenstraße" Chronik und Analyses eines Konflikts*, ed. Herrmann et al., 70–71.

82. See "Hafenstrasse: Bürgerkrieg oder was?" *Der Spiegel*, April 24, 1989, and "Beleidigte Diva," *Der Spiegel*, July 13, 1987.

83. "Echte Stätte der Phantasie," *Der Spiegel*, November 9, 1987.

84. "Den Kleinkrieg wird es geben," *Der Spiegel*, November 23, 1987.

85. Jan Guillou, *Der demokratische Terrorist*, trans. Hans-Joachim Maas (Munich: Piper, 1990).

86. *10 Meter Ohne Kopf*, 14.

87. Robert Pogue Harrison, "Hic Jacet," in *Landscape and Power*, 2nd ed., ed. W. J. T. Mitchell (Chicago: University of Chicago Press, 2002), 353.

88. On the role of duration within radical architecture, see Sean Keller, "Building Duration: Architecture Out of Adventure-Time," *Critical Inquiry* 50, no. 3 (Spring 2024): 472–93, https://doi.org/10.1086/728954.

89. Celia Applegate, *A Nation of Provincials: The German Idea of Heimat* (Berkeley: University of California Press, 1990), 242.

90. On housing exhibits, see, among others, Castillo, *Cold War on the Home Front*, and Wagner-Conzelmann, *Die Interbau 1957 in Berlin*.

91. Henri Lefebvre, *The Production of Space* (Malden: Blackwell, 1991), 385.

92. De Certeau, *The Practice of Everyday Life*, 106.

93. De Certeau, *The Practice of Everyday Life*, 108.

94. On ruins, see Dora Apel, *Beautiful Terrible Ruins: Detroit and the Anxiety of Decline* (New Brunswick: Rutgers University Press, 2015); Julia Hell, *The Conquest of Ruins: The Third Reich and the Fall of Rome* (Chicago: University of Chicago Press, 2019); Julia Hell and Andreas Schönle, eds., *The Ruins of Modernity* (Durham: Duke University Press, 2010); Susan Stewart, *The Ruins Lesson: Meaning and Material in Western Culture* (Chicago: University of Chicago Press, 2019); and Ann Laura Stoler, ed., *Imperial Debris: On Ruins and Ruination* (Durham: Duke University Press, 2013).

95. Caitlin DeSilvey and Tim Edensor, "Reckoning with Ruins," *Progress in Human Geography* 37, no. 4 (2012): 471, https://doi.org/10.1177/0309132512462271.

96. Butler, *Bodies that Matter*, 45. The parallels here between Butler's ideas of citation and Boym's notion of the off-modern are particularly noteworthy.

97. Boym, *The Future of Nostalgia*.

98. *Neubauprojekt: St. Pauli Hafenstraße* (Hamburg: Baugruppe Hafenstraße, 1993).

99. "Offener Brief," reproduced in *Gewalt Gegen Frauen*.

100. Simone Borgstede, "Liebeserklärung," *St. Pauli Einschnitt*, 5.

101. Simone Borgestede, "Volksküche," *St. Pauli Einschnitt*, 19.

102. "Zwei Briefe aus Saalfeld (ehemals DDR)," *St. Pauli Einschnitt*, 37.

103. For images and information on the art of the Hafenstraße, see Sigmund and Stroux, *Zu bunt*.

104. *10 Meter Ohne Kopf*, 13.

105. *Hafenstraße: Chronologie Eines Konflikts*, 5.

106. "Hafenstraße" (1987) [Rote Flora, Hafenstraße Flugblätter, 82–87].

107. *Der Kampf um die St. Pauli Hafenstraße* (Hamburg: Medienpädagogik Zentrum, 2004).

108. *Die Welt*, October 29, 1986, reproduced in *"Hafenstraße" Chronik und Analyses eines Konflikts*, ed. Herrmann et al., 87.

109. *Bild*, April 17, 1986, reproduced in *"Hafenstraße" Chronik und Analyses eines Konflikts*, ed. Herrmann et al., 87.

110. "Dr. Terror's House of Horrors," *Bild*, November 15, 1987, reproduced in *10 Meter Ohne Kopf*, 44.

111. Lenger, "Die Quelle des Chaos: Ein Pressespiegel" in *"Hafenstraße" Chronik und Analyses eines Konflikts*, ed. Herrmann et al., 93.

112. Quoted in Sigmund and Stroux, *Zu bunt*, 64.

CHAPTER SIX

1. On these campaigns, see Geronimo, *Fire and Flames: A History of the German Autonomist Movement*, rev. ed. (Oakland: PM Press, 2012); and AG Grauwacke, *Autonome in Bewegung*.

2. The connection between the Hafenstraße and squats in smaller cities is readily apparent in the 1987 film *Tanz auf dem Vulkan* (Gruppe Videotie Bochum, 1987). Residents of the squatted area in Bochum consistently refer to the Hafenstraße as an inspiration. They explicitly modeled their café and their strategies for forging connections to the surrounding neighborhood on the Hafenstraße.

3. See "Hafenstraße bleibt!" reproduced in *"Hafenstraße" Chronik und Analyses eines Konflikts*, ed. Herrmann et al., 40.

4. Although I have not come across any direct mention of it in the literature, it seems highly likely that the riots in Kreuzberg were at least partially facilitated by the rapid escalations of violence the previous month in Hamburg.

5. "Anti-Berlin," *Der Tagesspiegel*, May 3, 1987.

6. Carl-Wilhelm Busse, "Kreuzberger Nächte-Brandzeichen '87" *Westfalenblatt*, May 5, 1987.

7. Brigitte Fehrle, "Kreuzberg ist keine Spielweise," *Tageszeitung*, June 18, 1987.

8. Gerd Wartenburg, "Die Attitüde der Unangepaßtheit," *Volksblatt*, June 19, 1987. *Kiez* is a term that refers to traditional forms of locality and was often employed by leftists in reference to specific neighborhoods.

9. See, for example, "Über die Gewalttätigkeiten am 1. Mai 1987 und deren Ursachen (z.T. Auszüge aus einem Arbeitspapier Kreuzberger Kirchengemeinden)" [Landeskirchliche Archiv, 55.5/1044].

10. *Anarcho Sampler 87* (Berlin: Autofocus Archiv, 1987).

11. "1. Mai Diskussion zum Artikel: Wem hat's genutzt?—Fragen zum 1. Mai" *Interim* 55 (June 1, 1989).

12. For a comprehensive treatment of the events surrounding unification, see Timothy Garnton Ash, *The Magic Lantern: The Revolution of '89 Witnessed in Warsaw, Budapest, Berlin and Prague* (New York: Random House, 1990); Konrad Jarausch, *The Rush to German Unity* (Oxford: Oxford University Press, 1994); and Charles Maier, *Dissolution: The Crisis of Communism and the End of East Germany* (Princeton, NJ: Princeton University Press, 1997).

13. On the Round Tables, see Maier, *Dissolution*, 168–214.

14. See, for example, Uwe Rada, *Hauptstadt der Verdrängung: Berliner Zukunft zwischen Kiez und Metropole* (Berlin: Schwarze Risse, 1997).

15. On the malaise of East German intellectuals at the time of unification, see Konrad Jarausch, "The Double Disappointment: Revolution, Unification, and German Intellectuals," in *The Power of Intellectuals in Contemporary Germany*, ed. Michael Geyer (Chicago: University of Chicago Press, 2001).

16. On the multiple debates that raged in these years, see Michael Geyer, "The Long Goodbye: German Culture Wars in the Nineties," in *The Power of Intellectuals in Contemporary Germany*.

17. Günter Grass, "What Am I Talking For? Is Anybody Still Listening?" *New German Critique* 52 (1991): 66–72, https://doi.org/10.2307/488188.

18. Wolfgang Kaschuba, "Nowherelands and Residences: Recodifying Public Space in Berlin," in *Toward a New Metropolitanism: Reconstituting Public Culture, Urban Citizenship, and the Multicultural Imaginary in New York and Berlin*, ed. Günter Lenz, Friedrich Ulfers, and Antje Dallmann (Heidelberg: Winter, 2006), 235.

19. Kaschuba, "Nowherelands and Residences," 237.

20. The literature on these and related projects of historical memorialization is extensive. Some of the works include: Jennifer Allen, *Sustainable Utopias*; John Allen, "Ambient Power: Berlin's Potsdamer Platz and the Seductive Logic of Public Spaces," *Urban Studies* 43, no. 2 (2006): 441–55, http://www.jstor.org/stable/43197469; Dominik Bartmanski, *Matters of Revolution: Urban Spaces and Symbolic Politics in Berlin and Warsaw after 1989* (London: Routledge, 2022); Moritz Holfelder, *Palast der Republik: Aufstieg und Fall eines symbolischer Gebäudes* (Berlin: Ch. Links, 2008); Brian Ladd, *The Ghosts of Berlin: Confronting German History in the Urban Landscape* (Chicago: University of Chicago Press, 1997); Martin Sabrow, ed., *Errinerungsorte der DDR* (Munich: Beck, 2009); James Young, *At Memory's Edge: After-images of the Holocaust in Contemporary Art and Architecture* (New Haven: Yale University Press, 2000); and James Young, "Daniel Libeskind's Jewish Museum in Berlin: The Uncanny Arts of Memorial Architecture," *Jewish Social Studies* 6, no. 2 (2000): 1–23, https://dx.doi.org/10.1353/jss.2000.0007.

21. Claire Colomb, *Staging the New Berlin: Place Marketing and the Politics of Urban Reinvention Post-1989* (New York: Routledge, 2012). Colomb focused on the multiple different groups that took part in this rebranding, including not only governmental agencies but also public and private groups such as Berlin Tourismus Marketing and Partner für Berlin.

22. On the use of construction sites as tourist destinations, see Colomb, *Staging the New Berlin*, and Karen Till, *The New Berlin: Memory, Politics, Place* (Minneapolis: University of Minnesota Press, 2005).

23. This return to Western Civilization has become a central narrative in the historiography of the postwar period. See, for example, Jarausch, *After Hitler*; and Axel Schildt, *Ankunft im Westen: ein Essay zur Erfolgsgeschichte der Bundesrepublik* (Frankfurt: Fischer, 1999).

24. The most significant occupation in West Berlin at this time was the encampment and squatted house at the Einsteinufer. Other squatted houses such as the Urbanstr. 23 were quickly cleared by the police. See the flyer "Häuserkampf in Berlin seit Herbst 1988" [Papiertiger Archiv, Flugblätter ab 1988]. East Germany had a long history of squatting especially in neighborhoods such as Prenzlauer Berg. With some notable exceptions, however, these squats were not overtly political in nature. That is to say, the residents tended not to use the occupations as a political statement but as a way to find adequate housing. On this topic, see Udo Grashoff, *Schwarzwohnen: die Unterwanderung der staatlichen Wohnraumlenkung in der DDR* (Göttingen: V&R Unipress, 2011). It should be noted here that although many of the pre-unification squats in East Berlin were not political in nature, there were exceptions to this rule. The squatters at the house on Lychener Strasse 61, for example, claimed that their occupation was conducted in part to draw attention to the housing crisis in the city. In 1987, the house was searched, and the police confiscated copies of the West Berlin alternative paper *Zitty*. In 1988 the authorities were surprised to find the house empty and painted over with slogans such as "Aufruhr, Widerstand, die Lychener ist voll in unseren Hand," "Einsamer sucht Einsame zum Einsamen," and "Wir sind zwar raus, aber wir machen weiter." On this sequence of events, see "Durchsuchung eines 'öffentlichen Gebiets,'" *Umweltblätter* 7 (1987); "Behörden erneut gegen instandbesetzte Lychener 61," *Umweltblätter* 4 (1988); and "Lychener Straße 61 in Berlin-Prenzlauerberg am Ende?" *Umweltblätter* 10 (1988). See also Vasudevan, *Metropolitan Preoccupations*.

25. "Informationsblatt zur Besetzung der Schönhauser Allee 20" (December 22, 1989) [Robert Havemann Gesellschaft: Archiv der DDR Opposition, RTc09]. This house is often considered to be the first squatted house in East Berlin after the fall of the Wall.

26. "Untitled Flyer, Die Besetzer Scheinerstr. 47" (December 29, 1989) [Robert Havemann Gesellschaft: Archiv der DDR Opposition, RTc09].

27. In the late 1980s and early 1990s, East Berlin had hundreds of dilapidated, largely empty buildings. This was primarily a result of a failed housing policy on the part of the SED regime. Housing officials were simply unable—whether for financial or logistical reasons—to deal with the existing housing stock in inner-city neighborhoods.

28. "Umstrukturierung der Szene?" *Interim* 115 (September 13, 1990).

29. "Besetzte Häuser in Berlin/ Hauptstadt!" *Telegraph* 8 (April 26, 1990).

30. "Umstrukturierung der Szene?" *Interim* 115 (September 13, 1990): 7. See also "Hausbesetzung in Ostberlin—wir auch? Warum denn nicht!" *Interim* 97 (April 5, 1990).

31. *Kollektiv Mainzer Straße—Sag niemals nie* (1991). On the attack, see also "Information" (June 4, 1990) [Papiertiger Archiv, Flugblätter ab 88]; and "Pfingsten in Ostberlin. Neue Überfälle von Nazis und Hooligans" *Interim* 11 (June 18, 1990).

32. Interview in Amantine, *Gender und Häuserkampf* (Münster: Unrast Verlag, 2011), 185.

33. Wiesemann and Keller, dirs., *Petra Pan und Arumukha: Der Traum von ordentlichen Anarchisten* (Berlin: Autofocus Archiv, 1990).

34. For footage of the demonstration, see, among others, AK Kraak, dir., *Video Magazin # 3* (October 1990).

35. "DEUTSCHLAND, HALTS MAUL—ES REICHT!!! Für den Wiederzusammenbruch!" *Interim* 117 (September 27, 1990): 4.

36. Festival advertisement, back cover of the *Besetzerinnenzeitung Notausgabe* (August 4, 1990).

37. Susan Arndt, *Berlin, Mainzer Straße: Wohnen ist wichtiger als das Gesetz* (Berlin: Basisdruck Verlag, 1992), 151.

38. What I find more surprising than this tendency not to officially register with the police was the fact that many squatters actually *did* register, primarily in order to get library cards, bus passes, and the like.

39. Arndt, *Berlin, Mainzer Straße*, 158.

40. Julie Bashore, dir., *The Battle of Tuntenhaus* (Berlin: BBC Channel 4, 1991).

41. Arndt, *Berlin, Mainzer Straße*, 209.

42. Arndt, *Berlin, Mainzer Straße*, 209.

43. Arndt, *Berlin, Mainzer Straße*, 207.

44. According to theorists like Rosalyn Deutsche, this embrace of the unknown is one of the key elements of public space more broadly. See her essay "Agoraphobia," in *Evictions: Art and Spatial Politics* (Cambridge, MA: MIT Press, 1996).

45. Arndt, *Berlin, Mainzer Straße*, 44–45.

46. The Antiquariat itself seems to have been largely popular, however the name Max Hoelz initiated a serious controversy between the residents of the Tuntenhaus and the residents of the Mainzer Straße women's house, who argued that the name Max Hoelz was indicative of the left's inability to recognize the sexism of the earlier generations of socialists. After much back and forth, the proprietors of the Antiquariat decided to cross out the name Max Hoelz. On this affair, see "Stellungnahme zum 'Max Hoelz Antiquariat' in der Mainzer Strasse 4 in Berlin Friedrichshain" and "Zur Auseinandersetzung um die Bennenung des Max Hoelz Antiquariats," both of which can be found in the *Besetzerinnenzeitung* 8 (October 17, 1990).

47. Taken from the weekly schedule of events in *Besetzerinnenzeitung* 6 (September 25, 1990).

48. "Hausbesetzer. Selbstdarstellungen von 16 Projekten aus Friedrichshain Mitte und Prenzlauer Berg" (undated, likely late spring/early summer, 1990) 1 [Papiertiger Archiv, Flugblatter ab 88].

49. By this time the *Tageszeitung* had largely fallen out of favor among members of the radical left.

50. "Ein Einleitung ... zur Strukturdiskussion der Zeitung," *BesetzerinnenZeitung* 00 (August 6, 1990): unpaginated. See also the article "Konzept" in the same edition.

51. See, for example, *Alles schön wird verboten* (Hamburg: Medienpädagogik Zentrum, 1989); *Die Augen Schließen um besser zu sehen* (MPZ, 1986); *Bauwagen— weil's besser ist* (MPZ, 1989); *Hafenstraße—Ein Videoprojekt* (MPZ, 1988); *Irgendwie, Irgendwo, Irgendwann* (MPZ, 1988/89); *Das können die Soliden nicht verstehen* (MPZ, 1991); *Selbst das kleinste Licht durchbricht die Dunkelheit* (MPZ, 1990); *St. Pauli Hafentraße Nr. 7* (MPZ, 1995); *Terrible Houses in Danger* (MPZ, 1985); and *Zwischen Dachziegeln und Pflasterstein* (MPZ, 1986).

52. AK Kraak, dir., *Video Magazin #2* (September 1990).

53. "Bericht aus Greifswald," *Besetzerinnenzeitung* 1b:4 (June 27, 1991).

54. The radical left in Germany tends to support the football team FC St. Pauli from Hamburg. Supporters show up at games with pirate flags and chant antiracist slogans. See, for example, Brigitta Schmidt-Lauber, *FC St. Pauli: zur Ethnographie eines Vereins* (Münster: Lit Verlag, 2004).

55. Copy of a letter sent from residents of the Scharnweber 38 along with commentary. *Besetzerinnenzeitung* 00 (August 6, 1990).

56. See, for example, "SO GEHT ES NICHT WEITER—Diskussionspapier des Vertragsgremiums," *Besetzerinnenzeitung* 0 (August 15, 1990).

57. "Zwischenspiel im Ost-Berliner Häuserrat," *Telegraph* 13 (August 6, 1990): 33.

58. See Wiesemann and Keller, *Petra Pan und Arumukha: Der Traum von ordentlichen Anarchisten*, and Kollektiv Mainzer Straße, *Sag niemals nie*. In the first version of AK Kraak's *Video Magazin* series, the viewer witnessed a similar transition from abandoned buildings to riotous joy, signaled in this case by a panning shot of graffiti with the well-known phrase from the early 1980s: "You birthed us in concrete and now you wonder why we throw stones!" (AK Kraak, *Video Magazin #1*, August 1990).

59. Anton Waldt, "Trockeneis und Tränengas," in *Nachtleben Berlin. 1975 bis Heute*, ed. Wolfgang Farkas, Stefanie Seidl, and Heiko Zwirner (Berlin: Metrolit, 2013), 128.

60. Ulrich Gutmaier, *Die ersten Tage von Berlin. Der Sound der Wende* (Stuttgart: Tropen, 2013), 12.

61. Gutmaier, *Die ersten Tage von Berlin*, 27. My use of "wormhole" here is inspired by Claudia Verhoeven's analysis of the temporal imaginaries of Russian terrorists in her essay, "Wormholes in Russian History: Events 'Outside of Time' (Featuring Malevich, Morozov, and Mayakovsky)," in *Breaking up Time: Negotiating the Borders Between Past, Present and Future*, ed. Chris Lorenz and Berber Bevernage, (Göttingen: Vandenhoek & Ruprecht, 2013).

62. Gutmaier, *Die ersten Tage von Berlin*, 57.

63. Shannon Lee Dawdy, *Patina: A Profane Archaeology* (Chicago: University of Chicago Press, 2016).

64. Arndt, *Berlin, Mainzer Straße*, 45; Bashore, *The Battle of Tuntenhaus*.

65. Another example of this creative misuse of the discarded accoutrements of the GDR comes from a satirical piece in the *Besetzerinnenzeitung* titled "Advice for DDR Citizens: Learning from Capitalism," in which the authors ridiculed both the pedagogical conceit of West German capitalists and the naive eagerness with which many East

Germans embraced capitalist values by placing captions like "Even on vacation, one does not go shopping in a beach suit" over kitschy photos from the 1960s. See "Ratschlag für DDR-BürgerInnen: VOM KAPITALISMUS LERNEN," *Besetzerinnenzeitung* 6 (September 25, 1990): 11.

66. Quoted in Felix Denk and Sven von Thülen, eds., *Der Klang der Familie: Berlin, Techno, und die Wende* (Berlin: Suhrkamp, 2014), 170.

67. Gutmaier, *Die ersten Tage von Berlin*, 107.

68. Quoted in Anke Fesel and Chris Keller, eds., *Berlin Wonderland: Wild Years Revisited, 1990–1996* (Berlin: Gestalten, 2014), 184.

69. The dinner party scene was reproduced in *Sag niemals nie*.

70. "Werdet Wild und tut schöne Sachen!" Zentralrat der umherschweifenden HaschrebellInnen, *Dokumentation zur Mainzer Strasse, 12.-14. November* [Papier Tiger Flugblätter ab 88].

71. "Gebt den Tisch zurück!" *Tageszeitung*, August 27, 1990.

72. AK Kraak, *Video Magazin #1*.

73. Gutmaier, *Die ersten Tage von Berlin*, 193–94.

74. On techno in Berlin, see, among others, Denk and von Thülen, *Der Klang der Familie*; Tobias Rapp, *Lost and Sound: Berlin, Techno and the Easyjet Set* (Berlin: Innervisions, 2010); Albert Scharenberg, *Der Sound der Stadt: Musikindustrie und Subkultur in Berlin* (Münster: Westfälisches Dampfboot, 2005); and Anton Waldt, *Auf die Zwölf* (Berlin: Verbrecher Verlag, 2010).

75. Dmitri Hegemann, quoted in Rapp, *Lost and Sound*, 63. The idea that he could make this history his own is yet another indication of the ways in which these practices could be incorporated into modes of value creation suitable for capitalist economies.

76. Interview in Tilmann Künzel, dir., *Sub Berlin: The Story of Tresor* (Berlin: Filmlounge, 2012).

77. Denk and von Thülen, *Der Klang der Familie*, 141.

78. Aire, "Es soll Berghain Heissen," in *Nachtleben Berlin. 1975 bis Heute*, ed. Wolfgang Farkas, Stefanie Seidl, and Heiko Zwirner (Berlin: Metrolit, 2013), 187–88.

79. Slavko Stefanoski, quoted in Gutmaier, *Die ersten Tage von Berlin*, 207.

80. Gutmaier, *Die ersten Tage von Berlin*, 215.

81. For an excellent analysis of techno in these years, see Anja Schwanhäußer, *Kosmonauten des Underground: Ethnografie einer Berliner Szene* (Frankfurt: Campus, 2010).

82. Simon Frith, *Performing Rites: On the Value of Popular Music* (Cambridge, MA: Harvard University Press, 1996), 149.

83. Simon Reynolds, *Retromania: Pop Culture's Addiction to Its Own Past* (London: Faber & Faber, 2011), 313.

84. Andreas Busche, "Jeder kommt rein—oder auch nicht," in *Nachtleben Berlin. 1975 bis Heute*, ed. Wolfgang Farkas, Stefanie Seidl, and Heiko Zwirner (Berlin: Metrolit, 2013), 171–73. On the concept of "plunderphonics" and similar experimental music genres like "hauntology" and "echo jams," see Fisher, *Ghosts of My Life*; and Reynolds, *Retromania*.

85. "Germaneninfo Nr. 1" 0 (August 15, 1990) [Papiertiger Archiv, Flugblätter ab 88].

86. AK Kraak, dir., *Video Magazin #3* (October 1990).

87. The squat at the Auguststraße 10 had long been a locus of such subversive art projects. See, for example, the funeral parade for a large puppet that had graced the facade in AK Kraak, dir., *Video Magazin #8* (January 1993). See also the AK Kraak report on the outrageous "Männerpeapshow" at the house (AK Kraak, dir., *Video Magazin #12*, March 1995).

88. These houses were targeted because both had been occupied after July 24, the date from which the Magistrat of East Berlin declared no new squats would be tolerated.

89. Official documents noted that on November 14, 1990: 347 people were arrested (244 men, 103 women; 10 between 14 and 18, 51 between 18 and 21, 286 adults; 328 Germans, 19 foreigners; 278 living in Berlin, with 58 from the East and 51 from other Bundesländer). Data taken from "Dem Haftrichter zur Anordnung von Untersuchungshaft wegen Gewalttaten vorgeführte Straftäter, die am 14. November 1990 im Zusammenhang mit den Hausräumungen in Berlin Friedrichshain von der Polizei festgenommen wurden" [Papiertiger Archiv, Mainzer Straße].

90. Walter Momper, "Press Release" (November 14, 1990). "Pressemitteilung, Senatsverwaltung für Inneres, Pressestelle 331/1990," 17 [Papiertiger Archiv, Mainzer Straße].

91. "Editorial," *Telegraph* 16 (November 23, 1990).

92. "Herr Momper, Herr Mendiburu! Warum lügen sie uns Bürgerinnen und Bürger an???" *Besetzerinnenzeitung* 13 (November 21, 1990).

93. "Augenzeugenbericht," in Ulrike Engwicht and Dagmar Engwicht, "Ermittlungsausschuß" (November 18, 1990), 5 [Robert Havemann Gesellschaft, Archiv der DDR Opposition, TRc09 "Runder Tische Instandbesetzung"].

94. Letter from the Wohnungsbaugesellschaft Prenzlauer Berg to the Besetzerrat Prenzlauer Berg (November 16, 1990) [Papiertiger Archiv, Mainzer Straße].

95. The complete title of the agreement is "Vorvertrag auf Abschluß eines Vertrages über die bauliche Selbsthilfe und von Wohnungsmietverträgen sowie über gemeinschaftliche und gewerblich genutzte Räume und grundstückseigene Freiflächen." For documents on these negotiations, see Runder Tisch Instandbesetzung, Prenzlauer Berg, OW 01, OW 02, and RTc01–04 all in the Robert Havemann Gesellschaft, Archiv der DDR Opposition.

96. See, for example, "Friedrichshainer Häuserrat" [Robert Havemann Gesellschaft, Archiv der DDR Opposition, RTc05 DDR Archiv Runder Tische Instanbesetzung and "Prenzlauer Linie—das war's?" IBIS 05].

97. Form Letter to Potential Paten (undated) [Papiertiger Archiv, Mitte].

98. Volxsport, "Klarheit für Berlin," *Interim* 124 (November 22, 1990): 10.

99. Volxsport, "Klarheit für Berlin," *Interim* 124 (November 22, 1990): 12.

100. "Fight the Power: Ein Versuch nach vorne zu denken, denn wenn wir wissen, wo vorne ist, ist es klar, wo's lange geht," *Interim* 124 (November 22, 1990): 18.

101. See, for example, Andy Mathers, *Struggling for a Social Europe: Neoliberal Globalization and the Birth of a European Social Movement* (Burlington: Ashgate, 2007);

and Raphael Schlembach, *Against Old Europe: Critical Theory and Alter-Globalization Movements* (Farnham: Ashgate, 2014).

102. Waldt, "Trockeneis und Tränengas," 130.

103. Daniela Sandler, *Counterpreservation: Architectural Decay in Berlin since 1989* (Ithaca, NY: Cornell University Press, 2016), 40; Vasudevan, *Metropolitan Preoccupations*.

104. Smith, *Free Berlin*, 3.

105. Susan Buck-Morss, *The Dialectics of Seeing: Walter Benjamin and the Arcades Project* (Cambridge, MA: MIT Press, 1999), 159.

106. Vasudevan, *Metropolitan Preoccupations*.

EPILOGUE

1. David Wagner, "The Wish Fulfillment Zone," in *Berlin Wonderland: Wild Years Revisited, 1990–1996*, ed. Anke Fesel and Chris Keller (Berlin: Gestalten, 2014), 5.

2. Tsing, *The Mushroom at the End of the World*, 2.

3. De Certeau, *The Practice of Everyday Life*, 108.

4. On spectacle in late capitalism, see Guy Debord, *Society of the Spectacle* (Berkeley: Bureau of Public Secrets, 2014 [1968]).

5. "Kunst am Bahn." Text accompanying the 1. Mainzer Kunstaustellung, reproduced in *Besetzerinnenzeitung* 17 (December 19, 1990): 16.

6. "Diese Neubesetzung ist volkommen unpolitisch," *Besetzerinnenzeitung* 17 (December 19, 1990): 19. For an illuminating analysis of the broader intersections of art and activism in late twentieth-century Berlin, see Smith, *Free Berlin*.

7. Uwe Rada, "Die Fassade als lebendige Kulisse," *Tageszeitung*, October 16, 1998.

8. "Die Zeit künstlerischer Anarchie ist vorbei," *Tageszeitung*, October 16, 1998.

9. See, for example, Ingo Bader and Albert Scharenberg, "The Sound of Berlin: Subculture and the Global Music Industry," *International Journal of Urban and Regional Research* 34, no. 1 (2010): 76–91, https://doi.org/10.1111/j.1468-2427.2009.00927.x; Christina Heinen, *Tief in Neukölln: Soundkulturen zwischen Improvisation und Gentrifizierung in einem Berliner Bezirk* (Bielefeld: Transcript, 2013); Barbara Lang, *Mythos Kreuzberg: Ethnographie eines Stadtteils, 1961–1995* (Frankfurt: Campus, 1998); and Johannes Novy, "Städtetourismus, Stadtteiltourismus und der Mythos Städtischer Steuerung. Das Bespiel Berlin," in *Governance von Destinationen: Neue Ansätze für die erfolgreiche Steuerung touristischer Zielgebiete*, ed. Anja Saretzki and Karlheinz Wöhler (Berlin: Erich Schmidt Verlag, 2013).

10. See, for example, Claire Colomb, "Pushing the Urban Frontier: Temporary Uses of Space, City Marketing, and the Creative City Discourse in 2000s Berlin," *Journal of Urban Affairs* 34, no. 2 (2012): 131–52, https://doi.org/10.1111/j.1467-9906.2012.00607.x; Johannes Novy and Claire Colomb, "Struggling for the Right to the (Creative) City in Berlin and Hamburg: New Urban Social Movements, New 'Spaces of Hope'?" *International Journal of Urban and Regional Research* 37, no. 5 (September 2013): 1816–38, https://doi.org/10.1111/j.1468-2427.2012.01115.x; Geoff Stahl, ed., *Poor, but Sexy: Reflections on Berlin Scenes* (Bern: Peter Lang, 2014); and Quentin Stevens and Mhairi

Ambler, "Europe's City Beaches as post-Fordist placemaking," *Journal of Urban Design* 15, no. 4 (2010): 515–37, https://doi.org/10.1080/13574809.2010.502341.

11. Quoted in Colomb, *Staging the New Berlin*, 239.

12. See Andrej Holm, *Wir bleiben alle! Gentrifizierung—städtische Konflikte um Aufwertung und Verdrängung* (Muenster: Unrast Verlag, 2010).

13. Joe Perry, "Love Parade 1996: Techno Playworlds and the Neoliberalization of Post-Wall Berlin," *German Studies Review* 42, no. 3 (October 2019): 584, https://dx.doi.org/10.1353/gsr.2019.0081. Such arguments are not, of course, limited to Berlin. For Marxist geographers like David Harvey this incorporation of urban difference into strategies of capitalist accumulation is a global phenomenon. See, for example, David Harvey, "From Space to Place and Back Again: Reflections on the Condition of Postmodernity," in *Mapping the Futures: Local Cultures, Global Change*, ed. Jon Bird (London: Routledge, 1993). Cultural theorist Mark Fisher makes a similar argument in regard to current trends in popular culture in his book *Ghosts of My Life*.

14. For a historiographical overview of some of this literature, see Marcus Colla, "The Spectre of the Present: Time, Presentism, and the Writing of Contemporary History," *Contemporary European History* 30, no. 1 (February 2021): 124–35, https://doi.org/10.1017/S096077732000048X.

15. See, for example, Assmann, *Is Time out of Joint?*; Esposito and Becker, "The Time of Politics, the Politics of Time, and Politicized Time"; Lorenz and Bevernage, eds., *Breaking up Time*; Marek Tamm, "How to Reinvent the Future?" *History and Theory* 59, no. 3 (September 2020): 448–58, https://doi.org/10.1111/hith.12173; and Marek Tamm and Laurent Olivier, "Introduction," in *Rethinking Historical Time: New Approaches to Presentism*, ed. Marek Tamm and Laurent Olivier (New York: Bloomsbury, 2019); Tsing, *The Mushroom at the End of the World*.

16. Cornum, "Seizing the Alterity of Futures"; Freeman, *Time Binds*; Muñoz, *Cruising Utopia*; Tomba, *Insurgent Universality*; Anna Lowenhaupt Tsing, Heather Swanson, Elaine Gan, and Nils Bubandt, eds., *Arts of Living on a Damaged Planet: Ghosts and Monsters of the Anthropocene* (Minneapolis: University of Minnesota Press, 2017); and Wilder, *Concrete Utopianism*.

17. Freeman, *Time Binds*, xv. This argument is similar to the one Peter Osborne makes in regard to the politics of the avant-garde in his book *The Politics of Time: Modernity and the Avant-Garde* (London: Verso, 2011).

18. Freeman, *Time Binds*, xxii. Freeman is specifically discussing the radical potential of queer temporalities, but I would argue that these concepts can be more widely applied to other forms of temporal dissonance.

19. Wilder, *Concrete Utopianism*, 10.

20. Cornum, "Seizing the Alterity of Futures," 187, 189. Cornum's argument is indebted to Walter Benjamin's discussion of messianic time in his "Theses on the Philosophy of History."

21. Invisible Committee, *Now* (n.p.: Ill Will, 2017), 25.

22. Invisible Committee, *Now*, 52.

23. Agentur BILWET, *Bewegungslehre*, 11.

24. Vladimir Nabokov, *Transparent Things* (New York: Vintage Books, 1972), 1.

Bibliography

ARCHIVAL COLLECTIONS

Archiv Soziale Bewegungen in Freiburg

14.3.0 I
14.3.0 XIII
14.3.2 II
14.3.2 III
14.3.3.0 I
14.3.3.0 XIII
Brochures

Archiv der Sozialen Bewegungen, Rote Flora

Box 09.400 HH Hafenstraße I
Hafenstrasse Flügblätter, 82–87
Hafenstraße Flugblätter 88–89

Evangelisches Zentralarchiv, Berlin

686/730
686/7831

Kreuzbergmuseum

Inv. Nr. 2010/27, Lfd. Nr. 27

Landesarchiv Berlin

Brep 002
Brep 16495
Brep 16496
Brep 16497
Brep 16498
Brep 17124
Brep 17125
Brep 17127

Brep 17128
Brep 17438
Brep 27780
Brep 38292
Brep 6429

Landeskirchliche Archiv

55.5/1889
55.5/1044
55.5/1889

Papiertiger Archiv, Berlin

Brochures
Flugblätter ab 1988
Flugblätter bis 1988
Häuserkampf Berlin/W., September—November 1980
Häuserkampf Berlin/W., 12/1980
Mainzer Str
Mieten-Politik, Widerstand, Stadtteil Politik, Berlin
Mitte

Robert Havemann Gesellschaft, Archiv der DDR Opposition

RTc01-04
RTc05, IBIS 05
RTc09, OW 01
RTc09, OW 02

Staatsarchiv Hamburg

136-1, 4924
136-1, 4925
136-1, 4926
136-1, 4927
331-1 II, Ablieferung 41, 20.37-3

PUBLISHED SOURCES

Adelt, Ulrich. *Krautrock: German Music in the Seventies*. Ann Arbor: University of Michigan Press, 2016.

Adorno, Theodor. *Minima Moralia: Reflections from a Damaged Life*. London: Verso, 1978. First published Frankfurt: Suhrkamp Verlag, 1951.

AG Grauwacke. *Autonome in Bewegung: aus den ersten 23 Jahren*. Berlin: Assoziation A, 2003.

Agentur BILWET. *Bewegungslehre: Botschaften aus einer autonomen Wirklichkeit*. Amsterdam: Edition ID Archiv, 1991.

Aire. "Es soll Berghain heissen." In *Nachtleben Berlin. 1975 bis Heute*, edited by Wolfgang Farkas, Stefanie Seidl, and Heiko Zwirner. Berlin: Metrolit, 2013.

Allen, Jennifer. *Sustainable Utopias: The Art and Politics of Hope in Germany.* Cambridge, MA: Harvard University Press, 2022.
Allen, John. "Ambient Power: Berlin's Potsdamer Platz and the Seductive Logic of Public Spaces." *Urban Studies* 43, no. 2 (2006): 441–55. http://www.jstor.org/stable/43197469.
Aly, Götz. *Unser Kampf: 1968—ein irritierter Blick zurück.* Frankfurt: Fischer, 2007.
Amann, Rolf. *Der moralische Aufschrei: Presse und abweichendes Verhalten am Beispiel der Hausbesetzungen in Berlin.* Frankfurt: Campus Verlag, 1985.
Amantine. *Gender und Häuserkampf.* Münster: Unrast Verlag, 2011.
Anders, Freia. "Wohnraum, Freiraum, Widerstand. Die Formierung der Autonomen in den Konflikten um Hausbesetzungen Anfang der achtziger Jahre." In *Das Alternative Milieu: Antibürgerlicher Lebensstil und linke Politik in der Bundesrepublik Deutschland und Europa, 1968–1983,* edited by Sven Reichardt and Detlef Siegfried. Göttingen: Wallstein Verlag, 2010.
Anonymous. *A Woman in Berlin: Eight Weeks in the Conquered City.* New York: Picador, 2000.
Arndt, Susan. *Berlin, Mainzer Straße: Wohnen ist wichtiger als das Gesetz.* Berlin: Basisdruck Verlag, 1992.
Artkämpfer, Heiko. *Hausbesetzer, Hausbesitzer, Hausfriedensbruch.* Berlin: Springer Verlag, 1995.
Apel, Dora. *Beautiful Terrible Ruins: Detroit and the Anxiety of Decline.* New Brunswick: Rutgers University Press, 2015.
Applegate, Celia. *A Nation of Provincials: The German Idea of Heimat.* Berkeley: University of California Press, 1990.
Ash, Timothy Garnton. *The Magic Lantern: The Revolution of '89 Witnessed in Warsaw, Budapest, Berlin and Prague.* New York: Random House, 1990.
Assmann, Aleida. *Is Time out of Joint? On the Rise and Fall of the Modern Time Regime.* Ithaca: Cornell University Press, 2020.
Aust, Stefan. *Der Baader-Meinhof Komplex.* Hamburg: Hoffmann und Campe, 2008.
Bacia, Jürgen, and Klaus-Jürgen Scherer, eds. *Paßt bloß auf! Was will die neue Jugendbewegung?* Berlin: Olle und Wolter, 1981.
Bader, Ingo, and Albert Scharenberg. "The Sound of Berlin: Subculture and the Global Music Industry." *International Journal of Urban and Regional Research* 34, no. 1 (2010): 76–91. https://doi.org/10.1111/j.1468-2427.2009.00927.x.
Badura-Triska, Eva, and Hubert Klocker. "Vienna Actionism and its Context." In *Vienna Actionism: Art and Upheaval in 1960s Vienna,* edited by Eva Badura-Triska and Hubert Klocker. Cologne: Walther König, 2012.
Bartmanski, Dominik. *Matters of Revolution: Urban Spaces and Symbolic Politics in Berlin and Warsaw After 1989.* London: Routledge, 2022.
Baumann, Bommi. *How It All Began.* Vancouver: Pulp Press, 1977.
Becker, Tobias. "The Meaning of Nostalgia: Genealogy and Critique." *History and Theory* 57, no. 2 (June 2018): 234–50. https://doi.org/10.1111/hith.12059.
Benjamin, Walter. "Theses on the Philosophy of History." In *Illuminations: Essays and Reflections,* edited by Hannah Arendt, 253–64. New York: Schocken Books, 1968.
Benjamin, Walter. "The Work of Art in the Age of Mechanical Reproduction." In *Illuminations: Essays and Reflections,* edited by Hannah Arendt, 217–52. New York: Schocken Books, 1968.

Betts, Paul. *The Authority of Everyday Objects: A Cultural History of West German Industrial Design*. Berkeley: University of California Press, 2004.

Betts, Paul, and David Crowley. "Introduction." In "Domestic Dreamworlds: Notions of Home in Post-1945 Europe." Special issue, *Journal of Contemporary History* 40, no. 2 (2005): 213–36.

Biess, Frank. *Republik der Angst: Eine Andere Geschichte der Bundesrepublik*. Reinbeck bei Hamburg: Rowohlt, 2019.

Biess, Frank, and Astrid M. Eckert. "Introduction: Why Do We Need New Narratives for the History of the Federal Republic?" *Central European History* 52, no. 1 (2019): 1–18. https://doi.org/10.1017/S0008938919000013.

Black, Monica. *A Demon-Haunted Land: Witches, Wonder Doctors, and the Ghosts of the Past in Post-WWII Germany*. New York: Metropolitan Books, 2020.

Black, Monica. "Miracles in the Shadow of the Economic Miracle: The 'Supernatural '50s' in West Germany." *The Journal of Modern History* 84, no. 4 (2012): 833–60. https://doi.org/10.1086/667597.

Bloxham, Donald. *Genocide on Trial: War Crimes Trials and the Formation of Holocaust History*. Oxford: Oxford University Press, 2003.

Böckelmann, Frank, and Herbert Nagel, eds. *Subversive Aktion: der Sinn der Organisation ist ihr Scheitern*. Frankfurt am Main: Neue Kritik, 2002.

Bodenschatz, Harald, Volker Heise, and Jochen Korfmacher. *Schluss mit der Zerstörung? Stadterneuerung und städtische Opposition in West-Berlin, Amsterdam und London*. Giessen: Anabas, 1983.

Boltanski, Luc, and Ève Chiapello. *The New Spirit of Capitalism*. Rev. ed. Translated by Gregory Elliott. London: Verso, 2018.

Bondy, Curt. *Jugendliche stören die Ordnung: Bericht und Stellungnahme zu den Halbstarkenkrawallen*. Munich: Juventa-Verlag, 1957.

Bopp, Jörg. "Trauer-Power. Zur Jugendrevolte 1981." *Kursbuch* 65 (1981): 151–68.

Böttcher, Lutz, et al. "'Strategien für Kreuzberg.' Bericht der Vorprüfergruppe über den Wettbewerb." *ARCH+* 37 (1978): 63–73.

Bowie, Laura. *The Streets Echoed with Chants: The Urban Experience of Post-war Berlin*. Oxford: Peter Lang, 2022.

Boym, Svetlana. *The Future of Nostalgia*. New York: Basic Books, 2002.

Boym, Svetlana. *The Off-Modern*. New York: Bloomsbury, 2017.

Brown, Timothy Scott. *West Germany and the Global Sixties: The Antiauthoritarian Revolts, 1962–1978*. Cambridge: Cambridge University Press, 2013.

Brown, Timothy Scott. "1968 Underground: West German Radicals Between Subculture and Revolution." In *Subcultures, Popular Music and Social Change*, edited by William Osgerby, 219–34. Newcastle: Cambridge Scholars Publishing, 2014.

Brown, Timothy Scott, and Lorena Anton. "Introduction." In *Between the Avant-Garde and the Everyday: Subversive Politics in Europe from 1957 to the Present*, edited by Timothy Scott Brown and Lorena Anton, 1–8. New York: Berghahn Books, 2011.

Buck-Morss, Susan. *Dreamworld and Catastrophe: The Passing of Mass Utopia in East and West*. Cambridge, MA: MIT Press, 2002.

Buck-Morss, Susan. *The Dialectics of Seeing: Walter Benjamin and the Arcades Project*. Cambridge, MA: MIT Press, 1999.

Bude, Eva. *Verpisst euch! Sex and Drugs and Hardcore-Punk*. Hamburg: Europa Verlag, 2005.

Busche, Andreas. "Jeder kommt rein—oder auch nicht." In *Nachtleben Berlin. 1975 bis Heute*, edited by Wolfgang Farkas, Stefanie Seidl, and Heiko Zwirner. Berlin: Metrolit, 2013.
Butler, Judith. *Bodies That Matter: On the Discursive Limits of "Sex."* New York: Routledge, 1993.
Carter, Erica. *How German Is She? Postwar West German Reconstruction and the Consuming Woman.* Ann Arbor: University of Michigan Press, 1997.
Castillo, Greg. *Cold War on the Home Front: The Soft Power of Midcentury Design.* Minneapolis: University of Minnesota Press, 2010.
Castillo, Greg. "Domesticating the Cold War: Household Consumption as Propaganda in Marshall Plan Germany." In "Domestic Dreamworlds: Notions of Home in Post-1945 Europe." Special issue, *Journal of Contemporary History* 40, no. 2 (2005): 261–88. https://doi.org/10.1177/0022009405051553.
Castillo, Greg. "Marshall Plan Modernism in Divided Germany." In *Cold War Modern: Design, 1945–1970*, edited by David Crowley and Jane Pavitt, 66–72. London: V&A Publishing, 2008.
Cattaneo, Claudio, and Miguel Martinez, eds. *The Squatters' Movement in Europe: Commons and Autonomy as Alternatives to Capitalism.* London: Pluto, 2014.
Cerutti, Silvano. "Man bediente sich einfach bei dem was herumlag. Die Moral der hässlichkeit." In *Hot Love. Swiss Punk & Wave, 1976–1980*, edited by Lurker Grand. Zurich: Edition Patrick Frey, 2007.
Chatterjee, Partha. *The Nation and Its Fragments: Colonial and Postcolonial Histories.* Princeton, NJ: Princeton University Press, 1993.
Chin, Rita, and Heide Fehrenbach. "German Democracy and the Question of Difference, 1945–1995." In *After the Nazi Racial State: Difference and Democracy in Germany and Europe*, edited by Rita Chin, Heide Fehrenbach, Geoff Eley, and Atina Grossman. Ann Arbor: University of Michigan Press, 2009.
Cohn-Bendit, Daniel, and Gabriel Cohn-Bendit. *Obsolete Communism: The Left-Wing Alternative.* Oakland: AK Press, 2001 [1968].
Colomb, Claire. "Pushing the Urban Frontier: Temporary Uses of Space, City Marketing, and the Creative City Discourse in 2000s Berlin." *Journal of Urban Affairs* 34, no. 2 (2012): 131–52. https://doi.org/10.1111/j.1467-9906.2012.00607.x.
Colomb, Claire. *Staging the New Berlin. Place Marketing and the Politics of Urban Reinvention Post-1989.* New York: Routledge, 2012.
Colla, Marcus. "The Spectre of the Present: Time, Presentism, and the Writing of Contemporary History." *Contemporary European History* 30, no. 1 (February 2021): 124–35. https://doi.org/10.1017/S096077732000048X.
Confino, Alon. *A World Without Jews: The Nazi Imagination from Persecution to Genocide.* New Haven: Yale University Press, 2014.
Cornum, Lou. "Seizing the Alterity of Futures: Toward a Philosophy of History across Afrofuturism and Indigenous Futurism." *History of the Present* 13, no. 2 (October 2023): 166–91. https://doi.org/10.1215/21599785-10630116.
Crew, David, ed. *Consuming Germany in the Cold War.* New York: Berg, 2003.
Crowley, David, and Jane Pavitt, eds. *Cold War Modern: Design, 1945–1970.* London: V&A Publishing, 2008.
Dany, Hans-Christian. "Im Kohlenkeller eines neuen Dekadenzbewußtseins." In *Lieber zu viel als zu wenig: Kunst, Musik, Aktionen zwischen Hedonismus und Nihilismus (1976–1985)*. Berlin: Vice Versa, 2003.

Dawdy, Shannon Lee. *Patina: A Profane Archaeology*. Chicago: University of Chicago Press, 2016.

Dax, Max. *Dreissig Gespräche*. Frankfurt: Suhrkamp, 2008.

De Certeau, Michel. *The Practice of Everyday Life*. Berkeley: University of California Press, 1984.

Debord, Guy. *Society of the Spectacle*. Berkeley: Bureau of Public Secrets, 2014 [1968].

Del Pilar Blanco, María, and Esther Pereen, eds. *The Spectralities Reader: Ghosts and Haunting in Contemporary Cultural Theory*. London: Bloomsbury, 2013.

Deleuze, Gilles, and Félix Guattari. *A Thousand Plateaus: Capitalism and Schizophrenia*. Translated by Brian Massumi. Minneapolis: University of Minnesota Press, 1987.

Deleuze, Gilles, and Félix Guattari. *Anti-Oedipus: Capitalism and Schizophrenia*. New York: Penguin Classics, 2009.

DeSilvey, Caitlin, and Tim Edensor. "Reckoning with Ruins." *Progress in Human Geography* 37, no. 4 (2012): 465–85. https://doi.org/10.1177/0309132512462271.

Denk, Felix, and Sven von Thülen, eds. *Der Klang der Familie: Berlin, Techno und die Wende*. Berlin: Suhrkamp, 2014.

Deutsche, Rosalyn. *Evictions: Art and Spatial Politics*. Cambridge, MA: MIT Press, 1996.

Diederichsen, Detlef. "Wie ich mal meine Jugend verschwendete." In *Zurück zum Beton: die Anfänge von Punk und New Wave in Deutschland 1977–82. Kunsthalle Düsseldorf, 7. Juli—15. September 2002*, edited by Ulrike Groos and Peter Gorschlüter. Cologne: König, 2002.

Dreyer, Sven-Andre, Michael Wenzel, and Thomas Stelzmann, eds. *Keine Atempause: Musik aus Düsseldorf*. Düsseldorf: Droste Verlag, 2018.

Duivenvoorden, Eric. *Een voet tussen de deur: Geschiedenis van de kraakbeweging (1964–1999)*. Amsterdam: De Arbeiderspers, 2000.

Durkheim, Emile. *The Elementary forms of Religious Life*. New York: Free Press, 1995.

Dürr, Hans Peter. "Savage Ethnology." *Semiotext(e): The German Issue* 4, no. 2 (1982): 200–208.

Edelstein, Dan, Stefanos Geroulanos, and Natasha Wheatley, eds. *Power and Time: Temporalities and Conflict in the Making of History*. Chicago: University of Chicago Press, 2020.

Eitler, Pascal, and Jens Elberfeld, eds. *Zeitgeschichte des Selbst: Therapeutisierung, Politisierung, Emotionalisierung*. Bielefeld: Transcript, 2015.

Ermittlungsauschuss im Mehringhof. *Abgeräumt? 8 Häuser geräumt . . . Klaus-Jürgen Rattay tot. Ermittlungsausschuss. Eine Dokumentation*. Berlin: Ermittlungsausschuss, 1981.

Esch, Rüdiger. *Electri_City: The Düsseldorf School of Electronic Music*. London: Omnibus Press, 2016.

Esposito, Fernando. "Von *no future* bis Posthistoire: Der Wandel des temporalen Imaginariums nach dem Boom." In *Vorgeschichte der Gegenwart: Dimensionen des Strukturbruchs nach dem Boom*, edited by Anselm Doering-Manteuffel, Lutz Raphael, and Thomas Schlemmer, 393–424. Göttingen: Vandenhoeck and Ruprecht, 2016.

Esposito, Fernando, and Tobias Becker. "The Time of Politics, the Politics of Time, and Politicized Time: An Introduction to Chronopolitics." *History and Theory* 62, no. 4 (2023): 3–23. https://doi.org/10.1111/hith.12324.

Farkas, Wolfgang, Stefanie Seidl, and Heiko Zwirner, eds. *Nachtleben Berlin. 1975 bis heute*. Berlin: Metrolit, 2013.
Felsch, Philipp, and Frank Witzel. *BRD Noir*. Berlin: Mathes & Seitz, 2016.
Felsch, Philipp. *Der lange Sommer der Theorie: Geschichte einer Revolte, 1960–1990*. Munich: C.H. Beck, 2015.
Fesel, Anke, and Chris Keller, eds. *Berlin Wonderland: Wild Years Revisited, 1990–1996*. Berlin: Gestalten, 2014.
Fichter, Tilman, and Siegward Lönnendonker. *Kleine Geschichte des SDS*. Essen: Klartext, 2007.
Fisher, Mark. *Ghosts of My Life: Writings on Depression, Hauntology and Lost Futures*. 2nd ed. Winchester, UK: Zero Books, 2022.
Föllmer, Moritz. "Cities of Choice: Elective Affinities and the Transformation of Western European Urbanity from the Mid-1950s to the Early 1980s." *Contemporary European History* 24, no. 4 (2015): 577–96. https://doi.org/10.1017/S096077731500034X.
Forner, Sean. *German Intellectuals and the Challenge of Democratic Renewal: Culture and Politics after 1945*. Cambridge: Cambridge University Press, 2014.
Foucault, Michel. "Preface." In *Anti-Oedipus: Capitalism and Schizophrenia*, Gilles Deleuze and Félix Guattari (New York: Penguin Classics, 2009).
Foster, Hal. "Outmoded Spaces, 1993." In *Memory*, edited by Ian Farr, 49–59. Cambridge, MA: MIT Press, 2012.
Freeman, Elizabeth. *Time Binds: Queer Temporalities, Queer Histories*. Durham: Duke University Press, 2010.
Frith, Simon. *Performing Rites: On the Value of Popular Music*. Cambridge, MA: Harvard University Press, 1996.
Fulda, Daniel, Stefan-Ludwig Hoffmann, and Till van Rahden, eds. *Demokratie im Schatten der Gewalt. Geschichten des Privaten im deutschen Nachkrieg*. Göttingen: Wallstein, 2010.
Geronimo. *Fire and Flames: A History of the German Autonomist Movement*. Rev. ed. Oakland: PM Press, 2012.
Geyer, Michael. "Cold War Angst: The Case of West-German Opposition to Rearmament and Nuclear Weapons." In *The Miracle Years: A Cultural History of West Germany, 1949–1968*, edited by Hannah Schissler, 376–408. Princeton, NJ: Princeton University Press, 2001.
Geyer, Michael, ed. *The Power of Intellectuals in Contemporary Germany*. Chicago: University of Chicago Press, 2001.
Giesen, Bernhard. "Performing the Sacred: A Durkheimian perspective on the performative turn in the social sciences." In *Social Performance: Symbolic Action, Cultural Pragmatics, and Ritual*, edited by Jeffrey Alexander, Bernhard Giesen, and Jason Mast, 325–67. Cambridge: Cambridge University Press, 2006.
Gildea, Robert, James Mark, and Anette Warring, eds. *Europe's 1968: Voices of Revolt*. Oxford: Oxford University Press, 2013.
Giltcher-Holtey, Ingrid. *Die 68er Bewegung: Deutschland, Westeuropa, USA*. Munich: CH Beck, 2001.
Glaser, Peter. "Geschichte wird Gemacht." In *Zurück zum Beton. Die Anfänge von Punk und New Wave in Deutschland, 1977–1982. Kunsthalle Düsseldorf, 7. Juli—15. September 2002*, edited by Ulrike Groos and Peter Gorschlüter. Cologne: König, 2002.
Gordon, Avery. *Ghostly Matters: Haunting and the Sociological Imagination*. Minneapolis: University of Minnesota Press, 2008.

Graeber, David. *Direct Action: An Ethnography.* Oakland: AK Press, 2009.
Grand, Lurker, ed. *Hot Love: Swiss Punk & Wave, 1976–1980.* Zurich: Edition Patrick Frey, 2007.
Grashoff, Udo. *Schwarzwohnen: die Unterwanderung der staatlichen Wohnraumlenkung in der DDR.* Göttingen: V&R Unipress, 2011.
Grass, Günter. "What Am I Talking For? Is Anybody Still Listening?" *New German Critique* 52 (1991): 66–72. https://doi.org/10.2307/488188.
Greenberg, Udi. *The Weimar Century: German Emigres and the Ideological Foundations of the Cold War.* Princeton, NJ: Princeton University Press, 2014.
Groebner, Valentin. *Retroland: Geschichtstourismus und die Sehnsucht nach dem Authentischen.* Frankfurt: Fischer, 2018.
Groetz, Thomas. *Doris als Musikerin. Die Tödliche Doris, Band 2.* Berlin: Martin Schmitz Verlag, 1999.
Groetz, Thomas. *Kunst-Musik: deutscher Punk und New Wave in der Nachbarschaft von Joseph Beuys.* Berlin: Martin Schmitz Verlag, 2002.
Grolle, Joist. "Der Hamburger Hafenstraßenkonflikt und der Geisterkrieg um die Vergangenheit." *Zeitschrift des Vereins für Hamburgisch Geschichte* 91 (2005): 133–58.
Groos, Ulrike, and Peter Gorschlüter, eds. *Zurück zum Beton: die Anfänge von Punk und New Wave in Deutschland 1977–82. Kunsthalle Düsseldorf, 7. Juli—15. September 2002.* Cologne: König, 2002.
Grotum, Thomas. *Die Halbstarken: zur Geschichte einer Jugendkultur der 50er Jahre.* Frankfurt: Campus, 1994.
Grundmann, Gudrun, ed. *Sachschaden: Häuser und andere Kämpfe.* Frankfurt: Verlag die Tageszeitung, 1981.
Guillou, Jan. *Der demokratische Terrorist.* Translated by Hans-Joachim Maas. Munich: Piper, 1990.
Gumbrecht, Hans Ulrich. *Our Broad Present: Time and Contemporary Culture.* New York: Columbia University Press, 2014.
Gut, Gudrun. "Von alleine läuft gar nichts." In *Nachtleben Berlin. 1975 bis heute,* edited by Wolfgang Farkas, Stefanie Seidl, and Heiko Zwirner. Berlin: Metrolit, 2013.
Gutmaier, Ulrich. *Die ersten Tage von Berlin. Der Sound der Wende.* Stuttgart: Tropen, 2013.
Häberlen, Joachim. "Heterochronias: Reflections on the Temporal Exceptionality of Revolts." *European Review of History* 28, no. 4 (2021): 531–48. https://doi.org/10.1080/13507486.2021.1897530.
Häberlen, Joachim. "Sekunden der Freiheit: Zum Verhältnis von Gefühlen, Macht und Zeit in Ausnahmesituationen am Beispiel der Revolte 1980/81 in Berlin." In *Ausnahmezustände: Entgrenzungen und Regulierungen in Europa während des Kalten Krieges,* edited by Dirk Schumann and Cornelia Rau. Göttingen: Wallstein, 2015.
Häberlen, Joachim. "(Not) Narrating the History of the Federal Republic: Reflections on the Place of the New Left in West German History and Historiography." *Central European History* 52, no. 1 (2019): 107–24. https://doi.org/10.1017/S0008938919000074.
Häberlen, Joachim. *The Emotional Politics of the Alternative Left: West Germany, 1968–1984.* Cambridge: Cambridge University Press, 2018.
Häberlen, Joachim, and Jake P. Smith. "Struggling for Feelings: The Politics of Emotions in the Radical New Left in West Germany, c. 1968–84." *Contemporary*

European History 23, no. 4 (November 2014): 615–37. https://doi.org/10.1017
/S0960777314000344.
Habersbusch, Kuno. *Berliner Linie gegen Instandbesetzer: Die "Vernunft schlägt immer wieder zu!"* Berlin: N.p., 1981.
Hakemi, Sara. *Anschlag und Spektakel: Flugblätter der Kommune I, Erklärungen von Ensslin/Baader und den frühen RAF*. Bochum: Posth, 2008.
Halberstam, Jack. "Going Gaga: Anarchy, Chaos, and the Wild." *Social Text* 31, no. 3 (116) (Fall 2013): 123–34. https://doi.org/10.1215/01642472-2152873.
Hall, Mirko, Seth Howes, and Cyrus Shahan, editors. *Beyond No Future: Cultures of German Punk*. New York: Bloomsbury, 2016.
Haller, Michael, ed. *Aussteigen oder rebellieren. Jugendliche gegen Staat und Gesellschaft*. Reinbeck bei Hamburg: Rowohlt, 1981.
Hänny, Reto. "Freedom for Greenland—Melt the Pack Ice." *Semiotext(e): The German Issue* 4, no. 2 (1982): 290–92.
Hänny, Reto. *Zürich, Anfang September*. Frankfurt: Suhrkamp, 1981.
Hansen, Miriam. "Spaces of History, Language of Time: Kluge's *Yesterday Girl* (1966)." In *German Film and Literature: Adaptations and Transformations*, edited by Eric Rentschler, 193–216. New York: Methuen, 1986.
Hanshew, Karrin. "Daring More Democracy? Internal Security and the Social Democratic Fight against West German Terrorism." *Central European History* 43, no. 1 (2010): 117–47. http://www.jstor.org/stable/40601021.
Hanshew, Karrin. *Terror and Democracy in West Germany*. Cambridge: Cambridge University Press, 2012.
Hardt, Michael. *The Subversive Seventies*. Oxford: Oxford University Press, 2023.
Härlin, Benny. "Von Haus zu Haus—Berliner Bewegungsstudien." *Kursburch* 65 (1981): 1–28.
Harootunian, Harry. *Marx after Marx: History and Time in the Expansion of Capitalism*. New York: Columbia University Press, 2015.
Hartog, François. *Regimes of Historicity: Presentism and Experiences of Time*. Translated by Saskia Brown. New York: Columbia University Press, 2015.
Harvey, David. *The Conditions of Postmodernity*. Oxford: Wiley-Blackwell, 1990.
Harvey, David. "From Space to Place and Back Again: Reflections on the Condition of Postmodernity." In *Mapping the Futures: Local Cultures, Global Change*, edited by Jon Bird. London: Routledge, 1993.
Hayton, Jeff. *Culture from the Slums: Punk Rock in East and West Germany*. Oxford: Oxford University Press, 2022.
Hebdige, Dick. *Subculture. The Meaning of Style*. New York: Methuen, 1979.
Heinen, Christina. *Tief in Neukölln: Soundkulturen zwischen Improvisation und Gentrifizierung in einem Berliner Bezirk*. Bielefeld: Transcript, 2013.
Heisig, Matthias. "Das Politikum der Hausbesetzungen am Beispiel der Berliner Ereignisse 1980–1983." Diplomarbeit: Freie Universität Berlin, 1983.
Hell, Julia. *The Conquest of Ruins: The Third Reich and the Fall of Rome*. Chicago: University of Chicago Press, 2019.
Hell, Julia, and Andreas Schönle, eds. *The Ruins of Modernity*. Durham: Duke University Press, 2010.
Hentschel, Gitti. "Wenn die Munition verschossen ist." In *Sachschaden: Häuser und andere Kämpfe*, edited by Gudrun Grundmann (Frankfurt: Verlag die Tageszeitung, 1981).

Herf, Jeffrey. *Divided Memory: The Nazi Past in the Two Germanys*. Cambridge, MA: Harvard University Press, 1999.
Herrmann, Michael, Hans-Joachim Lenger, Jan Philipp Reemtsma, and Karl Heinz Roth, eds. *"Hafenstraße" Chronik und Analysen eines Konflikts*. Hamburg: Verlag am Galgenberg, 1987.
Hersche, Jeanne. *Antithesen zu den "Thesen zu den Jugendunruhen 1980" der Eidgenössischen Kommission für Jugendfragen: der Feind heisst Nihilismus*. Schaffhausen: Verlag Peter Meili, 1982.
Herzog, Dagmar. *Sex after Fascism: Memory and Morality in Twentieth-Century Germany*. Princeton, NJ: Princeton University Press, 2005.
Herzog, Dagmar. *Sexuality in Europe: A Twentieth-Century History*. Cambridge: Cambridge University Press, 2011.
Hezel, Lukas. "'Was gibt es zu verlieren, wo es kein Morgen gibt?' Chronopolitik und Radikalisierung in der Jugendrevolte 1980/81 und bei den Autonomen." In *Zeitenwandel: Transformationen Geschichtlicher Zeitlichkeit nach dem Boom*, edited by Fernando Esposito, 119–52. Göttingen: Vandenhoeck & Ruprecht, 2017.
Hillis, Faith. *Utopia's Discontents: Russian Emigres and the Quest for Freedom, 1830s–1930s*. Oxford: Oxford University Press, 2022.
Hockenos, Paul. *Joschka Fischer and the Making of the Berlin Republic: An Alternative History of Postwar Germany*. Oxford: Oxford University Press, 2007.
Hockenos, Paul. *Berlin Calling: A Story of Anarchy, Music, the Wall, and the Birth of the New Berlin*. New York: The New Press, 2017.
Hoffmann-Axthelm, Dieter, Otto Kallscheuer, and Eberhard Knödler-Bunte. *Zwei Kulturen. TUNIX, Mescalero und die Folgen*. Berlin: Verlag Ästhetik und Kommunikation, 1978.
Holfelder, Moritz. *Palast der Republik: Aufstieg und Fall eines symbolischer Gebäudes*. Berlin: Ch. Links, 2008.
Hollstein, Walter. "Autonome Lebensformen. Über die transbürgerliche Perspektive der Jugendbewegung." In *Aussteigen oder rebellieren. Jugendliche gegen Staat und Gesellschaft*, edited by Michael Haller, 197–216. Reinbeck bei Hamburg: Rowohlt, 1981.
Holm, Andrej. *Wir bleiben alle! Gentrifizierung—städtische Konflikte um Aufwertung und Verdrängung*. Münster: Unrast Verlag, 2010.
Horkheimer, Max, and Theodor Adorno. *Dialectic of Enlightenment*. Stanford: Stanford University Press, 2007. First published Amsterdam: Querido Verlag, 1947.
Horn, Eva. *The Future as Catastrophe: Imagining Disaster in the Modern Age*. New York: Columbia University Press, 2018.
Holmig, Alexander. "Die aktionistische Wurzeln der Studentenbewegung: Subversive Aktion, Kommune I und die Neudefinition des Politischen." In *1968: Handbuch zur Kultur- und Mediengeschichte der Studentenbewegung*, edited by Martin Klimke and Joachim Scharloth, 107–18. Stuttgart: J.B. Metzler, 2007.
Huyssen, Andreas. *Twilight Memories: Marking Time in a Culture of Amnesia*. New York: Routledge, 1995.
The Invisible Committee. *Now*. N.p.: Ill Will, 2017.
Isler, Vera, and Michael Haller. *Die Kunst der Verweigerung: Wandmalereien in den Autonomen Jugendzentren der Schweiz*. Zurich: Pro Juventue, 1982.
Jacobson, Sarah. "Redefining Urban Citizenship: Italian Migrants and Housing Occupations in 1970s Frankfurt am Main." *Contemporary European History* 33, no. 2 (2024): 634–50. https://doi.org/10.1017/S0960777322000662.

Jameson, Fredric. "Postmodernism, or the Cultural Logic of Late Capitalism." *New Left Review* 1/146 (July/August 1984): 53–92.

Jarausch, Konrad. *After Hitler: Recivilizing Germans, 1945–1995.* Translated by Brandon Hunziker. Oxford: Oxford University Press, 2006.

Jarausch, Konrad. "The Double Disappointment: Revolution, Unification, and German Intellectuals." In *The Power of Intellectuals in Contemporary Germany*, edited by Michael Geyer. Chicago: University of Chicago Press, 2001.

Jarausch, Konrad. *The Rush to German Unity.* Oxford: Oxford University Press, 1994.

Kadir, Nazima. "Myth and Reality in the Amsterdam Squatters' Movement, 1975–2012." In *The City Is Ours: Squatting and Autonomous Movements in Europe from the 1970s to the Present*, edited by Bart van der Steen and Ask Katzeff, 21–61. Oakland: PM Press, 2014.

Kandutsch, Kazuo. "The Event *Kunst und Revolution.*" In *Vienna Actionism: Art and Upheaval in 1960s Vienna*, edited by Eva Badura-Triska and Hubert Klocker. Cologne: Walther König. 2012.

Kaschuba, Wolfgang. "Nowherelands and Residences: Recodifying Public space in Berlin." In *Toward a New Metropolitanism: Reconstituting Public Culture, Urban Citizenship, and the Multicultural Imaginary in New York and Berlin*, edited by Günter Lenz, Friedrich Ulfers, and Antje Dallmann. Heidelberg: Winter, 2006.

Kasper, Sebastian. *Spontis: Eine Geschichte antiautoritärer Linker im roten Jahrzehnt.* Münster: Edition Assemblage, 2019.

Katsiaficas, Georgy. *The Subversion of Politics: European Autonomous Social Movements and the Decolonization of Everyday Life.* Amherst: Humanities Press International, 1997.

Keller, Sean. "Building Duration: Architecture Out of Adventure-Time." *Critical Inquiry* 50, no. 3 (Spring 2024): 472–93. https://doi.org/10.1086/728954.

Kempton, Richard. *Provo: Amsterdam's Anarchist Revolt.* Brooklyn: Autonomedia, 2007.

Kerstin, Franz-Werner. "Juvenile Left-Wing Radicalism, Fringe Groups, and Antipsychiatry in West Germany." In *Between Marx and Coca-Cola: Youth Cultures in Changing European Societies, 1960–1980*, edited by Axel Schildt and Detlef Siegfried, 353–75. New York: Berghahn, 2006.

Klein, Hans-Joachim. *Rückkehr in die Menschlichkeit: Appell eines ausgestiegenen Terroristen.* Reinbeck bei Hamburg: Rowohlt, 1979.

Klimke, Martin, and Joachim Scharloth. "Maos Rote Garden? '1968' zwischen kulturrevolutionärem Anspruch und subversiver Praxis—eine Einleitung." In *1968: Handbuch zur Kultur- und Mediengeschichte der Studentenbewegung*, edited by Martin Klimke and Joachim Scharloth, 1–10. Stuttgart: J.B. Metzler, 2007.

Klimke, Martin. *The Other Alliance: Student Protest in West Germany and the United States in the Global Sixties.* Princeton, NJ: Princeton University Press, 2010.

Koenen, Gerd. *Das rote Jahrzehnt: Unsere kleine deutsche Kulturrevolution, 1967–1977.* Cologne: Kiepenhauer & Witsche, 2001.

Kommission für Jugendfragen. *Thesen zu den Jugendunruhen.* Bern: Bundesamt für Kulturpflege, 1980.

Koshar, Rudy. *Germany's Transient Pasts: Preservation and National Memory in the Twentieth Century.* Chapel Hill: University of North Carolina Press, 1998.

Koshar, Rudy. *From Monuments to Traces: Artifacts of German Memory, 1870–1990.* Berkeley: University of California Press, 2000.

Kraushaar, Wolfgang. "Berliner Subkultur: Blues, Haschrebellen, Tupamaros und Bewegung 2. Juni." In *1968: Handbuch zur Kultur- und Mediengeschichte der Studentenbewegung*, edited by Martin Klimke and Joachim Scharloth, 261–75. Stuttgart: J.B. Metzler, 2007.

Kraushaar, Wolfgang. *Fischer in Frankfurt: Karriere eines Aussenseiters*. Hamburg: Hamburger Edition, 2001.

Kraushaar, Wolfgang. *Die RAF und linke Terrorismus*. Hamburg: Hamburger Edition, 2006.

Kraushaar, Wolfgang. "Thesen zum Verhältnis von Alternativ- und Fluchtbewegung. Am Beispiel der frankfurter scene." In *Autonomie oder Getto? Kontroversen über die Alternativbewegung*, edited by Wolfgang Kraushaar. Frankfurt: Verlag Neue Kritik, 1978.

Kuhn, Armin. *Vom Häuserkampf zur neoliberalen Stadt: Besetzungsbewegungen und Stadterneuerung in Berlin und Barcelona*. Münster: Westfälisches Dampfboot, 2014.

Kundani, Hans. *Utopia or Auschwitz? Germany's 1968 Generation and the Holocaust*. New York: Columbia University Press, 2009.

Kunzelmann, Dieter. *Leisten Sie keinen Widerstand! Bilder aus meinem Leben*. Berlin: Transit, 1998.

Ladd, Brian. *The Ghosts of Berlin: Confronting German History in the Urban Landscape*. Chicago: University of Chicago Press, 1997.

Landwehr, Achim. "Nostalgia and the Turbulence of Times." *History and Theory* 57, no. 2 (June 2018): 251–68. https://doi.org/10.1111/hith.12060.

Lang, Barbara. *Mythos Kreuzberg: Ethnographie eines Stadtteils, 1961–1995*. Frankfurt: Campus, 1998.

Laufer, Klaus. "Eingeschlossene Bergleute machen sich zum Beispiel durch Klofzeichen bemerkbar." In *Geniale Dilletanten*, edited by Wolfgang Müller. Berlin: Merve, 1982.

Laurisch, Bernd. *Kein Abriß unter dieser Nummer: 2 Jahre Instandbesetzung in der Cuvrystraße in Berlin-Kreuzberg*. Gießen: Anabas, 1981.

Lecorte, Thomas. *Wir tanzen bis zum Ende. Die Geschichte eines Autonomen*. Hamburg: Verlag am Galgenberg, 1992.

Lee, Mia. *Utopia and Dissent in West Germany: The Resurgence of the Politics of Everyday Life in the Long 1960s*. New York: Routledge, 2019.

Lefebvre, Henri. *The Production of Space*. Malden: Blackwell, 1991.

Lerner, Ben. *10:04*. New York: Faber and Faber, 2015.

Levy, William. "Aufruf zum Chaos." In *AMOK/KOMA. Ein Bericht zur Lage*, edited by Jürgen Ploog, Paciao, and W. Hartmann. Bonn: Expanded Media Editions, 1980.

Lorenz, Chris. "Out of Time? Some Critical Reflections on François Hartog's Presentism." In *Rethinking Historical Time: New Approaches to Presentism*, edited by Marek Tamm and Laurent Oliver, 23–42. New York: Bloomsbury, 2019.

Lorenz, Chris, and Berber Bevernage, eds. *Breaking up Time: Negotiating the Borders Between Past, Present and Future*. Göttingen: Vandenhoek & Ruprecht, 2013.

Maase, Kaspar. *BRAVO Amerika. Erkundungen zur Jugendkultur der Bundesrepublik in den fünfziger Jahren*. Hamburg: Junius, 1992.

Maasen, Sabine, Jens Elberfeld, Pascal Eitler, and Maik Tändler, eds. *Das beratene Selbst: zur Genealogie der Therapeutisierung in den 'langen' Siebzigern*. Bielefeld: Transcript, 2011.

Maier, Charles. *Dissolution: The Crisis of Communism and the End of East Germany.* Princeton, NJ: Princeton University Press, 1997.
Maier, Charles. *The Unmasterable Past: History, Holocaust, and German National Identity.* Cambridge, MA: Harvard University Press, 1988.
Mallet, Carl-Heinz. *Die Leute von der Hafenstraße: Über eine andere Art zu leben.* Hamburg: Lutz Schulenburg, 2000.
Marcus, Greil. *Lipstick Traces: A Secret History of the Twentieth Century.* Cambridge, MA: Harvard University Press, 1989.
Marcuse, Herbert. *Eros and Civilization: A Philosophical Inquiry into Freud.* 2nd ed. Boston: Beacon Press, 1966. First published New York: Vintage Books, 1955.
Marcuse, Herbert. *One-Dimensional Man.* Boston: Beacon Press, 1964.
März, Michael. *Linker Protest nach dem Deutschen Herbst. Eine Geschichte des linken Spektrums in Schatten des 'starken Staates', 1977–1979.* Bielefeld: Transcript, 2012.
Mathers, Andy. *Struggling for a Social Europe: Neoliberal Globalization and the Birth of a European Social Movement.* Burlington: Ashgate, 2007.
Mausbach, Wilfried. "'Burn, ware-house, burn!' Modernity, Counterculture, and the Vietnam War in West Germany." In *Between Marx and Coca-Cola: Youth Cultures in Changing European Societies, 1960–1980,* edited by Axel Schildt and Detlef Siegfried, 175–202. New York: Berghahn, 2006.
McKinney, Devin. *Magic Circles: The Beatles in Dream and History.* Cambridge, MA: Harvard University Press, 2004.
Meinecke, Thomas. "Neue Hinweise: Im Westeuropa Dämmerlicht (1981)" In *Mode & Verzweiflung,* edited by Thomas Meinecke. Frankfurt: Suhrkamp, 1986.
Mende, Silke. "Von der 'Anti-Parteien-Partei' zur 'ökologischen Reformpartei'. Die Grünen und der Wandel des Politischen." *Archiv für Sozialgeschichte* 52 (2012): 273–315.
Mende, Silke. "Das 'Momo'-Syndrom: Zeitvorstellungen im alternativen Milieu und in den 'neuen' Protestbewegungen." In *Zeitenwandel: Transformationen Geschichtlicher Zeitlichkeit nach dem Boom,* edited by Fernando Esposito, 153–92. Göttingen: Vandenhoeck & Ruprecht, 2017.
Milder, Stephen. *Greening Democracy: The Anti-nuclear Movement and Political Environmentalism in West Germany and Beyond, 1968–1983.* Cambridge: Cambridge University Press, 2017.
Mitchell, W. J. T., ed. *Landscape and Power.* 2nd ed. Chicago: University of Chicago Press, 2002.
Mitscherlich, Alexander. *Die Unwirtlichkeit unserer Städte: Anstiftung zum Unfrieden (The Inhospitality of Our Cities).* Frankurt: Suhrkamp, 1965.
Mitscherlich, Alexander, and Margarete Mitscherlich. *Die Unfähigkeit zu trauern. Grundlagen kollektiven Verhaltens.* Munich: Piper, 1967.
Möntmann, Nina. "Die treibende Kraft der mobilen Anpassung." In *Lieber zu viel als zu wenig: Kunst, Musik, Aktionen zwischen Hedonismus und Nihilismus (1976–1985).* Berlin: Vice Versa, 2003.
Moses, A. Dirk. *German Intellectuals and the Nazi Past.* Cambridge: Cambridge University Press, 2007.
Mrozek, Bodo. *Jugend—Pop—Kultur: Eine transnationale Geschichte.* Frankfurt: Suhrkamp, 2019.
Müller-Münch, Ingrid, Wolfgang Prosinger, Sabine Rosenbladt, and Linda Stibler, eds.

Besetzung—Weil das Wünschen nicht geholfen hat. Reinbeck bei Hamburg: Rowohlt Taschenbuch Verlag, 1981.

Müller, Wolfgang. *Subkultur Westberlin 1979–1989. Freizeit.* Hamburg: Philo Fine Arts, 2013.

Müller, Wolfgang. "Die wahren Dilletanten." In *Geniale Dilletanten*, edited by Wolfgang Müller. Berlin: Merve, 1982.

Müller, Wolfgang, and Martin Schmitz, eds. *Die Tödliche Doris—Kunst.* Berlin: Martin Schmitz Verlag, 1999.

Muñoz, José Esteban. *Cruising Utopia: The Then and There of Queer Futurity.* New York: New York University Press, 2009.

Nabokov, Vladimir. *Transparent Things.* New York: Vintage Books, 1972.

Nigg, Heinz, ed. *Wir wollen alles, und zwar subito! Die Achtziger Jugendunruhen in der Schweiz und ihre Folgen.* Zurich: Limmat Verlag, 2001.

Novy, Johannes. "Städtetourismus, Stadtteiltourismus und der Mythos Städtischer Steuerung. Das Beispiel Berlin." In *Governance von Destinationen: Neue Ansätze für die erfolgreiche Steuerung touristischer Zielgebiete*, edited by Anja Saretzki and Karlheinz Wöhler. Berlin: Erich Schmidt Verlag, 2013.

Novy, Johannes, and Claire Colomb. "Struggling for the Right to the (Creative) City in Berlin and Hamburg: New Urban Social Movements, New 'Spaces of Hope'?" *International Journal of Urban and Regional Research* 37, no. 5 (September 2013): 1816–38. https://doi.org/10.1111/j.1468-2427.2012.01115.x.

Oldenziel, Ruth, and Karin Zachmann, eds. *Cold War Kitchen: Americanization, Technology, and European Users.* Cambridge, MA: MIT Press, 2009.

Olick, Jeffrey. *In the House of the Hangman: The Agonies of German Defeat, 1943–1949.* Chicago: University of Chicago Press, 2005.

Osborne, Peter. *The Politics of Time: Modernity and the Avant-Garde.* London: Verso, 2011.

Ossowski, Leonie. *Wilhelm Meister's Abschied.* Weinheim und Basel: Beltz Verlag, 1982.

Owens, Lynn. *Cracking Under Pressure: Narrating the Decline of the Amsterdam Squatters' Movement.* University Park: Pennsylvania State University Press, 2009.

Owens, Linus, Ask Katzeff, Elisabeth Lorenzi, and Baptiste Colin. "At Home in the Movement: Constructing an Oppositional Identity through Activist Travel across European Squats." In *Understanding European Movements: New Social Movements, Global Justice Struggles, Anti-austerity Protest*, edited by Cristina Flesher Fominaya and Laurence Cox. London: Routledge, 2013.

Papenfuß, Bert. "Kunsterziehung durch Punk." In *Lieber zu viel als zu wenig: Kunst, Musik, Aktionen zwischen Hedonismus und Nihilismus (1976–1985).* Berlin: Vice Versa, 2003.

Pavitt, Jane. "Design and the Democratic Ideal." In *Cold War Modern: Design, 1945–1970*, edited by David Crowley and Jane Pavitt, 73–93. London: V&A Publishing, 2008.

Perry, Joe. "Love Parade 1996: Techno Playworlds and the Neoliberalization of Post-Wall Berlin." *German Studies Review* 42, no. 3 (October 2019): 561–79. https://dx.doi.org/10.1353/gsr.2019.0081.

Ploog, Jürgen, Paciao, and W. Hartmann, eds. *AMOK/KOMA. Ein Bericht zur Lage.* Bonn: Expanded Media Editions, 1980.

Ploog, Jürgen. "Showdown des Okzidents." In *AMOK/KOMA. Ein Bericht zur Lage*,

edited by Jürgen Ploog, Paciao, and W. Hartmann. Bonn: Expanded Media Editions, 1980.
Pogue Harrison, Robert. "Hic Jacet." In *Landscape and Power*, 2nd ed., edited by W. J. T. Mitchell, 350–65. Chicago: University of Chicago Press, 2002.
Poiger, Uta. *Jazz, Rock, and Rebels: Cold War Politics and American Culture in a Divided Germany*. Berkeley: University of California Press, 2000.
Postone, Moishe. *Time, Labor, and Social Domination: A Reinterpretation of Marx's Critical Theory*. Cambridge: Cambridge University Press, 1993.
Prinz, Ursula, ed. *Gefühl und Härte. Neuen Kunst aus Berlin, 8. Oktober bis 14. November 1982, Kunstverein München*. Munich: Kunstverein München, 1982.
Prognos, A. G. "Jugendprotest: Einstellungen und Motive von Jugendlichen in 8 ausgewählten Gruppen." In *Jugendprotest im demokratischen Staat. Enquete-Kommission des Deutschen Bundestages*, edited by Matthias Wissmann and Rudolf Hauck. Stuttgart: Edition Weitbrecht, 1983.
Prosinger, Wolfgang. "Krieg im Frieden: Die Gewaltsame Räumung des Dreisamecks in Freibug." In *Besetzung—Weil das Wünschen nicht geholfen hat*, edited by Ingrid Müller-Münch, Wolfgang Prosinger, Sabine Rosenbladt, and Linda Stibler. Reinbeck bei Hamburg: Rowohlt Taschenbuch Verlag, 1981.
Provenzano, Luca. "'Power Is in the Streets': Protest and Militancy in France, Italy and West Germany, 1968–1979." *Contemporary European History* (2023): 1–18. https://doi.org/10.1017/S096077732300022X.
R, Moritz. *Der Plan: Glanz und Elend der Neuen Deutschen Welle. Die Geschichte einer deutschen Band*. Kassel: Verlag Martin Schmitz, 1993.
Rabehl, Bernd. "Im Kampf gegen die Polizei werden sie die Gestalt der Polizei annehmen. Eine Einschätzung des aktuellen Jugendprotests. Gespräch mit Bernd Rabehl." In *Paßt bloß auf! Was will die neue Jugendbewegung?* edited by Jürgen Bacia and Klaus-Jürgen Sherer. Berlin: Olle und Wolter, 1981.
Rada, Uwe. *Hauptstadt der Verdrängung: Berliner Zukunft zwischen Kiez und Metropole*. Berlin: Schwarze Risse, 1997.
Rapp, Tobias. *Lost and Sound: Berlin, Techno and the Easyjet Set*. Berlin: Innervisions, 2010.
Regener, Sven. *Der kleine Bruder*. Frankfurt: Eichborn Berlin, 2008.
Reichardt, Sven. *Authentizität und Gemeinschaft: Linksalternatives Leben in den siebziger und frühen achtziger Jahren*. Berlin: Suhrkamp, 2014.
Reichardt, Sven, and Detlef Siegfried, eds. *Das Alternative Milieu: Antibürgerlicher Lebensstil und linke Politik in der Bundesrepublik Deutschland und Europa, 1968–1983*. Göttingen: Wallstein Verlag, 2010.
Reiche, Anne. *Auf der Spur*. Edition Cimarron, 2019.
Reichensperger, Petra. "Schlau sein—dabei sein." In *Lieber zu viel als zu wenig: Kunst, Musik, Aktionen zwischen Hedonismus und Nihilismus (1976–1985)*. Berlin: Vice Versa, 2003.
Renaud, Terence. *New Lefts: The Making of a Radical Tradition*. Princeton, NJ: Princeton University Press, 2021.
Reynolds, Simon. *Retromania: Pop Culture's Addiction to Its Own Past*. London: Faber & Faber, 2011.
Richter, Isabel. "Psychonauts and Seekers: West German Entanglements in the Spiritual Turn of the Global 1960s and 1970s." *Contemporary European History* 33, no. 1 (2024): 250–66. https://doi.org/10.1017/S0960777322000121.

Ross, Kristin. *Communal Luxury: The Political Imaginary of the Paris Commune*. London: Verso, 2015.
Ross, Kristin. *May '68 and Its Afterlives*. Chicago: University of Chicago Press, 2002.
Röttgen, Herbert. "Mythology in Revolution?" *Semiotext(e): The German Issue* 4, no. 2 (1982): 192–98.
Rubin, Eli. *Amnesiopolis: Modernity, Space, and Memory in East Germany*. Oxford: Oxford University Press, 2016.
Rutschky, Michael. *Erfahrungshunger: ein Essay über die siebziger Jahre*. Cologne: Kiepenhauer & Witsch, 1980.
Sabrow, Martin, ed. *Errinerungsorte der DDR*. Munich: Beck, 2009.
Sandler, Daniela. *Counterpreservation: Architectural Decay in Berlin since 1989*. Ithaca, NY: Cornell University Press, 2016.
Scharenberg, Albert. *Der Sound der Stadt: Musikindustrie und Subkultur in Berlin*. Münster: Westfällisches Dampfboot, 2005.
Scharloth, Joachim. "Ritualkritik und Rituale des Protests: Die Entdeckung des Performativen in der Studentenbewegung der 1960er Jahre." In *1968: Handbuch zur Kultur- und Mediengeschichte der Studentenbewegung*, edited by Martin Klimke and Joachim Scharloth, 75–87. Stuttgart: J.B. Metzler, 2007.
Schildt, Axel. "Across the Boder: West German Youth Travel to Western Europe." In *Between Marx and Coca-Cola: Youth Cultures in Changing European Societies, 1960–1980*, edited by Axel Schildt and Detlef Siegfried. New York: Berghahn Books, 2006.
Schildt, Axel. *Ankunft im Westen: ein Essay zur Erfolgsgeschichte der Bundesrepublik*. Frankfurt: Fischer, 1999.
Schildt, Axel, and Detlef Siegfried, eds. *Between Marx and Coca-Cola: Youth Cultures in Changing European Societies, 1960–1980*. New York: Berghahn Books, 2006.
Schildt, Axel, Detlef Siegfried, and Karl Chritian Lammers, eds. *Dynamische Zeiten. Die 60er Jahre in den beiden deutschen Gesellschaften* (Hamburg: Christians, 2003).
Schiller, Melanie. "Wie klingt die Bundesrepublik? Kraftwerk, *Autobahn* und die Suche nach der eigenen Identität." In *Mensch—Maschinen—Musik: Das Gesamtkunstwerk Kraftwerk*, edited by Uwe Schütte. Düsseldorf: C.W. Leske Verlag, 2018.
Schissler, Hanna, ed. *The Miracle Years: A Cultural History of West Germany, 1949–1968*. Princeton, NJ: Princeton University Press, 2001.
Schlembach, Raphael. *Against Old Europe: Critical Theory and Alter-Globalization Movements*. Farnham: Ashgate, 2014.
Schlicht, Uwe, ed. *Trotz und Träume: Jugend lehnt sich auf*. Berlin: Severin und Siedler, 1982.
Schmid, Thomas. "Autonomie von der Entwicklung – doch in der Entwicklung." In *Zwei Kulturen. TUNIX, Mescalero und die Folgen*, edited by Dieter Hoffmann-Axthelm, Otto Kallscheuer, and Eberhard Knödler-Bunte, 182–205. Berlin: Verlag Ästhetik und Kommunikation, 1978.
Schmidt-Lauber, Brigitta. *FC St. Pauli: zur Ethnographie eines Vereins*. Münster: Lit Verlag, 2004.
Schneider, Frank Apunkt. *Als die Welt noch Unterging: Von Punk zu NDW*. Mainz: Ventil, 2006.
Schneider, Peter. *Rebellion und Wahn*. Cologne: Kiepenheuer & Witsch, 2010.
Scholz, Natalie. "Ghosts and Miracles: The Volkswagen as Imperial Debris in Postwar

West Germany." *Comparative Studies in Society and History* 62, no. 3 (2020): 487–519. https://doi.org/10.1017/S0010417520000158.

Schulz-Hageleit, Peter, ed. *Lieber instandbesetzten als kaputtbesitzen! Unterrichts Materialien zur Wohnungspolitik*. Berlin: Basis Verlag, 1981.

Schumann, Dirk, and Cornelia Rau, eds. *Ausnahmezustände: Entgrenzungen und Regulierungen in Europa während des Kalten Krieges*. Göttingen: Wallstein, 2015.

Schütte, Uwe. *Kraftwerk: Future Music from Germany*. London: Penguin, 2020.

Schütte, Uwe, ed. *Mensch—Maschinen—Musik: Das Gesamtkunstwerk Kraftwerk*. Düsseldorf: C.W. Leske Verlag, 2018.

Schwanhäußer, Anja. *Kosmonauten des Underground: Ethnographie einer Berliner Szene*. Frankfurt: Campus, 2010.

Sedlmaier, Alexander. *Consumption and Violence: Radical Protest in Cold-War West Germany*. Ann Arbor: University of Michigan Press, 2014.

Sepp, Benedikt. *Das Prinzip Bewegung. Theorie, Praxis, und Radikalisierung in der West Berliner Linken 1961–1972*. Göttingen: Wallstein, 2023.

Shahan, Cyrus. *Punk Rock and German Crisis: Adaptation and Resistance after 1977*. New York: Palgrave, 2013.

Shahan, Cyrus. "The Sounds of Terror: Punk, Post-punk and the RAF after 1977." *Popular Music and Sound* 34, no. 3 (July 2011): 369–86. https://doi.org/10.1080/03007761003726258.

Sharpe, Christina. *In the Wake: On Blackness and Being*. Durham: Duke University Press, 2016.

Siegfried, Detlef. *Sound der Revolte: Studien zur Kulturrevolution um 1968*. Munich: Weinheim, 2008.

Siegfried, Detlef. *Time Is on My Side: Konsum und Politik in der Westdeutschen Jugendkultur der 60er Jahre*. Göttingen: Wallstein Verlag, 2006.

Sigmund, Monika, and Marily Stroux. *Zu bunt: Wandbilder in der Hafenstraße*. Hamburg: St. Pauli Archiv, 1996.

Sites, William. *Sun Ra's Chicago: Afrofuturism and the City*. Chicago: University of Chicago Press, 2020.

Slobodian, Quinn. *Foreign Front: Third World Politics in Sixties West Germany*. Durham: Duke University Press, 2012.

Smith, Briana. *Free Berlin: Art, Urban Politics, and Everyday Life*. Cambridge, MA: MIT Press, 2022.

Sneeringer, Julia. *A Social History of Early Rock 'n' Roll in Germany: Hamburg from Burlesque to the Beatles, 1956–69*. London: Bloomsbury, 2018.

Sneeringer, Julia. "Sites of Corruption, Sites of Liberation: Hamburg-St. Pauli and the Contested Spaces of Early Rock 'n' Roll." *Contemporary European History* 26, no. 2 (2017): 313–37. https://doi.org/10.1017/S0960777316000588.

Sontheimer, Michael. *"Natürlich kann geschossen werden": eine kurze Geschichte der Roten Armee Fraktion*. Munich: Deutsche Verlags-Anstalt, 2010.

Squatting Europe Kollective. *Squatting in Europe: Radical Spaces, Urban Struggles*. New York: Minor Compositions, 2013.

St. Pauli Einschnitt. Hamburg: Hafenrand verein für selbstbestimmtes Leben und Wohnen in St. Pauli e.V., 2000.

Stahl, Geoff, ed. *Poor, but Sexy: Reflections on Berlin Scenes*. Bern: Peter Lang, 2014.

Stevens, Quentin, and Mhairi Ambler. "Europe's City Beaches as post-Fordist placemaking." *Journal of Urban Design* 15, no. 4 (2010): 515–37. https://doi.org/10.1080/13574809.2010.502341.

Stewart, Susan. *On Longing: Narratives of the Miniature, the Gigantic, the Souvenir, the Collection*. Durham: Duke University Press, 1993.

Stewart, Susan. *The Ruins Lesson: Meaning and Material in Western Culture*. Chicago: University of Chicago Press, 2019.

Stock, Wolfgang Jean. "Vorwort." In *Gefühl und Härte. Neuen Kunst aus Berlin, 8. Oktober bis 14. November 1982, Kunstverein München*, edited by Ursula Prinz. Munich: Kunstverein München, 1982.

Stoler, Ann Laura, ed. *Imperial Debris: On Ruins and Ruination*. Durham: Duke University Press, 2013.

Strategien für Kreuzberg. Berlin: Senator für Bau- und Wohnungswesen, 1979.

Suttner, Andreas. *"Beton brennt": Hausbesetzer und Selbstverwaltung im Berlin, Wien und Zürich der 80er Jahre*. Vienna: Lit, 2011.

Tamm, Marek. "How to Reinvent the Future?" *History and Theory* 59, no. 3 (September 2020): 448–58. https://doi.org/10.1111/hith.12173.

Tamm, Marek, and Laurent Olivier, eds. *Rethinking Historical Time: New Approaches to Presentism*. New York: Bloomsbury, 2019.

Teipel, Jürgen. *Verschwende deine Jugend: Ein Doku-Roman über den deutschen Punk und New Wave*. Frankfurt: Suhrkamp, 2001.

Till, Karen. *The New Berlin: Memory, Politics, Place*. Minneapolis: University of Minnesota Press, 2005.

Tomba, Massimiliano. *Insurgent Universality: An Alternative Legacy of Modernity*. Oxford: Oxford University Press, 2019.

Tompkins, Andrew. *Better Active than Radioactive! Anti-nuclear Protest in 1970s France and West Germany*. Oxford: Oxford University Press, 2016.

Traverso, Enzo. *Left-Wing Melancholia: Marxism, History, and Memory*. New York: Columbia University Press, 2017.

Tsing, Anna Lowenhaupt. *The Mushroom at the End of the World: On the Possibility of Life in Capitalist Ruins*. Princeton, NJ: Princeton University Press, 2015.

Tsing, Anna Lowenhaupt, Heather Swanson, Elaine Gan, and Nils Bubandt, eds. *Arts of Living on a Damaged Planet: Ghosts and Monsters of the Anthropocene*. Minneapolis: University of Minnesota Press, 2017.

Untermöhlen, Nikolaus. "Doris als Musikerin." In *Geniale Dilletanten*, edited by Wolfgang Müller. Berlin: Merve, 1982.

Untermöhlen, Nikolaus. "Grundlagen zur Molekularstructur der Musik in den verschiedenen Zuständen." In *Geniale Dilletanten*, edited by Wolfgang Müller. Berlin: Merve, 1982.

Van der Steen, Bart, and Knud Andresen, eds. *A European Youth Revolt: European Perspectives on Youth Protest and Social Movements in the 1980s*. New York: Palgrave, 2016.

Van der Steen, Bart, and Ask Katzeff, eds. *The City Is Ours: Squatting and Autonomous Movements in Europe from the 1970s to the Present*. Oakland: PM Press, 2014.

Van Rahden, Till. "Clumsy Democrats: Moral Passions in the Federal Republic." *German History* 29, no. 3 (September 2011): 485–504. https://doi.org/10.1093/gerhis/ghr050.

Varon, Jeremy. *Bringing the War Home: The Weather Underground, the Red Army Faction, and Revolutionary Violence in the Sixties and Seventies. Berkeley: University of California Press, 2004.

Vasudevan, Alexander. Metropolitan Preoccupations: The Spatial Politics of Squatting in Berlin. Malden: Wiley Blackwell, 2015.

Verhoeven, Claudia. "Time of Terror, Terror of Time: On the Impatience of Russian Revolutionary Terrorism (Early 1860s–Early 1880s)." Jahrbücher Für Geschichte Osteuropas 58, no. 2 (2010): 254–73. http://www.jstor.org/stable/41052430.

Verhoeven, Claudia. "'Now Is the Time for Helter Skelter': Terror, Temporality, and the Manson Family." In Power and Time: Temporalities in Conflict and the Making of History, edited by Dan Edelstein, Stefanos Geroulanos, and Natasha Wheatley. Chicago: University of Chicago Press, 2020.

Verhoeven, Claudia. "Wormholes in Russian History: Events 'Outside of Time' (Featuring Malevich, Morozov, and Mayakovsky)." In Breaking up Time: Negotiating the Borders Between Past, Present and Future, edited by Chris Lorenz and Berber Bevernage, 109–23. Göttingen: Vandenhoek & Ruprecht, 2013.

Vidon, Alain. "Der Tag, an dem Calvin ausflippte." In Hot Love: Swiss Punk & Wave, 1976–1980, edited by Lurker Grand. Zurich: Edition Patrick Frey, 2007.

Volmer, Ludger. Die Grünen: von der Protestbewegung zur etablierten Partei. Eine Bilanz. Munich: Bertelsmann, 2009.

Von Dirke, Sabine. All Power to the Imagination! The West German Counterculture from the Student Movement to the Greens. Lincoln: University of Nebraska Press, 1996.

Von Hodenberg, Christina. The Other '68: A Social History of West Germany's Revolt. Oxford: Oxford University Press, 2024.

Von Moltke, Johannes. No Place Like Home: Locations of Heimat in German Cinema. Berkeley: University of California Press, 2005.

Von Saldern, Adelheid. Häuserleben: zur Geschichte städtischen Arbeiterwohnens vom Kaiserreich bis heute. Bonn: JHW Dietz, 1995.

Wagner, David. "The Wish Fulfillment Zone." In Berlin Wonderland: Wild Years Revisited, 1990–1996, edited by Anke Fesel and Chris Keller. Berlin: Gestalten, 2014.

Wagner-Conzelmann, Sandra. Die Interbau 1957 in Berlin. Stadt von Heute—Stadt von Morgen. Städtebau und Gesellschaftskritik der 50er Jahre. Petersberg: Michael Imhof Verlag, 2007.

Waldt, Anton. Auf die Zwölf. Berlin: Verbrecher Verlag, 2010.

Waldt, Anton. "Trockeneis und Tränengas." In Nachtleben Berlin. 1974 bis Heute, edited by Wolfgang Farkas, Stefanie Seidl, and Heiko Zwirner. Berlin: Metrolit, 2013.

Wartenburg, J. C. Kreuzberg K36. Leben in [der] Bewegung. Kreuzberg inside bis zum Fall der Mauer. Berlin: self-published, 2003.

Was wird in den besetzten Häusern gemacht? Eine Dokumentation am Beispiel von. 13. Besetzten Häusern. Berlin: Architekteninitiative Schöneberger Planung, 1981.

Wenzel, Axel, Jürgen Roth, and Häuserrat Frankfurt. Frankfurt. Zerstörung. Terror. Folter. Im Namen des Gesetzes. Frankfurt: Megapress, 1974.

Wiesen, S. Jonathan. "Miracles for Sale: Consumer Displays and Advertising in Postwar West Germany." In Consuming Germany in the Cold War, edited by David Crew, 151–78. New York: Berg, 2003.

Wildenhain, Michael. Zum beispiel k. Berlin: Rotbuch Verlag, 1983.

Wilder, Gary. Concrete Utopianism: The Politics of Temporality and Solidarity. New York: Fordham University Press, 2022.

"*Wir wollen niemals auseinandergehen...*" Berlin: SHIK, 1983.
Wirth, Hans-Jürgen. *Die Schärfung der Sinne: Jugendprotest als persönliche und kulturelle Chance*. Frankfurt: Syndikat, 1984.
Wissmann, Matthias, and Rudolf Hauck, eds. *Jugendprotest im demokratischen Staat. Enquete-Kommission des Deutschen Bundestages*. Stuttgart: Edition Weitbrecht, 1983.
Womack, Ytasha. *Afrofuturism: The World of Black Sci-Fi and Fantasy Culture*. Chicago: Lawrence Hill, 2013.
Young, James. *At Memory's Edge: After-images of the Holocaust in Contemporary Art and Architecture*. New Haven: Yale University Press, 2000.
Young, James Edward. "Daniel Libeskind's Jewish Museum in Berlin: The Uncanny Arts of Memorial Architecture." *Jewish Social Studies* 6, no. 2 (2000): 1–23. https://dx.doi.org/10.1353/jss.2000.0007.
Zahl, Peter-Paul. "Eisbrecher, Mitten in den Strassen, Volldampf Voraus." In *Instandbesetzer Bilderbuch*, edited by Wolfgang Krolow. Berlin: Lit Pol, 1981.
Züfle, Manfred, and Jürg Meier, eds. *Paranoia City oder Zürich ist überall*. Reinbeck bei Hamburg: Rowohlt Taschenbuch, 1982.

Periodicals

Der Abend
Agit 883
Akut und Praktisch
ARCH +
ASTA Häuserrat, *Häuserkampf-info*
Badische Zeitung
Berliner Morgenpost
Berliner Zeitung
Besetzerinnenzeitung
Bild
epd Landesdienst Berlin
Frankfurter Allgemeine Zeitung
Frankfurter Rundschau
Hamburger Abendblatt
Hamburger Rundschau
Instandbesetzerpost
Interim
KAMIKAZE
Kiez Depesche
Kommunistische Volkszeitung
Kursbuch
Netzwerk Rundbrief
Neue Zürcher Zeitung
Radikal
Schwarze Kanal
Der Spiegel
Stilett

Subito
Süddeutsche Zeitung
Südost Express
Tagesanzeiger
Tagesspiegel
Die Tageszeitung
Telegraph
Umweltblätter
Volksblatt
Die Welt
Welt am Sonntag
Westfalenblatt
Wiener
Winterfeldt Plazette
Die Zeit

Films and albums

AK Kraak, dir. *Video Magazin # 3*. Berlin, October 1990.
AK Kraak, dir. *Video Magazin #1*. Berlin, August 1990.
AK Kraak, dir. *Video Magazin #12*. Berlin, March 1995.
AK Kraak, dir. *Video Magazin #2*. Berlin, September 1990.
AK Kraak, dir. *Video Magazin #8*. Berlin, January 1993.
Anarcho Sampler 87. Berlin: Autofocus Archiv, 1987.
Die Augen Schließen um besser zu sehen. Hamburg: Medienpädagogik Zentrum, 1986.
Bashore, Juliet, dir. *The Battle of Tuntenhaus*. Berlin: BBC Channel 4, 1991.
Bauwagen—weil's besser ist. Hamburg: Medienpädagogik Zentrum, 1989.
Behrendt, Jens-Peter, and Bernd Liebner, dirs. *Am Anfang war doch nicht der Pflasterstein*. Vorhang auf, Film ab!, 1982.
Cybulski, Tamara, Bettina van Nes, and Gottlieb Renz, dirs. *Wo die Angst ist Geht's Lang*. Berlin: dffb, 1981.
Fassbinder, Rainer Werner, dir. *Die Ehe der Maria Braun* (*The Marriage of Maria Braun*). Berlin: Albatros Filmproduktion, 1979.
Fassbinder, Rainer Werner, et al., dir. *Deutschland im Herbst* (*Germany in Autumn*). West Germany: ABS Filmproduktion, 1978. Facets Video, 2010. DVD.
Fehlfarben. "Ein Jahr (es geht voran)," track 8 on *Monarchie und Alltag*, EMI Studios, 1980.
Gramming, Walter, dir. "Hammer und Sichel." 1978. In *Berlin Super 80: Music & Film Underground West Berlin, 1978–1984*. Berlin: Monitorpop Entertainment, 2005. DVD.
Gruppe Videotie, dir. *Tanz auf dem Vulkan*. Bochum: Videotie, 1987.
Hafenstraße—Ein Videoprojekt. Hamburg: Medienpädagogik Zentrum, 1988.
Irgendwie, Irgendwo, Irgendwann. Hamburg: Medienpädagogik Zentrum, 1988/89.
Jelinski, Manfred, and Jörg Buttergeit, dirs. *So war das S.O. 36: Ein Abend des Nostalgie*. Berlin, Cinema Vitesse: 1984.
Der Kampf um die St. Pauli Hafenstraße. Hamburg: Medienpädagogik Zentrum, 2004.

Kollektiv Mainzer Straße, dir. *Sag niemals nie (Never Say Never)*. Berlin: Autofocus Videowerkstatt, 1991.
Das können die Soliden nicht verstehen. Hamburg: Medienpädagogik Zentrum, 1991.
Kluge, Alexander, dir. *Abschied von Gestern (Yesterday Girl)*. Frankfurt: Independent Film, 1966.
Künzel, Tilmann, dir. *Sub Berlin: The Story of Tresor*. Berlin: Filmlounge, 2012.
Maschmann, Anette, and Axel Brand, dirs. "E Dopo?" 1981/82. In *Berlin Super 80: Music & Film Underground West Berlin, 1978–1984*. Berlin: Monitorpop Entertainment, 2005. DVD.
Maye, Ingrid, and Volker Rendschmidt, dirs. "Ohne Liebe gibt es keinen Tod." 1980. In *Berlin Super 80: Music & Film Underground West Berlin, 1978–1984*. Berlin: Monitorpop Entertainment, 2005. DVD.
Notorische Reflexe. "*Fragment Video*." 1983. In *Berlin Super 80: Music & Film Underground West Berlin, 1978–1984*. Berlin: Monitorpop Entertainment, 2005. DVD.
Regiekollektiv Medienwerkstatt Freiburg. *Freiburg—Polizeiburg*. Freiburg: Medienwerkstatt, 1980.
Regiekollektiv Medienwerkstatt Freiburg. *Paßt bloß auf! Ein Film aus der Kultur von unten*. Freiburg: Medienwerkstatt, 1981. 75 min.
Seelen, Joost, dir. *De Stad was van ons*. Stichting Zuidenwind Filmprodukties, 1996.
Selbst das kleinste Licht durchbricht die Dunkelheit. Hamburg: Medienpädagogik Zentrum, 1990.
Sieber, Markus, Ronnie Wahli, Marcel Müller, and Thomas Krempke, dirs. *Züri brännt (Zurich Is Burning)*. Zurich: Videoladen Zurich, 1980.
Staudte, Wolfgang, dir. *Die Mörder sind unter uns (The Murderers Are among Us)*. 1946; Deutsche Film.
Terrible Houses in Danger. Hamburg: Medienpädagogik Zentrum, 1985.
Die Tödliche Doris, dir. "Berliner Küchenmusik." 1982. In *Berlin Super 80: Music & Film Underground West Berlin, 1978–1984*. Berlin: Monitorpop Entertainment, 2005. DVD.
Uhlmann, René, dir. *Punk Cocktail. Zurich Scene, 1976–1980*. 2006. DVD, 55 min.
Wenders, Wim, dir. *Im Lauf der Zeit (Kings of the Road)*. Westdeutscher Rundfunk (WDR), 1976.
Wiesemann and Keller, dirs. *Petra Pan und Arumukha: Der Traum von ordentlichen Anarchisten (Petra Pan and Arumukha: The Dream of Orderly Anarchists)*. Berlin: Autofocus Archiv, 1990.
Wolkenstein, Rolf, and Horst Markgraf, dirs. "Hüpfen '82." 1982. In *Berlin Super 80: Music & Film Underground West Berlin, 1978–1984*. Berlin: Monitorpop Entertainment, 2005. DVD.
Das Zögern ist Vorbei. Berlin: MOB, 1981.
Zwischen Dachziegeln und Pflasterstein. Hamburg: Medienpädagogik Zentrum, 1986.

Index

Page numbers in italics refer to figures.

Abschied von Gestern (Kluge film), 18, 23–24
Abwärts, 49–50
academics: left-leaning, 43, 205n7; and organizing temporality, 17; reform-minded, 120
Action Center for Independent and Socialist Students (AUSS), 27–28
activism: aesthetics, 85; and alternative futures, 169; anarchist, 35, 38, 172–74; antiauthoritarian, 2–3, 26–27, 35, 190n7; and art, 1–2, 31–32, 172, 188, 230n6; and autonomy, 81–82, 102, 105–8, 139, 155; and Christian groups, 116–18; and counterculture, 29, 65, 88–89, 95–96, 105, 171; creative and productive dimensions of, 8; decentralized, self-controlled, self-organized forms of, 168; dialectical, 4, 48; and disillusionment, 40; insurgent, 221n77; Kinderladen, 32, 38; left, 1–4, 29–30, 34, 37–38, 40–41, 45, 65, 75, 85, 105–6, 119, 126, 156–57; left-alternative, 42–44, 48, 65, 118; and marginal edges of meaning, 174; militant, 26–27; and negotiations, 118; in neighborhoods, 41, 44–45, 108, 159–60, 166; and philosophy, 33; political, 93; postprogressive, 183–84, 186; progressive, 45; and provocation, 56; and radicalism, 80, 99; of Red Decade, 37; and reform, 115–16; reform-minded/oriented, 66, 120; representational, 3–4; and resistance, 48; and revolution, 29–35, 37–38, 40, 48–49, 66, 81–82, 110; and squatting, 1, 110, 168–69, 172–74; and transnationalism, 108–9, 111–12; travel networks of, 213n41; urban, 46, 78, 100, 138, 157; and violence, 40, 83, 156–57; youth, 2–3, 27–28, 50, 66–67, 73, 78, 83–84, 87, 99, 104, 108, 111–18, 142–43, 172, 190n15, 191n19, 213n53. *See also* demonstrations; protests; riots
Adalbertstraße squats, 48, 80
Adenauer, Konrad, 19
Adorno, Theodor, 23–24, 196n32, 205n7
Afrofuturism, 174, 191n28, 193n40, 222n80
AG Grauwacke, 120
Agentur BILWET group, 89, 109–10
Agit 883 (journal), 30–31
AJZ youth center (Zurich), 77–78, 94, 100, 107, 112, 129
AK Kraak, 167, 176, 227n58, 229n87
Aktionsgemeinschaft Westend, 37
Aktionsgruppe Paula Panther/Karl Krallmich, 213n45
alienation, 63, 83, 109–10, 117, 138, 142
Allen, Jennifer, 44, 66, 187–88, 224n20
alternate reality, 89–90, 109
Alternative List, 81, 179, 212n31, 215n70. *See also* Green Alternative List (GAL)
alternative milieu, 5, 9, 33, 42–43, 48, 65–66, 72–73, 96, 113, 134, 159, 185, 190n16

256 ‹ INDEX

Aly, Götz, 38, 199n83
Am Anfang war doch nicht der Pflasterstein (film), 105
AMOK/KOMA. Ein Bericht zur Lage (ed. Ploog et al.), 56–57
Amsterdam: anarchists, 81; squatting in, 74–76, 79–80, 92, 108, 129–30, 139, 155
anarchy and anarchists: and activism, 35, 38, 172–74; and antiauthoritarianism, 34–35, 190n15; and capitalism, 183–84; and destruction, 89; dispossessed, 125–26; and ideology, 190n8; and negation, 5–6, 107, 168, 176; relationality of, 144; Russian, 193n40; of squatting, 2–3, 7, 111, 125, 172–74; temporal, 174; of youth movements and revolts, 3, 5–7, 81, 125–27, 175–76, 182; in Zurich, 193n40
Andreas Dorau und die Marinas (music group), 69–70
antiauthoritarianism: and activism, 2–3, 26–27, 35, 190n7; and anarchist practices, 34–35, 190n15; and autonomy, 3, 36–37; and body/subjectivity, 31; and counterculture, 30, 35; and cultural forms, 24; demonstrations, 109; and dialectical progress, 36–38; disillusioned, 45; and experimentation, 85; and Gammlers, 26, 31; ideological positions of, 49; and Kommune I, 28; and leftist movements, 3, 24, 31, 38, 43, 47, 49, 51, 57, 97–98, 173, 183, 190n7, 190n15; and Marxism, 190n15; and off-modern, 183; and politics, 116; politics of, 116; and pop culture, 28, 38; and postwar, 31; and power, 190n7; and progress, 36–37; and punks, 57; radical, 3, 47; and radical autonomy, 3; and raised fist symbol, 51; and rebel idea, 35; and reconstruction years, 10; and revolution, 3, 27–28, 30–32, 34–37, 43, 57; and squatting, 2–3, 85, 173; and student movements, 116; symbols, 57; and urban renewal, 45, 97–98; and violent opposition, 34; of youth movements and revolts, 3, 34–35, 85, 109, 116

Anti-Oedipus (Deleuze and Guattari), 32–33
Antiquariat, 166, 226n46
APO, 4, 55
apocalypse, 41–42, 44, 55–56, 58, 60, 70, 89, 98, 114, 134, 169
APO-OPAs, 4
Arch+ (journal), 44–45
archives, 10, 138, 166
art: and activism, 1–2, 31–32, 172, 188, 230n6; and catharsis, 32; experimental, 9–10, 52–53, 58–61, 78, 93, 98, 106–7, 126–28, 171–73; impressionistic, 106; as occupation, 182–83; and politics, 202n34; radical, 31–32, 34; and squatting, 1–2, 182–83; and subversion, 229n87; and transgression, 107; and violence, 34; of youth movements and revolts, 9–10, 106–7, 182–84, 229n87
Art and Culture Center of Kreuzberg. *See* KuKuCK
assemblage, polyphonic, 91
Assmann, Aleida, 17
AtaTak Gallery, 52
AUSS. *See* Action Center for Independent and Socialist Students (AUSS)
Autonomen movement, 126, 128, 156–61, 164, 177–78
Autonomie (journal), 41
Autonomie: Neue Folge (journal), 48
autonomy: and activism, 81–82, 102, 105–8, 139, 155; and antiauthoritarianism, 3, 36–37; and authenticity, 66; and diversity, 167; and negation, 79; and objects, 92; and protests, 82; and radicalism, 82; and revolution, 4; and social connections, 73–74; of squatting, 2–4, 6, 8, 66, 79, 89–90, 107–8, 132–42, 154–55, 165, 167, 179; of youth activists, 66–67, 73–74
avant-garde, 26, 28, 52, 113, 127, 147, 231n17

Baader, Andreas, 36, 39
Badische Zeitung (newspaper), 104
Bakunin, Mikhail Alexandrovich, 70, 144
Bargeld, Blixa, 55, 69, 143
Baudrillard, Jean, 205n7

Baumann, Michael "Bommi," 26–27, 35
Beatles, 24–26, 130, 147, 196n36
Benjamin, Walter, 7, 11, 58, 87, 171, 231n20
Berghain (club), 175
Berlin: anomalous temporal qualities, 170; as capital of new German art scene, 107; contemporary, 184; as creative city, 184; creative destruction in, 13, 155–80, 223–30n; as global city, 158–59; and global youth market, 184; hipness, 184; oppositional modes of dwelling in, 167–68; postwar, 15, 18; radically increasing property, 184; squatting movement in, 13, 81, 117, 155–80, 223–30n; tourism in, 224–25nn21–22; and transgressive cultural forms, 184–85; urban landscape of, 158–60, 169, 184. *See also* East Berlin; West Berlin
Berlin-Mitte, 157–58, 160, 170, 175–76, 178–79, 181, 183
Berlin Partner's marketing group, 184
Berlin Wall, 157–58, 169–74, 225n25
"Berliner Küchenmusikk" (Tödliche Doris film), 127
Berliner Morgenpost (newspaper), 81, 103, 122–23
Besetzerinnenzeitung / BesetzerInnen Zeitung (alternative newspaper), 162–68, *163*, *177*, 177–78, 183, 227n65
Besetzerinnenzeitung Notausgabe (periodical), 226n36
Besetzerrat. *See* Squatter(s) Council
Beuys, Joseph, 50, 52
Bewegungslehre (Agentur BILWET book), 92–95, 98, 100–102, 186
Bey, Hakim, 179
BI SO36 squats, 46–48, 79, 201n22
Biermann, Wolf, 132
Bild (reactionary tabloid newspaper), 41, 153
Blau ist Rot (film), 156
Blockupy movement (Frankfurt), 179
Blues (militant group), 34
Blumenschein, Tabea, 128
Bölke, Marco, 172
Bopp, Jörg, 115, 213–14n56
bourgeois, 15–16, 20, 26, 28, 31, 33, 36, 43, 50–51, 81, 91, 97–98, 113, 119–20, 135–36, 142, 145–46, 156, 162–64
Boym, Svetlana, 12, 65, 149, 193n41, 222n96
Brus, Günter, 32
Brussels, Belgium, 28
Buback, Siegfried, Attorney General, 39–40
Buback-Nachruf, 40, 55
Buck-Morss, Susan, 29–30
Bude, Eva, 62, 213n43
built environments: asynchronicities in, 172; and capitalism, 24; and counterculture, 44–45; destruction of, 98–99; Nazism removed from, 19; palimpsestic, 10; and postprogressive practices, 12–13; postwar, 19, 31; and progressive temporalities, 7; and squatting, 66, 98–99, 128, 134–35; and state power, 2; symbolism of, 98–99, 110; temporal qualities of, 128, 134–35. *See also* housing
Butler, Judith, 62, 149, 222n96
Buttergeit, Jörg, 73, 206n16

capitalism, 3–5; and accumulation, 209n86; and alienation, 63, 142; and alternative temporal logics, 185; and anarchist practices, 183–84; ascent of in West Germany, 9; and built environments, 24; chronopolitical rebellions against, 185; constraints of emotional regime of, 84; and consumerism, 19–20, 23, 27, 41, 159; and counterculture, 169; and creative destruction, 185; and culture industries, 23; defying, 97–98; and democracy, 24, 27; as destructive, 23; and disruption, 185; embraced by Germans, 227–28n65; emotional damage inflicted by, 84; expansion of, 169; and fascism, 203n64; and fragmentation, 9, 12, 185, 209n86; fragmentation of, 9; global, 23, 159, 179–80, 184–85; and hierarchy, 3; and housing, 161, 180; and imperialism, 23; and incursions, 180; logics of, 128; a mobile, and flexible accumulation,

capitalism (*continued*)
209n86; and modernity, 11, 17, 23–24, 43, 47, 60, 73, 114, 143–45, 147, 154, 180; and modern regime of time, 17; and negation, 128; neoliberal, 160; and objects, 20; oppressive emotional regimes of, 84; overturning, 3; and past, 23; political and economic contradictions of, 37; post-, 3; postindustrial, 209n86; and postmodernism, 83; postwar, 19–20, 148; and power, 3–4, 24, 183–84; and presentism, 7; and progress, 14, 20, 23, 185; protestant ethics of, 33; and rent-profiteers, 81; and revolution, 27, 41; spatial logics of, 209n86; and spatiotemporal practices, 9; spectacle in, 230n4; and squatting, 81–83, 141; and state, 82–83; and state violence, 55–56; static temporal logics of, 183–84; and techno, 184; and technology, 23; and time, 17; and transgressive cultural forms, 184–85; and value creation, 17, 38, 147, 174, 182, 184, 228n75; and violence, 81, 83, 141, 156. *See also* consumerism and consumption
carnival, of negation, 49, 160, 169, 173, 176, 178
Carnival against Capitalism, anti-G8 protests (Genoa), 179
carnivalesque, postprogressive practices, 183; and anarchist creativity, 181; and creative destruction, 13, 155–80, 223–30n
Castillo, Greg, 21, 195n24, 222n90
CDU. *See* Christian Democratic Union party (CDU)
Chaoten (chaos makers), 103, 107–8, 125, 153
Chatterjee, Partha, 195n17
Christian Democratic Union party (CDU), 19, 27, 122–23, 130–31, 133, 140–41, 212n31
chrononormativity, 17–18, 82, 89, 105, 135, 143, 148–49, 153, 184–85
Citizens' Initiatives, 37, 44–47
city planning, 48. *See also* urban renewal

Clash, The (band), 78
classification, and hierarchy, 95
Cold War, 21, 171
Colomb, Claire, 159, 224–25nn21–22
colonialism: anti-, 27, 31, 34; and imperialism, 145; and marginalization, 3; post-, 195n17; and violence, 34, 145
commerce, and gentrification, 183
communes and communal living, 2, 4, 40, 81, 111, 117, 146, 150. *See also* Kommune I
communism, 21, 30–31, 81, 144, 157–58, 162
consumerism and consumption: and capitalism, 19–20, 23, 27, 41, 159; and democracy, 19–22, 27, 85; and domesticity, 21–22; and modernity, 22, 38; and objects, 19–20, 92; postwar, 19–25, 38; and progress, 22–23; and renewal, 24–25; and self-creation, 24–25; youth culture, 24–25. *See also* capitalism
Cornum, Lou, 222n80, 231n20
counterculture: and activism, 29, 65, 88–89, 95–96, 105, 171; and antiauthoritarianism and antiauthoritarian movement, 30, 35; and capitalism, 169; ideology of, 43–44; and left, 8–9, 41, 65, 95, 161, 180; and logics of progress, 11; milieus, 1, 11–12, 27, 83; and off-modern, 12, 40–67, 200–205n; and perpetual motion, 58–59; and politics, 27–28; postprogressive, 12; and progress, 32; and punks, 48–65; and radical change, 88–89; and rebellion, 72; and revolution, 27–28, 30, 34–35, 197n43; sociabilities of, 28; and squatting, 154, 180; and violence, 53–54; of youth movements and revolts, 66–67. *See also* youth movements; youth revolts
counterterrorism, elite West German unit, 39
creative destruction: in Berlin (new), 13, 155–80, 223–30n; and capitalism, 185; and carnival time, 13, 155–80, 223–30n; and modernity, 17; and negation, 70, 99, 128, 141, 160, 173,

176, 181–82; and punk movement, 58, 70, 92, 142–43, 157, 163–64, 168–69, 172; and radicalism, 92; and rebellion, 72; of squatting, 13, 155–80, 223–30n; transgressive, 5, 99; and vengeance, 91; of youth movements and revolts, 78, 92, 94, 100, 114, 120, 128, 156, 164, 167–70, 176, 179

criminality and criminalization: and squatting, 119–20; and violence, 35, 120, 133

cultural: appropriation, 43; capital, 184; production, 9–10, 78, 92, 94

Culture and Life Project (KuLe), 176, 183

cybernetics, 51, 65

Dany, Hans-Christian, 64, 204n86

Dawdy, Shannon Lee, 171, 227n63

DDR. *See* German Democratic Republic (DDR) [East Germany]

de Certeau, Michel, 11, 66, 148–49, 182

Death Mills, The (film), 18

Debord, Guy, 56, 230n4

Debray, Jules Régis, 27, 34

Deleuze, Gilles, 5–6, 32–33, 61, 191n18

Delgado, Gabi, 52–55, 64, 94, 147

democracy: and capitalism, 24, 27; and consumerism, 19–22, 27, 85; and domesticity, 21–22; and economy, 19; liberal, 19, 27; and mainstream politics, 40; and modernity, 19, 22–24; and politics, 19, 40; postwar, 19

Demokratische Terrorist, Der (Guillou), 146, 222n85

demonstrations: of Action Week, 207n37; and activism, 108–9; and alternate reality, 109; antiauthoritarian, 109; by AtaTak Gallery (Wuppertal), 52; and auratic contexts, 109; and autonomous spaces, 165; in Berlin, 74; in Berlin (May Day), 107; in Berlin (post-Reagan visit), *110*; Black Friday, 108–9, 212n31; conservative, 212n31; and counterpublic discourses/values, 166; and discontents, 109; and Dutch activists of Agentur BILWET group, 89; against eviction of squat on Winterfeldstrasse, 78, 106; in Freiburg, 79–80, 109, 207n30; as gateways into alternate reality, 109; Grunewald, 122–23; in Hamburg, 155; in Kreuzberg (May Day), 155–57; leftist counter-, 162; and living contradictions, 162; mass, 81, 109, 123, 155; and power, 109; and professional revolutionaries, 212n31; against reunification, 162; and revolution, emotional rush of, 109; and revolutionaries, professional, 212n31; ritually reenacting moments of original transgressions, 107; at Rote Fabrik building (Zurich), 75; as self-referential exercises in simulating feelings of collective transgression, 109; and street theater skirmish, 80, 207n35; and transnational unity, 108–9; unanchored, borderless quality of, 109; and violence, 75, 79; in West Berlin, 73, 78, 80–81, 100, 108–9, 126, 212n31; in Wuppertal, 52; of youth movements and revolts, 98, 105, 108–10. *See also* activism; protests; riots

Der Plan (band), 52, 56, 63–64

DeSilvey, Caitlin, 149, 222n95

destruction, creative. *See* creative destruction

Deutsch Amerikanische Freundschaft (German American Friendship), 52–53

Deutsche, Rosalyn, 226n44

Deutschland im Herbst (film), 40

Dialectic of the Enlightenment (Horkheimer and Adorno), 23

dialectics, 65–66

Didaktische Einheit (music group), 126–27, 217n101

Diederichsen, Detlef, 52, 202n42

dilettantism, 58–59

Dinger, Klaus, 50

discontents: and demonstrations, 109; and postwar housing policy, 199n79; and power, 109

dispossessed, 125–26

diversity: and autonomy, 167; and squatting, 96, 112, 118

Dohnanyi, Mayor, 132–33, 141, 219n28

domesticity, 15, 17, 20–22, 148, 151, 153, 195n22
domination, 2–3, 23, 35, 57, 180, 185
Dreamtime: On the Border between Wilderness and Civilization (Dürr), 43
Drexciya, 174
Duntze, Klaus, 117
Durkheim, Emile, 94, 101, 210n3
Dürr, Hans Peter, 43, 201n15
Dutschke, Rudi, 28, 30, 34, 40, 183
Düül, Amon, 51

E Dopo? (film), 60–61
East Berlin, 158, 160–61, 164–65, 169–75, 179–80, 225n27, 225nn24–25, 229n88. *See also* Berlin; West Berlin
East Germany, 23–24, 157–72, 224n15, 225n24. *See also* German Democratic Republic (DDR) [East Germany]; German Democratic Republic (GDR) [East Germany]; West Germany
Ebert, Erika, 104, 211n18
echo jams, 228n84
ecology movements, 37
Edensor, Tim, 149, 222n95
8oer Jahre, Die (journal/magazine), 52, 55
Einstürzende Neubauten/Collapsing New Buildings (band), 55, 64, 69
Eisenman, Peter, 158
Elektro (club), 173–75
Elon, Amos, 14, 193n1
Emotional Politics of the Alternative Left, The (Häberlen), 84
Engler, Jürgen, 53, 203n44
Ensslin, Gudrun, 36, 39, 199n75
environmental movements, 41–42
Erhard, Ludwig, 19
experimentation: and activism, 8; aesthetic, 9–10; Afrofuturist, 193n40; and alternative social/cultural forms, 40; anarchist, 184; and antiauthoritarianism, 85; and art, 9–10, 52–53, 58–61, 78, 93, 98, 106–7, 126–28, 171–73; and collective living, 1; and community, 94; and comportment, 53; and counterculture, 8–9, 12, 18, 27–28, 95, 105, 146, 171; and creative destruction, 100; and cultural production, 9–10, 78; and illegal occupations, 40, 47–48; leftist, 9, 30, 40, 48, 85, 95; and logics of progress, 30; and modernity, 8, 10; and modes of being, 11–12; and modes of embodiment, 6; and music, 10, 25–26, 40, 50–52, 58–61, 85, 106, 126, 147, 174–75, 228n84; and New Left, 30; off-modern, 12, 41, 68, 85; philosophical, 10; and philosophy, 10; and politics, 12; postprogressive temporal imaginaries, 10; and progress, 30, 49, 171, 181; and punk movement, 49–50, 52, 66, 68, 70, 98; and radicalism, 198n57; and rebelliousness, 115; and revolution, 31–39; sexual, 28; and sociability, 2, 98, 100–101, 143, 182; spatiotemporal framework of, 142; and squatting, 2, 108, 141, 179; and subjectivity, 143, 182; and temporal imaginaries, 7, 10; and temporalities, 100, 143; and temporal logics, 8, 11–12, 48, 59, 171, 182; and time, 40–41, 65, 181; transnational analysis of leftist, 198n57; of youth movements and revolts, 8–9, 24–27, 85, 95, 98, 100–101, 106, 115, 184
exploitation, and violence, 14

Fanon, Frantz, 34
fascism: anti-, 107, 145, 161, 165–66, 178; and capitalism, 203n64; and communication, 50; and counterculture, 51; and disciplinary normalization, 33; and industrialism, 55; neo-, 186; and past, 17, 31–33, 36, 57; and power, 33, 35; and punks, 54; and repression, 32, 36; revival of, 162; and vengeance, 36; and violence, 156, 162
Fashion & Doubt/Mode & Verzweiflung (journal), 65
Fassbinder, Rainer Werner, 22, 86–87
Faust, 51
FDJ. *See* Free German Youth (FDJ)
FDP. *See* Free Democratic Party (FDP)
Federal Republic (of Germany), 14–15, 19, 23–24, 27, 30, 40, 70

Fehlfarben (band), 5
Felsch, Philipp, 15, 193n35, 196n32, 205n7
Felscherinow, Christiane, 68
Fenstermacher, Frank, 54
Fischer, Joschka, 40, 43, 201n14
Fischli, Peter, 57–58, 203n65
football, 168, 227n54
Foucault, Michel, 32–33, 190n7, 198nn63–64
fragmentation: and capitalism, 9, 12, 185, 209n86; and collapse, 186; and destabilization, 98; and disruption, 185; of progress, 145; of progressive temporalities, 98; and punks, 98; and separation, 186; and squatting, 185–86
Frankfurt, Germany, 24; squatting in, 37, 112, 179, 199n80; student revolutionaries in, 34
Frankfurter Allgemeine Zeitung (newspaper), 139
Free Democratic Party (FDP), 104
Free German Youth (FDJ), 171
freedom: postwar, 23; pseudo-, 23; of squatting, 96, 104, 136–37, 173. *See also* liberation
Freeman, Elizabeth, 17–18, 185, 231n18
Freiburg, Germany, 1, 10, 104, 108–9, 171, 207n30; anarchists, 81; demonstrations in, 79–80; dispossessed anarchists of, 125–26; Schwarzwaldhof squat in, 80, 95, 100, 108, 112, 125–29; squatting, 79–80, 86, 95, 97–98, 100, 125, 129–30; youth movements and revolts in, 78–82, 86, 95, 97–98, 100, 129–30
Freiwillige Selbstkontrolle/F.S.K. (music group), 56, 65, 205n89
Freizeit '81/Freetime '81 (radical group), 91–92; brochure/flyer, 88, 208n65
Friedrich, Jörg, 123
Frith, Simon, 175, 228n82
Fun Guerillas (*Spaßguerilla*), 108
future: alternative, 48, 164, 169; catastrophic, 42, 44; fear about, 83–84; humane, 115; and living historically, 185; openness of, 7; and past, 5–6, 7, 9, 10, 12, 15–22, 29, 31–33, 36, 38–39, 47–48, 52, 66, 81–82, 87, 91, 182, 185–86; and present, 5–6, 10, 12, 19–21, 29–30, 33, 38–39, 52, 83, 87, 91, 171, 185–86; and progress, 66–67, 69, 89; progressive, 7; and redemption of oppressed, 185; and revolution, 29, 31–32, 38; and ruination, 87; and time, 64, 148; utopian, 4–5, 12, 31–32, 38–39, 42–44, 85–87, 94, 98, 117, 142–43. *See also* past; present

GAL. *See* Green Alternative List (GAL)
Gammlers, 107, 125; and antiauthoritarianism, 26, 31; and revolution, 26–27
Gäng, Peter, 27, 35, 197n44
GDR. *See* German Democratic Republic (GDR) [East Germany]
Gemeinschaft ("community"), 150
Geniale Dilettanten festival, 55, 58–59, 174
Geniale Dilettanten (ed. Müller), 61
genocide, 17–18, 36, 162
gentrification, 37, 98, 155, 159, 183. *See also* urban renewal
German Autumn (1977), 39–41, 43–45, 49, 55, 65–66, 68, 215n70
German Democratic Republic (DDR) [East Germany], 19, 150, 166, 227n65. *See also* East Germany
German Democratic Republic (GDR) [East Germany], 19, 150, 159–61, 166, 171–73, 181, 227n65. *See also* East Germany
"Getting Stoned and Revolution" (journal article), 30–31
ghettoization, politics of, 47
Glaser, Peter, 70
Global South, 27, 34
Glowing Pickle art gallery, 173
Goethe, Johann Wolfgang von, 51
Goethe Institute (Copenhagen), 139
Goldman, Emma, 144
Gollwitzer, Helmut, 117–18, 214n68
Gramming, Walter, 60, 204n74
Grass, Günter, 24, 117, 158, 214n67, 224n17
Grätz, Fred, 123
Grauzone (music group), 74–75, 204n72
Green Alternative List (GAL), 132. *See also* Alternative List

Green movement, 42
Green Party, 44, 159, 200n4
Greifswald, Germany, 167–68
Groetz, Thomas, 62
Grolle, Joist, 220n49
Guattari, Félix, 5–6, 32, 61, 191n18
Guevara, Che, 31
Guillou, Jan, 146, 222n85
Gumbrecht, Hans Ulrich, 7–8, 83
Gut, Gudrun, 105, 211n19
Gutmaier, Ulrich, 170, 172, 174

Häberlen, Joachim, 43, 84, 208n50, 212n33, 214n57
Habermas, Jürgen, 116, 183
Hafenstraße (Hamburg), 161, 165–69, 172; art of, 223n103; embattled history of, 153–54; as inspiration, 223n2; insurgent dwelling and cultivation of place in, 12–13, 129–55, 177–78, 217–23n; ownership of houses in, 219n26; and radicalism, 220n49; and squats in smaller cities, 223n2; as symbolic, 154
Haig, Alexander, Secretary of State, 213n33
Halberstam, Jack, 64, 204n85
Halbstarke (youth group), 24
Hamburg, Germany: activists in, 171; archives in, 10; Beatles' New Years Eve in, 26; demonstrations and protests in, 155; punk clubs in, 53; riots and violence in, 223n4; squatting in (Ekhofstraße), 199n80; Star Club in, 25; St. Pauli neighborhood, 24–25; youth culture in, 24–25. *See also* Hafenstraße (Hamburg)
Hamburger Abendblatt (newspaper), 131, 139
"Hammer und Sichel" (Gramming film), 60, 204n74
Hänny, Reto, 76
Hanseatic League, 145
Härlin, Benny, 1–7, 21, 118
Hartog, François, 7–8, 18, 171
Harvey, David, 209n86, 231n13
Hash Rebels (militant group), 30–31, 34–35, 173

haunted and haunting: past, 10–11, 23, 87, 147; places/spaces, 10–11, 23, 147; and dwelling authenticity, 182
hauntology, 11, 182, 193n39, 228n84
Häuserkämpfe. *See* housing, struggles and battles
Häuserkampf-info 1 (brochure), 37
Hebdige, Dick, 57
Hegel, Georg Wilhelm Friedrich, 56
Hegemann, Dmitri, 174, 228n75
Heimat ("home"), 117; films, 73, 148; and squatting, 148–50. *See also* housing
Heimat for Drag-Queens, 175
Heisig, Matthias, 96, 209nn88–89
Hendrix, Jimi, 31
heritage sites, 7–8, 191n25
Herrmann, Michael, 132
HERTZ (band), 61, 204n76
Hezel, Lukas, 83–84
hierarchy: and classification, 95; as unacceptable, 168
hippies, 31, 65, 107, 164
historicism and historicity: and modernity, 17, 185; modern regime of, 17–18; and progress, 185
history: battle against demons of, 36; embodiment of, 9–10; off-beat movements of, 12; and past, 7; and presentism, 7–8; and revolution, 36; telos of, 42; and time, 5. *See also* past
"History of an old House" (documentary film), 104
Hoelz, Max, 166, 226n46
Hollstein, Walter, 116, 214n58
home. *See Heimat* ("home"); housing
homelessness, 23, 37, 150–51, 159
homogeneity, 145
Hönkelrausch (film), 156
Horkheimer, Max, 23
housing: affordable, 180, 216n87; in Berlin, 178; and capitalism, 161, 180; collective, 117; and displacements, 37–38; exhibits, 148, 195n24, 222n90; failures, 225n27; in inner-city neighborhoods, 225n27; and insurgent dwelling, 130; legalized, 119, 126; and modernity, 20–21, 37; older, 104, 146–47, 151, 161; policies, 117, 126, 199n79,

215n70, 225n27; politics, 216n79; postwar, 20–22, 96, 147–50, 199n79; and progress, 20–21; and rebirth, 21; as romanticized spheres of postwar moral and aesthetic idealism, 20; shortages, 75, 123, 216n87; stock, 161, 170, 225n27; struggles and battles, 37. *See also* built environments; communes and communal living; Heimat (home); urban renewal
Huber, Josef, 119
Hülbrock, Klaus (Göttinger Mescalero), 40
Humphrey, Hubert, Vice President, 28
"Hüpfen '82" (film), 60, 204n73
Hütter, Ralf, 51

identities, 19, 91, 93, 164, 184–85
ideology: and anarchy, 190n8; of antiauthoritarianism, 49; of counterculture, 43–44; of insurgent dwelling, 134–35; leftist, 60–61; of New Left, 7; of postwar Germany, 7; of punks, 6, 54–56; and ritualization, 101, 103; of squatting movement, 134–35, 173; symbols, 173; temporal, 17; of temporal progress, 7; of youth movements and revolts, 6, 101
Iggy Pop, 54
immigrants, 37, 45, 137, 157, 159, 197n43
imperialism, 33, 164; anti-, 36, 72, 164; and capitalism, 23; and colonialism, 145; and liberation, 179; TAZ, 122; and violence, 145
individualism, 135
individuality, 184; de-, 33; and objects, 20; and politics, 33; postwar, 23; and power, 33; pseudo-, 23
individualization, and resignation, 161
industrialism, and fascism, 55
injustice: resistance to, 215n70; and violence, 23
Instandbesetzerpost (magazine), 89, 97, 102–3, 112
Instandbesetzungen (squatting tactic), 47, 80, 123
insurgent dwelling: and cultivation of place in Hamburg's Hafenstraße, 12–13, 129–55, 177–78, 217–23n; ideology of, 134–35; and negation, 164–65, 182; and perpetual motion, 147; of youth movements and revolts, 134–35, 141, 142, 143–44, 147–48. *See also* squatting movement
insurrection, 30; anarchist, 35–36; global, 34; and revolution, 34–36; and violence, 34
Interim (alternative newspaper), 156–57, 160–61, 166, 179
International Essen Song Days (festival, 1968), 28
internationalism, 144
Invisible Committee (French anarchist collective), 186
"Invocation of Chaos" (Levy poem), 69

Jameson, Fredric, 8, 83
Journey through a Haunted Land (Elon), 14
June 2nd Movement (militant group), 34–36, 135
Jungsozialisten in der SPD (JUSOS), 26
JUSOS. *See* Jungsozialisten in der SPD (JUSOS)

K-Gruppen, 30–31, 55
Kant, Immanuel, 24, 51
Karl-Marx-Allee, 161
Kaschuba, Wolfgang, 158
Katholisch Kitsch (band), 56
Kemner, Michael, 58
Kennedy, Robert, 32
Kiesinger, Kurt Georg, 27
Kiez. See neighborhoods
Kiez Depesche (newspaper), 102
Kinderladen activists and movement, 32, 38
Kings of the Road (Wenders film), 20, 195n21
Kino Anschlag, 166
Klaus, Dr., 119, 129, 215n76, 218n4
Kleenex/LiLiPUT (music group), 56
Kleine Bruder, Der (Regener), 113–14, 213n50
Kluge, Alexander, 18, 23–24
Knapp, Udo, 30

Koenen, Gerd, 34
Kohl, Helmut, 133, 216n87
Kommune I, 26–28, 87, 173; and antiauthoritarianism, 28; and pop culture, 28
Kraaker Bewegig. See squatting movement
Kracauer, Siegfried, 21, 196n27
Kraftwerk (electronic music group), 50–52, 147, 202n36
Kramer, Jürgen, 52, 55
Kraushaar, Wolfgang, 48, 183, 198n70
Krautrock music groups, 50
Kreuzberg district/neighborhood, Berlin: activists in, 45, 47, 82, 122, 155–56, 171; and alternative milieu, 159; alternative milieu of, 113, 159; counterculture in, 63; Cuvrystraße building, 47; evolutionary landscape of, 114; Feuerwache building in, 45; Fränkelufer squat in, 81, *101*; freedom in, 105; Manteuffelstraße squat in, 104, 211n18; music in, 174; protests and riots in, 82, 155–56, 223n4; squatting in, 66, 92, 94–97, *101*, 103–4, 113, 115–16, 122, 142, 155–56, 211n18; and traditional placeworlds, 66; urban renewal of, 45–47
Kropotkin, Peter (Pyotr Alexeyevich), 144
Krupps, Die (band), 55
Kruse, Bishop, 104, 214n64
KuKuCK, 2, 92–93, *93*, 102–3, 129
KuLe. *See* Culture and Life Project (KuLe)
Kunc, Milan, 52
Kunzelmann, Dieter, 26, 28, 34, 116
Kursbuch (leftist journal), 1

Lang, Fritz, 51
Lange, Volker, Senator, 130, 219n28
Lecorte, Thomas, 73, 82–83, 120
Lefebvre, Henri, 148, 222n91
left: activism, 1–2, 34, 37–38, 40–41, 65; anarchism, 74–75; and Christian groups, 116–18; counterattacks, 1–2; and counterculture, 8–9, 41, 65, 95, 161, 180; and cultural production, 9–10; defensive certainties of, 4; disaffected, 52–53; ideology of, 60–61; militant, 70–71; and Nazism, 9; old, 30; and pop culture, 24, 38, 68; postrevolutionary, 43, 72, 80–82, 103, 108, 216n85; postwar, 5, 24, 30–31, 205n7; and power, 190n7; and progress, 30, 36–37; progressive teleologies of, 64; protests, 1; radical, 27, 29, 35, 38–41, 55, 70–75, 80–85, 89, 95–96, 142, 155–57, 160, 162, 168–69, 199n85, 226n49, 227n54; and revolution, 27, 29, 34, 40–41, 118; traditional, 30; and transformations, 9. *See also* New Left
left-alternative, 9, 33, 37, 40–44, 48, 53, 61–62, 65–66, 72–73, 96, 118, 134, 145
leftist movements, 3, 18, 24, 42, 111, 114–15, 173, 191n19
leftist politics: and activism, 3–4; European new, 3; and pop culture, 24; and punks, 48–49, 70–71, 78; and revolution, 118; and squatting, 3; of youth movements and revolts, 3–4, 89, 118
Lenin, Vladimir, 30, 34, 158, 171
Lerner, Ben, 11–12, 193n42
Levy, William, 69
liberation: existential, 142; international, 144; of past, 87; and renewal, 183–84; of squatting, 2, 4–5, 96, 142, 179; from state power, 2; weapons of, 143; of West German society, 9; of youth movements and revolts, 126–27. *See also* freedom
Libeskind, Daniel, 158
living co-ops *(Wohngemeinschaften)*, 2, 42
Lochte, Christian, 131, 141, 151
Loewy, Raymond, 21
Lorenz, Peter, 35
Lotta Continua Italian autonomist groups, 36–37
Love Parade (Berlin club), 175
Löwenthal, Leo, 21, 196n27, 196n32
Lummer, Heinrich, 108, 116, 118–19, 129, 212n31

Mahler, Horst, 36
Mainzer Straße, Berlin, 160–66, *165*, 171–73, *172*, 176–84, 226n46
Malaria! (band), 105
Mallet, Carl-Heinz, 135
Mao Zedong, 27, 34, 50
Maoists, 81
Marcus, Greil, 49
Marcuse, Herbert, 23, 27, 37
marginalized groups and populations: and activists, 174; and anarchist negation, 107; and dialectical theory, 3; as excluded, 35; and leftist progress, 36–37; and leftist revolution, 3; and off-modern, 12; politicized, 44–45, 94; and power, 3–4; and revolution, 3–4, 27, 35, 37; and ruins, 149; and transnationalism, 107
Maris, Bastian, 172–73
Marley, Bob, 75–76
Marriage of Maria Braun, The (Fassbinder film), 22, 86–87
Marx, Karl, 31
Marxism, 3, 5, 7, 8, 11, 31, 34, 190n15, 209n86, 231n13
Material für Nachkriegszeit (Müller and Untermöhlen film), 62–63
materiality, 96, 98, 110. *See also* postmaterialism
Meinecke, Thomas, 65, 205n89
Meinhof, Ulrike, 36
memory studies, 7–8
Mende, Silke, 42
Merve Verlag (publishing house), 61, 205n7
Mescalero, Göttinger (Klaus Hülbrock), 40
Metropolis (Lang film), 51
middle class, 132
militance, 2, 4, 26, 33–41, 70–72, 79, 82, 86, 110, 126, 131, 135–37, 139, 146, 149, 151, 155–57, 190n6. *See also* violence
minorities, racialized, 3
Mitscherlich, Alexander, 37
Mitscherlich, Alexander and Margarete, 23
Mitte. *See* Berlin-Mitte

Mode & Verzweiflung/Fashion & Doubt (journal), 65
modern time regimes, 11, 13, 17–18, 38, 65, 84
modernity: and capitalism, 11, 17, 23–24, 43, 47, 60, 73, 114, 143–45, 147, 154, 180; and constant becoming, 7; and consumerism, 22, 38; and creative destruction, 17; and democracy, 19, 22–24; and difference, 185; and historicism, 17, 185; and housing, 20–21, 37; and past, 20–21; and presentism, 8; and progress, 17, 19–23, 65, 185; progressive, 6–8, 147, 185; temporalities of, 6, 8–10, 17, 50–51, 185; and time, 5–8, 11, 13, 17–18, 65; urban, 158. *See also* postmodernism
Mollis, 114, 119–20, 122–23, 134, 144, 179. *See also* Müslis
Muehl, Otto, 32, 52–53
Müller, Herr, 145
Müller, Wolfgang, 55, 58–59, 62–63, 128
Munich, Germany: Schwabing neighborhood, 26, 27
Murderers Are among Us, The (Staudte film), 15–16, *16*, 22, 48
Müslis, 114, 119–20, 134, 178. *See also* Mollis
Mutoid Waste Company, as art venue, 173
Muzak (fanzine), 56, 64

Nabokov, Vladimir, 186, 231n24
narcissism, 35, 104, 183
national identity (German), 151, 158–59
nationalism, 17, 54, 157–65, 186, 195n17
NATO, 2, 19, 144
Nazis and Nazism, 9, 14–23, 27, 31, 33, 36, 51–59, 64, 82, 86, 122–23, 137–38, 141, 148, 157–62, 168, 192n32, 193nn2–3, 194n13, 203n64, 220n49
negation: anarchist, 5–6, 107, 168, 176; authentic, 44, 49, 65–66, 73–74, 120, 145; and autonomy, 79; and becoming, 173; and boundless optimism, 178; and capitalism, 128; carnival of, 49, 160, 169, 173, 176, 178; collective, 76, 109; and creation,

negation (*continued*)
171; and creative becoming, 181–82; and creative destruction, 70, 99, 128, 141, 160, 173, 176, 181–82; destructive, 88–89; dialectical, 58, 66, 134–35, 149; directionless, 128, 149, 168; endless, 85, 125, 128, 142; and endless becoming, 5–6, 85, 182; and insurgent dwelling, 164–65, 182; and order, 70; perpetual, 143, 147; and politics, 31; and pop culture, 28–29; practiced, 75; and progress, 49; and punks, 49; radical, 29, 76, 91–92, 99, 134–35, 141–42, 144, 153, 157; and resistance/revolution, 3, 28–29, 31, 35, 111, 145, 183; of social conditions, 142, 151; and squatting, 125, 165–66, 169; transgressive, 5, 99, 136; and transnationalism, 107; and utopias, 98

neighborhoods, 223n8; activism in, 41, 44–45, 108, 159–60, 166; at-risk, 45; gentrification of, 159; historic, 45; housing stock in inner-city, 225n27; improvement projects for, 45; squatting in, 66, 96–97, 123, 161, 166, 178, 225n24; traditional placeworlds of, 66; up-and-coming, 184; and urban renewal, 37, 45; youth culture in, 24–27. *See also* specific neighborhood(s)

Nekromantik (Buttergeit film), 206n16
Nena, 100
neoliberalism, 160, 172
Netzbau, 118, 215n73
Netzwerk Selbsthilfe, 81, 118–19, 125, 215n70, 216n85
Neue Wilden, 106–7, 213n51
Neue Zürcher Zeitung (newspaper), 76
Neumann, Hans-Jürgen, 150
Neu! (electronic music group), 50–52
Never Say Never/Sag niemals nie (film), 162, 169, 226n31, 228n69
"New Directions: In the Twilight of Western Europe" (Meinecke essay), 65
New Kreuzberg Center, 63
New Left: aesthetics, 191n19; and experimentation, 30; and marginalized populations, 3; and Marxism, 3, 5; nascent, 23; and negation, 29; and off-modern, 12; politicized, 210n95; postwar, 23; prefigurative traditions of, 3, 5; and progressive temporalities postwar period, 9; and revolution, 3, 5, 27, 28–30; temporal dimensions of, 9; and temporal progress, 7

New Wave. *See* punk movement
Nietzsche, Friedrich, 205n7
Nikolaikirche, in Leipzig, 158
Notorische Reflexe, 107, 211n26

objects: abandoned, 172–73; and adventurous reality, 92; asynchronous, 181, 184; and autonomy, 92; and bodies, 22, 148, 186; and capitalism, 20; and consumerism, 19–20, 92; cultural, 95; discarded, 93, 95–96; and environments, 22, 87, 93, 143, 173, 184, 186; and identities, 91; and individuality, 20; and past, 186; and places, 186; and progress, 20; and renewal, 20; and rituals, 101; and spaces, 136, 181–82; and temporal logics, 19–20; and time, 20
off-modern: activism, 66; and antiauthoritarian left, 183; and citation, 51–52, 55–57, 222n96; and counterculture, 12, 40–67, 200–205n; defined/described, 65; instantiations of, 65; and marginal mode of being in time, 12; and New Left, 12
"Ohne Liebe gibt es keinen Tod" (film), 60–61
Ohnesorg, Benno, 34
Olles, Werner, 30–31, 198n56
One-Dimensional Man (Marcuse), 23
OPAs, 4
opposition: international forms of, 145; international network of, 143–44; and new cultural forms, 27; symbols of, 126, 162; and transgression, 180
oppression, 84, 107, 138, 142, 144, 185
Osborne, Peter, 231n17
Ossis, 164
Ossowski, Leonie, 142–43, 221n70

Osterkorn, Thomas, 131, 218n14
Overath, Wolfgang, 55

pacifism, 31, 164
paranoia, 32–33, 97, 134, 139, 146
Paris Commune, 30, 191n29
Paßt bloß auf! (film), 86–87, 95
past: alternative versions of, 149; battle against demons of, 36; and capitalism, 23; cavernous emptiness of, 95; dreams of, 96; and fascism, 36; fascist, 17, 31–33, 36, 57; forgotten, 95–96; and future, 5–6, 7, 9, 10, 12, 15–22, 29, 31–33, 36, 38–39, 47–48, 52, 66, 81–82, 87, 91, 182, 185–86; ghosts of, 11, 24, 31, 64, 147; and history, 7; liberation from, 22; and living historically, 185; mastered, 149; and modernity, 20–21; national, 19; obfuscating or overcoming, 6; and objects, 186; and places, 186; poetry of, 3; postwar, 15–24; and present, 3, 5–6, 10, 12, 17–21, 24, 26, 29, 31, 33, 36, 38–39, 52, 57, 87, 91, 98, 185–86, 199n84; and presentism, 8; and progress, 22–23, 48, 87, 89; and progressive time, 22; repressed, 32; and revolution, 33; ruins of, 15; shadows of, 86; and squatting, 6–7, 10–11, 95–96; traumatic, 31; unmastered, 7; unruly, 6; violent, 32–33. See also future; history; present
Paten movement, 117–18, 214n68, 216n85
patriarchy, and violence, 156
perpetual motion: and counterculture, 58–59; and insurgent dwelling, 147; and negation, 143, 147; and ritualization/rebirth of youth movements and revolts, 12, 100–128, 210–17n; spaces of, 95
Perry, Joe, 184–85, 231n13
Perschau, Hartmut, 140–41
Petra Pan und Arumukha (film), 162, 169–70
Pflumm, Daniel, 173–74
philosophy: and activism, 33; and experimentation, 10; of life, 175; of youth movements and revolts, 9–10

places: cultivation of in Hamburg's Hafenstraße, 12–13, 129–54, 177–78, 217–23n; haunted, 11; and insurgent dwelling, 12–13, 129–54, 217–23n; and objects, 186; and past, 186; and polyphonic assemblages, 91; self in, grounded, 151; and spaces, 147; temporalities of, 66–67, 143; and time, 11, 174. See also insurgent dwelling; spaces
placeworlds, 66, 184
Playtime (Tati film), 64–65
Ploog, Jürgen, 66–67, 70
Plünderer, Die, 88, 90, 208n65
"Plunderer, The" (brochure), 89
"Plunderers—from the Movement, for the Movement, The" (brochure), 86
plunderphonics, 176, 228n84
politics: alternative integration, 122; antiauthoritarian, 116; and art, 202n34; of avant-garde, 231n17; confrontational, 71, 89; and counterculture, 27–28; democratic, 19, 40; dialectical, 4; and experimentation, 12; geo-, 157; of ghettoization, 47; housing, 216n79; and individual rights, 33; international symbols of, 156; leftist, 3–4, 24, 48–49, 70–71, 78, 89, 118; mainstream, 44; and negation, 31; oppositional, 27; and pop culture, 26; postprogressive, 182; progressive, 216n79; radical, 48, 70–71; reform-minded, 120; regenerative of youth movements and revolts, 126; representational, 3–4, 190n15; and revolution, 29, 34, 37; and rights of individual, 33; of spaces, 27; and squatting, 118–21, 176; static state of, 72; symbols of, 6, 156; and urban renewal, 37; of youth movements and revolts, 120–21, 126
polyphonic assemblages, 91
Ponto, Jürgen, 39
pop (popular) culture, 231n13; American, 56; and antiauthoritarianism, 28, 38; and insurgent dwelling, 146; and Kommune I, 28; and left, 24, 38, 68; music, 25–26, 28, 147; and negations

pop (popular) culture (*continued*)
of polite society, 28–29; and politics, 26; and progress, 25–26; and punks, 57, 147; and revolution, 38
post-adolescence, 114–16, 213n52
postmaterialism, 9. *See also* materiality
postmodernism, 8, 83, 158. *See also* modernity
postprogressive: activism, 183–84, 186; imaginaries, 66–67, 146, 169, 171; sensibilities, 143
postprogressive temporalities, 8–12, 41, 66–67, 134–35, 160, 171, 183–85. *See also* progressive temporalities
postwar: and allure of progress, 12, 14–39, 193–99n; films, 15, 18, 20, 22, 23–24; and free choice, 195n16; left, 5, 24, 30–31, 205n7; order, 23, 31, 69, 73–74, 87, 139, 141, 143; power, 98, 149; progress, 14–39, 48, 87, 91, 149; progressive myths of, 141; reconstructionists, 64; revolution, 14–39; temporal progress, 16–19; and Western Civilization, return to, 225n23
power: and antiauthoritarianism, 190n7; and capitalism, 3–4, 24, 183–84; counteracting, 3–4, 92, 143–44; and demonstrations, 109; and discontents, 109; and everyday life, 190n7; and fascism, 33, 35; and individuality, 33; international symbols of, 155–56; and left, 190n7; and marginalized groups, 3–4; postwar, 98, 149; regimes of, 148–49; state, 1–3, 35, 79, 137, 144, 183–84; and subjectivity, 33; symbols of, 155–56; and temporalities, 17; and time, 8
Practice of Everyday Life, The (de Certeau), 66, 148–49
present: divergent temporal rhythms in, 11; and future, 5–6, 10, 12, 19–21, 29–30, 33, 38–39, 52, 83, 87, 91, 171, 185–86; homogenous time-web of, 145; and living historically, 185; and past, 3, 5–6, 10, 12, 17–21, 24, 26, 29, 31, 33, 36, 38–39, 52, 57, 87, 91, 98, 185–86, 199n84; radical potential of, and youth movements/revolts, 12, 68–99, 205–10n; and revolution, 29. *See also* future; past; presentism
presentism: as broad present, 8; and capitalism, 7; defined/described, 7; and experimental temporal imaginaries, 7; and history, 7–8; and modernity, 8; and past, 8; and postmodernism, 8; and progressive temporal logics, 8; and squatting, 8; and technologies, 8; of youth movements and revolts, 8. *See also* present
Production of Space, The (Lefebvre), 148, 222n91
progress: allure of in postwar Germany, 12, 14–39, 193–99n; and antiauthoritarianism, 36–37; and capitalism, 14, 20, 23, 185; and consumerism, 22–23; and counterculture, 32; dialectical, 36–38; feelings of, 18, 69; fragmentation of, 145; and future, 66–67, 69, 89; and future landscapes, 171; handrails of, 182; and historicism, 185; integrationist iterations of, 85; iron-cage logics of, 91; and left, 30, 36–37; logics of, 6–7, 11, 30, 33, 91–96, 147, 171, 181, 185; and modernity, 17, 19–23, 65, 185; narrative logics of, 181; narratives of, 185; and negation, 49; and objects, 20; and past, 22–23, 48, 87, 89; and polyphonic assemblage, 91; and pop culture, 25–26; postwar, 14–39, 48, 87, 91, 149; prescribed paths of, 66–67; and radicalism, 42; and revolution, 14–39, 51; subverting, 7; and temporalities of place, 66–67; temporal logics of, 6, 169, 171, 185; and time, 44, 181; and urban landscape, 169. *See also* temporal progress
progressive imaginaries, 51
progressive temporalities, 10, 12, 182, 186; fragmentation of, 98; postwar, 7, 20–22, 26, 38–39, 128; of squatting, 7, 66, 87, 128; of youth movements and revolts, 9, 72, 84, 87. *See also* postprogressive temporalities; temporal progress

Project Commission, 45, 201n19
proletariat, 30–31
propaganda, 21, 29–30
protests: and activism, 1; and autonomy, 82; destructive, 81; left, 1; and leftist, 1; militant, 79; and nonrepresentational revolutionary movement, 4; against nuclear power, 37, 41–42; and radicalism, 82; during Red Decade, 1–2; and squatting, 4, 75, 78–83, 122–23; and violence, 34, 79–83, 155; by youth, 27–28; of youth movements and revolts, 79–83, 105, 119–20, 143. *See also* activism; demonstrations; riots
Pudding Attack, 28
punk movement, *63*, *74*; and abnormalities, 62; aesthetics, 52, 55–56, 58, 70–72, 76–82, 89–91, 98; and anarchy, 151; and antiauthoritarianism, 57; apocalyptic aesthetics, 55–56, 58, 70, 89, 98; and art, 41, 52–65, 76, 92–93, 107, 114, 147, 202n33, 204n71, 211n25; art journal, 52; audiovisual techniques, 59–60; burgeoning (1970s-1980), 48–49, 52, 57; centers of (cities), 50, 53; citational practices, 55–57, 76; and civilizational decline, and dystopian, nihilistic images of, 54–55; and counterculture, 48–65; and creative destruction, 58, 70, 92, 142–43, 157, 163–64, 168–69, 172; and creative pastiche, 208n75; and cultural forms, 92; and Dada, 50, 51; and demonstrations, *74*; and destruction/chaos, 50, 53, 68, 72–74, 79, 81, 91–92, 98, 107, 147; détournements of, 87; and dilettantism, 59; and directionless dialectics, 66; European milieu, 72; fanzines, 53–54, 56, 70, 72; and fascism, 54; fashion and clothing, 6, 54–55, 57, 64–65, 95, 153; in film, 62–65; and fringe groups, 130; and future/new, 64–65; in German-speaking countries, 202n30; ideology of, 6, 54–56; and insurgent dwelling, 131, 141; and leftist politics, 48–49, 70–71, 78; masculine orientation of, 203n47; and media, 58, 66, 204n71, 205n8; music of, 1, 6, 49–64, 66, 69–70, 76, 78–79, 100, 105, 107, 114, 137, 144, 151, 163–64, 202n35, 203n47, 203n57, 203n64, 204n72, 205n8; and negation/rejection, 49–50, 58–59, 66, 69, 85, 91, 136–37; and New Wave, 41, 56, 58–59, 62–74, 80–82, 85, 89–92, 98, 107, 141–43, 147; "no future" attitude of, 49, 54–55, 58, 69–70, 84, 90–93, 95, 113, 154; politically oriented fanzine, 72; and progressive breakthrough, 147; and progressive time, 85; and provocation, shock, disturbance, 53–54, 56–57; and radical actions, 53; and radical leftist politics, 55, 58, 70–71, 74, 78, 85; real, 53; and revolution, 41, 49, 57, 66, 72–73, 85, 144; and spatiotemporal imaginary, 66; subcultures, 52–53, 57, 95, 208n75; Swiss, 60, 89, 203n65, 204n72; and youth movements/revolts, 73, 82, 92, 100; in Zurich, 59. *See also* student movements; youth movements; youth revolts

queer: temporalities, 17–18, 231n18; theory, 8

Rabehl, Bernd, 28, 116, 183
racialized minorities, 3
Rada, Uwe, 183
radicalism and radicalization: and activism, 80, 99; and autonomy, 82; and creative destruction, 92; and duration within architecture, 222n88; and experimentation, 198n57; and impatience, 197n41; and left, 27, 29, 33–42, 55, 85, 142, 156, 198n57, 199n85; and negation, 29, 76, 91–92, 99, 134–35, 141–42, 144, 153, 157; and politics, 48, 70–71; and progress, 42; and protests, 82; and reunification, 181; and revolution, 36–38, 40–41, 85; and social transformation, 35; of squatting, 68–99, 143, 150–54, 180–81, 205–10n; and techno, 184; and violence, 33–34, 40–41, 65, 156; of youth, 27; of youth movements and revolts, 12, 68–99, 128, 205–10n

Radikal (far-left journal), 4, 70–72, 71, 80–82, 93, 122
RAF. *See* Red Army Faction (RAF)
Raspe, Jan-Carl, 39
Ratinger Hof (club/venue), 52–53
Rattay, Klaus-Jürgen, 85, 100, 123, 211n20
Reagan, Ronald, 110, 156
rebellions, 27, 72, 185
Rebel without a Cause (film), 24
rebirth: and housing, 21; postwar, 10–11, 14–15, 17, 21; and ritualization, and perpetual motion of youth, 12, 100–128, 210–17n
reconstruction, 10, 49, 64, 85, 87, 155
Red Army, 36, 170
Red Army Faction (RAF), 35–36, 38–41, 44, 53–56, 70, 127, 129–33, 146, 151, 162, 198–99n73, 199n77
Red Decade (1967–77), 1–2, 27, 30, 37, 70, 98, 145, 157
Reemtsma, Jan Philipp, 132
Regener, Sven, 113, 213n50
Reich, Wilhelm, 32
Reichardt, Sven, 190n16
Reiche, Anne, 135, 137
Reiche, Reimut, 27, 35
Reiser, Rio, 50
relationality, anarchist, 144
Renaud, Terence, 3, 198n51, 199n85
Residents, The (band), 203n64
resignification, 93–94
resistance: and activism, 48; and domesticity, 151; to injustice, 215n70; leftist, 48, 150; militant, 2; and negation, 3, 145; and squatting, 168, 176, 185; of youth movements and revolts, 80–81
restoration, nationalist, 186
reunification, 158, 162, 181. *See also* unification
revolts. *See* revolution; youth revolts
revolution: and abstraction, 34; and activism, 29–35, 37–38, 40, 48–49, 66, 81–82, 110; anarchist, 35–36, 38; and antiauthoritarianism, 3, 27–28, 30–32, 34–37, 43, 57; and autonomy, 4; and capitalism, 27, 41; and counterculture, 27–28, 30, 34–35, 197n43; and demonstrations, 109, 212n31; and dialectical logics, 3; and future, 29, 31–32, 38; and Gammlers, 26–27; global, 108; and guerrilla tactics, 35–36; and hedonism, 36; and history, 36; and insurrection, 34–36, 109–10; leftist, 27, 29, 34, 40–41, 85, 118, 166–67; and marginalized groups, 3–4, 27, 37; and marginalized groups and populations, 35; mythologization of, 38; and negation, 3, 28–29, 31, 35, 111, 183; and New Left, 3, 5, 27, 28–30; nonrepresentational, 3–5; and past, 33; and politics, 29, 34, 37; and pop culture, 38; postwar, 14–39; prepolitical, 3; and present, 29; professional, 109–10, 212n31; and progress, 14–39, 51; and radicalism, 36–38, 40–41, 85; reimagined, 41; representational, 33; and social transformation, 34; and squatting, 37–38, 108, 151; and time, 5–6, 66; transnational, 111–12; and violence, 31–36, 40–41, 156; of youth movements and revolts, 5–6, 26–31, 87–89, 106
Reynolds, Simon, 175
riots, 26, 111, 178; and protests, 75–77, 81; and radicalization, 75; and squatting, 76–82, 155–56; and violence, 35, 86, 108, 156, 223n4; and youth movements/revolts, 75–82, 85–89, 91, 94. *See also* activism; demonstrations; protests; violence
ritualization: and ideology, 101, 103; and rebirth, and perpetual motion of youth, 12, 100–128, 210–17n
Rohner, Meinrad, 41, 200n5
Rolling Stones (band), 24
romanticism, 20, 43–44, 65–66, 73, 145, 149–50
Ross, Kristin, 30, 191n29
Rother, Michael, 52, 202n40
Rotten, Johnny, 49–50
Röttgen, Herbert, 43
ruin dwellers, 6–7, 11–12, 15, 180–86, 222n94, 230–31n; and counterculture, 48, 58; and creative destruction, 158, 169–70, 172, 174–76; and insurgent

dwelling, 147–49, 154; and new worlds, 87, 180; punks as, 172; of youth movements and revolts, 69, 87. *See also* squatting movement

Sachs, Michael, 145–46
Sandler, Daniela, 180, 230n103
Scheytan, Firiz, 61, 81, 207n42
Schiller, Margit, 36, 199n74
Schleyer, Hans "Hanns" Martin, 39, 55, 127, 150–51
Schneider, Peter, 29, 32
Schultz-Hageleit, Peter, 115–16, 214n57
Schütte, Uwe, 51, 202n36
Schwarze Kanal, Der (radical West Berlin paper), 100, 120–26, *124*
Schwebel, Thomas, 54
SDS, 27, 30, 35
SED regime, 157, 225n27
Seelen, Joost, 206n20
Seibert, Che, 202n41
self: conceptions of, 9; denormalized, 33; and environments, 72–73, 85; modern, 6; new sense of, and youth movements, 73; and normalization, 33; *vs.* other, 6; and world, 29, 143
self-centered, 48
self-congratulatory, 173
self-control, 65, 168
self-creation, 25, 184
self-destructive, 48
self-determined, 4
self-esteem, 156–57
self-help, 45, 97, 114, 167
self-initiative, 48
self-introductions, 97, 102, 166–67, 176
self-irony, 183
self-realization, 33, 116
self-recognition, 30
Sex Pistols, 49
sexual conservatism, and social conformity, 24–25
Sharpe, Christina, 11
SHIK, 118
"Sickness" (flyer), 125
Sid Vicious, 50
Siegfried, Detlef, 27, 29
Situationists, 56

Slobodian, Quinn, 34, 198n69
Smith, Briana, 180
Sneeringer, Julia, 24–25, 196n35
Sniper (bar), 176
So war das S.O. 36: Ein Abend des Nostalgie (Buttergeit documentary film), 73
sociabilities: and belonging, 168–69; of counterculture, 28; and punks, 53, 98; and squatting, 2, 73, 110–11, 143; and subjectivities, 169, 175, 181–82; of youth movements and revolts, 31, 105
social: conformity, and sexual conservatism, 24–25; logics, 83, 154; movements, 186
social order, 73, 76–77, 86, 142
social theory and theorists, 49, 101
socialism, 27–28, 30–32, 40, 71–72, 157–58, 161, 171–73, 226n46
Socialist Austrian Student Union, 32
Society for Self-governed Dwelling, 118
sociotemporal logics, 80
solidarity, 26–27, 33, 91, 108–9, 117–18, 129–30, 132, 144–45, 162–63, 168, 179–80
spaces: ahistorical, 89–91; of alterity, 96; authentic, 66; autonomous, 134, 154, 165; communal, 150; demarcated, 143; domestic, 20–21, 98–99, 143, 148–49; free, 4, 110, 113, 141, 179; illegal, 2, 218n8; interstitial, 60, 170–71, 175, 182; liberated, 96, 138, 164–65; liminal, 11, 171; and objects, 136, 181–82; of perpetual metamorphosis, 95; and places, 147; and polyphonic assemblages, 91; public, and embrace of unknown, 226n44; sacred, 110; and squatting, 2, 10–11; and time, 62, 91, 100, 174–75, 182; urban, 10–11, 91, 98–99, 134–35. *See also* places
spatiotemporal: imaginaries, 66–67, 142; *Kiez*, 156; logics and contexts, 96, 141–44; practices, 9; qualities, 135, 156
SPD, 26–27, 130–31, 141, 179
Spiegel, Der, 68, 76, 145
Spontis, 36–38, 41, 131
Squatter(s) Council, 1–2, 85, 97, 103, 106, 111–12, 121, 168, 207n37, 213n53

squatting movement, 1–10, 12, 21, *101*, 101–6, 112, 122–23, 130, 162, 164–66, *165*, 176, 180–86, 189n2, 199n80, 206n19, 230–31n; aesthetics of, 2; and agitation, 93; and ahistorical spaces, 89–90; alterity of, 216n87; and alternate forms of community, 94; and alternative milieu, 5, 95–96; as antihierarchical, 3; and art, commerce, fashion, 183; asynchronous qualities of, 6, 11; auratic nature of, 96, 109, 134, 138, 142, 146, 148–49, 169; and being in the world, 6; as beneficial, 210n91; in Berlin (new), 13, 81, 117, 155–80, 223–30n; and bodies that mattered, 153; Christian support for, 116–18, 214nn64–65; and collective living, 1–2; and counterculture, 65–66; and counterpublic network, 166; defeats, 129; and demonic exorcism (eviction), 127; and dialogue with youth, 120–21, *121*; and diversity, 112; documentaries, 104–5; and domestic transgression, 4; and duration within radical architecture, 222n88; evictions, 101, 120, 127, 178; as global revolution, 108, 143–44; goals and desires of, 104; images and videos of, 167; infrastructure of, 2–3; and insubordination, 149; maximalist dreams of, 180; and misuse of living space as illegal, 218n8; newspaper and press coverage, 100–105, 166–67, 217n89; oppositional lifestyles of, 96–97; peculiar and mystical landscapes of, 98–99; and politics, 118–21; and polyphonic assemblages, 91; as postrevolutionary protest, 95–96; and prefigurative traditions, 5; and psychoterrorists, 122; as regenerative, 96–97; and registration with police, 226n38; and resignification, 93–94; and restorative nostalgia, 149–50; and sabotage, 93; self-produced media of, 1; slogans of, 4; and spaces of perpetual metamorphosis, 95; as strangers in dead land, 6; and symbolic power of houses, 98–99, 110–11; tangible assistance from sympathetic citizens, 117; topology of secret signs, 93–94; and total solution, 119; and uniqueness of houses, 92; and unknown, embrace of, 226n44; and urban nostalgia, 96; and youth culture, 1; and youth movements/revolts, 12, 67–99, 141, 205–10n. *See also* insurgent dwelling; ruin dwellers; student movements; youth movements; youth revolts

St. Pauli Einschnitt, 150

Stad was van ons, De (Seelen documentary), 206n20

"Stadtteilzentrum Feuerwache," 46

Stalinism, 160, 165

Star Club (Hamburg), 25–26

state violence: and capitalism, 55–56; denunciations of, 137; forms of, 85; protests against, 155

Staudte, Wolfgang, 15–16, 193n5

Stefanoski, Slavko, 175

Stewart, Susan, 19–20

Stieler, Johnie, 174–75

Stilett (fanzine), 72, 111

Stillstand, 123

Stock, Wolfgang Jean, 106–7, 211n25

Störtebeker, Klaus, 144–45, 221n78

Strategien für Kreuzberg, 45, 68–69, 201n22

student movements: anarchist, 34; and antiauthoritarianism, 116; and consumerism, 24–25; and insurrection, 34; and left, 38; and liberation, 9; postwar, 24–25; and revolution, 34, 38; and self-recognition, 30; spatial logics of, 197n40; and squatting, 2, 119. *See also* punk movement; squatting movement; youth movements; youth revolts

Styrene, Poly, 49–50

subcultures, 24–26, 31, 52–53, 57, 83, 95, 127–28, 165, 208n75. *See also* youth culture

Subito, 77, 87–89, 92

subjectivities: and body, 31–32; and power, 33; and sociabilities, 169, 175, 181–82; and squatting, 96, 143, 175–76
subversion, 2, 7–8, 10–11, 65, 76, 78, 85, 146, 184, 229n87
Subversive Aktion, Provo-inspired political group, 28, 197n46
Süddeutsche Zeitung, 103–4
Südost Express, 47, 201n23
Suzuki, Damo, 51
Swabians, 112, 213n43
S.Y.P.H. (band), 54–56, 127

Tacheles (art/squat project in Berlin-Mitte), 170, 181–83
Tagesspiegel, 103–4, 123
Tageszeitung, Die, 40, 81, 103–4, 107–8, 121–23, 126, 131, 156, 173, 183, 201n23, 216nn85–86, 226n49
Talking Heads, 54–55
Tati, Jacques, 64–65
techno music, 170, 174–76, 180, 184, 228n74, 228n81
Telegraph, 161, 166, 168, 178
teleology, 5–6, 12, 64
telos, 42, 44
temporal: anarchy, 174; change, 8, 66; consciousness, 7, 83, 185, 194n10; continuity and continuum, 148, 169; disruption, 185–86; dissonance, 185, 231n18; dynamics, 10, 38–39, 51–52; ideologies, 17; pastiche, 6; perception, 59, 61; practices, 6, 9, 17, 44, 84, 87, 95, 98, 108, 134, 160, 174–76, 182–84; regimes, 11–12, 19, 21–22, 38–39, 84, 87, 182; regulation, 17–18; structures, 59, 61; transcendence, 95–96; transgression, 89, 101
temporal imaginaries, 5–8, 10, 14, 17–18, 65–67, 87, 89, 134, 142, 171, 178–79, 183, 185, 193n3, 199n77, 227n61
temporal logics: alternative, 185; and being, 11–12; collapsing, 182; and counterculture, 64; destructive, 6; diverse, 185; and dwellings, 171; and experimentation, 8, 11–12, 48, 59, 171, 182; interstices of, 174–75; of modernity, 6, 185; and objects, 19–20; and postrevolutionary activism, 43–44; of progress, 6, 169, 171, 185; progressive, 8, 12; and techno, 175; of youth movements and revolts, 92
temporal progress, 7, 16–19, 38–39, 51–52, 87, 116, 169, 172. *See also* progressive temporalities
temporalities, 8–12; alternative, 185; and experimentation, 100, 143; historicizing of, 17; of modernity, 6, 8–10, 17, 50–51, 185; postwar, 148; and power, 17, 148; and squatting, 143; and time, 17; of youth movements and revolts, 9, 84, 101, 192n32. *See also* postprogressive temporalities; progressive temporalities
10 Meter Ohne Kopf, 140, 152
terrorism: and chaos, 69; leftist, 22, 139; mass struggle-, 35; political, 155–56; Russian, 199n77, 227n61; and squatting, 103, 107, 117–18, 122, 131, 133, 136, 140–41, 146, 151, 212n31; and violence, 35, 140–41. *See also* violence
Third World, 34
time: being in, 11–12, 14, 18, 20, 65, 84–89, 101, 143, 148, 172, 181–85; and capitalism, 17; and collapse of modern regime, 13; crisis of, 7–8; disciplinary, chrononormative dimensions of, 185; and future, 64, 148; historicizing of, 17; and history, 5; Messianic/messianic, 11, 231n20; and modernity, 5–8, 11, 13, 17–18, 65; and music, 61, 175; narrative, 61; and objects, 20; and places, 11, 174; postprogressive, 11, 41, 182; and power, 8; and progress, 44, 181; progressive, 5–7, 12, 22, 40, 49, 52, 64–65, 85, 87, 142, 148–49, 186, 190n15; progressive temporal forms of, 186; and revolution, 5–6, 66; slowing or stopping passage of, 5, 41–42, 44, 59, 175; and space, 62, 91, 100, 174–75, 182; speeding up, 5; and squatting, 6–7; structuring of, 8; and temporalities, 17; and youth movements/revolts, 5–7. *See also* future; modern time regime; past; present
Tin Drum, The (Grass), 24

Tödliche Doris, Die (music group), 58–59, 61–62, 127–28
Ton Steine Scherben, 50, 202n34
totalitarianism, 55, 147
transgression: and artistic representations, 107; of boundaries, 53; collective, 109–10; innovative, 102; and opposition, 180; original acts of, 101; and perpetual becoming, 95–96; representational spaces of, 180; temporal, 89, 101
transnationalism: and activism, 108, 111–12; and leftist experimentation/radicalism, 198n57; and marginalized groups, 107; and negation, anarchist, 107; and revolution, 111–12; and youth culture, 24, 111–12
Tresor (techno club), 174–75, 180, 182
Tsing, Anna Lowenhaupt, 49, 91, 143, 182
TUNIX festival, 41, 43, 54, 60, 118, 200n6
Tupamaros (militant group), 34–35
TUWAT festival, 107–8

Uhlmann, René, 59, 204n72
underground clubs, 2, 4
unification, 158, 171, 224n12, 224n15. *See also* reunification
Unreality of Our Cities (Mitscherlich), 37
Untermöhlen, Nikolaus, 61, 62–63
urban landscape: of Berlin (creative city), 158–60, 169, 184; palimpsestic qualities of, 169; and progress, 169
urban renewal, 201n23; alternative visions of, 114; and antiauthoritarianism, 45, 97–98; destructive, 85, 116–17; and equitable housing sacrificed, 138; facilitation of, 130; failure of, 47; humane, resident-oriented forms of, 46–47; inner-city, 37; and neighborhoods, 37, 45; opposition and resistance to, 37, 45, 97, 116–18, 178; and politics, 37; squatters' critiques of, 117; and violence, 178. *See also* city planning; gentrification; housing
utopias and utopianism, 3–5, 23–25, 29, 42–49, 73, 80, 119, 129; concrete, 185; fractured, 95–96; future, 4–5, 12, 31–32, 38–39, 42–45, 85–87, 94, 98, 117, 142–43; and negation, 98; politics of, 47; and squatting, 94–96; sustainable, 44, 47, 66; and temporal change, 66

vandalism, and violence, 156
Vasudevan, Alexander, 180
vengeance: and destruction, 91; and fascism, 36
Verein Hafenstraße, 132–33, 145
Verein SO36, 201n22
Verhoeven, Claudia, 197n41, 199n77, 209n79, 227n61
Vertragsgremium, 167–68, 227n58
Video Magazin (AK Kraak), 167, 227n58
Vidon, Alain, 89, 208n66
Vienna Actionists (radical artists), 31–32, 52–53
Vietnam War, 27–28, 34, 36
violence: and activism, 40, 83, 156–57; alternatives to, 41; and art, 34; and capitalism, 81, 83, 141, 156; and colonialism, 34, 145; and counterculture, 53–54; and criminality, 35, 120, 133; and demonstrations, 75, 79; disorganized and regenerative, 108; and disruptions, 178; and exploitation, 14; of extraparliamentary opposition, 34; and fascism, 156; and housing policies, 81, 215n70; and injustice, 23; and insurrection, 34; irreverent forms of, 156; leftist, 155–56; of past, 32–33; and patriarchy, 156; police, 41, 79, 178, 183; and protests, 34, 79–83, 155; as punishment, 36; and radicalism, 33–34, 40–41, 65, 156; regenerative, 108; rejection of, 126; and resistance, 35; retaliatory acts of, 139; and revolution, 31–36, 40–41, 156; and riots, 35, 86, 108, 156, 223n4; sinister forms of, 86; and social order, 86; and squatting, 120, 137, 141, 156; state, 55–56, 85, 137, 155; structural, 86; structures of, 122, 141; subtle forms of, 86; and subversion, 85; symbolic, 34, 156; and terrorism, 35, 140–41; and vandalism, 156; of youth movements and revolts,

85. *See also* creative destruction; militance; riots; terrorism
Völkischer Beobachter (Nazi-era newspaper), 6
Volksblatt, 156
Volxsport, 155–56, 179
von Braun, Werner/Wernher, 51
Voscherau, Mayor, 133, 151

Wagner, David, 181, 230n1
Wagner, Senator, 145, 219n28
Wagner-Conzelmann, Sandra, 195n24, 222n90
Waldschmidt, Armin, 117, 214n63
Waldt, Anton, 170, 180
Wartenberg, J. C., 94–95, 113
Welt, Die, 129
Wende, 157, 170–71, 181
Wenders, Wim, 20, 195n21
Wessis, 164
West Berlin: activists in, 107, 126; "Bathtub" on Nürnberger Straße in, 25; Gedächtniskirche neighborhood, 26; leftist critics in, 183; radical movements in, 9, 82; riots in, 155; squatting movement in, 1–2, 73, 79–82, 85, 94–98, 100, 102, 104–5, 108, 112, 116–23, 126, 128–29, 155, 199n80, 210n92, 225n24; student revolutionaries in, 34; youth culture in, 27; youth movements and revolts in, 82, 100, 105–7, 126, 128–29. *See also* Berlin; East Berlin
West German Parliamentary Commission, 114–15, 120–21
West Germany, 161; afterlives of 1968 in, 9–12; Economic Miracle of 1950s, 15, 18, 21–22, 24, 25, 38, 51, 55–56, 194n6; as machine, apparatus, computer, 1; national traditions of, 19; postwar, 12, 14–39; squatting in, 218n8. *See also* East Germany
Western Europe, 1, 96, 189n2
Westfallenblatt, 156
WGs. *See Wohngemeinschaften* (WGs)
Wild Ones, The (film), 24
Wildenhain, Michael, 78, 102–3, 206n26
Wilder, Gary, 185

Wilhelm Meister's Abschied (Ossowski), 142–43, 221n70
Wirtschaftswunder (band), 56, 64
Witzel, Frank, 15, 194n7
Wo die Angst ist Geht's Lang (film), 105, 211n20
Wohlrabe, Jürgen, 122–23
Wohngemeinschaften (WGs), 2, 42
Woman in Berlin, A (anonymous), 14–15, 22, 193n4
Women's Movement, 190n7
working classes, 3, 27, 57

youth centers and clubs, 2, 4, 11, 26, 74–79, 95, 122. *See also* AJZ youth center (Zurich)
youth cultures, 1, 10, 24, 28–31, 48, 57, 160, 196n33. *See also* subcultures
youth movements, 3–10, 12, 92–122, 125–29, 181–82, 189n2, 209n82; and absurdism, 4; aesthetic and cultural dimensions, 9–10, 105; analyses of, 83–84; as anarchist, 3, 5–7, 125–27; and antiauthoritarianism, 3, 85, 116; and breaking through, 5, 10; and break with known, 5; brochures, flyers, pamphlets, 105–6, 209n82; and chaos, 69, 114; and chaos makers, 103; Christian support for, 116–18; and citational maelstrom, 176; and destruction, 98–99; end of, 129–30; fashion/clothes/style of, 6, 31; feelings and harshness of, 73; inclusiveness of, 114; language of, emerged in Zurich, 206n25; leftist, 1–4, 27, 118, 210n95; and media, 10; music of, 106–7; peculiar, mystical landscapes of, 98–99; and perpetual transgression, 5; and post-adolescence, 114–16, 213n52; revitalization and rebirth of, and perpetual motion, 12, 100–128, 210–17n; and simulated dissent, 114; as state of being, 4–5; study of, 114–15; and transhistorical imaginaries, 89. *See also* activism, youth; counterculture; punk movement; squatting movement; student movements; youth revolts

youth revolts, 8, 205–17n; aesthetics of, 101; and changes, 179; and constraints of adolescence, 4; and dancing, 81, 84, 92, 95; and dissatisfaction, 91–92; experimental social, cultural, aesthetic forms emerged from, 101; jumpstarted, 66–67; and leftist activism, 1–2; and novelty/adventure, 82; and radical potential of present, 12, 68–99, 205–10n; and rebellions, 27; revitalization and rebirth of, and perpetual motion, 12, 100–128, 210–17n; and squatting movement, 12, 67–99, 141, 205–10n. *See also* counterculture; punk movement; squatting movement; student movements; youth movements

Zahl, Peter-Paul, 116, 214n60
Züri brännt (film), 78
Zurich, Switzerland: anarchists in, 193n40; youth movements and revolts in, 68, 75–82, 88–89, 91, 94, 100, 112–13, 129–30, 139, 206n25

www.ingramcontent.com/pod-product-compliance
Lightning Source LLC
Chambersburg PA
CBHW022042290426
44109CB00014B/949